THE
NEW
CANADIAN
ANTHOLOGY

THE
NEW
CANADIAN
ANTHOLOGY:

POETRY
AND SHORT FICTION
IN ENGLISH

Edited by
ROBERT LECKER & JACK DAVID

© Nelson Canada,
A Division of International Thomson Limited, 1988

Published in 1988 by
Nelson Canada,
A Division of International Thomson Limited
1120 Birchmount Road
Scarborough, Ontario
M1K 5G4

Canadian Cataloguing in Publication Data

Main entry under title:

The New Canadian Anthology

Includes bibliographies and index.
ISBN 0-17-603413-7

1. Canadian poetry (English).*   2. Short stories,
Canadian (English).*   3. Canadian fiction (English).*
I. Lecker, Robert, 1951–   . II. David, Jack,
1946–   .

PS8273.N49 1988   C811'.008   C88-093536-7
PR9195.23.N49 1988

Cover: "Forked Lightning," Paterson Ewen,
    acrylic, metal, etc. . . . on plywood, 1971
    122 × 244 cm
    ABBA 72/3-1670

Printed and bound in Canada

2 3 4   88   92 91

List of Contributing Critics

Peter Buitenhuis, Simon Fraser University
Susan Copoloff-Mechanic, Montreal
Michael Darling, University of Western Ontario
Jack David, Centennial College
Stan Dragland, University of Western Ontario
L. R. Early, York University
Robert Gibbs, University of New Brunswick
Ronald Hatch, University of British Columbia
Michael Helm, Toronto
John F. Hulcoop, University of British Columbia
Ed Jewinski, Wilfrid Laurier University
W. J. Keith, University of Toronto
David A. Kent, Centennial College
David Latham, University of Lethbridge
Robert Lecker, McGill University
Jean Mallinson, Vancouver
Francis Mansbridge, Cranbrook, B.C.
Leslie Monkman, Queen's University
Ann Munton, University of British Columbia
Shirley Neuman, University of Alberta
Ken Norris, University of Maine
Peter O'Brien, Toronto
John Orange, King's College
David O'Rourke, Centennial College
Zailig Pollock, Trent University
Stephen Scobie, University of Victoria
David Staines, University of Ottawa
Clara Thomas, York University
Lee Briscoe Thompson, University of Vermont
Louise Vanier-Gagnon, Vancouver
Terry Whalen, St. Mary's University
Bruce Whiteman, McGill University
Janice Williamson, Toronto
George Woodcock, Vancouver
Lorraine York, McGill University

· CONTENTS ·

Preface xi

Introduction
GEORGE WOODCOCK xiii

POETRY

SHORT FICTION

· PREFACE ·

The New Canadian Anthology collects some of the finest English-Canadian poetry and short fiction written since the late 1800s. Although its thrust is intentionally modern, the importance of maintaining a sense of historical perspective has not been forgotten.

We have attempted to provide a chronological and developmental perspective by dating each work. The date that appears in brackets at the end of each selection is the *date of first publication in any form*. For previously unpublished material, we give the estimated date of composition. In all cases, we have sought to reproduce the most authoritative text *currently* available; this text frequently differs from that of the first publication. A list of the texts we have employed appears in the permissions acknowledgements. Except in the case of excerpted material, line numbers are provided for all poems of more than forty lines.

In making our selections we were often assisted by the many scholars and critics whose contributions to this volume make it unique: this is the first single-volume anthology of English-Canadian poetry and short fiction that contains bio-critical essays written by experts on the various authors whose works appear here. These contributors have also provided the helpful lists of works by and on each author which appear at the end of each bio-critical entry. In this sense, *The New Canadian Anthology* is a genuinely collaborative effort, and we wish to thank all of the contributors. Their input helped us make a better anthology; whatever flaws remain are strictly ours.

A number of people made special contributions to the editing and preparation of this volume. Our many thanks are due to Jamie Gaetz, W. J. Keith, Nanette Norris, and Francesca Worrall. As well, our debt to Peter Milroy is profound; this book is in many ways the product of his faith, intelligence, and vision.

ROBERT LECKER
JACK DAVID

· INTRODUCTION ·

by George Woodcock

An anthology that sets out to represent a literary tradition is rather like an exhibition in one gallery of a great museum, in which the curators have set out to assemble a representative collection from the best works they have available. There, carefully selected, well lit and labelled, the exhibits stand, and the way they are arranged reflects a pattern which in the curator's mind represents the essence of the culture that is presented. But, as the experienced museum-goer knows, the other galleries and even the cellars and attics of the museum are packed with works not on display, works often as good, which have been left out perhaps because one can have too much of any class of good things, or perhaps because the objects are too large to fit easily into the show, or perhaps because they belong to formative periods about which critical judgments are still uncertain.

Wise viewers take the whole show in—the excellence of the objects shown and the conclusions to which the curator is gently trying to edge them by arrangement and emphasis. But if the exhibition has been a good one, they go away happy but not quite content, for the selection of objects in that bright room will have aroused their curiosity about what lies unseen in the other galleries, in the cellars and attics, and they will not be satisfied until they have seen them.

It is the same with anthologies. No one ever learns a literature completely from an anthology, since each is deliberately a sampling, with its limitations of size, of period, of choice. But whatever its approach, the good anthology will not merely provide its readers with a few hours of stimulating reading and a collection of quotable passages to be used in impressing others. It will also stir their curiosity and lead them to find for themselves the other necessary works and writers in the tradition, so that the anthology will indeed be an introduction, an opening of awareness to a new field of experience.

This kind of introduction is, I suggest, what Robert Lecker and Jack David have provided in *The New Canadian Anthology: Poetry and Short Fiction in English.*

Collections like *The New Canadian Anthology*, which present a broad spectrum of Canadian poetry and fiction for the general reader, do not have many predecessors. There have been numerous anthologies of verse, of which the best known are those by A. J. M. Smith, Margaret Atwood, and Ralph Gustafson, together with the two-volume *Canadian Poetry*, which Lecker and David themselves prepared more recently, and these collections have been influential in establishing the critical, accepted canon of Canadian poetry. There have been quite a number of good anthologies of short stories, notably those compiled by Robert Weaver and by David Helwig. But of broader collections that bring in the whole field of creative writing, poetry and prose, there have been comparatively few. One was *The Oxford Anthology of Canadian Literature* (1973), by Weaver and William Toye, and even that was prepared with one eye on the academic market. Another was Mordecai Richler's *Canadian Writing Today* (1970), published with a view to introducing Canadian writers to an international and particularly to a British readership.

It is interesting to compare Richler's collection with the present one, prepared more than a decade and a half later, for it shows considerable changes not only in Canadian writing itself but also in our attitudes toward it. Richler seemed at first an odd figure to pick for such a task. He was living in England, and had been an expatriate from Canada for over ten years, while he was well known for his deprecatory remarks about Canadian writers and writing. But in fact both his physical distance from Canada and his modest expectation of what Canadian writers could produce were editorial advantages, and he put together in the end the kind of workmanlike and provisional collection, introducing quite a number of new and not yet very well tried talents, which was appropriate at the time. What Richler found was that when he looked at his country's writing at the end of the 1960s, many years after his departure for Europe, there was more to admire than he had expected, and the general tentativeness yet hopefulness of his effort was summarized in a paragraph toward the end of his introduction:

> *This anthology, then, is of writers embarking on settlement. It is not meant to be historical or definitive. It entertains no over-large claims unless it be considered such to say (and this is a real measure of recent Canadian literary achievement) that I believe it to be sufficiently fresh and talented to engage the interest not only of dutiful buyers of Canadiana but of a broader, more exacting, audience, appreciative of good new writing whatever its origins.*

The time has come, in the late 1980s, when there is a sufficiently large and varied body of Canadian writing for us to regard it as a literature that *has* reached its maturity and that we can have no doubt merits the interest of the "broader, more exacting" audience to which Richler refers. We have moved from diffidence toward certainty, and the editors of *The New Canadian Anthology* have shown their sense of this fact in the decisiveness of their choices, which explains both the deliberate limitations and the particular advantages of this volume. They have realized that as a literature changes and matures a new kind of anthology is needed, and they have acted accordingly.

The limitations are of proportion and of period as well as—inevitably—of choice. There are obviously some works of literature, notably novels, and the long poems of writers like E. J. Pratt, that cannot be anthologized except in fragments. The editors have, I think, been wisely cautious about using extracts from such longer works since, charming or impressive though a fragment of such a poem or novel may be, it will almost always seem diminished by comparison with a short complete work. I believe I am right in saying that among hundreds of items the excerpt from Pratt's *Brébeuf and His Brethren* is the only actual fragment chosen for this anthology, and it works because Pratt tends to be an episodic poet.

This limitation on extracting from larger works has of course meant that a number of leading contemporary Canadian authors are excluded because they are by nature writers of books, dealing at their best with large integrated structures, and none of their smaller works seemed adequate to represent them faithfully. Excellent novelists such as Hugh MacLennan, Robertson Davies, and Timothy Findley are among them, and anyone who enjoys this anthology is urged to supplement it by seeking out their books, if he does not know them already.

The limitations of period are perhaps more debatable. The poetry extends just over a century, for it was in the 1880s that Isabella Valancy Crawford, Charles G. D. Roberts, and Archibald Lampman, the earliest poets represented here, published their first volumes, with Bliss Carman and Duncan Campbell Scott following in the 1890s. The prose covers an even more restricted period; the earliest of it dates from after World War I. The editors have not attempted to be representative of the whole scope of Canadian writing, for many early writers included by earlier anthologists like A. J. M. Smith and Margaret Atwood in the interests of historical completeness have been deliberately ignored.

This has meant sacrificing a good deal of interesting but not necessarily first-rate work, for there have been writers active in Canada almost since the time of the earliest settlement. The first in English was Robert Hayman, whose *Quodlibets, Lately Come Over from New Britaniola, Old Newfoundland*, was published in London in 1628, two and a half centuries before the first poem in the present volume was written. And throughout the nineteenth century, especially after the influx of immigrants from Britain after the Napoleonic Wars, men and women were hard at work producing the poems, novels, and memoirs which we now regard as representing the colonial period in our literature. Some of these writers, like James de Mille and Rosanna Leprohon and Susanna Moodie, became accomplished professional writers of a kind, while others, like the poets Alexander McLachlan and Charles Heavysege, revealed strains of undisciplined and often bizarre originality.

But all these writers in their own way remained transient, still committed to the literary language and attitudes of a distant mother culture and inclined to that fear of the still so proximate wilderness which Northrop Frye has described as "the garrison mentality." Furthermore, until the appearance late in the nineteenth century of Isabella Valancy Craw-

ford and the Confederation poets (such as Roberts), and of Sara Jeannette Duncan and Stephen Leacock as prose-fiction writers a little later,
not much writing was being done in Canada that would bear comparison
either with contemporary British writing or with the kind of later Canadian writing from which this anthology has been selected. What value
we should place on the early Canadian writers has always been a matter
of debate, with their advocates tending to defend them because they
existed at all in so hostile a land, and their critics tending to dismiss them
because of their lack of evident quality. Much of the argument over past
anthologies of Canadian writing has centred on the "dear bad poets,"
as James Reaney once called them:

Who wrote
Early in Canada
And never were of note.

Not very long ago, indeed, the appreciation of writing in Canada was
largely in the hands of the literary historians, because at that time it
seemed as though we had so little to offer that we could not afford to
be rigorously selective. When the first edition of the *Literary History of*
Canada appeared, as recently as 1965, Northrop Frye remarked in his
Conclusion that if evaluation had been the guiding principle of the book
it would have ended as "a huge debunking project, leaving Canadian
literature a poor naked *alouette* plucked of every feather of decency and
dignity." He added:

And Canada has produced no author who is a classic in the sense of possessing
a vision greater in kind than that of his best readers. (Canadians themselves
might argue about one or two, but in the perspective of the world at large the
statement is true.) There is no Canadian writer of whom we can say what we
can say of the world's major writers, that their readers can grow up inside their
work without ever being aware of a circumference.

Now, a mere twenty years later, we have accumulated a body of writing
that has grown immensely in variety and in strength, and we have cause
to be proud of it. Our pride, moreover, is reinforced by assurances
from outside. Not long ago I read a review in which Anthony Burgess
discussed Robertson Davies's novel, *What's Bred in the Bone*, which he
described as "high art." Burgess concluded:

If Canada is not proud of producing Robertson Davies it is the provincial
backwater that its southern neighbour thinks it is. But I have too much respect
for that great country to suppose that it cannot reconcile ice hockey with literary
greatness.

The form the present anthology takes is a sign that we have indeed
found our pride, that we are no longer afraid to judge our literature by
standards of excellence rather than provenance; the creativity of our

writers and the growing independence of our critics has relieved us of the need for the literary-historical crutch, the crutch of an approach that enabled us uneasily to avoid the responsibility of critical judgement. The editors are justified in their recognition that, in an anthology that does not claim to be historical, writers like Charles Heavysege and Susanna Moodie have no place beside far better writers like Earle Birney and Mavis Gallant. Which does not mean that we reject the "dear bad" ones; they have their own virtues, which are largely those of social history, and they will keep their places in the museum if not in the select gallery. It does mean that we are celebrating the coming of age of literature in Canada by presenting our best writers in all the variety that is one of the true signs of growth in any artistic tradition.

Apart from the fact that it is evaluative in the sense of seeking to pick the best works by the best Canadian writers, *The New Canadian Anthology* also continues the essentially critical function initiated by A. J. M. Smith's *Book of Canadian Poetry* in 1943 by presenting not only biographical notes but also concise critiques of each of the poets and prose writers included. In this sense it adds a further dimension to our view of Canadian writing; since these introductory pieces are prepared by various critics and scholars, the poems and short stories are supplemented by nearly fifty miniature individual essays which show the range and fertility of approach that in recent years have emerged among Canadian critics.

Vitality of criticism is one sign of the maturity of a literary tradition. The others, I suggest, are individuality and variegation, the constant moving away from models. Emerging literatures tend to be self-conscious in their search for identity, but once the tradition is established it forms a space within which individual writers can develop according to their own talents and inclinations. What this anthology shows best is the way in which Canadian literature has reached this situation.

Among the earlier writers included in these pages we become aware of the kinds of urge that mark the emergence of a national literary culture. Poets like Crawford and Roberts, Lampman and D. C. Scott, represent the first transitional stage, when Canadians realized that they must write from Canadian experience, but in general did so while continuing to use the forms and the diction of another tradition—that of English late romanticism. Even here the sense of a need to find forms more appropriate for the poetic charting of a new land appeared fitfully in the later poems of Duncan Campbell Scott and Charles G. D. Roberts, with their tendency towards a freer verse and towards a more imagistic kind of perception. E. J. Pratt provided a more self-conscious extension of the same process, taking themes that reflect the emergence of Canadian national sentiment, but often going back as far as the English seventeenth century and Butler's *Hudibras* to find the verse forms in which he could give these themes expression.

But it soon became obvious that there was a disparity between content and form. Canadian geography and Canadian history shaped experience and perceptions of it in ways that could not find expression in a poetic language developed in the English mid-nineteenth century, a language that in an increasingly industrialized age even English poets were finding inadequate. And so, over the next generation, the Canadian poets whose work was vital enough to survive were those who set out on a deliberate crusade of modernism in poetry, which was partly encouraged by similar currents elsewhere in the English-speaking world, but also expressed a mounting sense of cultural nationalism. So we have the various groupings of poets who centred on the avant-garde magazines of the times: the *McGill Fortnightly Review* group of the 1920s, who produced the anthology *New Provinces* in 1936, and among whom A. J. M. Smith, F. R. Scott, and later A. M. Klein were most important; and in the 1940s the partisans of the two rival Montreal magazines, *Preview*, with which P. K. Page and again Scott and Klein were associated, and *First Statement*, edited by John Sutherland, in which Irving Layton and Louis Dudek were closely involved.

Since there was no native model for a kind of poetry that might fit the Canadian experience, these writers tended paradoxically to become international in order to express their sense of nationality. They followed the work of poets elsewhere who were mounting their own rebellions against established conventions, hoping to find the formal clues that they could apply to their own situation.

The imagists—Ezra Pound and especially H. D.—strongly influenced W. W. E. Ross, who can perhaps be regarded as the first true Canadian modernist, and to a lesser extent both Smith and Scott. The latter two were also influenced by the English poets of the thirties generation (Smith actually published in English avant-garde magazines of the time like *New Verse*); Dorothy Livesay, in her autobiographical miscellany, *Right Hand Left Hand*, has told how reading Auden and Spender helped her to reconcile her fervent Marxism with her desire to write a genuine lyric poetry. The inclination to follow English examples was continued in the *Preview* group, one of whose leading figures was an English expatriate poet, Patrick Anderson.

But the *First Statement* group oriented themselves toward American mentors, theoretically because they saw themselves not merely as Canadian but also as linked to an American rebellion against old-world values, and practically because they found American speech more like their own than English. Through them the influence of Ezra Pound and William Carlos Williams entered most deeply into Canadian poetry and contributed to its rapid colloquialization. Inevitably, considering the fact of geographical proximity, developments in American poetry have continued to have their impact in Canada, as happened again in the early 1960s when, particularly on the West Coast, a number of younger poets fell under the influence of Charles Olson and other Black Mountain poets and their theories of poetic sound and its relation to breath rhythms.

But such influences have usually been quickly absorbed, and the poets subjected to them, such as George Bowering in the 1960s, have emerged as very individual voices.

Indeed, I think one of the striking characteristics of the whole period when Canadian poetry was emerging into modernism is the way in which—while poets were acting together to liberate their literature from the domination of the past, and in doing so were accepting influences from outside—there was little inclination for Canadians to write in such a derivative way that they could have fitted easily into the English 1930s or the American beat generation. This showed a completely different attitude from that of the colonial period, when poets like Oliver Goldsmith the younger and Charles Sangster and their contemporaries wrote like poets transported from England—even, in the case of Charles Heavysege and his grandiose verse dramas, from an England lost in the past. The urge to create a native and independent literature encouraged a personal individuality among its adherents, so that although we have been talking about groups in the 1920s and 1940s, these were largely associations for convenience, created for the immediate purpose of enabling poets to publish work for which there was as yet no commercial market. One has only to glance at the writings of this transitional period to realize how much, even when they were closely associated, the poets differed from each other. Placing the cool agnostic rationalism of an F. R. Scott beside the intense Jewish mysticism of an A. M. Klein not only reveals vastly differing attitudes toward life and the universe but also different uses of language and imagery; another pattern of striking contrasts can be found by comparing the ways in which Irving Layton and Raymond Souster, who collaborated in *Northern Review*, the successor to *Preview* and *First Statement*, developed into very different poets, the one bardically self-assertive and the other patiently constructing a unique urban vision out of modest perceptions recorded in the manner of latter-day imagism.

The individuality which even at this early period of the 1930s and 1940s already characterized the more vital Canadian poets then emerging led to the extraordinary variegation that appeared already in the 1950s with poets inclined towards the mythic and the metaphysical like James Reaney, Jay Macpherson, and to a lesser degree Eli Mandel, and has become the most striking feature of the 1970s and 1980s in Canadian writing, both poetry and prose. Liberated within an assured tradition, writers in recent years have tended to follow their own idiosyncratic courses without being dominated by the imperatives of either nationalism or conventional avant-gardism, and it would be hard to find much in common between the youngest poets in this collection—Margaret Atwood, Daphne Marlatt, Michael Ondaatje, bp Nichol, Mary di Michele, and Roo Borson—except the fact that they are all Canadian. Writers from the 1930s and 1940s, like Dorothy Livesay and Earle Birney and

P. K. Page, who got their second winds of inspiration during the 1960s, re-emerged at a higher stage of poetic self-realization, as one can see in the case of Birney by comparing "The Bear on the Delhi Road" with "Vancouver Lights"; or in the case of Dorothy Livesay by comparing "Ice Age" with "Day and Night." In each case the earlier poem is covertly didactic, making an obliquely political point; the later poem is the lyrically intense recording of a gratuitous perception about existence.

Studying the poets from E. J. Pratt onwards, one becomes aware— among the echoes of foreign influences—of the emergence of a distinctive tone one can only call Canadian: a gruff, ironic tone of self-recognition and self-deprecation (projected in the image of the poet as clown appearing so often in writers like Birney, Purdy, and Layton) that finds its expression in an easily colloquial language or in the kind of laconic pattern of short lines that was first developed in Canada by W. W. E. Ross, whose brief 1939 poem, "Loon" (not included in this collection), I take the liberty of quoting because in its close sense of the land, in its tendency to identify with wild creatures, in its modesty, directness, and clarity of diction, and yet in its contained simplicity, it epitomizes so much that is characteristic of the best in recent Canadian poetry:

> *Black and white*
> *the loon glides at approach of night*
> *on the lake. The moon*
> *nearly full will soon*
>
> *fill the lake with eerie glow*
> *and the rocks around will soon*
> *echo over the water below*
> *the wild calling of the loon.*

Up to now I have concentrated on poetry, and this is not only because there are more poets than prose writers in this anthology. It is also because poetry has been the cutting edge of new developments in Canadian literature for the past century, a national fiction following on the heels of a national poetry, and poets themselves often becoming the most strikingly experimental of novelists. No less than three poets included in this anthology—Robert Kroetsch, Leonard Cohen, and Margaret Atwood—are among the more important Canadian fiction writers, while others, like Earle Birney, P. K. Page, and George Bowering, have written interesting individual novels.

The accidents of publication—it was often easier for a book of substantial length to appear in Boston or New York than in Toronto or Montreal—had created in the nineteenth century a tendency for Canadian fiction writers to look southward over the border, and even when Canada began to produce novelists and storytellers of some stature and individuality, like Sara Jeannette Duncan and Stephen Leacock, they seemed to fit as much into a continental as into a Canadian pattern.

Duncan's great masters were William Dean Howells and Henry James, and Leacock was in many respects an heir to the American humourist tradition represented by Mark Twain; yet they wrote best, as Duncan did in *The Imperialist* and Leacock in *Sunshine Sketches of a Little Town*, when they wrote drawing deeply on their Canadian experience. This inclination was carried on into the 1920s, especially by Morley Callaghan, who in his earlier days tended to seek and find an audience in the United States and who learnt much about the writing of fiction from his association with Ernest Hemingway—which did not prevent him from writing some of the best novels of Canadian urban life.

Indeed, it is among the fiction writers—more than among the poets—that the pattern of departure and return, the tradition of the Canadian expatriate writer, has been most evident. Mavis Gallant, for example, has spent virtually all her writing life in Paris and has contributed most of her stories, before publication in volume form, to the *New Yorker*. Mordecai Richler wrote most of his novels in England, where Margaret Laurence also lived for a long period, having already spent years in Africa. But this did not make these writers less Canadian; they did not become successful transplants into the new environment, like Canadian actors in Hollywood. Rather, they added their new experiences to their old ones, which they had acquired during those first twenty years of life that, as Richler once remarked, provide a novelist with the ideas and impressions on which he or she works for the whole of his or her career. As their frequent homecomings in fiction demonstrate, it is impossible to think of Richler or Gallant without the Montreal childhoods they have so vividly re-created. Margaret Laurence's African experiences, once she had translated them into literature in books like *This Side Jordan* (1960) and *The Prophet's Camel Bell* (1963), turned out to be merely the prelude to a deep immersion in her prairie background. This in turn led her to write that remarkable sequence of books, from *The Stone Angel* (1964) to *The Diviners* (1974), which may well constitute the greatest Canadian achievement in fiction to date. It certainly represents the peak of the urge—which the Canadian novelists in the years after World War II shared with the poets—to give the Canadian land and its inhabitants a shaping myth that would do justice to its splendid geography and also to its history as a unique community of peoples. Now the pattern of expatriation—which was so characteristic of the transitional 1950s, when writers were trying to establish their identities in a shifting world—is less evident; indeed, a reverse pattern is perceptible, for some of the best story writers in this anthology, like Leon Rooke and Audrey Thomas (American in origin) and John Metcalf (English in origin), began work in other settings before they brought their talents to enrich Canadian literature.

More than the poems, the stories in this volume act as pointers to larger works that cannot be represented here, for all but a few of their creators have written novels as well. To get the full flavour of Canadian fiction, the reader who admires Sinclair Ross's "The Painted Door" or Morley Callaghan's "Now that April's Here" or Ethel Wilson's "From Flores" should carry on to read Ross's *As For Me and My House*—one of the finest prairie novels—or *They Shall Inherit the Earth* and the other splendid moral fables in the form of novels that Callaghan produced during the 1930s—or Wilson's sensitive novels set in British Columbia, like *Hetty Dorval* and *Swamp Angel*, which so intriguingly combine an Edwardian sensibility with a modern intelligence.

But it would be wrong to regard the stories as merely introductions to their writers' larger works, or in any way as specimens of a minor genre. Only in size is the short story less than the novel: in the hands of a fine writer it can produce a vision of life as intense—though necessarily not so complex—as that of a novel, and Canadian writers have long been attracted to this briefer form. Generally speaking, the story is one of the less profitable literary genres, and one of the less popular among publishers and editors of periodicals, and there were times—particularly during the 1950s and 1960s—when it was hard even to get stories published. But for reasons that critics have not satisfactorily explained, Canadian writers continued to produce them. For a long time their principal patron was the CBC, where, from the 1940s, Robert Weaver (later also the editor of the *Tamarack Review*) broadcast stories, paid their writers, and even arranged for their publication in anthologies. Some of the best story writers—such as Alice Munro and Hugh Hood—developed under his encouragement, and so the story continued as a living form until, from the late 1960s onward, publishers began to take risks with short fiction again and new and vital story-tellers appeared. Some of the best are represented here, and among them are excellent writers who have made the story their special genre and have not yet chosen to go beyond it, like Keath Fraser.

Poetry and short fiction, of course, are not all the constituents of a literary tradition. Behind the story looms the novel, and we have already noted how impossible it is to convey any sense of the intricate architecture of such a form through a chapter picked for inclusion in a miscellany. Behind poetry stands drama, which was once its natural blank-verse extension, but which in more recent centuries has become a meeting ground where the prose and poetry of customary dialogue meet. But there is an inevitable colloquial diffusiveness about contemporary drama that makes it difficult to bring into a volume with more compact forms like the poem and the short story.

There are also the other, non-fictional and non-poetic forms of writing that sometimes verge on imaginative literature, like history—whose need to make comprehensible patterns often edges it over into myth—and like biography and autobiography, which are often infused with the imaginative intensity of fiction, as the biographer seeks to enter the mind of his subject or the autobiographer seeks to find a pattern in his own past. Again, these are forms too peripheral to find a place in such a collection as this, though one can conceive an ideal Canadian anthology, of several volumes and three thousand pages, where every kind of writing representative of our culture would have its place. One day, perhaps, we shall see it.

Over the last century, what was once a scattering of writers working largely in isolation across a vast country, has gradually been transformed into a literary community. It is this literary community, come of age, that *The New Canadian Anthology: Poetry and Short Fiction in English* presents. The days when "Canadian literature" was a phrase used either with diffidence or with mockery have come to an end. English-Canadian writers and writing can stand with pride, as these offerings show, beside those of any other English-writing community.

•POETRY•

· ISABELLA VALANCY CRAWFORD ·

1850–1887

If any single writer can be regarded as marking the beginning of the change from the dependent colonial tradition in Canadian poetry represented by Heavysege and Sangster in the mid-Victorian age, it is Isabella Valancy Crawford. She stands at the beginning of the emergent Canadian tradition of the last decades of the century, though her recognition and what influence she had were entirely posthumous.

Isabella Crawford was born in Dublin of a Highland Scottish family in 1850. Her father, who was a physician, brought his family to Canada in 1858, where he tried to survive through a country practice in the pioneer settlement of Paisley in Canada West. After being involved in a humiliating scandal, when he was prosecuted and convicted of misappropriating public funds as township treasurer of Paisley, Dr. Crawford moved to Lakefield and then to Peterborough. However, continuing ill fortune and ineptitude prevented him from making an adequate living for his family, even though almost all his twelve or thirteen children died young from an inherited heart disease.

Following the only profession then acceptable for a lady, Isabella Valancy Crawford began her literary career when she set out to help the family by selling the short stories and poems she wrote to newspapers and magazines in Toronto. Her father died in 1875, and the following year, when her remaining invalid sister also died, she and her mother moved to Toronto, where they took rooms over a grocery store on King Street. There, to keep the two of them alive in shabby gentility, Isabella evolved a Canadian variant of the Grub Street life, turning out a series of writings in prose and verse which she hawked around the few available sources of publication. She even wrote a novel, *The Little Bacchante*, which appeared as a serial in the *Toronto Evening Globe*. In 1884, having scraped and saved enough money by meagre living, she published at her own expense the only book of hers to appear in her lifetime, a collection of poems, 224 pages long, entitled *Old Spookses' Pass, Malcolm's Katie, and Other Poems*. Forbiddingly titled, shoddily bound, and, as Isabella herself said, "decorated with press errors as a Zulu chief is laden with beads," the book was a disappointing failure; in spite of friendly reviews in both English and Canadian papers, only fifty of the thousand copies that were printed sold.

Nevertheless, a subdued interest in Crawford's poetry continued after her sudden death of the family sickness in 1887. *Old Spookses' Pass* was reprinted in 1898, and in 1905 Crawford was "discovered" by that early enthusiast of Canadian literature, John William Garvin, founder of the short-lived *Master Works of Canadian Literature* series, who in 1905 published *The Collected Poems of Isabella Valancy Crawford*, which added fifty-two poems that had never before appeared in volume form. In spite of its erratic editing, Garvin's volume marked the turning point in the establishment of Crawford's reputation. But, though in recent years James Reaney has been eloquent in presenting Crawford as an important mythopoeic poet, it is really to A. J. M. Smith that we owe her serious acceptance into the recognized canon of Canadian poetry through his ample selections from her work in *The Book of Canadian Poetry* and later in the *Oxford Book of Canadian Verse*.

While the more extravagant recent claims for Crawford's major standing can be somewhat discounted, it is certainly with a real sense of something new entering Canadian poetry that one compares her work with that of her immediate predecessors. In terms of its form her poetry is not very innovative. In diction, imagery, and metrical shape her poems resemble those of the later English romantics, and her luminous visualizations put one in mind of the pre-Raphaelite painters and even, at times, of Landseer. She thought and felt like the High-Victorian colonial she was. What is new in her is the way she gives herself to her poetry. For her Canadian predecessors, poetry had been part of the cultural wall that pioneer groups raised against a hostile world, and the defensiveness became an inhibition that negated both passion and originality. But Crawford used poetry to liberate rather than to defend, and the prosodic clichés with which her work abounds are fired by the needs of a passionate nature and a sometimes grotesque mind. Her poems grip our imaginations because they are moved by frustrated passion, and by the power of an inner vision that had little to do with the objective world in which the poet lived. When Crawford did face that world openly, she could only deal with it, at best, in terms of satire, as in such interestingly uncharacteristic pieces as "A Wooing" and "The Rolling-Pin." Her work was uneven, and long stretches of her narrative poems can only be described as tedious, bad verse, because she was trying to tell an obvious tale or point an obvious moral. The Crawford we value is the woman of obscure life whose bizarre hidden personality emerges so strikingly when she draws conventional imagery into the fantastic, as in that strange multiple conceit of a poem, "Said the Canoe":

They hung the slaughter'd fish like swords
On saplings, slender—like scimitars
Bright, and ruddied from new-dead wars,
Blaz'd in the light—the scaly hordes.

· —————— ·

Works by Crawford include *Old Spookses' Pass, Malcolm's Katie, and Other Poems* (1884); *The Collected Poems of Isabella Valancy Crawford*, ed. John Garvin (1905); *Isabella Valancy Crawford: Makers of Canadian Literature*, ed. Katherine Hale (1923); *Selected Stories of Isabella Valancy Crawford*, ed. Penny Petrone (1975); *Fairy Tales of Isabella Valancy Crawford*, ed. Penny Petrone (1977); *Hugh and Ion*, ed. Glenn Clever (1977); and *The Halton Boys: A Story for Boys*, ed. Frank Tierney (1979).

Works on Crawford include Frank Bessai, "The Ambivalence of Love in the Poetry of Isabella Valancy Crawford," *Queen's Quarterly* 77 (1970): 404–18; Mary F. Martin, "The Short Life of Isabella Valancy Crawford," *Dalhousie Review* 52.3 (1972): 390–400; Ann Yeoman, "Towards a Native Mythology: The Poetry of Isabella Valancy Crawford," *Canadian Literature* 52 (1972): 39–47; Lynn Suo, "An Annotated Bibliography on Isabella Valancy Crawford," *Essays on Canadian Writing* 11 (1977): 289–314; *The Isabella Valancy Crawford Symposium*, ed. and intro. Frank Tierney (1979); and Dorothy Farmiloe, *Isabella Valancy Crawford: The Life and the Legends* (1983).

GEORGE WOODCOCK

THE ROMAN ROSE-SELLER

Not from Pæstum come my roses; Patrons, see
My flowers are Roman-blown; their nectaries
Drop honey amber, and their petals throw
Rich crimsons on the lucent marble of the shrine
Where snowy Dian lifts her pallid brow,
As crimson lips of Love may seek to warm
A sister glow in hearts as pulseless hewn.
Cæsar from Afric wars returns to-day;
Patricians, buy my royal roses; strew
10 His way knee-deep, as though old Tiber roll'd
A tide of musky roses from his bed to do
A wonder, wond'rous homage. Marcus Lucius, thou
To-day dost wed; buy roses, roses, roses,
To mingle with the nuptial myrtle; look,
I strip the polish'd thorns from the stems,
The nuptial rose should be a stingless flower;
Lucania, pass not by my roses. Virginia,
Here is a rose that has a canker in't, and yet
It is most glorious-dyed and sweeter smells
20 Than those death hath not touched. To-day they bear
The shield of Claudius with his spear upon it,
Close upon Cæsar's chariot—heap, heap it up
With roses such as these; 'tis true he's dead
And there's the canker! but, Romans, he
Died glorious, there's the perfume! and his virtues
Are these bright petals; so buy my roses, Widow.
No Greek-born roses mine. Priestess, priestess!
Thy ivory chariot stay; here's a rose and not
A white one, though thy chaste hands attend
30 On Vesta's flame. Love's of a colour—be it that
Which ladders Heaven and lives amongst the Gods;
Or like the Daffodil blows all about the earth;
Or, Hesperus like, is one sole star upon
The solemn sky which bridges some sad life,
So here's a crimson rose: Be thou as pure
As Dian's tears iced on her silver cheek,
And know no quality of love, thou art
A sorrow to the Gods! Oh mighty Love!
I would my roses could but chorus Thee.
40 No roses of Persepolis are mine. Helot, here—
I give thee this last blossom: A bee as red

As Hybla's golden toilers sucked its sweets;
A butterfly, wing'd like to Eros, nipp'd
Its new-pinked leaves; the sun, bright despot, stole
The dew night gives to all. Poor slave, methinks
A bough of cypress were as gay a gift, and yet
It hath some beauty left! a little scarlet—for
The Gods love all; a little perfume, for there is no life,
Poor slave, but hath its sweetness. Thus I make
50 My roses Oracles. O hark! the cymbals beat
In god-like silver bursts of sound; I go
To see great Cæsar leading Glory home,
From Campus Martius to the Capitol!

[1874]

THE DARK STAG

A startled stag, the blue-grey Night,
  Leaps down beyond black pines.
Behind—a length of yellow light—
  The hunter's arrow shines:
His moccasins are stained with red,
  He bends upon his knee,
From covering peaks his shafts are sped,
The blue mists plume his mighty head,—
  Well may the swift Night flee!

10 The pale, pale Moon, a snow-white doe,
  Bounds by his dappled flank:
They beat the stars down as they go,
  Like wood-bells growing rank.
The winds lift dewlaps from the ground,
  Leap from the quaking reeds;
Their hoarse bays shake the forests round,
With keen cries on the track they bound,—
  Swift, swift the dark stag speeds!

  Away! his white doe, far behind,
20   Lies wounded on the plain;
Yells at his flank the nimblest wind,

His large tears fall in rain;
Like lily-pads, small clouds grow white
   About his darkling way;
From his bald nest upon the height
The red-eyed eagle sees his flight;
He falters, turns, the antlered Night,—
   The dark stag stands at bay!

His feet are in the waves of space;
30   His antlers broad and dun
He lowers; he turns his velvet face
   To front the hunter, Sun;
He stamps the lilied clouds, and high
   His branches fill the west.
The lean stork sails across the sky,
The shy loon shrieks to see him die,
   The winds leap at his breast.

Roar the rent lakes as thro' the wave
   Their silver warriors plunge,
40 As vaults from core of crystal cave
   The strong, fierce muskallunge;
Red torches of the sumach glare,
   Fall's council-fires are lit;
The bittern, squaw-like, scolds the air;
The wild duck splashes loudly where
   The rustling rice-spears knit.

Shaft after shaft the red Sun speeds:
   Rent the stag's dappled side,
His breast, fanged by the shrill winds, bleeds,
50   He staggers on the tide;
He feels the hungry waves of space
   Rush at him high and blue;
Their white spray smites his dusky face,
Swifter the Sun's fierce arrows race
   And pierce his stout heart thro'.

His antlers fall; once more he spurns
   The hoarse hounds of the day;
His blood upon the crisp blue burns,
   Reddens the mounting spray;
60 His branches smite the wave—with cries
   The loud winds pause and flag—

He sinks in space—red glow the skies,
The brown earth crimsons as he dies,
    The strong and dusky stag.

[1883]

SAID THE CANOE

My masters twain made me a bed
Of pine-boughs resinous, and cedar;
Of moss, a soft and gentle breeder
Of dreams of rest; and me they spread
With furry skins and, laughing, said:
"Now she shall lay her polished sides
As queens do rest, or dainty brides,
Our slender lady of the tides!"

My masters twain their camp-soul lit;
10 Streamed incense from the hissing cones:
Large crimson flashes grew and whirled;
Thin golden nerves of sly light curled
Round the dun camp; and rose faint zones,
Half way about each grim bole knit,
Like a shy child that would bedeck
With its soft clasp a Brave's red neck,
Yet sees the rough shield on his breast,
The awful plumes shake on his crest,
And, fearful, drops his timid face,
20 Nor dares complete the sweet embrace.

Into the hollow hearts of brakes—
Yet warm from sides of does and stags
Passed to the crisp, dark river-flags—
Sinuous, red as copper-snakes,
Sharp-headed serpents, made of light,
Glided and hid themselves in night.

My masters twain the slaughtered deer
Hung on forked boughs with thongs of leather:
Bound were his stiff, slim feet together,

30 His eyes like dead stars cold and drear.
   The wandering firelight drew near
   And laid its wide palm, red and anxious,
   On the sharp splendour of his branches,
   On the white foam grown hard and sere
      On flank and shoulder.
   Death—hard as breast of granite boulder—
      Under his lashes
   Peered thro' his eves at his life's grey ashes.

   My masters twain sang songs that wove—
40 As they burnished hunting-blade and rifle—
   A golden thread with a cobweb trifle,
   Loud of the chase and low of love:

   "O Love! art thou a silver fish,
   Shy of the line and shy of gaffing,
   Which we do follow, fierce, yet laughing,
   Casting at thee the light-winged wish?
   And at the last shall we bring thee up
   From the crystal darkness, under the cup
      Of lily folden
50   On broad leaves golden?

   "O Love! art thou a silver deer,
   With feet as swift as wing of swallow,
   While we with rushing arrows follow?
   And at the last shall we draw near
   And o'er thy velvet neck cast thongs
   Woven of roses, stars and songs—
      New chains all moulden
      Of rare gems olden?"

   They hung the slaughtered fish like swords
60   On saplings slender; like scimitars,
      Bright, and ruddied from new-dead wars,
   Blazed in the light the scaly hordes.

   They piled up boughs beneath the trees,
      Of cedar web and green fir tassel.
      Low did the pointed pine tops rustle,
   The camp-fire blushed to the tender breeze.

   The hounds laid dewlaps on the ground
      With needles of pine, sweet, soft and rusty,

Dreamed of the dead stag stout and lusty;
70 A bat by the red flames wove its round.

The darkness built its wigwam walls
  Close round the camp, and at its curtain
  Pressed shapes, thin, woven and uncertain
As white locks of tall waterfalls.

[1884]

THE LILY BED

His cedar paddle, scented, red,
He thrust down through the lily bed;

Cloaked in a golden pause he lay,
Locked in the arms of the placid bay.

Trembled alone his bark canoe
As shocks of bursting lilies flew

Thro' the still crystal of the tide,
And smote the frail boat's birchen side;

Or, when, beside the sedges thin
10 Rose the sharp silver of a fin;

Or when, a wizard swift and cold,
A dragon-fly beat out in gold

And jewels all the widening rings
Of waters singing to his wings;

Or, like a winged and burning soul,
Dropped from the gloom an oriole

On the cool wave, as to the balm
Of the Great Spirit's open palm

The freed soul flies. And silence clung
20 To the still hours, as tendrils hung,

In darkness carven, from the trees,
Sedge-buried to their burly knees.

Stillness sat in his lodge of leaves;
Clung golden shadows to its eaves,

And on its cone-spiced floor, like maize,
Red-ripe, fell sheaves of knotted rays.

The wood, a proud and crested brave;
Bead-bright, a maiden, stood the wave.

And he had spoke his soul of love
30 With voice of eagle and of dove.

Of loud, strong pines his tongue was made;
His lips, soft blossoms in the shade,

That kissed her silver lips—her's cool
As lilies on his inmost pool—

Till now he stood in triumph's rest,
His image painted in her breast.

One isle 'tween blue and blue did melt,—
A bead of wampum from the belt

Of Manitou—a purple rise
40 On the far shore heaved to the skies.

His cedar paddle, scented, red,
He drew up from the lily bed;

All lily-locked, all lily-locked,
His light bark in the blossoms rocked.

Their cool lips round the sharp prow sang,
Their soft clasp to the frail sides sprang,

With breast and lip they wove a bar.
Stole from her lodge the Evening Star;

With golden hand she grasped the mane
50 Of a red cloud on her azure plain.

It by the peaked, red sunset flew;
Cool winds from its bright nostrils blew.

They swayed the high, dark trees, and low
Swept the locked lilies to and fro.

With cedar paddle, scented, red,
He pushed out from the lily bed.

[1884]

· CHARLES G. D. ROBERTS ·

1860–1943

Cousin to Bliss Carman, Charles G. D. Roberts was born in Douglas, New Brunswick, on 10 January 1860. The family moved to Westcock, New Brunswick, the same year, where, eventually tutored by his father and by the spiritual tenor of the Tantramar Marshes, Roberts accumulated a storehouse of images for the fiction and poetry he would later write. Roberts's father became Canon of Christ Church Cathedral, Fredericton, in 1874. In Fredericton Roberts graduated from the University of New Brunswick in 1879 and he married in 1880. In the same year his *Orion and Other Poems* established him as a major Canadian writer, one who also inspired other "Confederation" poets to work with a new vigour and a sense of national pride. He was a high-school headmaster in Chatham, New Brunswick, from 1879 to 1882, and he received an MA from the University of New Brunswick in 1881. After a politically difficult editorship at the *Week* in 1883, and a financially difficult attempt at freelance work, he became a professor at King's College, Windsor, Nova Scotia, in 1885. He remained there for ten years, writing poetry, fiction, and history in his spare time. He was elected a fellow of the Royal Society of Canada in 1890 and of the Royal Society of Literature in 1893. After 1895 he attempted another two-year period of freelancing in Fredericton, but left for New York in 1897 to become an assistant editor at the *Illustrated American* for nine months. In 1898 he was elected the only non-American charter member of the National Institute of Arts and Letters, and lived in New York until he moved to Europe in 1907. He settled in London in 1912, and served in World War I. He lived in Europe and then in England until 1925, re-turning to Canada in that year as a popular writer and lecturer. In 1926 he became president of the Canadian Authors' Association and was awarded the Lorne Pierce Gold Medal of the Royal Society of Canada. He was knighted in 1935, and, when not on tour, he lived in Toronto, where he remarried very late in life, and where he died on 26 November 1943.

Roberts's major output as a poet was in the years 1880 to 1898, when he published such volumes as *Orion and Other Poems* (1880), *In Divers Tones* (1886), *Songs of the Common Day, and Ave: An Ode for the Shelley Centenary* (1893), and *New York Nocturnes and Other Poems* (1898). Increasingly, after the turn of the century, Roberts was to pour his creative energies into the writing of wilderness and romance fiction, and his achievement as a poet is therefore largely visible in the poetry he wrote before middle age. His first two volumes established him as a poet who knew the received forms of classical and British poetry (Shelley, Keats, Wordsworth, Tennyson, and Swinburne are his usually cited mentors) and could also eloquently employ such forms to his own end of evoking the mystery and solitude of his own Canadian region. James Cappon said of him that all of his poetry has the "cosmic touch," and this is true of his many poems of place and nostalgia such as "The Tantramar Revisited" in *In Divers Tones*. In addition to long, lofty poems expressive of an evolutionary idealism, Roberts wrote many shorter poems such as "The Sower" and "The Potato Harvest" in *In Divers Tones* and "In an Old Barn" in *Songs of the Common Day, and Ave*, which blend a Wordsworthian regard for ordinary labour with an Emersonian gift for noticing the miracle in the common. Roberts's shorter poems are his most memorable ones, and in *New York Nocturnes and Other Poems* he also departed interestingly from his nature themes with a series of Swinburne- and Baudelaire-inspired love lyrics which critics have only recently begun to respect for their modernity. That volume also contains Roberts's "The Solitary Woodsman," a poem which summarily renders in cameo the sensitivity he prized the most in his canon; a temporary sense of peace which is felt when, in solitude, the spirit contemplates that which in his fiction he calls "the heart of the ancient wood." Roberts's *Selected Poems* (1936) contains his later poems; and while it houses his accomplished "The Iceberg," it does not match the measure of his two very best volumes, *In Divers Tones* and *Songs of the Common Day, and Ave.*

Roberts's works include *Orion and Other Poems* (1880); *In Divers Tones* (1886); *Songs of the Common Day, and Ave: An Ode for the Shelley Centenary* (1893); *New York Nocturnes and Other Poems* (1898); *Selected Poems* (1936); and *The Collected Poems of Sir Charles G. D. Roberts* (1985).

Works on Roberts include James Cappon, *Charles G. D. Roberts and the Influences of His Time* (1905); E. M. Pomeroy, *Sir Charles G. D. Roberts: A Biography* (1943); W. J. Keith, *Charles G. D. Roberts* (1969); Fred Cogswell, "Charles G. D. Roberts," *Canadian Writers and Their Works*, ed. Robert Lecker, Jack David, and Ellen Quigley (1983), Poetry Series 2: 187–226; Carrie MacMillan, ed., *The Proceedings of the Sir Charles G. D. Roberts Symposium, Mount Allison University* (1984); Glenn Clever, *The Sir Charles G. D. Roberts Symposium* (1984); and John Coldwell Adams, *Sir Charles God Damn* (1986).

TERRY WHALEN

TANTRAMAR REVISITED

Summers and summers have come, and gone with the flight of the
    swallow;
Sunshine and thunder have been, storm, and winter, and frost;
Many and many a sorrow has all but died from remembrance,
Many a dream of joy fall'n in the shadow of pain.
Hands of chance and change have marred, or moulded, or
    broken,
Busy with spirit or flesh, all I most have adored;
Even the bosom of Earth is strewn with heavier shadows,—
Only in these green hills, aslant to the sea, no change!
Here where the road that has climbed from the inland valleys and
    woodlands,
10 Dips from the hill-tops down, straight to the base of the hills,—
Here, from my vantage-ground, I can see the scattering houses,
Stained with time, set warm in orchards, and meadows, and wheat,

Dotting the broad bright slopes outspread to southward and
   eastward,
Wind-swept all day long, blown by the south-east wind.

Skirting the sunbright uplands stretches a riband of meadow,
Shorn of the labouring grass, bulwarked well from the sea,
Fenced on its seaward border with long clay dykes from the turbid
Surge and flow of the tides vexing the Westmoreland shores.
Yonder, toward the left, lie broad the Westmoreland marshes,—
20 Miles on miles they extend, level, and grassy, and dim,
Clear from the long red sweep of flats to the sky in the distance,
Save for the outlying heights, green-rampired Cumberland Point;
Miles on miles outrolled, and the river-channels divide them,—
Miles on miles of green, barred by the hurtling gusts.

Miles on miles beyond the tawny bay is Minudie.
There are the low blue hills; villages gleam at their feet.
Nearer a white sail shines across the water, and nearer
Still are the slim, grey masts of fishing boats dry on the flats.
Ah, how well I remember those wide red flats, above tide-mark
30 Pale with scurf of the salt, seamed and baked in the sun!
Well I remember the piles of blocks and ropes, and the net-reels
Wound with the beaded nets, dripping and dark from the sea!
Now at this season the nets are unwound; they hang from the
   rafters
Over the fresh-stowed hay in upland barns, and the wind
Blows all day through the chinks, with the streaks of sunlight, and
   sways them
Softly at will; or they lie heaped in the gloom of a loft.

Now at this season the reels are empty and idle; I see them
Over the lines of the dykes, over the gossiping grass,

Now at this season they swing in the long strong wind, thro' the
   lonesome
40 Golden afternoon, shunned by the foraging gulls.
Near about sunset the crane will journey homeward above them;
Round them, under the moon, all the calm night long,
Winnowing soft grey wings of marsh-owls wander and wander,
Now to the broad, lit marsh, now to the dusk of the dike.
Soon, thro' their dew-wet frames, in the live keen freshness of
   morning,
Out of the teeth of the dawn blows back the awakening wind.
Then, as the blue day mounts, and the low-shot shafts of the
   sunlight
Glance from the tide to the shore, gossamers jewelled with dew

Sparkle and wave, where late sea-spoiling fathoms of drift-net
50 Myriad-meshed, uploomed sombrely over the land.

Well I remember it all. The salt, raw scent of the margin;
While, with men at the windlass, groaned each reel, and the net,
Surging in ponderous lengths, uprose and coiled in its station;
Then each man to his home,—well I remember it all!

Yet, as I sit and watch, this present peace of the landscape,—
Stranded boats, these reels empty and idle, the hush,
One grey hawk slow-wheeling above yon cluster of haystacks,—
More than the old-time stir this stillness welcomes me home.
Ah, the old-time stir, how once it stung me with rapture,—
60 Old-time sweetness, the winds freighted with honey and salt!
Yet will I stay my steps and not go down to the marshland,—
Muse and recall far off, rather remember than see,—
Lest on too close sight I miss the darling illusion,
Spy at their task even here the hands of chance and change.

[1883]

THE SOWER

A brown, sad-coloured hillside, where the soil
    Fresh from the frequent harrow, deep and fine,
    Lies bare; no break in the remote sky-line,
Save where a flock of pigeons streams aloft,
Startled from feed in some low-lying croft,
    Or far-off spires with yellow of sunset shine;
    And here the Sower, unwittingly divine,
Exerts the silent forethought of his toil.

Alone he treads the glebe, his measured stride
    Dumb in the yielding soil; and tho' small joy
    Dwell in his heavy face, as spreads the blind
Pale grain from his dispensing palm aside,
    This plodding churl grows great in his employ;—
    Godlike, he makes provision for mankind.

[1884]

THE POTATO HARVEST

A high bare field, brown from the plough, and borne
  Aslant from sunset; amber wastes of sky
  Washing the ridge; a clamour of crows that fly
In from the wide flats where the spent tides mourn
To yon their rocking roosts in pines wind-torn;
  A line of grey snake-fence that zigzags by
  A pond and cattle; from the homestead nigh
The long deep summonings of the supper horn.

Black on the ridge, against that lonely flush,
  A cart, and stoop-necked oxen; ranged beside
    Some barrels; and the day-worn harvest-folk,
Here emptying their baskets, jar the hush
  With hollow thunders. Down the dusk hillside
    Lumbers the wain; and day fades out like smoke.

[1886]

IN AN OLD BARN

Tons upon tons the brown-green fragrant hay
  O'erbrims the mows beyond the time-warped eaves,
  Up to the rafters where the spider weaves,
Though few flies wander his secluded way.
Through a high chink one lonely golden ray,
  Wherein the dust is dancing, slants unstirred.
  In the dry hush some rustlings light are heard,
Of winter-hidden mice at furtive play.

Far down, the cattle in their shadowed stalls,
  Nose-deep in clover fodder's meadowy scent,
    Forget the snows that whelm their pasture streams,
The frost that bites the world beyond their walls.
  Warm housed, they dream of summer, well content
    In day-long contemplation of their dreams.

[1893]

· BLISS CARMAN ·

1861–1929

Cousin to Charles G. D. Roberts, Bliss Carman was born in Fredericton, New Brunswick, on 15 April 1861. He graduated from the University of New Brunswick in 1881, and he was also a graduate of what Roberts was to call the "strange aesthetic ferment" of the Fredericton cultural scene during his youth. Typical of what was to become his vagabond identity as a writer, he wandered somewhat aimlessly (as an overseas student in Britain, as a teacher in Fredericton, as an unhappy lover) until, after an M.A. from the University of New Brunswick, he went to Harvard University in 1866 and absorbed the lectures and the works of Josiah Royce, Francis Child, and George Santayana. It was there that he also met Richard Hovey, the poet of the open road who convinced Carman to dedicate his life to poetry. Some of Carman's individual poems had already appeared in the *Week*, the *Harvard Monthly*, and the *Atlantic Monthly* when he left Harvard in 1888 for a life of travelling, visiting, writing, and editorial work. His first volume was *Low Tide on Grand Pré: A Book of Lyrics* (1893), and its reception as the work of a major Canadian nature mystic gave Carman the courage to write his way through more than thirty volumes of verse during his lifetime. His accomplishment as a poet is uneven because he tried to earn his living by writing poetry, and by performing editorial tasks for such publications as the *Independent, Current Literature, Cosmopolitan*, the *Boston Transcript*, the *Atlantic Monthly*, and the *Chap Book*. The latter publication he established with the help of Hovey in 1894. This publication, and his bachelor lifestyle as a world traveller, placed him in close contact and discussion with many world-class poets of his day. By the turn of the century he was received and acclaimed on both sides of the Atlantic—and he was more firmly appreciated in the United States than in Canada. From about 1897 onwards he spent much of his time visiting Mary Perry King and her husband in Connecticut, and in 1908 his interest in Mrs. King and in her Delsartean ideas led him to settle there, using it as his base for the rest of his life. After an illness in 1920 provoked fresh interest in him in Canada, he travelled across Canada several times during that decade. He was honoured at the inaugural dinner of the Canadian Authors' Association in Montreal in 1922. Other honours in the 1920s included a series of honorary degrees, election as a corresponding member of the Royal Society of Canada, and a commission, in 1927, to edit *The Oxford Book of American Verse*. By the time of his death in New Canaan, Connecticut, on 8 June 1929, his poetry was already being regarded as somewhat antique, too romantic in sentiment and traditional in craft for the taste of a more complicated world.

While Carman adopted many masks and mythologies during his career—he is variously a nature mystic, bohemian poet of the open road, love poet, Canadian symbolist, sea-balladist, Maritime poet of witness, Delsartean philosopher, elegist, and poet of nostalgia—he is best known in Canada for two kinds of poems which initially seem to contradict each other: poems of unscreened melancholy and poems of unscreened joy. "Low Tide on Grand Pré," a poem that Desmond Pacey called "the most nearly perfect single poem to come out of Canada," is an example of the melancholy order, and "Vagabond Song" is an example in the order of joy. Both of these poems are paradigmatic of Carman's ability, at his best to contain a frankness of emotion wi' carefully crafted bounds set by traditional stanzaic patterns. Carman was not a great technical innovator—he once described free verse as "4% beer"—but his best poems indicate a grace of traditional craftsmanship that demonstrates that perhaps the genie is powerful precisely because he *is* in the bottle, because he is restrained from chaos by boundaries. Carman's poetry is, for all the range of its tones, unified in its love of beauty and its high regard for intuitive mystical states. Recent critics have begun to uncover a philosophical vigour which had previously been overlooked in his canon, a freshness of sensibility after the vogue of modernist poetics, and a delicacy in his love poetry, especially in his *Sappho: One Hundred Lyrics* (1905), all of which help to retrieve his reputation as an important Canadian poet.

Carman's works include *Low Tide on Grand Pré: A Book of Lyrics* (1893); *Behind the Arras: A Book of the Unseen* (1895); *Sappho: One Hundred Lyrics* (1905); *Ballads and Lyrics* (1923); John Robert Sorfleet, ed., *The Poems of Bliss Carman* (1976); and H. Pearson Gundy, ed., *Letters of Bliss Carman* (1982).

Works on Carman include H. D. C. Lee; *Bliss Carman: A Study in Canadian Poetry* (1912); Odell Shepard, *Bliss Carman* (1923); James Cappon, *Bliss Carman and the Literary Currents and Influences of His Time* (1930); Muriel Miller, *Bliss Carman: A Portrait* (1935); Donald Stephens, *Bliss Carman* (1966); Terry Whalen, "Bliss Carman," *Canadian Writers and Their Works*, ed. Robert Lecker, Jack David, and Ellen Quigley (1983), Poetry Series 2: 77–132; and Muriel Miller, *Bliss Carman: Quest and Revolt* (1985).

.———————.

TERRY WHALEN

LOW TIDE ON GRAND PRÉ

The sun goes down, and over all
  These barren reaches by the tide
Such unelusive glories fall,
  I almost dream they yet will bide
  Until the coming of the tide.

And yet I know that not for us,
  By any ecstasy of dream,
He lingers to keep luminous
  A little while the grievous stream,
10 Which frets, uncomforted of dream—

A grievous stream, that to and fro
  Athrough the fields of Acadie
Goes wandering, as if to know

Why one beloved face should be
So long from home and Acadie.

Was it a year or lives ago
We took the grasses in our hands,
And caught the summer flying low
Over the waving meadow lands,
20   And held it there between our hands?

The while the river at our feet—
A drowsy inland meadow stream—
At set of sun the after-heat
Made running gold, and in the gleam
We freed our birch upon the stream.

There down along the elms at dusk
We lifted dripping blade to drift,
Through twilight scented fine like musk,
Where night and gloom awhile uplift,
30   Nor sunder soul and soul adrift.

And that we took into our hands
Spirit of life or subtler thing—
Breathed on us there, and loosed the bands
Of death, and taught us, whispering,
The secret of some wonder-thing.

Then all your face grew light, and seemed
To hold the shadow of the sun;
The evening faltered, and I deemed
That time was ripe, and years had done
40   Their wheeling underneath the sun.

So all desire and all regret,
And fear and memory, were naught;
One to remember or forget
The keen delight our hands had caught;
Morrow and yesterday were naught.

The night has fallen, and the tide . . .
Now and again comes drifting home,
Across these aching barrens wide,
A sigh like driven wind or foam:
50   In grief the flood is bursting home.

[1886]

A VAGABOND SONG

There is something in the autumn that is native to my blood!
Touch of manner, hint of mood;
And my heart is like a rhyme,
With the yellow and the purple and the crimson keeping time.

The scarlet of the maples can shake me like a cry
Of bugles going by.
And my lonely spirit thrills
To see the frosty asters like a smoke upon the hills.

There is something in October sets the gypsy blood astir;
We must rise and follow her,
When from every hill of flame
She calls and calls each vagabond by name.

[1895]

I LOVED THEE, ATTHIS, IN THE LONG AGO

I loved thee, Atthis, in the long ago,
When the great oleanders were in flower
In the broad herded meadows full of sun.
And we would often at the fall of dusk
Wander together by the silver stream,
When the soft grass-heads were all wet with dew
And purple-misted in the fading light.
And joy I knew and sorrow at thy voice,
And the superb magnificence of love,—
The loneliness that saddens solitude,
And the sweet speech that makes it durable,—
The bitter longing and the keen desire,
The sweet companionship through quiet days
In the slow ample beauty of the world,

And the unutterable glad release
Within the temple of the holy night.
O Atthis, how I loved thee long ago
In that fair perished summer by the sea!

[1902]

VESTIGIA

I took a day to search for God,
And found Him not. But as I trod
By rocky ledge, through woods untamed,
Just where one scarlet lily flamed,
I saw His footprint in the sod.

Then suddenly, all unaware,
Far off in the deep shadows, where
A solitary hermit thrush
Sang through the holy twilight hush—
I heard His voice upon the air.

And even as I marvelled how
God gives us Heaven here and now,
In a stir of wind that hardly shook
The poplar leaves beside the brook—
His hand was light upon my brow.

At last with evening as I turned
Homeward, and thought what I had learned
And all that there was still to probe—
I caught the glory of His robe
Where the last fires of sunset burned.

Back to the world with quickening start
I looked and longed for any part
In making saving Beauty be . . .
And from that kindling ecstasy
I knew God dwelt within my heart.

[1920]

· ARCHIBALD LAMPMAN ·

1861–1899

Born at Morpeth, Canada West, into a family of United Empire Loyalist descent, Archibald Lampman grew up in several small towns in east central Ontario, and graduated from Trinity College, Toronto, with a B.A. in classics. In 1883 he secured an appointment as a clerk in the Post Office Department of the civil service in Ottawa, where he became the centre of a circle of aspiring writers which included Duncan Campbell Scott, Wilfred Campbell, and, more distantly, Charles G. D. Roberts and Bliss Carman. Lampman's first book, *Among the Millet*, was published in 1888 to favourable reviews in Canada, the United States, and England. *Lyrics of Earth* eventually appeared in 1896, and *Alcyone* was in press when he died in 1899 at the age of thirty-seven, when severe pneumonia aggravated a heart condition that had originated in a childhood illness.

Lampman's poetry has always had admirers, even at the height of the modernist attack on romantic poetry during the 1920s and 1930s. Only as more of his work has been made available has its range become clear. The nature poems in his first two volumes reveal him as an eloquent heir to the romantic vision of an ideal beauty and the restorative power in nature. In "Among the Timothy" he takes up the familiar Wordsworthian theme of dejection and imaginative renewal, in its familiar context, the meditative landscape poem. In "The Frogs" he develops a meditation on dreams and reality, while, at the same time, evoking Keats's "Ode on a Grecian Urn"—perhaps in an attempt to resolve his fascination with a poet by whom he felt possessed. His lyrical affirmations were, however, accompanied by persistent uncertainties. In the luminous stanzas of "Heat" and again in the more sombre land-scape of "In November" he explores the essential significance and inherent limitations of visionary nature poetry.

It was Lampman's sense of these limitations that led him to other themes in the 1890s. Certain aspects of his Christian upbringing, as well as his sympathy with romantic values, led him toward a socialist point of view in politics, and toward a tenuous philosophy of evolutionary idealism. His concern with such issues is expressed in his essays, many of which first appeared in "At the Mermaid Inn," the column that Lampman, Scott, and Campbell wrote for the Toronto *Globe* in 1892–93. While he continued to write nature lyrics, Lampman turned more frequently to other kinds of poetry. Psychological and symbolic allegories, moral sonnets, and narrative and dramatic verse reflect the changing emphasis in his work as it shifts away from natural landscape, toward the urban and social landscape of human relations and human suffering. This more vexed theme, which had always shadowed Lampman's brighter visions, is unforgettably expressed in the urgent rhythms and lurid symbolism of his apocalyptic poem "The City of the End of Things."

Lampman's later poems have never received their proper share of attention, perhaps because of their unresolved contradictions and uneven quality. To some extent, these problems reflect a period of crisis and frustration involving his hapless passion for Katherine Waddell as well as his unrealized poetic ambitions. Nevertheless, his later work does contain more than enough courage, craftsmanship, and imaginative richness to reward attentive reading. Although "The Story of an Affinity," his long domestic idyll, belongs to a genre that is unlikely ever to regain its once popular appeal, it remains a work of considerable depth and interest. The same can be said of other late poems such as "The Minstrel," the Temiscamingue sonnets of 1896-97, and "The Lake in the Forest." Indeed, Lampman's final poem, the austere and lovely sonnet "Winter Uplands," written twelve days before his death, stands as an enduring testimony to the vitality of his talent.

. ———— .

Lampman's works include *Among the Millet, and Other Poems* (1888); *Lyrics of Earth* (1895); *Alcyone* (1899); *The Poems of Archibald Lampman* (1900); *At the Long Sault and Other New Poems* (1943); *Archibald Lampman: Selected Prose* (1975); *Lampman's Kate: Late Love Poems of Archibald Lampman* (1975); *At the Mermaid Inn: Wilfred Campbell, Archibald Lampman, Duncan Campbell Scott in the* Globe *1892-3* (1979); and *An Annotated Edition of the Correspondence Between Archibald Lampman and Edward William*

Thomson 1890-1898 (1980). A scholarly edition of the poetry is in preparation.

Works on Lampman include Carl Y. Connor, *Archibald Lampman: Canadian Poet of Nature* (1929); Munro Beattie, "Archibald Lampman," *Our Living Tradition* (1957); Desmond Pacey, "Archibald Lampman," *Ten Canadian Poets* (1958); Michael Gnarowski, ed., *Archibald Lampman* (1970); George Woodcock, ed., *Colony and Confederation: Early Canadian Poets and Their Background* (1974); Lorraine McMullen, ed., *The Lampman Symposium* (1976); George Wicken, "Archibald Lampman: An Annotated Bibliography," *The Annotated Bibliography of Canada's Major Authors*, ed. Robert Lecker and Jack David (1980), 2: 97–146; D. M. R. Bentley, "Watchful Dreams and Sweet Unrest: An Essay on the Vision of Archibald Lampman," *Studies in Canadian Literature* 6 (1981): 188–210 and 7 (1982): 5–26; and L. R. Early, *Archibald Lampman* (1986).

L. R. EARLY

AMONG THE TIMOTHY

Long hours ago, while yet the morn was blithe,
    Nor sharp athirst had drunk the beaded dew,
A mower came, and swung his gleaming scythe
    Around this stump, and, shearing slowly, drew
    Far round among the clover, ripe for hay,
        A circle clean and gray;
And here among the scented swathes that gleam,
    Mixed with dead daisies, it is sweet to lie
    And watch the grass and the few-clouded sky,
10   Nor think but only dream.

For when the noon was turning, and the heat
    Fell down most heavily on field and wood,

I too came hither, borne on restless feet,
  Seeking some comfort for an aching mood.
  Ah! I was weary of the drifting hours,
    The echoing city towers,
The blind gray streets, the jingle of the throng,
  Weary of hope that like a shape of stone
  Sat near at hand without a smile or moan,
    And weary most of song.

And those high moods of mine that sometime made
20   My heart a heaven, opening like a flower
  A sweeter world where I in wonder strayed,
    Begirt with shapes of beauty and the power
    Of dreams that moved through that enchanted clime
      With changing breaths of rhyme,
Were all gone lifeless now, like those white leaves
  That hang all winter, shivering dead and blind
  Among the sinewy beeches in the wind,
30   That vainly calls and grieves.

Ah! I will set no more mine overtaskèd brain
  To barren search and toil that beareth nought,
For ever following with sore-footed pain
  The crossing pathways of unbournèd thought;
  But let it go, as one that hath no skill,
    To take what shape it will,
An ant slow-burrowing in the earthy gloom,
  A spider bathing in the dew at morn,
  Or a brown bee in wayward fancy borne
40   From hidden bloom to bloom.

Hither and thither o'er the rocking grass
  The little breezes, blithe as they are blind,
Teasing the slender blossoms pass and pass,
  Soft-footed children of the gipsy wind,
  To taste of every purple-fringèd head
    Before the bloom is dead;
And scarcely heed the daisies that, endowed
  With stems so short they cannot see, up-bear
  Their innocent sweet eyes distressed, and stare
50   Like children in a crowd.

Not far to fieldward in the central heat,
  Shadowing the clover, a pale poplar stands
With glimmering leaves that, when the wind comes, beat

Together like innumerable small hands,
And with the calm, as in vague dreams astray,
Hang wan and silver-gray;
Like sleepy maenads, who in pale surprise,
Half-wakened by a prowling beast, have crept
Out of the hidden covert, where they slept,
60   At noon with languid eyes.

The crickets creak, and through the noonday glow,
That crazy fiddler of the hot mid-year,
The dry cicada plies his wiry bow
In long-spun cadence, thin and dusty sere;
From the green grass the small grasshoppers' din
Spreads soft and silvery thin;
And ever and anon a murmur steals
Into mine ears of toil that moves alway,
The crackling rustle of the pitch-forked hay
70   And lazy jerk of wheels.

As so I lie and feel the soft hours wane,
To wind and sun and peaceful sound laid bare,
That aching dim discomfort of the brain
Fades off unseen, and shadowy-footed care
Into some hidden corner creeps at last
To slumber deep and fast;
And gliding on, quite fashioned to forget,
From dream to dream I bid my spirit pass
Out into the pale green ever-swaying grass
80   To brood, but no more fret.

And hour by hour among all shapes that grow
Of purple mints and daisies gemmed with gold
In sweet unrest my visions come and go;
I feel and hear and with quiet eyes behold;
And hour by hour, the ever-journeying sun,
In gold and shadow spun,
Into mine eyes and blood, and through the dim
Green glimmering forest of the grass shines down,
Till flower and blade, and every cranny brown,
90   And I are soaked with him.

[1888]

HEAT

From plains that reel to southward, dim,
　The road runs by me white and bare;
Up the steep hill it seems to swim
　Beyond, and melt into the glare.
Upward half-way, or it may be
　Nearer the summit, slowly steals
A hay-cart, moving dustily
　With idly clacking wheels.

By his cart's side the wagoner
10　Is slouching slowly at his ease,
Half-hidden in the windless blur
　Of white dust puffing to his knees.
This wagon on the height above,
　From sky to sky on either hand,
Is the sole thing that seems to move
　In all the heat-held land.

Beyond me in the fields the sun
　Soaks in the grass and hath his will;
I count the marguerites one by one;
20　Even the buttercups are still.
On the brook yonder not a breath
　Disturbs the spider or the midge.
The water-bugs draw close beneath
　The cool gloom of the bridge.

Where the far elm-tree shadows flood
　Dark patches in the burning grass,
The cows, each with her peaceful cud,
　Lie waiting for the heat to pass.
From somewhere on the slope near by
30　Into the pale depth of the noon
A wandering thrush slides leisurely
　His thin revolving tune.

In intervals of dreams I hear
　The cricket from the droughty ground;
The grasshoppers spin into mine ear
　A small innumerable sound.
I lift mine eyes sometimes to gaze:

The burning sky-line blinds my sight:
The woods far off are blue with haze:
40   The hills are drenched in light.

And yet to me not this or that
    Is always sharp or always sweet;
In the sloped shadow of my hat
    I lean at rest, and drain the heat;
Nay more, I think some blessèd power
    Hath brought me wandering idly here:
In the full furnace of this hour
    My thoughts grow keen and clear.

[1888]

IN NOVEMBER

With loitering step and quiet eye,
Beneath the low November sky,
I wandered in the woods, and found
A clearing, where the broken ground
Was scattered with black stumps and briers,
And the old wreck of forest fires.
It was a bleak and sandy spot,
And, all about, the vacant plot
Was peopled and inhabited
10 By scores of mulleins long since dead.
A silent and forsaken brood
In that mute opening of the wood,
So shrivelled and so thin they were,
So gray, so haggard, and austere,
Not plants at all they seemed to me,
But rather some spare company
Of hermit folk, who long ago,
Wandering in bodies to and fro,
Had chanced upon this lonely way,
20 And rested thus, till death one day
Surprised them at their compline prayer,
And left them standing lifeless there.

There was no sound about the wood
Save the wind's secret stir. I stood
Among the mullein-stalks as still
As if myself had grown to be
One of their sombre company,
A body without wish or will.
And as I stood, quite suddenly,
30 Down from a furrow in the sky
The sun shone out a little space
Across that silent sober place,
Over the sand heaps and brown sod,
The mulleins and dead goldenrod,
And passed beyond the thickets gray,
And lit the fallen leaves that lay,
Level and deep within the wood,
A rustling yellow multitude.

And all around me the thin light,
40 So sere, so melancholy bright,
Fell like the half-reflected gleam
Or shadow of some former dream;
A moment's golden revery
Poured out on every plant and tree
A semblance of weird joy, or less,
A sort of spectral happiness;
And I, too, standing idly there,
With muffled hands in the chill air,
50 Felt the warm glow about my feet,
And shuddering betwixt cold and heat,
Drew my thoughts closer, like a cloak,
While something in my blood awoke,
A nameless and unnatural cheer,
A pleasure secret and austere.

[1890]

ON THE COMPANIONSHIP
WITH NATURE

Let us be much with Nature; not as they
That labour without seeing, that employ
Her unloved forces, blindly without joy;
Nor those whose hands and crude delights obey
The old brute passion to hunt down and slay;
But rather as children of one common birth,
Discerning in each natural fruit of earth
Kinship and bond with this diviner clay.
Let us be with her wholly at all hours,
With the fond lover's zest, who is content
If his ear hears, and if his eye but sees;
So shall we grow like her in mould and bent,
Our bodies stately as her blessèd trees,
Our thoughts as sweet and sumptuous as her flowers.

[1892]

THE CITY OF THE END
OF THINGS

Beside the pounding cataracts
Of midnight streams unknown to us
'Tis builded in the leafless tracts
And valleys huge of Tartarus.
Lurid and lofty and vast it seems;
It hath no rounded name that rings,
But I have heard it called in dreams
The City of the End of Things.

Its roofs and iron towers have grown
10 None knoweth how high within the night,
But in its murky streets far down
A flaming terrible and bright
Shakes all the stalking shadows there,

Across the walls, across the floors,
And shifts upon the upper air
From out a thousand furnace doors;
And all the while an awful sound
Keeps roaring on continually,
And crashes in the ceaseless round
20 Of a gigantic harmony.
Through its grim depths re-echoing
And all its weary height of walls,
With measured roar and iron ring,
The inhuman music lifts and falls.
Where no thing rests and no man is,
And only fire and night hold sway;
The beat, the thunder and the hiss
Cease not, and change not, night nor day.

And moving at unheard commands,
30 The abysses and vast fires between,
Flit figures that with clanking hands
Obey a hideous routine;
They are not flesh, they are not bone,
They see not with the human eye,
And from their iron lips is blown
A dreadful and monotonous cry;
And whoso of our mortal race
Should find that city unaware,
Lean Death would smite him face to face,
40 And blanch him with its venomed air:
Or caught by the terrific spell,
Each thread of memory snapt and cut,
His soul would shrivel and its shell
Go rattling like an empty nut.

It was not always so, but once,
In days that no man thinks upon,
Fair voices echoed from its stones,
The light above it leaped and shone:
Once there were multitudes of men,
50 That built that city in their pride,
Until its might was made, and then
They withered age by age and died.
But now of that prodigious race,
Three only in an iron tower,
Set like carved idols face to face,
Remain the masters of its power;

And at the city gate a fourth,
Gigantic and with dreadful eyes,
Sits looking toward the lightless north,
60 Beyond the reach of memories;
Fast rooted to the lurid floor,
A bulk that never moves a jot,
In his pale body dwells no more,
Or mind or soul,—an idiot!

But sometime in the end those three
Shall perish and their hands be still,
And with the master's touch shall flee
Their incommunicable skill.
A stillness absolute as death
70 Along the slacking wheels shall lie,
And, flagging at a single breath,
The fires shall moulder out and die.
The roar shall vanish at its height,
And over that tremendous town
The silence of eternal night
Shall gather close and settle down.
All its grim grandeur, tower and hall,
Shall be abandoned utterly,
And into rust and dust shall fall
80 From century to century;
Nor ever living thing shall grow,
Or trunk of tree, or blade of grass;
No drop shall fall, no wind shall blow,
Nor sound of any foot shall pass:
Alone of its accursèd state,
One thing the hand of Time shall spare,
For the grim Idiot at the gate
Is deathless and eternal there.

[1894]

WINTER UPLANDS

The frost that stings like fire upon my cheek,
The loneliness of this forsaken ground,
The long white drift upon whose powdered peak
I sit in the great silence as one bound;
The rippled sheet of snow where the wind blew
Across the open fields for miles ahead;
The far-off city towered and roofed in blue
A tender line upon the western red;
The stars that singly, then in flocks appear,
Like jets of silver from the violet dome,
So wonderful, so many and so near,
And then the golden moon to light me home—
The crunching snowshoes and the stinging air,
And silence, frost and beauty everywhere.

[1900]

· DUNCAN CAMPBELL SCOTT ·

1862–1947

Just as the fathers of Charles G. D. Roberts and Archibald Lampman were Anglican clergymen, Duncan Campbell Scott was the son of a Methodist minister. Born in Ottawa on 2 August 1862, he shared a generation with the other "poets of Confederation" but lived through almost half of the twentieth century and published three books in the last year of his life. After his early education in the small towns of Ontario and Quebec where his father was posted, Scott was forced by financial circumstances to relinquish his ambition to enter university and become a doctor; instead, at seventeen, he began a career in the Canadian civil service. There, in contrast to Lampman, he enjoyed great success, becoming Deputy Superintendent-General of the Department of Indian Affairs in 1913 and holding that position until he retired in 1932. In recognition of his contribution to Canadian literature, Scott received honorary doctorates from Queen's University and from the University of Toronto, and in 1927 he was awarded the Lorne Pierce Medal. Although he was overshadowed throughout much of his writing career by more flamboyant contemporaries such as Roberts and Carman, Scott's reputation as a writer of both poetry and fiction has risen steadily since his death.

In 1880, Roberts's *Orion and Other Poems* galvanized Lampman's hopes for Canadian poetry, and a few years later Lampman, in turn, served Scott as instigating force after their meeting in 1883: "It never occurred to me . . . to write a line of prose or poetry until I was about twenty-five and after I had met Archibald Lampman." Inspired by his friend, Scott had published his first poem and short story by the end of the 1880s, and in 1893 his first volume of poetry appeared. In *The Magic House and Other Poems* (1893), Scott displays many of the concerns and influences of Victorian romanticism also evident in his contributions to "At the Mermaid Inn," a weekly column for the Toronto *Globe* on which he collaborated with Lampman and Wilfred Campbell in 1892–93. If the impact of European romanticism pervades *The Magic House*, the book also anticipates more distinctive concerns in Scott's subsequent work: a fascination with experiments in metre and line length, a talent for exploiting intense visual contrasts, an attraction to dream visions of the interpenetrating forces of art and life.

With its presentation of two sonnets focused on Indian women, a second volume, *Labor and the Angel* (1898), initiates the association of Scott as writer with the cultures of Canada's indigenous peoples. Like most of his contemporaries, Scott saw the assimilation and eventual disappearance of native cultures as inevitable. As a civil servant he saw his role as one of easing the slow but relentless process of extinction, through mediation and education. As a writer, Scott repeatedly celebrates the values and vitality of these doomed cultures; his fatalistic perspective is that of the outsider, while the language and forms of his poetry are those of Europe.

The title of Scott's third volume, *New World Lyrics and Ballads* (1905), suggests an awareness of the need to adapt a European discourse to Canadian experience; and in their varied levels of focus and achievement, the poems reflect the difficulty and complexity of such adaptation. Scott's best-known poem, "The Forsaken," exploits the dialectic between past and present seen earlier in "The Onondaga Madonna," celebrating courage, stoicism, and dignity as appropriate responses to the violently opposed contraries within both nature and human existence. The narrative intensity of "On the Way to the Mission" suggests the power of the best of Scott's stories and of longer poems which appeared in subsequent collections of poetry, such as "At Gull Lake: August, 1810," "The Height of Land," and "Lines in Memory of Edmund Morris."

· ———— ·

Scott's works include *In the Village of Viger* (1896, 1945); *Lundy's Lane and Other Poems* (1916); *Beauty and Life* (1921); *The Witching of Elspie, a Book of Stories* (1923); *The Collected Poems of D. C. Scott* (1926); *The Green Cloister, Later Poems* (1935); *The Circle of Affection and Other Pieces in Prose and Verse* (1947); *Selected Poems* (1951); and *Untitled Novel* (1979). He also edited four collections of poems by Archibald Lampman.

Works on Scott include Stan Dragland, ed., *Duncan Campbell Scott: A Book of Criticism* (1974); K. P. Stich, ed., *The Duncan Campbell Scott Symposium* (1980); D. M. R. Bentley, "Duncan Campbell Scott," *Profiles in Canadian Literature*, ed. Jeffrey M. Heath (1980) 1: 25–32; and Gordon Johnston, "Duncan Campbell Scott," *Canadian Writers and Their Works*, ed. Robert Lecker, Jack David, and Ellen Quigley (1983), Poetry Series 2: 235–89. Useful discussions of Scott's writing also appear in George Woodcock, ed., *Colony and Confederation: Early Canadian Poets and Their Background* (1974); and in Tom Marshall, *Harsh and Lovely Land: The Major Canadian Poets and the Making of a Canadian Tradition* (1979).

LESLIE MONKMAN

THE ONONDAGA MADONNA

She stands full-throated and with careless pose,
This woman of a weird and waning race,
The tragic savage lurking in her face,
Where all her pagan passion burns and glows;
Her blood is mingled with her ancient foes,
And thrills with war and wildness in her veins;
Her rebel lips are dabbled with the stains
Of feuds and forays and her fathers' woes.

And closer in the shawl about her breast,
The latest promise of her nation's doom,
Paler than she her baby clings and lies,
The primal warrior gleaming from his eyes;
He sulks, and burdened with his infant gloom,
He draws his heavy brows and will not rest.

[1894]

THE FORSAKEN

I

Once in the winter
Out on a lake
In the heart of the north-land,
Far from the Fort
And far from the hunters,
A Chippewa woman
With her sick baby,
Crouched in the last hours
Of a great storm.
10 Frozen and hungry,
She fished through the ice
With a line of the twisted
Bark of the cedar,
And a rabbit-bone hook
Polished and barbed;
Fished with the bare hook
All through the wild day,
Fished and caught nothing;
While the young chieftain
20 Tugged at her breasts,
Or slept in the lacings
Of the warm *tikanagan*.
All the lake-surface
Streamed with the hissing
Of millions of iceflakes,
Hurled by the wind;
Behind her the round
Of a lonely island
Roared like a fire
30 With the voice of the storm
In the deeps of the cedars.
Valiant, unshaken,
She took of her own flesh,
Baited the fish-hook,
Drew in a grey-trout,
Drew in his fellows,
Heaped them beside her,
Dead in the snow.
Valiant, unshaken,

40 She faced the long distance,
Wolf-haunted and lonely,
Sure of her goal
And the life of her dear one;
Tramped for two days,
On the third in the morning,
Saw the strong bulk
Of the Fort by the river,
Saw the wood-smoke
Hang soft in the spruces,
50 Heard the keen yelp
Of the ravenous huskies
Fighting for whitefish:
Then she had rest.

II

Years and years after,
When she was old and withered,
When her son was an old man
And his children filled with vigour,
They came in their northern tour on the verge of winter,
To an island in a lonely lake.
60 There one night they camped, and on the morrow
Gathered their kettles and birch-bark
Their rabbit-skin robes and their mink-traps,
Launched their canoes and slunk away through the islands,
Left her alone forever,
Without a word of farewell,
Because she was old and useless,
Like a paddle broken and warped,
Or a pole that was splintered.
Then, without a sigh,
70 Valiant, unshaken,
She smoothed her dark locks under her kerchief,
Composed her shawl in state,
Then folded her hands ridged with sinews and corded with veins,
Folded them across her breasts spent with the nourishing of
   children,
Gazed at the sky past the tops of the cedars,
Saw two spangled nights arise out of the twilight,
Saw two days go by filled with the tranquil sunshine,
Saw, without pain, or dread, or even a moment of longing:

Then on the third great night there came thronging and
    thronging
80 Millions of snowflakes out of a windless cloud;
    They covered her close with a beautiful crystal shroud,
    Covered her deep and silent.
    But in the frost of the dawn,
    Up from the life below,
    Rose a column of breath
    Through a tiny cleft in the snow,
    Fragile, delicately drawn,
    Wavering with its own weakness,
    In the wilderness a sign of the spirit,
90 Persisting still in the sight of the sun
    Till day was done.
    Then all light was gathered up by the hand of God and hid in His
      breast,
    Then there was born a silence deeper than silence,
    Then she had rest.

[1905]

ON THE WAY TO THE MISSION

    They dogged him all one afternoon,
    Through the bright snow,
    Two whitemen servants of greed;
    He knew that they were there,
    But he turned not his head;
    He was an Indian trapper;
    He planted his snow-shoes firmly,
    He dragged the long toboggan
    Without rest.

10 The three figures drifted
    Like shadows in the mind of a seer;
    The snow-shoes were whisperers
    On the threshold of awe;
    The toboggan made the sound of wings,
    A wood-pigeon sloping to her nest.

The Indian's face was calm.
He strode with the sorrow of fore-knowledge,
But his eyes were jewels of content
Set in circles of peace.

20 They would have shot him;
But momently in the deep forest,
They saw something flit by his side:
Their hearts stopped with fear.
Then the moon rose.
They would have left him to the spirit,

But they saw the long toboggan
Rounded well with furs,
With many a silver fox-skin,
With the pelts of mink and of otter.
30 They were the servants of greed;
When the moon grew brighter
And the spruces were dark with sleep,
They shot him.
When he fell on a shield of moonlight
One of his arms clung to his burden;
The snow was not melted:
The spirit passed away.

Then the servants of greed
Tore off the cover to count their gains;
40 They shuddered away into the shadows,
Hearing each the loud heart of the other.
Silence was born.

There in the tender moonlight,
  As sweet as they were in life,
Glimmered the ivory features,
  Of the Indian's wife.

In the manner of Montagnais women
  Her hair was rolled with braid;
Under her waxen fingers
50   A crucifix was laid.

He was drawing her down to the Mission,
  To bury her there in spring,

When the bloodroot comes and the windflower
  To silver everything.

But as a gift of plunder
  Side by side were they laid,
The moon went on to her setting
  And covered them with shade.

[1905]

AT GULL LAKE: AUGUST, 1810

Gull Lake set in the rolling prairie—
Still there are reeds on the shore,
As of old the poplars shimmer
As summer passes;
Winter freezes the shallow lake to the core;
Storm passes,
Heat parches the sedges and grasses,
Night comes with moon-glimmer,
Dawn with the morning-star;
10 All proceeds in the flow of Time
As a hundred years ago.

Then two camps were pitched on the shore,
The clustered teepees
Of Tabashaw Chief of the Saulteaux.
And on a knoll tufted with poplars
Two gray tents of a trader—
Nairne of the Orkneys.
Before his tents under the shade of the poplars
Sat Keejigo, third of the wives
20 Of Tabashaw Chief of the Saulteaux;
Clad in the skins of antelopes
Broidered with porcupine quills
Coloured with vivid dyes,
Vermilion here and there
In the roots of her hair,

A half-moon of powder-blue
On her brow, her cheeks
Scored with light ochre streaks.
Keejigo daughter of Launay
30 The Normandy hunter
And Oshawan of the Saulteaux,
Troubled by fugitive visions
In the smoke of the camp-fires
In the close dark of the teepee,
Flutterings of colour
Along the flow of the prairies,
Spangles of flower tints
Caught in the wonder of dawn,
Dreams of sounds unheard—
40 The echoes of echo,
Star she was named for
Keejigo, star of the morning,
Voices of storm—
Wind-rush and lightning,—
The beauty of terror;
The twilight moon
Coloured like a prairie lily,
The round moon of pure snow,
The beauty of peace;
50 Premonitions of love and of beauty
Vague as shadows cast by a shadow.
Now she had found her hero,
And offered her body and spirit
With abject unreasoning passion,
As Earth abandons herself
To the sun and the thrust of the lightning.
Quiet were all the leaves of the poplars,
Breathless the air under their shadow,
As Keejigo spoke of these things to her heart
60 In the beautiful speech of the Saulteaux.

The flower lives on the prairie,
The wind in the sky,
I am here my beloved;
The wind and the flower.

The crane hides in the sand-hills,
Where does the wolverine hide?
I am here my beloved,
Heart's-blood on the feathers
The foot caught in the trap.

70   *Take the flower in your hand,*
     The wind in your nostrils;
     I am here my beloved;
     Release the captive
     Heal the wound under the feathers.

     A storm-cloud was marching
     Vast on the prairie,
     Scored with livid ropes of hail,
     Quick with nervous vines of lightning—
     Twice had Nairne turned her away
80   Afraid of the venom of Tabashaw,
     Twice had the Chief fired at his tents
     And now when two bullets
     Whistled above the encampment
     He yelled "Drive this bitch to her master."

     Keejigo went down a path by the lake;
     Thick at the tangled edges,
     The reeds and the sedges
     Were gray as ashes
     Against the death-black water;
90   The lightning scored with double flashes
     The dark lake-mirror and loud
     Came the instant thunder.
     Her lips still moved to the words of her music,
     "Release the captive,
     Heal the wound under the feathers."

     At the top of the bank
     The old wives caught her and cast her down
     Where Tabashaw crouched by his camp-fire.
     He snatched a live brand from the embers,
100 Seared her cheeks,
     Blinded her eyes,
     Destroyed her beauty with fire,
     Screaming, "Take that face to your lover."
     Keejigo held her face to the fury
     And made no sound.
     The old wives dragged her away
     And threw her over the bank
     Like a dead dog.

     Then burst the storm—
110 The Indians' screams and the howls of the dogs
     Lost in the crash of hail

That smashed the sedges and reeds,
Stripped the poplars of leaves,
Tore and blazed onwards,
Wasting itself with riot and tumult—
Supreme in the beauty of terror.

The setting sun struck the retreating cloud
With a rainbow, not an arc but a column
Built with the glory of seven metals;
120 Beyond in the purple deeps of the vortex
Fell the quivering vines of the lightning.
The wind withdrew the veil from the shrine of the moon,
She rose changing her dusky shade for the glow
Of the prairie lily, till free of all blemish of colour
She came to her zenith without a cloud or a star,
A lovely perfection, snow-pure in the heaven of midnight.
After the beauty of terror the beauty of peace.

But Keejigo came no more to the camps of her people;
Only the midnight moon knew where she felt her way,
130 Only the leaves of autumn, the snows of winter
Knew where she lay.

[1935]

· E. J. PRATT ·

1882–1964

Born in Western Bay, Newfoundland, 4 February 1882, Edwin John Pratt was the son of a Yorkshire-bred Methodist preacher. He was educated in local schools and St. John's Methodist College, and worked both as a teacher and as a preacher-probationer on the island before going to Toronto's Victoria College in 1907. There he studied philosophy, theology, and psychology. He finally completed his studies in 1917, having earned a B.A., a B.D., an M.A., and a Ph.D. To support himself through these years of study, he worked as a demonstrator in psychology and as an itinerant preacher.

Towards the end of this arduous period of study he discovered his true vocation—literature. He published his first book, *Rachel: A Sea Story of Newfoundland in Verse*, in 1917 and in 1920 he was appointed to the department of English at Victoria College. He remained at Victoria College for the rest of his professional life, teaching Shakespeare, romantic and nineteenth-century poetry, and modern drama. He inspired the admiration of students and colleagues, which still persists in those who knew him. Many honours came to him as a result of his many books of poetry. He was elected to the Royal Society of Canada in 1930 and won three Governor General's Awards for poetry. He was awarded a Canada Council Medal for distinction in literature in 1961 and made a commander of the Order of St. Michael and St. George by the King in 1946. He died in Toronto on 26 April 1964.

Pratt became a poet relatively late in life, and was conservative in his poetic techniques. He owed more to Thomas Hardy than to his contemporaries T. S. Eliot and Ezra Pound. In 1923 he collected his early work in *Newfoundland Verse*, which includes two of the poems reprinted in this anthology: "Newfoundland" and "The Shark." The partnership of man with the elements—sea, wind, and land—in "Newfoundland" creates the vitality of the island, a vitality born of struggle which sometimes ends with the harvest of the sea and sometimes with the harvest of death. In "The Shark," Pratt celebrates the absolute efficiency of a sea-creature whose design seems to belong more to the realm of the machine than to nature. The other two poems in this anthology come from a later collection, *Still Life and Other Verse* (1943). In "The Truant," Pratt pits man against the mechanical power that seems to have created the shark, the Panjandrum. "The Truant"—a central poem in the Pratt canon—asserts that man, suffering, defeated, dying, can still triumph over this ruthless power of the universe.

Most of Pratt's best-known poetry is in the form of the epic. His particular *forte* is the sea story. In *The Roosevelt and the Antinoe* (1930), *The Titanic* (1935), *Dunkirk* (1941), and *Behind the Log* (1947), he chronicles man's eternal contest against the sea, which when encountered courageously and humbly can be life-giving, but when encountered with pride and presumption can be savagely destructive. In his two epics of the land, *Brébeuf and His Brethren* (1940) and *Towards the Last Spike* (1952), Pratt has given Canadian history a new depth and excitement. *Brébeuf* relates the seventeenth-century saga of the Jesuit missionaries' attempt to convert the Indians—an attempt which ended in disaster and martyrdom. *Towards the Last Spike* chronicles the building of the Canadian Pacific Railway to the West Coast—an achievement which triumphantly confirmed Confederation.

Pratt's poems are distinctive by virtue of their energy and coherence. His language is sinewy and evocative. He was equally at home in blank verse, iambic tetrameter, and rhyming couplets; in sonnets, quatrains, and odes. In writing his long poems he was both a careful researcher and a scrupulous craftsman.

From the beginning of his career he was a keen supporter of Canadian poetry and a promoter of his fellow poets. For a younger generation—D. G. Jones, Margaret Atwood, and Dennis Lee, among others—he has been important as a strong, original voice, whose nationalism was deep but never strident, and who demonstrated that the imagination could respond to the Canadian environment with familiarity as well as with fear.

Pratt's works include *Newfoundland Verse* (1923); *The Witches' Brew* (1925); *The Iron Door: An Ode* (1927); *The Roosevelt and the Antinoe* (1930); *The Titanic* (1935); *Brébeuf and His Brethren* (1940); *Towards the Last Spike* (1952); and *The Collected Poems*, ed. Northrop Frye (1958).

Works on Pratt include Earle Birney, "E. J. Pratt and His Critics," *Our Living Tradition*, ed. Robert McDougall (1959), 123–47; Sandra Djwa, *E. J. Pratt: The Evolutionary Vision* (1974); Glenn Clever, ed., *The E. J. Pratt Symposium* (1977); Lila and Raymond Laakso, "E. J. Pratt: An Annotated Bibliography," *The Annotated Bibliography of Canada's Major Authors*, ed. Robert Lecker and Jack David (1980), 2: 147–220; and David Pitt, *E. J. Pratt: The Truant Years, 1882–1927* (1984).

PETER BUITENHUIS

NEWFOUNDLAND

Here the tides flow,
And here they ebb;
Not with that dull, unsinewed tread of waters
Held under bonds to move
Around unpeopled shores—
Moon-driven through a timeless circuit
Of invasion and retreat;
But with a lusty stroke of life
Pounding at stubborn gates,
10 That they might run
Within the sluices of men's hearts,
Leap under throb of pulse and nerve,
And teach the sea's strong voice
To learn the harmonies of new floods,
The peal of cataract,
And the soft wash of currents

Against resilient banks,
Or the broken rhythms from old chords
Along dark passages
20 That once were pathways of authentic fires.

Red is the sea-kelp on the beach,
Red as the heart's blood,
Nor is there power in tide or sun
To bleach its stain.
It lies there piled thick
Above the gulch-line.
It is rooted in the joints of rocks,
It is tangled around a spar,
It covers a broken rudder,
30 *It is red as the heart's blood,*
And salt as tears.

Here the winds blow,
And here they die,
Not with that wild, exotic rage
That vainly sweeps untrodden shores,
But with familiar breath
Holding a partnership with life,
Resonant with the hopes of spring,
Pungent with the airs of harvest.
40 They call with the silver fifes of the sea,
They breathe with the lungs of men,
They are one with the tides of the sea,
They are one with the tides of the heart,
They blow with the rising octaves of dawn,
They die with the largo of dusk,
Their hands are full to the overflow,
In their right is the bread of life,
In their left are the waters of death.

Scattered on boom
50 *And rudder and weed*
Are tangles of shells;
Some with backs of crusted bronze,
And faces of porcelain blue,
Some crushed by the beach stones
To chips of jade;
And some are spiral-cleft
Spreading their tracery on the sand
In the rich veining of an agate's heart;

And others remain unscarred,
60 *To babble of the passing of the winds.*

Here the crags
Meet with winds and tides—
Not with that blind interchange
Of blow for blow
That spills the thunder of insentient seas;
But with the mind that reads assault
In crouch and leap and the quick stealth,
Stiffening the muscles of the waves.
Here they flank the harbours,
70 Keeping watch
On thresholds, altars and the fires of home,
Or, like mastiffs,
Over-zealous,
Guard too well.

Tide and wind and crag,
Sea-weed and sea-shell
And broken rudder—
And the story is told
Of human veins and pulses,
80 *Of eternal pathways of fire,*
Of dreams that survive the night,
Of doors held ajar in storms.

[1923]

THE SHARK

He seemed to know the harbour,
So leisurely he swam;
His fin,
Like a piece of sheet-iron,
Three-cornered,
And with knife-edge,
Stirred not a bubble
As it moved
With its base-line on the water.

His body was tubular
And tapered
And smoke-blue,
And as he passed the wharf
He turned,
And snapped at a flat-fish
That was dead and floating.
And I saw the flash of a white throat,
And a double row of white teeth,
And eyes of metallic grey,
Hard and narrow and slit.

Then out of the harbour,
With that three-cornered fin
Shearing without a bubble the water
Lithely,
Leisurely,
He swam—
That strange fish,
Tubular, tapered, smoke-blue,
Part vulture, part wolf,
Part neither—for his blood was cold.

[1923]

FROM *BRÉBEUF AND HIS BRETHREN*

March 16, 1649

Three miles from town to town over the snow,
Naked, laden with pillage from the lodges,
The captives filed like wounded beasts of burden,
Three hours on the march, and those that fell
Or slowed their steps were killed.
                              Three days before
Brébeuf had celebrated his last mass.

And he had known it was to be the last.
There was prophetic meaning as he took
The cord and tied the alb around his waist,
Attached the maniple to his left arm
And drew the seamless purple chasuble
With the large cross over his head and shoulders,
Draping his body: every vestment held
An immediate holy symbol as he whispered—
"Upon my head the helmet of Salvation.
So purify my heart and make me white;
With this cincture of purity gird me,
O Lord.
    May I deserve this maniple
Of sorrow and of penance.
               Unto me
Restore the stole of immortality.
My yoke is sweet, my burden light.
             Grant that
I may so bear it as to win Thy grace."

Entering, he knelt before as rude an altar
As ever was reared within a sanctuary,
But hallowed as that chancel where the notes
Of Palestrina's score had often pealed
The *Assumpta est Maria* through Saint Peter's.
For, covered in the centre of the table,
Recessed and sealed, a hollowed stone contained
A relic of a charred or broken body
Which perhaps a thousand years ago or more
Was offered as a sacrifice to Him
Whose crucifix stood there between the candles.
And on the morrow would this prayer be answered:—
"Eternal Father, I unite myself
With the affections and the purposes
Of Our Lady of Sorrows on Calvary.
And now I offer Thee the sacrifice
Which Thy Beloved Son made of Himself
Upon the Cross and now renews on this,
His holy altar . . .
          Graciously receive
My life for His life as He gave His life
For mine . . .
       This is my body.
              In like manner . . .
Take ye and drink—the chalice of my blood."

No doubt in the mind of Brébeuf that this was the last
Journey—three miles over the snow. He knew
That the margins as thin as they were by which he escaped
From death through the eighteen years of his mission toil
Did not belong to this chapter: not by his pen
Would this be told. He knew his place in the line,
For the blaze of the trail that was cut on the bark by Jogues
Shone still. He had heard the story as told by writ
And word of survivors—of how a captive slave
Of the hunters, the skin of his thighs cracked with the frost,
He would steal from the tents to the birches, make a rough cross
From two branches, set it in snow and on the peel
Inscribe his vows and dedicate to the Name
In "litanies of love" what fragments were left
From the wrack of his flesh; of his escape from the tribes;
Of his journey to France where he knocked at the door of the College
Of Rennes, was gathered in as a mendicant friar,
Nameless, unknown, till he gave for proof to the priest
His scarred credentials of faith, the nail-less hands
And withered arms—the signs of the Mohawk fury.
Nor yet was the story finished—he had come again
Back to his mission to get the second death.
And the comrades of Jogues—Goupil, Eustache and Couture,
Had been stripped and made to run the double files
And take the blows—one hundred clubs to each line—
And this as the prelude to torture, leisured, minute,
Where thorns on the quick, scallop shells to the joints of the thumbs,
Provided the sport for children and squaws till the end.
And adding salt to the blood of Brébeuf was the thought
Of Daniel—was it months or a week ago?
So far, so near, it seemed in time, so close
In leagues—just over there to the south it was
He faced the arrows and died in front of his church.

But winding into the greater artery
Of thought that bore upon the coming passion
Were little tributaries of wayward wish
And reminiscence. Paris with its vespers
Was folded in the mind of Lalemant,
And the soft Gothic lights and traceries
Were shading down the ridges of his vows.
But two years past at Bourges he had walked the cloisters,
Companioned by Saint Augustine and Francis,
And wrapped in quiet holy mists. Brébeuf,
His mind a moment throwing back the curtain

Of eighteen years, could see the orchard lands,
The *cidreries*, the peasants at the Fairs,
The undulating miles of wheat and barley,
Gardens and pastures rolling like a sea
From Lisieux to Le Havre. Just now the surf
Was pounding on the limestone Norman beaches
And on the reefs of Calvados. Had dawn
This very day not flung her surplices
Around the headlands and with golden fire
Consumed the silken argosies that made
For Rouen from the estuary of the Seine?
A moment only for that veil to lift—
A moment only for those bells to die
That rang their matins at Condé-sur-Vire.

By noon St. Ignace! The arrival there
The signal for the battle-cries of triumph,
The gauntlet of the clubs. The stakes were set
And the ordeal of Jogues was re-enacted
Upon the priests—even with wilder fury,
For here at last was trapped their greatest victim,
Echon. The Iroquois had waited long
For this event. Their hatred for the Hurons
Fused with their hatred for the French and priests
Was to be vented on this sacrifice,
And to that camp had come apostate Hurons,
United with their foes in common hate
To settle up their reckoning with *Echon.*

* * *

Now three o'clock, and capping the height of the passion,
Confusing the sacraments under the pines of the forest,
Under the incense of balsam, under the smoke
Of the pitch, was offered the rite of the font. On the head,
The breast, the loins and the legs, the boiling water!
While the mocking paraphrase of the symbols was hurled
At their faces like shards of flint from the arrow heads—
"We baptize thee with water . . .
                    That thou mayest be led
To Heaven . . .
                To that end we do anoint thee.
We treat thee as a friend: we are the cause
Of thy happiness; we are thy priests; the more
Thou sufferest, the more thy God will reward thee,
So give us thanks for our kind offices."

The fury of taunt was followed by fury of blow.
Why did not the flesh of Brébeuf cringe to the scourge,
Respond to the heat, for rarely the Iroquois found
A victim that would not cry out in such pain—yet here
The fire was on the wrong fuel. Whenever he spoke,
It was to rally the soul of his friend whose turn
Was to come through the night while the eyes were uplifted in
   prayer,
Imploring the Lady of Sorrows, the mother of Christ,
As pain brimmed over the cup and the will was called
To stand the test of the coals. And sometimes the speech
Of Brébeuf struck out, thundering reproof to his foes,
Half-rebuke, half-defiance, giving them roar for roar.
Was it because the chancel became the arena,
Brébeuf a lion at bay, not a lamb on the altar,
As if the might of a Roman were joined to the cause
Of Judaea? Speech they could stop for they girdled his lips,
But never a moan could they get. Where was the source
Of his strength, the home of his courage that topped the best
Of their braves and even out-fabled the lore of their legends?
In the bunch of his shoulders which often had carried a load
Extorting the envy of guides at an Ottawa portage?
The heat of the hatchets was finding a path to that source.
In the thews of his thighs which had mastered the trails of the
   Neutrals?
They would gash and beribbon those muscles. Was it the blood?
They would draw it fresh from its fountain. Was it the heart?
They dug for it, fought for the scraps in the way of the wolves.
But not in these was the valour or stamina lodged;
Nor in the symbol of Richelieu's robes or the seals
Of Mazarin's charters, nor in the stir of the *lilies*
Upon the Imperial folds; nor yet in the words
Loyola wrote on a table of lava-stone
In the cave of Manresa—not in these the source—
But in the sound of invisible trumpets blowing
Around two slabs of board, right-angled, hammered
By Roman nails and hung on a Jewish hill.

The wheel had come full circle with the visions
In France of Brébeuf poured through the mould of St. Ignace.
Lalemant died in the morning at nine, in the flame
Of the pitch belts. Flushed with the sight of the bodies, the foes
Gathered their clans and moved back to the north and west
To join in the fight against the tribes of the Petuns.
There was nothing now that could stem the Iroquois blast.

However undaunted the souls of the priests who were left,
However fierce the sporadic counter attacks
Of the Hurons striking in roving bands from the ambush,
Or smashing out at their foes in garrison raids,
The villages fell before a blizzard of axes
And arrows and spears, and then were put to the torch.

The days were dark at the fort and heavier grew
The burdens on Ragueneau's shoulders. Decision was his.
No word from the east could arrive in time to shape
The step he must take. To and fro—from altar to hill,
From hill to altar, he walked and prayed and watched.
As governing priest of the Mission he felt the pride
Of his Order whipping his pulse, for was not St. Ignace
The highest test of the Faith? And all that torture
And death could do to the body was done. The Will
And the Cause in their triumph survived. Loyola's mountains,
Sublime at their summits, were scaled to the uttermost peak.
Ragueneau, the Shepherd, now looked on a battered fold.
In a whirlwind of fire St. Jean, like St. Joseph, crashed
Under the Iroquois impact. Firm at his post,
Garnier suffered the fate of Daniel. And now
Chabanel, last in the roll of the martyrs, entrapped
On his knees in the woods met death at apostate hands.

The drama was drawing close to its end. It fell
To Ragueneau's lot to perform a final rite—
To offer the fort in sacrificial fire!
He applied the torch himself. *"Inside an hour,"*
He wrote, *"we saw the fruit of ten years' labour*
Ascend in smoke,—then looked our last at the fields,
Put altar-vessels and food on a raft of logs,
And made our way to the island of St. Joseph."
But even from there was the old tale retold—
Of hunger and the search for roots and acorns;
Of cold and persecution unto death
By the Iroquois; of Jesuit will and courage
As the shepherd-priest with Chaumonot led back
The remnant of a nation to Quebec.

THE MARTYRS' SHRINE

Three hundred years have passed, and the winds of God
Which blew over France are blowing once more through the pines
That bulwark the shores of the great Fresh Water Sea.

Over the wastes abandoned by human tread,
Where only the bittern's cry was heard at dusk;
Over the lakes where the wild ducks built their nests,
The skies that had banked their fires are shining again
With the stars that guided the feet of Jogues and Brébeuf.
The years as they turned have ripened the martyrs' seed,
And the ashes of St. Ignace are glowing afresh.

The trails, having frayed the threads of the cassocks, sank
Under the mould of the centuries, under fern
And brier and fungus—there in due time to blossom
Into the highways that lead to the crest of the hill
Which havened both shepherd and flock in the days of their trial.
For out of the torch of Ragueneau's ruins the candles
Are burning today in the chancel of Sainte Marie.
The Mission sites have returned to the fold of the Order.
Near to the ground where the cross broke under the hatchet,
And went with it into the soil to come back at the turn
Of the spade with the carbon and calcium char of the bodies,
The shrines and altars are built anew; the *Aves*
And prayers ascend, and the Holy Bread is broken.

[1940]

THE TRUANT

"What have you there?" the great Panjandrum said
To the Master of the Revels who had led
A bucking truant with a stiff backbone
Close to the foot of the Almighty's throne.

"Right Reverend, most adored,
And forcibly acknowledged Lord
By the keen logic of your two-edged sword!
This creature has presumed to classify
10 Himself—a biped, rational, six feet high
And two feet wide; weighs fourteen stone;
Is guilty of a multitude of sins.
He has abjured his choric origins,
And like an undomesticated slattern,

Walks with tangential step unknown
Within the weave of the atomic pattern.
He has developed concepts, grins
Obscenely at your Royal bulletins,
Possesses what he calls a will
Which challenges your power to kill."

20 "What is his pedigree?"

"The base is guaranteed, your Majesty—
Calcium, carbon, phosphorus, vapour
And other fundamentals spun
From the umbilicus of the sun,
And yet he says he will not caper
Around your throne, nor toe the rules
For the ballet of the fiery molecules."
"His concepts and denials—scrap them, burn them—
To the chemists with them promptly."

30   "Sire,
The stuff is not amenable to fire.
Nothing but their own kind can overturn them.
The chemists have sent back the same old story—
'With our extreme gelatinous apology,
We beg to inform your Imperial Majesty,
Unto whom be dominion and power and glory,
There still remains that strange precipitate
Which has the quality to resist
Our oldest and most trusted catalyst.
40 It is a substance we cannot cremate
By temperatures known to our Laboratory.' "

And the great Panjandrum's face grew dark—
"I'll put those chemists to their annual purge,
And I myself shall be the thaumaturge
To find the nature of this fellow's spark.
Come, bring him nearer by yon halter rope:
I'll analyse him with the cosmoscope."

Pulled forward with his neck awry,
The little fellow six feet short,
50 Aware he was about to die,
Committed grave contempt of court
By answering with a flinchless stare
The Awful Presence seated there.

The ALL HIGH swore until his face was black.
He called him a coprophagite,
A genus *homo*, egomaniac,
Third cousin to the family of worms,
A sporozoan from the ooze of night,
Spawn of a spavined troglodyte:
60 He swore by all the catalogue of terms
Known since the slang of carboniferous Time.
He said that he could trace him back
To pollywogs and earwigs in the slime.
And in his shrillest tenor he began
Reciting his indictment of the man,
Until he closed upon this capital crime—
"You are accused of singing out of key,
(A foul unmitigated dissonance)
Of shuffling in the measures of the dance,
70 Then walking out with that defiant, free
Toss of your head, banging the doors,
Leaving a stench upon the jacinth floors.
You have fallen like a curse
On the mechanics of my Universe.

"Herewith I measure out your penalty—
Hearken while you hear, look while you see:
I send you now upon your homeward route
Where you shall find
Humiliation for your pride of mind.
80 I shall make deaf the ear, and dim the eye,
Put palsy in your touch, make mute
Your speech, intoxicate your cells and dry
Your blood and marrow, shoot
Arthritic needles through your cartilage,
And having parched you with old age,
I'll pass you wormwise through the mire;
And when your rebel will
Is mouldered, all desire
Shrivelled, all your concepts broken,
90 Backward in dust I'll blow you till
You join my spiral festival of fire.
Go, Master of the Revels—I have spoken."

And the little genus *homo*, six feet high,
Standing erect, countered with this reply—
"You dumb insouciant invertebrate,
You rule a lower than a feudal state—
A realm of flunkey decimals that run,

Return; return and run; again return,
Each group around its little sun,
100 And every sun a satellite.
There they go by day and night,
Nothing to do but run and burn,
Taking turn and turn about,
Light-year in and light-year out,
Dancing, dancing in quadrillions,
Never leaving their pavilions.

"Your astronomical conceit
Of bulk and power is anserine.
Your ignorance so thick,
110 You did not know your own arithmetic.
We flung the graphs about your flying feet;
We measured your diameter—
Merely a line
Of zeros prefaced by an integer.
Before we came
You had no name.
You did not know direction or your pace;
We taught you all you ever knew
Of motion, time and space.
120 We healed you of your vertigo
And put you in our kindergarten show,
Perambulated you through prisms, drew
Your mileage through the Milky Way,
Lassoed your comets when they ran astray,
Yoked Leo, Taurus, and your team of Bears
To pull our kiddy cars of inverse squares.

"Boast not about your harmony,
Your perfect curves, your rings
Of *pure and endless light*—'Twas we
130 Who pinned upon your Seraphim their wings,
And when your brassy heavens rang
With joy that morning while the planets sang
Their choruses of archangelic lore,
'Twas we who ordered the notes upon their score
Out of our winds and strings.
Yes! all your shapely forms
Are ours—parabolas of silver light,
Those blueprints of your spiral stairs
From nadir depth to zenith height,
140 Coronas, rainbows after storms,

Auroras on your eastern tapestries
And constellations over western seas.

"And when, one day, grown conscious of your age,
While pondering an eolith,
We turned a human page
And blotted out a cosmic myth
With all its baby symbols to explain
The sunlight in Apollo's eyes,
Our rising pulses and the birth of pain,
150 Fear, and that fern-and-fungus breath
Stalking our nostrils to our caves of death—
That day we learned how to anatomize
Your body, calibrate your size
And set a mirror up before your face
To show you what you really were—a rain
Of dull Lucretian atoms crowding space,
A series of concentric waves which any fool
Might make by dropping stones within a pool,
Or an exploding bomb forever in flight
160 Bursting like hell through Chaos and Old Night.

"You oldest of the hierarchs
Composed of electronic sparks,
We grant you speed,
We grant you power, and fire
That ends in ash, but we concede
To you no pain nor joy nor love nor hate,
No final tableau of desire,
No causes won or lost, no free
Adventure at the outposts—only
170 The degradation of your energy
When at some late
Slow number of your dance your sergeant-major Fate
Will catch you blind and groping and will send
You reeling on that long and lonely
Lockstep of your wave-lengths towards your end.

"We who have met
With stubborn calm the dawn's hot fusillades;
Who have seen the forehead sweat
Under the tug of pulleys on the joints,
180 Under the liquidating tally
Of the cat-and-truncheon bastinades;
Who have taught our souls to rally

To mountain horns and the sea's rockets
When the needle ran demented through the points;
We who have learned to clench
Our fists and raise our lightless sockets
To morning skies after the midnight raids,
Yet cocked our ears to bugles on the barricades,
And in cathedral rubble found a way to quench
190 A dying thirst within a Galilean valley—
No! by the Rood, we will not join your ballet."

[1942]

MISSING: BELIEVED DEAD: RETURNED

Steady, the heart!
Can you not see
You must not break
Incredulously?

The dead has come back,
He is here at the sill;
Try to believe
The miracle.

Give me more breath,
Or I may not withstand
The thrill of his voice
And the clasp of his hand.

Be quiet, my heart,
Can you not see
In the beat of my pulse
Mortality?

[1943]

· W. W. E. ROSS ·

1894–1966

William Wrightson Eustace Ross was an important but curiously lonely figure in the early years of Canadian poetic modernism. He had a strong sense of the Canadian land, and the physical nature of the northern wilderness is rendered in his best poems with as sharp a visuality as it is in the landscapes of the Group of Seven. But he does not seem to have had a great feeling of identity with the movements of literary nationalism that were stirring at the time, and as a consequence it was long before his importance in the developing tradition was recognized.

Undoubtedly this was in part a matter of Canadian distances, and also of differing backgrounds. Ross was born in 1894 at Peterborough, Ontario, and he was educated at the University of Toronto; trained as a scientist, he worked for most of his life as a geophysicist in the Agincourt Magnetic Observatory. His scientific training may well have a bearing on his choice, as a poet, of the precisions of imagist vision, but he remained detached from the Montreal groups, which in varying guises dominated the modern movement in English poetry in Canada from the late 1920s through to the late 1940s. He does not seem to have been in close contact with the writers associated with the *McGill Fortnightly Review*; he did not contribute to *New Provinces*.

Ross was publishing his first imagist poetry as early as 1923, in American magazines like *Poetry* (Chicago) and the *Dial*, so that he could hardly have been unknown to an assiduous student of the modern movement like A. J. M. Smith. By the 1940s Smith was aware enough of Ross's merits to include in *The Book of Canadian Poetry* a selection of his works, which subsequently increased from edition to edition. It seems evident that, unlike his fellow Toronto poets, E. J. Pratt and Robert Finch, both of whom contributed to *New Provinces*, Ross held himself aloof from the Montreal poets and thus from their self-consciously Canadian modernism. The affinities he seems to have elected were with contemporary American poets, and especially with Marianne Moore; they were in touch and praised each other's work.

This was in spite of the fact that Ross's poems were mainly concerned with the landscape and the natural life with which he was familiar, which were both Canadian. His attitude in this direction was one he shared with other imagists, who saw it as the poet's concern to reflect in his verse the world of immediate experience, wherever he was, yet who saw the tendency they represented as a cosmopolitan one, which indeed it was, being initiated by the English poet T. E. Hulme and carried to its height by the Americans Ezra Pound and H. D.

Apart from some of Raymond Souster's work, it is hard to find in Canada a better example of imagism than in the poetry of W. W. E. Ross, and it is significant that Souster was so largely responsible for the recognition of Ross's importance in the canon of Canadian poetry. The two books Ross published in his early career, *Laconics* (1930) and *Sonnets* (1932), aroused relatively little attention. After that he dropped out of sight, writing little, but still read by some of the younger poets, until Souster was responsible for the appearance in 1956 of a collection of his best work, *Experiment 1923–1929*, and later, with John Robert Colombo, for the definitive posthumous collection of his poems, *Shapes and Sounds: Poems of W. W. E. Ross*, which appeared in 1968, two years after his death.

In his earlier poems Ross, like a good

imagist, emphasized his visual and auditory experiences and avoided the development of obvious themes. He sought a form that, as he put it, "expresses now," by which he meant the world of actual, urgent experience. Later on he was inclined to give expression to the reflections that emerged from these moments of experience, and in this sense he departed eventually from the logical extremities of imagism. He also evaded the extremities of free verse, for though he did not write metrically regular verse, he did write quite carefully arranged syllabic verse; his most characteristic poems contained three eight-line stanzas, with four or five syllables a line. In his early poems he also used such devices as grammatical repetition and assonant line endings, and in his later poems he would sometimes resort to rhyme, particularly, of course, in the sonnets. But it was his insistence on the sharpness and freshness of the image which "expresses now," that made him such an important influence on a later generation of Canadian poets and gave his verse its special gemlike flame.

.——————.

Works by W. W. E. Ross include *Laconics* (1930); *Sonnets* (1932); *Experiment 1923–1929*, ed. Raymond Souster (1956); *Shapes and Sounds: Poems of W. W. E. Ross*, eds. Raymond Souster and John Robert Colombo (1968); and *A Literary Friendship: The Correspondence of Ralph Gustafson and W. W. E. Ross*, ed. Bruce Whiteman (1984).

Works on W. W. E. Ross include Peter Stevens, "On W. W. E. Ross," *Canadian Literature* 39 (1969): 43–61; Michael Darling, ed., "On Poetry and Poets: The Letters of W. W. E. Ross to A. J. M. Smith," *Essays on Canadian Writing* 16 (1979–80): 78–125; and David Latham, "W. W. E. Ross," *The Oxford Companion to Canadian Literature*, ed. William Toye (1983).

GEORGE WOODCOCK

THE CREEK

The creek, shining,
out of the deep woods
comes with its rippling of
water over pebbly bottom.

Moving between
banks crowded with raspberry
bushes, the ripe red
berries in their short season

to deepen slowly
among tall pines, athletes in
the wind, then the swampy
ground low-lying and damp

where sunlight strikes
glints on the gliding surface
of the clear cold
creek winding towards the shore

of the lake, blue,
not far through reeds and rushes,
where with a plunge, a small
waterfall, it disappears

among the waves
hastening from far to meet
the stranger, the stream issuing
from depths of green unknown.

[1930]

THE DIVER

I would like to dive
Down
Into this still pool
Where the rocks at the bottom are safely deep,

Into the green
Of the water seen from within,
A strange light
Streaming past my eyes—

Things hostile;
You cannot stay here, they seem to say;
The rocks, slime-covered, the undulating
Fronds of weeds—

And drift slowly
Among the cooler zones;
Then, upward turning,
Break from the green glimmer

Into the light,
White and ordinary of the day,
And the mild air,
With the breeze and the comfortable shore.

[1930]

THIS FORM

This form expresses now.
At other times other forms.
Now, this form.
This form seems effective now.
It is monotonous, crude.
It may be called "primitive."
A primitive form.
No form, a lack of form.
Nevertheless, it expresses.
It is expressive now.
At other times other forms.
This form now. Expressive now.

[1930]

ROCKY BAY

The iron rocks
slope sharply down
into the gleaming
of northern water,
and there is a shining
to northern water
reflecting the sky
on a keen cool morning.

A little bay,—
and there the water
reflects the trees
upside down,
and the coloured rock,
inverted also
in the little
shining bay.

Above, on the rock,
stand trees, hardy,
gripping the rock
tenaciously.
The water repeats them
upside down,
repeats the coloured
rock inverted.

[1930]

· F. R. SCOTT ·

1899–1985

Francis Reginald (Frank) Scott was born 1 August 1899 in Quebec City. He received a B.A. from Bishop's College in 1919, and was awarded a Rhodes scholarship to Oxford, where he earned a B.A. in 1922 and a B.Litt. in 1923. He enrolled in the McGill Law school in 1924, graduating with his B.C.L. in 1927. He soon joined the faculty at McGill, where he remained for the rest of his professional life, becoming Dean of Law in 1961. A committed socialist, Scott was instrumental in the founding of the League for Social Reconstruction and the Co-operative Commonwealth Federation. His achievements in the fields of constitutional law, social theory, and literature earned him many awards, including the Lorne Pierce Medal, the Molson Prize, and the Governor General's Award.

With his friend A. J. M. Smith, Frank Scott played a seminal role in the modernization of Canadian poetry. Recognizing that new subjects demanded new forms, Scott turned to imagism in the late twenties and to social satire in the thirties, wittily attacking the injustices of the capitalist system. Later, his verse would become more metaphysical, but all his best poetry is united by a concern with man's relationship to his environment and his potential as a social being. A profoundly humanist poet, Scott remained enough of a romantic to stress the importance of love and compassion, and enough of a classicist to mould his ideas in precise diction and regular rhythms.

As an observer of nature, Scott presents vivid depictions of the northern landscape in tightly controlled imagist poems such as "March Field" and "Trees in Ice." More typical, however, of his approach to nature is "Lakeshore," a complex metaphysical speculation on the place of man in the pattern of evolution. The poem's evocative diction, especially evident in the witty punning of the eighth stanza, is characteristic of Scott's mature verse. His language is always subtle and suggestive but never obscure, while his handling of rhythm and rhyme is confident and satisfying.

As a social satirist and philosopher, Scott demonstrates his awareness of both man's inhumanity to man and the as yet unrealized possibilities of human endeavour. While the exploitation of workers and the suffering of the poor move him to bitterly ironic comments on our society, Scott remains positive in his vision of social progress. "This is an hour / Of new beginnings," he writes in "Overture," a time in which every frontier is open to man. To balance the evil of social and economic inequalities that he attacks in some poems, Scott offers elsewhere the transcendent human qualities of hope and love, compassion and understanding.

· ———— ·

Scott's works include *Overture* (1945); *Events and Signals* (1954); *The Eye of the Needle* (1957); *Civil Liberties and Canadian Federalism* (1959); *Signature* (1964); *Selected Poems* (1966); *Trouvailles: Poems from Prose* (1967); *The Dance Is One* (1973); *Essays on the Constitution: Aspects of Canadian Law and Politics* (1977); and *The Collected Poems of F. R. Scott* (1981). He was the dominant force in the creation of *New Provinces: Poems of Several Authors* (1936) and translated *Poems of French Canada* (1977).

Works on Scott include Louis Dudek, "F. R. Scott and the Modern Poets," *Northern Review* 4 (1950–51): 4–15; Desmond Pacey, "F. R. Scott," *Ten Canadian Poets: A Group of Biographical and Critical Essays* (1958) 223–53; Stephen Scobie, "The Road Back to Eden: The

Poetry of F. R. Scott," *Queen's Quarterly* 79.3 (1972): 314–23; A. J. M. Smith, "F. R. Scott and Some of His Poems," *Towards a View of Canadian Letters: Selected Critical Essays, 1928–1971* (1973); 115–24; Sandra Djwa, "F. R. Scott," *Canadian Poetry: Studies/Documents/Reviews* 4 (1979); 1–16; Sandra Djwa and R. St J. Macdonald, ed., *On F. R. Scott* (1983); and Robert Still, "F. R. Scott: An Annotated Bibliography," *The Annotated Bibliography of Canada's Major Authors*, ed. Robert Lecker and Jack David (1983), 4: 205–65.

MICHAEL DARLING

THE CANADIAN AUTHORS MEET

Expansive puppets percolate self-unction
Beneath a portrait of the Prince of Wales.
Miss Crotchet's muse has somehow failed to function,
Yet she's a poetess. Beaming, she sails

From group to chattering group, with such a dear
Victorian saintliness, as is her fashion,
Greeting the other unknowns with a cheer—
Virgins of sixty who still write of passion.

The air is heavy with Canadian topics,
And Carman, Lampman, Roberts, Campbell, Scott,
Are measured for their faith and philanthropics,
Their zeal for God and King, their earnest thought.

The cakes are sweet, but sweeter is the feeling
That one is mixing with the *literati*;
It warms the old, and melts the most congealing.
Really, it is a most delightful party.

Shall we go round the mulberry bush, or shall
We gather at the river, or shall we
Appoint a Poet Laureate this fall,
Or shall we have another cup of tea?

O Canada, O Canada, O can
A day go by without new authors springing
To paint the native maple, and to plan
More ways to set the selfsame welkin ringing?

[1927]

MARCH FIELD

Now the old folded snow
Shrinks from black earth.
Now is thrust forth
Heavy and still
The field's dark furrow.

Not yet the flowing
The mound-stirring
Not yet the inevitable flow.

There is a warm wind, stealing
From blunt brown hills, loosening
Sod and cold loam
Round rigid root and stem.

But no seed stirs
In this bare prison
Under the hollow sky.

The stone is not yet rolled away
Nor the body risen.

[1929]

TRANS CANADA

Pulled from our ruts by the made-to-order gale
We sprang upward into a wider prairie
And dropped Regina below like a pile of bones.

Sky tumbled upon us in waterfalls,
But we were smarter than a Skeena salmon
And shot our silver body over the lip of air
To rest in a pool of space
On the top storey of our adventure.

A solar peace
And a six-way choice.

Clouds, now, are the solid substance,
A floor of wool roughed by the wind
Standing in waves that halt in their fall.
A still of troughs.

The plane, our planet,
Travels on roads that are not seen or laid
But sound in instruments on pilots' ears,
While underneath
The sure wings
Are the everlasting arms of science.

Man, the lofty worm, tunnels his latest clay,
And bores his new career.

This frontier, too, is ours.
This everywhere whose life can only be led
At the pace of a rocket
Is common to man and man.
And every country below is an I land.

The sun sets on its top shelf,
And stars seem farther from our nearer grasp.

I have sat by night beside a cold lake
And touched things smoother than moonlight on still water,
But the moon on this cloud sea is not human,
And here is no shore, no intimacy,
Only the start of space, the road to suns.

[1944]

OVERTURE

In the dark room, under a cone of light,
You precisely play the Mozart sonata. The bright
Clear notes fly like sparks through the air
And trace a flickering pattern of music there.

Your hands dart in the light, your fingers flow.
They are ten careful operatives in a row
That pick their packets of sound from steel bars
Constructing harmonies as sharp as stars.

But how shall I hear old music? This is an hour
Of new beginnings, concepts warring for power,
Decay of systems—the tissue of art is torn
With overtures of an era being born.

And this perfection which is less yourself
Than Mozart, seems a trinket on a shelf,
A pretty octave played before a window
Beyond whose curtain grows a world crescendo.

[1945]

LAKESHORE

The lake is sharp along the shore
Trimming the bevelled edge of land
To level curves; the fretted sands
Go slanting down through liquid air
Till stones below shift here and there
Floating upon their broken sky
All netted by the prism wave
And rippled where the currents are.

I stare through windows at this cave
10 Where fish, like planes, slow-motioned, fly.
Poised in a still of gravity
The narrow minnow, flicking fin,
Hangs in a paler, ochre sun,
His doorways open everywhere.

And I am a tall frond that waves
Its head below its rooted feet
Seeking the light that draws it down
To forest floors beyond its reach
Vivid with gloom and eerie dreams.

20 The water's deepest colonnades
   Contract the blood, and to this home
   That stirs the dark amphibian
   With me the naked swimmers come
   Drawn to their prehistoric womb.

   They too are liquid as they fall
   Like tumbled water loosed above
   Until they lie, diagonal,
   Within the cool and sheltered grove
   Stroked by the fingertips of love.

30 Silent, our sport is drowned in fact
   Too virginal for speech or sound
   And each is personal and laned
   Along his private aqueduct.

   Too soon the tether of the lungs
   Is taut and straining, and we rise
   Upon our undeveloped wings
   Toward the prison of our ground
   A secret anguish in our thighs
   And mermaids in our memories.

40 This is our talent, to have grown
   Upright in posture, false-erect,
   A landed gentry, circumspect,
   Tied to a horizontal soil
   The floor and ceiling of the soul;
   Striving, with cold and fishy care
   To make an ocean of the air.

   Sometimes, upon a crowded street,
   I feel the sudden rain come down
   And in the old, magnetic sound
50 I hear the opening of a gate
   That loosens all the seven seas.
   Watching the whole creation drown
   I muse, alone, on Ararat.

[1950]

· A. J. M. SMITH ·

1902–1980

Arthur James Marshall Smith was born 8 November 1902 in Westmount, Quebec. He attended McGill University, where he earned a B.Sc. and an M.A. and, with F. R. Scott, founded the *McGill Fortnightly Review*. He obtained his Ph.D. from the University of Edinburgh in 1931, and taught at Michigan State University from 1936 to 1972. He contributed to many of the leading literary magazines of his day, including *The Dial*, *Poetry*, and *New Verse*. As poet, critic, and anthologist, Smith championed the cause of modernism in Canadian poetry, and received many honours, including the Governor General's Award for Poetry, the Lorne Pierce Medal, and the Canada Council Medal.

The literary career of A. J. M. Smith is a paradigm of the development of Canadian poetry in the first half of this century. He reacted against his own attraction to late Victorian romanticism by espousing the tenets of an impersonal, austere imagism, which then gave way to an interest in an intellectually challenging metaphysical poetry. In the Depression years, he practised a more socially committed verse leavened by satire, and in his later work grappled in a personal way with the themes of mutability and death. The various subjects and styles of Smith's poetry are united, however, by a lifelong commitment to craftsmanship, highlighted by careful attention to the exigencies of rhyme, rhythm, and precise diction.

Smith's early poetry, of which "The Lonely Land" is the finest example, is characterized by the same romantic sensibility he later condemned in his "Rejected Preface" to *New Provinces* (1936). It is perhaps for this reason that Smith chose not to reprint "The Lonely Land" in his own anthologies, although it came to be regarded as a Canadian classic in his lifetime. The poem es-chews the "mechanically correct" rhymes and rhythms of the celebrated Canadian versifiers of the time in favour of an organic rhythm and irregular rhyme scheme which effectively convey the spirit of the Canadian north and link it with later works such as "The Creek" and "Swift Current" that are more obviously in the imagist tradition.

Influenced by the poetry and criticism of T. S. Eliot, Smith soon turned from imagism to a poetic more suited to the exploration of the complexities of modern life. "Like an Old Proud King in a Parable," revised in 1932 to its present form, exhibits both a distrust of lush romanticism and a simultaneous awareness of the limitations of classical austerity. Typifying Smith's metaphysical stance, the poem stresses the ironic conflict involved in any choice between competing realities.

As a satirist, Smith demonstrates the same metaphysical concerns. In "News of the Phoenix," for example, what appears to be a straightforward attack on the tendency of the modern bureaucratic state to suppress unpleasant news becomes an oblique comment on the impossibility of getting at any ultimate truth, as the irony undercuts the speaker as well as his ostensible target.

Commenting on the desirability of satirical verse in Canada, Smith remarks in his "Rejected Preface": "Detachment, indeed, or self-absorption is (for a time only, I hope) becoming impossible." It is the parenthetical qualification that gives away Smith's true feelings: his preference for "pure poetry" always made him unhappy with the role of social critic. In this respect, "The Archer," written not long after "News of the Phoenix," is closer to his central concern with the relationship between art and life, brilliantly expressing the poet's conviction that art will triumph over death. A preoccupation with death and rebirth informs many of the later poems, including "Metamorphosis," a particularly fine example of Smith's ability to manipulate sounds into patterns which give his poems the unity of well-wrought aesthetic objects.

· ———— ·

Smith's works include *News of the Phoenix and Other Poems* (1943); *A Sort of Ecstasy* (1954); *Collected Poems* (1962); *Poems: New and Collected* (1967); *Towards a View of Canadian Letters: Selected Critical Essays, 1928–1971* (1973); *On Poetry and Poets* (1977); and *The Classic Shade: Selected Poems* (1978). He edited numerous anthologies, including *The Book of Canadian Poetry* (1943) and *The Oxford Book of Canadian Verse* (1960).

Works on Smith include M. L. Rosenthal, " 'Poor Innocent': The Poetry of A. J. M. Smith," *Modern Poetry Studies* 8 (1977): 1–13; Sandra A. Djwa, "A. J. M. Smith: Of Metaphysics and Dry Bones," *Studies in Canadian Literature* 3 (1978): 17–34; Leon Edel, "The Worldly Muse of A. J. M. Smith," *University of Toronto Quarterly* 47 (1978): 200–13; John Ferns, *A. J. M. Smith* (1979); Michael E. Darling, *A. J. M. Smith: An Annotated Bibliography* (1981); a special issue of *Canadian Poetry: Studies/Documents/Reviews* 11 (1982); and Anne Burke, "A. J. M. Smith: An Annotated Bibliography," *The Annotated Bibliography of Canada's Major Authors*, ed. Robert Lecker and Jack David (1983), 4: 267–370.

MICHAEL DARLING

THE LONELY LAND

Cedar and jagged fir
uplift sharp barbs
against the gray
and cloud-piled sky;
and in the bay
blown spume and windrift
and thin, bitter spray
snap
at the whirling sky;
and the pine trees
lean one way.

A wild duck calls
to her mate,
and the ragged
and passionate tones

stagger and fall,
and recover,
and stagger and fall,
on these stones—
are lost
in the lapping of water
on smooth, flat stones.

This is a beauty
of dissonance,
this resonance
of stony strand,
this smoky cry
curled over a black pine
like a broken
and wind-battered branch
when the wind
bends the tops of the pines
and curdles the sky
from the north.

This is the beauty
of strength
broken by strength
and still strong.

[1926]

SWIFT CURRENT

This is a visible
and crystal wind:
no ragged edge,
no splash of foam,
no whirlpool's scar;
only
—in the narrows,
sharpness cutting sharpness,
arrows of direction,
spears of speed.

[1930]

LIKE AN OLD PROUD KING
IN A PARABLE

A bitter king in anger to be gone
From fawning courtier and doting queen
Flung hollow sceptre and gilt crown away,
And breaking bound of all his counties green
He made a meadow in the northern stone
And breathed a palace of inviolable air
To cage a heart that carolled like a swan,
And slept alone, immaculate and gay,
With only his pride for a paramour.

O who is that bitter king? It is not I.

Let me, I beseech thee, Father, die
From this fat royal life, and lie
As naked as a bridegroom by his bride,
And let that girl be the cold goddess Pride:

And I will sing to the barren rock
Your difficult, lonely music, heart,
Like an old proud king in a parable.

[1932]

NEWS OF THE PHOENIX

They say the Phoenix is dying, some say dead.
Dead without issue is what one message said,
But that has been suppressed, officially denied.

I think myself the man who sent it lied.
In any case, I'm told, he has been shot,
As a precautionary measure, whether he did or not.

[1933]

THE ARCHER

Bend back thy bow, O Archer, till the string
Is level with thine ear, thy body taut,
Its nature art, thyself thy statue wrought
Of marble blood, thy weapon the poised wing
Of coiled and aquiline Fate. Then, loosening, fling
The hissing arrow like a burning thought
Into the empty sky that smokes as the hot
Shaft plunges to the bullseye's quenching ring.

So for a moment, motionless, serene,
Fixed between time and time, I aim and wait;
Nothing remains for breath now but to waive
His prior claim and let the barb fly clean
Into the heart of what I know and hate—
That central black, the ringed and targeted grave.

[1937]

METAMORPHOSIS

This flesh repudiates the bone
    With such dissolving force,
In such a tumult to be gone,
    Such longing for divorce,
As leaves the livid mind no choice
    But to conclude at last
That all this energy and poise
    Were but designed to cast
A richer flower from the earth
    Surrounding its decay,
And like a child whose fretful mirth
    Can find no constant play,
Bring one more transient form to birth
    And fling the old away.

[1957]

· EARLE BIRNEY ·

1904–

Born 13 May 1904 in Calgary, then part of the Northwest Territories, Alfred Earle Birney was an only child. Reared in the wilderness of Alberta and British Columbia, Birney developed a love of books and nature simultaneously. From two years of manual work after completing high school, he saved enough money to pay his tuition at the University of British Columbia, eventually transferring from the science program to English literature. He subsequently completed his M.A. and Ph.D. at the University of Toronto. Much of his adult life has been taken up with teaching English and creative writing, with world travel, with political forays, and with writing.

As a young man, Birney wrote criticism, stories, and poetry, but he did not become an active writer seeking publication until the mid-1930s. Sensing his youth about to evaporate, and the world about to explode, he wrote "Vancouver Lights" in 1941. His first book, *David and Other Poems* (1942), catapulted Birney into the Canadian literary scene, and earned him the Governor General's Award for poetry. Fresh, intelligent, and *Canadian*, Birney's vigorous style was commended for its technical artistry and narrative power.

Out of his World War II experiences came the comic novel *Turvey* (1949), subtitled *A Military Picaresque*. And early in the 1950s he wrote his second and final novel, *Down the Long Table* (1955), about politics and personal relationships. Following a round-the-world trip in 1958–59, Birney entered an energetic phase, as exemplified in his volumes of poetry *Ice Cod Bell or Stone: A Collection of New Poems* (1962) and *Near False Creek Mouth: New Poems* (1964). These two splendid books demonstrated a more relaxed, colloquial tone,

and provided a glimpse into his personal life as well.

In the mid-1960s Birney began to admire the young poets bill bissett and bpNichol, who showed Birney how to liberate spelling and grammar, and how to spring letters and words from their typographical straitjackets. Dubbed "the oldest hippie in Canada," Birney began to give many public readings, and to take up anti-war and pro-nature themes once again in his writing. The books *pnomes jukollages & other stunzas* (1969) and *what's so big about GREEN?* (1973) exhibit this new-found exhilaration.

His support of young and emerging writers has continued all his life. Birney initiated one of the first courses in creative writing in Canada, and founded the first full program at the University of British Columbia. He also supported other writers through his backing of ACTRA and the League of Canadian Poets, and through his advice in letters and conversations, and his participation on Canada Council juries. Among the many who benefited from his help are Al Purdy, Joe Rosenblatt, bill bissett, and Joy Kogawa.

Throughout the 1970s and 1980s Birney consolidated the publication of his other works. *Big Bird in the Bush: Selected Stories and Sketches* (1978) collected his short fiction, *Spreading Time: Remarks on Canadian Writers and Writing: Book I* (1980) was the first of his memoirs, *Chaucer and Irony* (1985) collected his essays on Chaucer. Several other collections are pending, including a volume of his political writings (he visited Trotsky in 1935) and several volumes of his unpublished poetry. His massive correspondence is held by the Fisher Rare Book Library at the University of Toronto.

Birney's later poetry, including "Father Grouse" and "My Love Is Young," reflects a philosophical appreciation of life and death, and an opening up of the poet's inner heart to his readers. As all earlier personae are discarded—from the alliterative, the adjectival, the tourist, the activist—finally the man, unmasked, appears. His love for a younger woman, and his detachment from death, reveal a poet exercising his craft in a highly personal manner.

.————.

Birney's works include *The Creative Writer* (1966); *The Cow Jumped Over the Moon: The Writing and Reading of Poetry* (1972); *The Collected Poems of Earle Birney* (1975); *Ghost in the Wheels: Selected Poems* (1977); *Fall by Fury and Other Makings* (1978); and *Copernican Fix* (1985).

Works on Birney include Frank Davey, *Earle Birney* (1971); Richard Robillard, *Earle Birney* (1971); Bruce Nesbitt, ed., *Earle Birney* (1974); Peter Aichinger, *Earle Birney* (1979); *Perspectives on Earle Birney* (1981); Peter Noel-Bentley, "Earle Birney: An Annotated Bibliography," *The Annotated Bibliography of Canada's Major Authors*, ed. Robert Lecker and Jack David (1983), 4: 13–128; and Peter Aichinger, "Earle Birney," *Canadian Writers and Their Works*, ed. Robert Lecker, Jack David, and Ellen Quigley (1985), Poetry Series 5: 27–71.

JACK DAVID

BUSHED

He invented a rainbow but lightning struck it
shattered it into the lake-lap of a mountain
so big his mind slowed when he looked at it

Yet he built a shack on the shore
learned to roast porcupine belly and
wore the quills on his hatband

At first he was out with the dawn
whether it yellowed bright as wood-columbine
or was only a fuzzed moth in a flannel of storm
But he found the mountain was clearly alive
sent messages whizzing down every hot morning
boomed proclamations at noon and spread out
a white guard of goat
before falling asleep on its feet at sundown

When he tried his eyes on the lake   ospreys
would fall like valkyries

choosing the cut-throat
He took then to waiting
till the night smoke rose from the boil of the sunset

But the moon carved unknown totems
out of the lakeshore
owls in the beardusky woods derided him
moosehorned cedars circled his swamps and tossed
their antlers up to the stars
Then he knew   though the mountain slept   the winds
were shaping its peak to an arrowhead
poised

And now he could only
bar himself in and wait
for the great flint to come singing into his heart

[1951]

THE BEAR ON THE DELHI ROAD

Unreal   tall as a myth
by the road the Himalayan bear
is beating the brilliant air
with his crooked arms
About him two men   bare
spindly as locusts   leap

One pulls on a ring
in the great soft nose   His mate
flicks   flicks with a stick
up at the rolling eyes

They have not led him here
down from the fabulous hills
to this bald alien plain
and the clamorous world   to kill
but simply to teach him to dance

They are peaceful both   these spare
men of Kashmir   and the bear
alive is their living   too
If   far on the Delhi way
around him galvanic they dance
it is merely to wear   wear
from his shaggy body the tranced
wish forever to stay
only an ambling bear
four-footed in berries

It is no more joyous for them
in this hot dust to prance
out of reach of the praying claws
sharpened to paw for ants
in the shadows of deodars
It is not easy to free
myth from reality
or rear this fellow up
to lurch   lurch with them
in the tranced dancing of men

Srinagar 1958–Île des Porquerolles 1959 [1960]

EL GRECO: *ESPOLIO*

The carpenter is intent on the pressure of his hand

on the awl   and the trick of pinpointing his strength
through the awl to the wood   which is tough
He has no effort to spare for despoilings
or to worry if he'll be cut in on the dice
His skill is vital to the scene   and the safety of the state
Anyone can perform the indignities   It's his hard arms
and craft that hold the eyes of the convict's women
There is the problem of getting the holes exact
(in the middle of this elbowing crowd)
and deep enough to hold the spikes
after they've sunk through those bared feet
and inadequate wrists he knows are waiting behind him

He doesn't sense perhaps that one of the hands
is held in a curious gesture over him—
giving   or asking   forgiveness?—
but he'd scarcely take time to be puzzled by poses
Criminals come in all sorts
as anyone knows who makes crosses
are as mad or sane as those who decide on their killings
Our one at least has been quiet so far
though they say he talked himself into this trouble
a carpenter's son who got notions of preaching

Well here's a carpenter's son who'll have carpenter sons
God willing   and build what's wanted
temples or tables   mangers or crosses
and shape them decently
working alone in that firm and profound abstraction
which blots out the bawling of rag-snatchers
To construct with hands   knee-weight   braced thigh
keeps the back turned from death

But it's too late now for the other carpenter's boy
to return to this peace before the nails are hammered

Bowen Island [1960]

BILLBOARDS BUILD FREEDOM
OF CHOICE
—Courtesy, Oregon Chambers of Commerce—

(*billboard on coastal highway*)

Yegitit?
Look see
     AMERICA BUILDS BILLBOARDS
so billboards kin bill freedoma choice
between—yeah between billbores no
     WAIT
its yedoan hafta choose no more between
say like trees and billbores lessa course
wenna buncha trees is flattint out inta
10   BILLB—
yeah yegotit
youkin pick between well
hey!   see!   like dat!
     ALL VINYL GET WELL DOLLS $6.98
or—watch wasdat comin up?
     PRE PAID CAT?
     PREPAID CATASTROPHE COVERAGE
yeah hell youkin have damnear anythin
     FREE 48 INCH TV IN EVERY ROOM
20 see!   or   watchit!
     OUR PIES TASTE LIKE MOTHERS
yeah but look bud no chickenin out
because billbores build
     AM—
yeah an AMERICAN BUILDS MORE
buildbores to bill more—
sure yugotta! yugotta have
     FREEDOM TO
hey! you doan wannem godam fieldglasses!
30 theys probly clouds on Mount Raneer
but not on
     MOUNT RAINIER THE BEER THAT CHEERS

and not on good old yella
    SHELL
keepin de windoff yuh from allose clammy beaches
Landscapes is for the birds fella
yegotta choose between well like
between two a de same
hell like de man said Who's got time
40 for a third tit? *two* parties is *Okay*
    that's   DEMOC   sure but yegit three
yegot COMMIES I'm tellinyeh
is like dose damfool niggers in
in Asia someweres all tryin to be nootrul
I tellyeh treesa crowd   a crowda
godamatheisticunamericananti
    BILLBORES
yeah an yewanna help Burma?   help
    BURMA SHAVE
50 yewanna keep the longhairs from starvin?
    BUY HANDMADE TOY SOLDIERS
yegotta choose fella yegotta
choose between
    AMERICA and UN—
between KEE-RISPIES and KEE-RUMPIES
between KEE-RYEST and KEE-ROOST-SHOVE
and brother if you doan pick
    RIGHT
you better
60 git this heap
tahelloffn
our
    FREEWAY

1961/1962 [1963]

CANADA COUNCIL

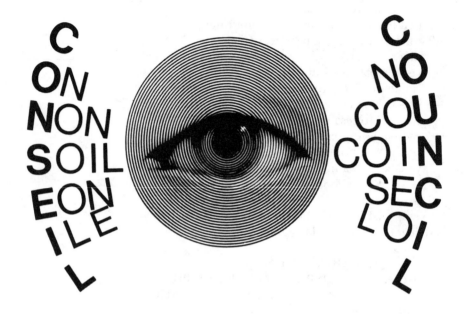

[1969]

FATHER GROUSE

some mornings trying to write
i get like an old ruffed partridge
flopping off & on the nest
scared somebody'll steal
those handsome brown eggs
i've never quite laid yet

flinching from cloud shadows
hearing a fox behind every bush
snakes in the grass
shots on the hill—
limping & trembling around
from what looked like a man

but was only a dumb moose—
till i crumple down beat
with nothing done
& then the phone rings

but listen!
it isnt another mag salesman
or the Poets' League about dues
out of that lovely earpiece
comes a voice spreading sunshine
all through the woods
& i sit back drumming softly
to the loveliest partridge of all
(whose eggs they really are)
& feeling energy-control
right down to my wingtips

after we hang up
quietly i'm warming the eggs again
if i cant lay i can hatch
maybe something of me
will show in the chicks

Alexander St., July 1974 [1976]

MY LOVE IS YOUNG

my love is young & i am old
she'll need a new man soon
but still we wake to clip and talk
to laugh as one
to eat and walk
beneath our twelve-year moon

good moon   good sun
that we do love
i pray the world believe me
& never tell me when it's time
that i'm to die
or she's to leave me

[1977]

· A. M. KLEIN ·

1909–1972

A. M. Klein was born in 1909 in Ratno in the Ukraine, and in 1910 his family moved to Montreal where he lived for the rest of his life. After graduating from McGill, he studied law at the Université de Montréal. Throughout most of his career, Klein combined his law practice with editing the *Canadian Jewish Chronicle* and acting as a speechwriter and public-relations adviser to Samuel Bronfman. In 1949 he received the Governor General's Award for *The Rocking Chair and Other Poems* (1948). The same year he was an unsuccessful federal candidate for the Co-operative Commonwealth Federation, and in 1949 he went on a fact-finding trip to Israel for the Canadian Jewish Congress. In the early fifties he suffered the first of a series of breakdowns, and after 1955 withdrew from active life, including writing, entirely. He died in 1972.

Klein received a solid Jewish education and, although he abandoned religious orthodoxy at an early age, he always retained a deep interest in the Jewish community and its values; Zionism, in particular, remained a central concern throughout his life. Klein's Jewish background is reflected in his first book, *Hath Not a Jew....* Published in 1940 (though consisting almost entirely of poems written in the late twenties and early thirties), *Hath Not a Jew ...* presents a picture of Jewish life and customs reflecting, for the most part, the traditions of the central European *shtetl*. Although many of these traditions were still alive in the Montreal of Klein's youth; there is, in general, remarkably little sense in these poems (or in any of Klein's poems for that matter), of contemporary Jewish life in Montreal. The contrast with Layton or Richler in this regard is striking. Many of the poems in the collec-

tion are among Klein's most beautiful, but they often substitute a quaint charm for genuine intensity. An important exception is "Out of the Pulver and the Polished Lens," a poem inspired by Spinoza's excommunication by the Jewish community of Amsterdam. Klein had little first-hand knowledge of Spinoza's philosophy, but as a symbol of the creative individual at odds with but unavoidably bound to an uncomprehending community, Spinoza's appeal to the young Klein is understandable.

The thirties were a difficult time for Klein, who was deeply affected by the Depression and by the rise of Fascism. In the late thirties he wrote little; the poems he did produce, a series of satires of a vaguely leftist cast, are largely unsuccessful, giving evidence, in their uncertainty of tone, of Klein's sense of confusion and helplessness. World War II came as a relief; issues achieved a terrible clarity and Klein found a voice once more as a spokesman for his community and for all humanity against the evils of Nazism. In 1944 *Poems* was published, in which an anguished Klein confronts the horrors of his day more directly than he had done before. In *The Hitleriad* (1944), a largely unsuccessful satire on Hitler in the manner of Pope's *Dunciad*, Klein's total revulsion from Hitler and all he stands for makes it almost impossible for him to rise above the level of ultimately trivializing abuse.

Much of Klein's writing in the early 1940s reflects a sense of alienation and futility, but at the same time a commitment to his art and to its social function. The finest expression of this attitude is "Portrait of the Poet as Landscape," which appears at the end of *The Rocking Chair and Other Poems* (1948), but was written before the other poems in the volume. *The Rocking Chair* is Klein's finest achievement; although most of the poems deal with the French Canadian culture of Quebec, Klein is able to express through them (see especially "The Rocking Chair" and "Political Meeting") his richly ambivalent feelings about his relationship to his own community in a way that never seemed possible to him in his specifically Jewish poems.

Throughout the 1940s, Klein developed an interest in dialectical modes of thought as a means of making sense of the negative aspects of experience, which threatened to overwhelm him. "Sestina on the Dialectic" is one example of this interest; a more important one is his poetic novel, *The Second Scroll* (1951), in which he struggles to interpret the Holocaust and the founding of the state of Israel in dialectical terms that owe much to the Kabbalah. In his last (mostly unpublished) writings, most notably an unfinished novel on the legend of the golem, the struggle to "negate the negation" is increasingly seen to be futile; the struggle ends, finally, in silence.

Klein's works include *Hath Not a Jew . . .* (1940); *Poems* (1944); *The Hitleriad* (1944); *The Rocking Chair and Other Poems* (1948); *The Second Scroll* (1951). See also Volumes I, II, and III of Klein's collected works—*Beyond Sambation: Selected Essays and Editorials 1928–1955*, ed. M. W. Steinberg and Usher Caplan (1982); *A. M. Klein: Short Stories*, ed. M. W. Steinberg (1983); and *Literary Essays and Reviews*, ed. Usher Caplan and M. W. Steinberg (1987).

Works on Klein include Miriam Waddington, *A. M. Klein* (1970); T. A. Marshall, ed., *A. M. Klein* (1970); G. K. Fischer, *In Search of Jerusalem: Religion and Ethics in the Writings of A. M. Klein* (1975); Seymour Mayne, ed., *The A. M. Klein Symposium* (1975); Usher Caplan, *Like One That Dreamed: A Portrait of A. M. Klein* (1982); Solomon Spiro, *Tapestry for Designs: Judaic Allusions in* The Second Scroll *and* The Collected Poems *of A. M. Klein* (1984); and Zailig Pollock, ed., "A. M. Klein's Montreal," a special issue of the *Journal of Canadian Studies* 19 (1985).

ZAILIG POLLOCK

HEIRLOOM

My father bequeathed me no wide estates;
No keys and ledgers were my heritage;
Only some holy books with *yahrzeit* dates
Writ mournfully upon a blank front page—

Books of the Baal Shem Tov, and of his wonders;
Pamphlets upon the devil and his crew;
Prayers against road demons, witches, thunders;
And sundry other tomes for a good Jew.

Beautiful: though no pictures on them, save
The scorpion crawling on a printed track;

The Virgin floating on a scriptural wave,
Square letters twinkling in the Zodiac.

The snuff left on this page, now brown and old,
The tallow stains of midnight liturgy—
These are my coat of arms, and these unfold
My noble lineage, my proud ancestry!

And my tears, too, have stained this heirloomed ground,
When reading in these treatises some weird
Miracle, I turned a leaf and found
A white hair fallen from my father's beard.

[1935]

PORTRAIT OF THE POET
AS LANDSCAPE

I

Not an editorial-writer, bereaved with bartlett,
mourns him, the shelved Lycidas.
No actress squeezes a glycerine tear for him.
The radio broadcast lets his passing pass.
And with the police, no record. Nobody, it appears,
either under his real name or his alias,
missed him enough to report.

It is possible that he is dead, and not discovered.
It is possible that he can be found some place
10 in a narrow closet, like the corpse in a detective story,
standing, his eyes staring, and ready to fall on his face.
It is also possible that he is alive
and amnesiac, or mad, or in retired disgrace,
or beyond recognition lost in love.

We are sure only that from our real society
he has disappeared; he simply does not count,
except in the pullulation of vital statistics—

somebody's vote, perhaps, an anonymous taunt
of the Gallup poll, a dot in a government table—
20 but not felt, and certainly far from eminent—
in a shouting mob, somebody's sigh.

O, he who unrolled our culture from his scroll—
the prince's quote, the rostrum-rounding roar—
who under one name made articulate
heaven, and under another the seven-circled air,
is, if he is at all, a number, an x,
a Mr. Smith in a hotel register,—
incognito, lost, lacunal.

II

The truth is he's not dead, but only ignored—
30 like the mirroring lenses forgotten on a brow
that shine with the guilt of their unnoticed world.
The truth is he lives among neighbours, who, though they will allow
him a passable fellow, think him eccentric, not solid,
a type that one can forgive, and for that matter, forgo.

Himself he has his moods, just like a poet.
Sometimes, depressed to nadir, he will think all lost,
will see himself as throwback, relict, freak,
his mother's miscarriage, his great-grandfather's ghost,
and he will curse his quintuplet senses, and their tutors
40 in whom he put, as he should not have put, his trust.

Then he will remember his travels over that body—
the torso verb, the beautiful face of the noun,
and all those shaped and warm auxiliaries!
A first love it was, the recognition of his own.
Dear limbs adverbial, complexion of adjective,
dimple and dip of conjugation!

And then remember how this made a change in him
affecting for always the glow and growth of his being;
how suddenly was aware of the air, like shaken tinfoil,
50 of the patents of nature, the shock of belated seeing,
the lonelinesses peering from the eyes of crowds;
the integers of thought; the cube-roots of feeling.

Thus, zoomed to zenith, sometimes he hopes again,
and sees himself as a character, with a rehearsed role:

the Count of Monte Cristo, come for his revenges;
the unsuspected heir, with papers; the risen soul;
or the chloroformed prince awaking from his flowers;
or—deflated again—the convict on parole.

III

He is alone; yet not completely alone.
60 Pins on a map of a colour similar to his,
each city has one, sometimes more than one:
here, caretakers of art, in colleges;
in offices, there, with arm-bands, and green-shaded;
and there, pounding their catalogued beats in libraries,—

everywhere menial, a shadow's shadow.
And always for their egos—their outmoded art.
Thus, having lost the bevel in the ear,
they know neither up nor down, mistake the part
for the whole, curl themselves in a comma,
70 talk technics, make a colon their eyes. They distort—

such is the pain of their frustration—truth
to something convolute and cerebral.
How they do fear the slap of the flat of the platitude!
Now Pavlov's victims, their mouths water at bell,
the platter empty.
                          See they set twenty-one jewels
into their watches; the time they do not tell!

Some, patagonian in their own esteem,
and longing for the multiplying word,
80 join party and wear pins, now have a message,
an ear, and the convention-hall's regard.
Upon the knees of ventriloquists, they own,
of their dandled brightness, only the paint and board.

And some go mystical, and some go mad.
One stares at a mirror all day long, as if
to recognize himself; another courts
angels,—for here he does not fear rebuff;
and a third, alone, and sick with sex, and rapt,
doodles him symbols convex and concave.

90 O schizoid solitudes! O purities
    curdling upon themselves! Who live for themselves,
    or for each other, but for nobody else;
    desire affection, private and public loves;
    are friendly, and then quarrel and surmise
    the secret perversions of each other's lives.

    IV

    He suspects that something has happened, a law
    been passed, a nightmare ordered. Set apart,
    he finds himself, with special haircut and dress,
    as on a reservation. Introvert.
100 He does not understand this; sad conjecture
    muscles and palls thrombotic on his heart.

    He thinks an impostor, having studied his personal biography,
    his gestures, his moods, now has come forward to pose
    in the shivering vacuums his absence leaves.
    Wigged with his laurel, that other, and faked with his face,
    he pats the heads of his children, pecks his wife,
    and is at home, and slippered, in his house.

    So he guesses at the impertinent silhouette
    that talks to his phone-piece and slits open his mail.
110 Is it the local tycoon who for a hobby
    plays poet, he so epical in steel?
    The orator, making a pause? Or is that man
    he who blows his flash of brass in the jittering hall?

    Or is he cuckolded by the troubadour
    rich and successful out of celluloid?
    Or by the don who unrhymes atoms? Or
    the chemist death built up? Pride, lost impostor'd pride,
    it is another, another, whoever he is,
    who rides where he should ride.

    V

120 *Fame*, the adrenalin: to be talked about;
    to be a verb; to be introduced as *The*;
    to smile with endorsement from slick paper; make

caprices anecdotal; to nod to the world; to see
one's name like a song upon the marquees played;
to be forgotten with embarrassment; to be—
to be.

It has its attractions, but is not the thing;
nor is it the ape mimesis who speaks from the tree
ancestral; nor the merkin joy . . .
130 Rather it is stark infelicity
which stirs him from his sleep, undressed, asleep
to walk upon roofs and window-sills and defy
the gape of gravity.

VI

Therefore he seeds illusions. Look, he is
the nth Adam taking a green inventory
in world but scarcely uttered, naming, praising,
the flowering fiats in the meadow, the
syllabled fur, stars aspirate, the pollen
whose sweet collision sounds eternally.
140 For to praise

the world—he, solitary man—is breath
to him. Until it has been praised, that part
has not been. Item by exciting item—
air to his lungs, and pressured blood to his heart.—
they are pulsated, and breathed, until they map,
not the world's, but his own body's chart!

And now in imagination he has climbed
another planet, the better to look
with single camera view upon this earth—
150 its total scope, and each afflated tick,
its talk, its trick, its tracklessness—and this,
this he would like to write down in a book!

To find a new function for the déclassé craft
archaic like the fletcher's; to make a new thing;
to say the word that will become sixth sense;
perhaps by necessity and indirection bring
new forms to life, anonymously, new creeds—
O, somehow pay back the daily larcenies of the lung!

These are not mean ambitions. It is already something
160 merely to entertain them. Meanwhile, he
makes of his status as zero a rich garland,
a halo of his anonymity,
and lives alone, and in his secret shines
like phosphorus. At the bottom of the sea.

[1945]

THE ROCKING CHAIR

It seconds the crickets of the province. Heard
in the clean lamplit farmhouses of Quebec,—
wooden,—it is no less a national bird;
and rivals, in its cage, the mere stuttering clock.
To its time, the evenings are rolled away;
and in its peace the pensive mother knits
contentment to be worn by her family,
grown-up, but still cradled by the chair in which she sits.

It is also the old man's pet, pair to his pipe,
the two aids of his arithmetic and plans,
plans rocking and puffing into market-shape;
and it is the toddler's game and dangerous dance.
Moved to the verandah, on summer Sundays, it is,
among the hanging plants, the girls, the boy-friends,
sabbatical and clumsy, like the white haloes
dangling above the blue serge suits of the young men.

It has a personality of its own;
is a character (like that old drunk Lacoste,
exhaling amber, and toppling on his pins);
it is alive; individual; and no less
an identity than those about it. And
it is tradition. Centuries have been flicked
from its arcs, alternately flicked and pinned.
It rolls with the gait of St. Malo. It is act

and symbol, symbol of this static folk
which moves in segments, and returns to base,—

a sunken pendulum: *invoke, revoke*;
loosed yon, leashed hither, motion on no space.
O, like some Anjou ballad, all refrain,
which turns about its longing, and seems to move
to make a pleasure out of repeated pain,
its music moves, as if always back to a first love.

[1945]

POLITICAL MEETING
(For Camillien Houde)

On the school platform, draping the folding seats,
they wait the chairman's praise and glass of water.
Upon the wall the agonized Y initials their faith.

Here all are laic; the skirted brothers have gone.
Still, their equivocal absence is felt, like a breeze
that gives curtains the sounds of surplices.

The hall is yellow with light, and jocular;
suddenly some one lets loose upon the air
the ritual bird which the crowd in snares of singing

catches and plucks, throat, wings, and little limbs.
Fall the feathers of sound, like *alouette's*.
The chairman, now, is charming, full of asides and wit,

building his orators, and chipping off
the heckling gargoyles popping in the hall.
(Outside, in the dark, the street is body-tall,

flowered with faces intent on the scarecrow thing
that shouts to thousands the echoing
of their own wishes.) The Orator has risen!

Worshipped and loved, their favourite visitor,
a country uncle with sunflower seeds in his pockets,
full of wonderful moods, tricks, imitative talk,

he is their idol: like themselves, not handsome,
not snobbish, not of the *Grande Allée! Un homme!*
Intimate, informal, he makes bear's compliments

to the ladies; is gallant; and grins;
goes for the balloon, his opposition, with pins;
jokes also on himself, speaks of himself

in the third person, slings slang, and winks with folklore;
and knows now that he has them, kith and kin.
Calmly, therefore, he begins to speak of war,

praises the virtue of being *Canadien,*
of being at peace, of faith, of family,
and suddenly his other voice: *Where are your sons?*

He is tearful, choking tears; but not he
would blame the clever English; in their place
he'd do the same; maybe.

Where *are* your sons?
                    The whole street wears one face,
shadowed and grim; and in the darkness rises
the body-odour of race.

[1946]

SESTINA ON THE DIALECTIC

Yes yeasts to No, and No is numinous with Yes. All is a hap, a haze,
a hazard, a do-doubtful, a flight from, a travel to. Nothing will keep,
but eases essence,—out!—outplots its plight. So westers east, and so each
teaches an opposite: a nonce-thing still.

A law? Fact or flaw of the fiat, still—a law. It binds us, braided, wicker
and withe. It stirs the seasons, it treads the tides, it so rests in our life
there's nothing, there's not a sole thing that from its workings will not
out.

The antics of the antonyms! From, to; stress, slack, and stress,—a rhythm running to a reason, a double dance, a shivering still.

Even the heart's blood, bursting in, bales out, an ebb and flow; and even the circuit within which its pulsebeat's beam—man's morse—is a something that grows, that grounds,—treks, totters. So.

O dynasties and dominions downfall so! Flourish to flag and fail, are potent to a pause, a panic precipice, to a picked pit, and thence—rubble rebuilding,—still rise resurrective,—and now see them, with new doers in dominion!

They, too, dim out.

World's sudden with somersault, updown, inout, overandunder. And, note well: also that other world, the two-chambered mind, goes with it, ever kaleidoscopic, one scape to another, suffering change that changes still, that focuses and fissions *the* to *a*.

When will there be arrest? Consensus? A marriage of the antipathies, and out of the vibrant deaths and rattles the life still? O just as the racked one hopes his ransom, so I hope it, name it, image it, the together-living, the together-with, the final synthesis. A stop.

But so it never will turn out, returning to the rack within, without. And no thing's still.

[c. 1946]

· DOROTHY LIVESAY ·

1909–

Dorothy Kathleen May Livesay was born in Winnipeg, Manitoba, on 12 October 1909 to journalist parents who encouraged her writing career from the start. She spent her first decade on the prairies, before the family moved east to Toronto. In 1931 Livesay graduated from the University of Toronto (B.A., Honours in modern languages) and went on to earn a Diplôme d'études supérieures at the Sorbonne in 1932, with a thesis on modern English poetry. Deeply moved by social issues during the Great Depression, she worked as a social worker in Toronto, Montreal, New Jersey, and eventually Vancouver, participating as well in politicized cultural groups and writing for leftist periodicals such as *New Frontier*. Livesay settled in Vancouver, married a fellow activist in 1937, and bore children in 1940 and 1942. From the end of World War II through to the 1960s, she taught, directed adult education programs, and wrote, in Canada, Europe, and then Africa. Livesay has since served as writer-in-residence at nine Canadian universities and colleges, travelled and lectured widely, founded and edited a periodical of poetry and reviews called *CV/II*, and nurtured many writers. From *Green Pitcher* in 1928 to *The Self-Completing Tree* in 1986, Livesay has published some two dozen books of poetry and prose. She has received two Governor General's Awards for Poetry, honorary doctorates and medals from several universities, the Queen's Canada Medal, the Governor General's Persons Award, and the Order of Canada. These honours, in addition to a recent documentary film about her, affirm Livesay's status as one of this century's most important Canadian poets.

Livesay's early poetry was imagistic, introspective, and intensely conscious of the natural world and private emotion. Praised by the critics for its precision and delicacy, the poetry of *Green Pitcher* and of *Signpost* (1932) was nonetheless soon rejected by its young author as irrelevant in the face of the social upheaval of the 1930s. After several years of uncertainty, during which she confined herself to artistically unsatisfying agitation-propaganda drama, exhortatory prose, and social short stories, Livesay found in the English social poets—Spender, Auden, and Day Lewis—a literary model for reconciling a social imperative with the lyrical impulses of poetry. The result was such powerful poems as "Day and Night" (1936), which used industrial, jazz, and black spiritual rhythms, complicated juxtapositions, multiple voices, and working-class artefacts to capture the horrors of modern factory life and capitalist oppression. Social injustice, the Spanish Civil War, and the onset of World War II were other major preoccupations of her poetry in the late 1930s.

In the 1940s Livesay continued to publish highly political poetry, so compelling even to conservative Canadians that the collection entitled *Day and Night* carried off the 1944 Governor General's Award for Poetry. In these years Livesay also turned her sophisticated sensibility and softened socialism to linking the larger world with a microcosm not previously treated seriously in Canadian poetry: that of wife and mother. Her 1947 *Poems for People*, a second Governor General's Award winner, shows an even more accomplished level of richly restrained diction, energy, humanism, and the ability to project herself into the experience of others. It was this talent for seeing through others' eyes that influenced most of her writing—both poetic and journalistic—of the post-war years. Using the exciting new option of radio verse-drama and what she dubbed a "documentary" poetic form, Livesay directed her attention to the plight of minority groups such as Japanese Canadians and the Métis.

In the 1950s Livesay's poetic concerns became less passionate, social, and public, and more cerebral, contemplative, and artistic. When she commented on society, it tended to be as an astute but subdued observer, and she has referred to that decade as one of "almost an existential despair" in which her consolations were abstract and her poetry was deliberately formally structured.

Then three electric years of teaching English in Zambia gave Livesay the driving rhythms and strong images which would, upon her return to Canada in 1963, inform a great outpouring of poetry. *The Unquiet Bed* (1967) and *Plainsongs* (1969) were astonishing in their sexual and emotional candour, their penetrating analysis of male-female relationships and of women's perspectives; their freewheeling metrics and evident pleasure in the natural rhythms of human speech. Livesay also pursued with increasing sharpness the theme of aging and the plight of the elderly in a youth-oriented society. And, expanding her long-standing interest in the Canadian experience, she published in a series of perceptive backward glances, a collection of quasi-historical poems (*The Documentaries*, [1968]), evocative short stories about her prairie origins (*Beginnings: A Winnipeg Childhood*, [1973]), and a retrospective collage of her life in the Great Depression (*Right Hand Left Hand*, [1977]).

In the late 1970s and the 1980s Livesay's poetry has focused upon three particular areas: the phases of love, the personal march toward death, and the precarious state of the world—environmental, social, and spiritual. Firmly committed to a clean, accessible free verse in style, and to "plain talk" in content, Livesay continues to spurn safe positions or serene detachment, steadfastly arguing the centrality of the human heart.

· ——————— ·

Livesay's works include *Green Pitcher* (1928); *Signpost* (1932); *Day and Night* (1944); *Poems for People* (1947); *Call My People Home* (1950); *New Poems* (1955); *Selected Poems of Dorothy Livesay* (1957); *The Colour of God's Face* (1964); *The Unquiet Bed* (1967); *The Documentaries* (1968); *Plainsongs* (1969); *Disasters of the Sun* (1971); *Collected Poems: The Two Seasons* (1972); *Beginnings: A Winnipeg Childhood* (1973); *Nine Poems of Farewell 1972–1973* (1973); *Ice Age* (1975); *The Woman I Am: Best Loved Poems from One of Canada's Best Loved Poets* (1977); *The Raw Edges: Voices from Our Time* (1981); *The Phases of Love* (1983); *Feeling the Worlds: New Poems* (1984); *Right Hand Left Hand* (1977); and *The Self-Completing Tree* (1986). She has edited the *Collected Poems of Raymond Knister* (1949); *40 Women Poets of Canada* (1971); *Woman's Eye: 12 B.C. Poets* (1978); and the journals *New Frontier, Contemporary Verse, Northern Review, White Pelican,* and *CV/II*.

Works on Livesay include Peter Stevens, "Out of the Silence and Across the Distance," *Queen's Quarterly* 78 (1971): 579–91; D. Leland, "Dorothy Livesay: Poet of Nature," *Dalhousie Review* 51 (1971): 404–12; B. Mitchell, " 'How Silence Sings' in the Poetry of Dorothy Livesay," *Dalhousie Review* 54 (1974): 510–28; Peter Stevens, "Dorothy Livesay: The Love Poetry," *Poets and Critics: Essays from "Canadian Literature" 1966–1974*, ed. George Woodcock (1974): 33–52; Debbie Foulks, "Livesay's Two Seasons of Love," *Canadian Literature* 74 (1977): 63–73; a special issue of *Room of One's Own* 5.1–2 (1979); Alan Ricketts, "Dorothy Livesay: An Annotated Bibliography," *The Annotated Bibliography of Canada's Major Authors,* ed. Robert Lecker and Jack David (1983), 4: 129–203; and Lee Briscoe Thompson, *Dorothy Livesay* (1987).

LEE BRISCOE THOMPSON

FIRE AND REASON

I cannot shut out the night—
Nor its sharp clarity.

The many blinds we draw,
You and I,
The many fires we light
Can never quite obliterate
The irony of stars,
The deliberate moon,
The last, unsolved finality of night.

[1928]

GREEN RAIN

I remember long veils of green rain
Feathered like the shawl of my grandmother—
Green from the half-green of the spring trees
Waving in the valley.

I remember the road
Like the one which leads to my grandmother's house,
A warm house, with green carpets,
Geraniums, a trilling canary
And shining horse-hair chairs;
And the silence, full of the rain's falling
Was like my grandmother's parlour
Alive with herself and her voice, rising and falling—
Rain and wind intermingled.

I remember on that day
I was thinking only of my love
And of my love's house.
But now I remember the day
As I remember my grandmother.
I remember the rain as the feathery fringe of her shawl.

[1930]

BARTOK AND THE GERANIUM

She lifts her green umbrellas
Towards the pane
Seeking her fill of sunlight
Or of rain;
Whatever falls
She has no commentary
Accepts, extends,
Blows out her furbelows,
Her bustling boughs;

And all the while he whirls
Explodes in space,
Never content with this small room:
Not even can he be
Confined to sky
But must speed high and higher still
From galaxy to galaxy,
Wrench from the stars their momentary notes
Steal music from the moon.

She's daylight
He is dark
She's heaven-held breath
He storms and crackles
Spits with hell's own spark.

Yet in this room, this moment now
These together breathe and be:
She, essence of serenity,
He in a mad intensity
Soars beyond sight
Then hurls, lost Lucifer,
From heaven's height.

And when he's done, he's out:
She leans a lip against the glass
And preens herself in light.

[1952]

LAMENT

for J.F.B.L.

What moved me, was the way your hand
Lay in my hand, not withering,
But warm, like a hand cooled in a stream
And purling still; or a bird caught in a snare
Wings folded stiff, eyes in a stare,
But still alive with the fear,
Heart hoarse with hope—
So your hand, your dead hand, my dear.

And the veins, still mounting as blue rivers,
10 Mounting towards the tentative finger-tips,
The delta where four seas come in—
Your fingers promontories into colourless air
Were rosy still—not chalk (like cliffs
You knew in boyhood, Isle of Wight):
But blushed with colour from the sun you sought
And muscular from garden toil;
Stained with the purple of an iris bloom,
Violas grown for a certain room;
Hands seeking faïence, filagree,
20 Chinese lacquer and ivory—
Brussels lace; and a walnut piece
Carved by a hand now phosphorus.

What moved me, was the way your hand
Held life, although the pulse was gone.
The hand that carpentered a children's chair,
Carved out a stair
Held leash upon a dog in strain
Gripped wheel, swung sail,
Flicked horse's rein
30 And then again
Moved kings and queens meticulous on a board,
Slashed out the cards, cut bread, and poured
A purring cup of tea;
The hand so neat and nimble
Could make a tennis partner tremble,
Write a resounding round
Of sonorous verbs and nouns—
Hand that would not strike a child, and yet
Could ring a bell and send a man to doom.

40 And now unmoving in this Spartan room
The hand still speaks:
After the brain was fogged
And the tight lips tighter shut,
After the shy appraising eyes
Relinquished fire for the sea's green gaze—
The hand still breathes, fastens its hold on life;
Demands the whole, establishes the strife.

What moved me, was the way your hand
Lay cool in mine, not withering;
50 As bird still breathes, and stream runs clear—
So your hand; your dead hand, my dear.

[1953]

ON LOOKING INTO
HENRY MOORE

1

Sun, stun me, sustain me
Turn me to stone:
Stone, goad me and gall me
Urge me to run.

When I have found
Passivity in fire
And fire in stone
Female and male
I'll rise alone
Self-extending and self-known.

2

The message of the tree is this:
Aloneness is the only bliss

Self-adoration is not in it
(Narcissus tried, but could not win it)

Rather, to extend the root
Tombwards, be at home with death

But in the upper branches know
A green eternity of fire and snow.

3

The fire in the farthest hills
Is where I'd burn myself to bone:
Clad in the armour of the sun
I'd stand anew, alone

Take off this flesh, this hasty dress
Prepare my half-self for myself:
One unit, as a tree or stone
Woman in man, and man in womb.

[1956]

ICE AGE
(for Laura Damania)

In this coming cold
devouring our wheat fields
and Russia's
there'll be no shadow
nor sign of shadow
all cloud, shroud
endless rain
eternal snow

In this coming cold
which we have fashioned
out of our vain jet-pride,
the supersonic planes
will shriek destruction
upon the benign
yin yang
ancient and balanced universe

Worse than an animal
man tortures his prey
given sun's energy
and fire's blaze
he has ripped away
leaf
    bird
       flower
is moving to destroy
the still centre
heart's power.

Now who among us
will lift a finger
to declare *I am of God, good?*
Who among us
dares to be righteous?

[1975]

· IRVING LAYTON ·

1912–

Irving Layton was born Israel Lazarovitch in 1912 in the Romanian village
of Tirgul Neamt. The next year his
family immigrated to Montreal, which
ever since has provided Layton with his
personal and literary focus. He received a B.Sc. from MacDonald College in 1939, and an M.A. in political
economy from McGill in 1946. In the
1940s he was, with Louis Dudek and
John Sutherland, a core member of the
First Statement group which worked to
imbue Canadian poetry with a greater
energy and proletarian vigour. For
many years he held a variety of teaching jobs: at Sir George Williams University, Herzliah High School, and other
schools, until in 1969 he accepted a
professorship at York University. After retiring from teaching in 1978 he
moved back to Montreal where he is
currently living with his fifth wife, Anna
Pottier. His numerous awards and
honours include the Governor General's Award (1959), the Order of Canada (1976), a Life Achievement Award
from the Encyclopaedia Britannica
(1978), nomination for the Nobel Prize
(1982), and honorary degrees from
Bishop's University and Concordia.

For the past half century Layton has
been a central and controversial figure
in Canadian poetry. His poetry has often
shocked with its explicit sensuality and
outspoken invective, while his frequent
public appearances have helped make
the writing and reading of poetry a
more acceptable activity in Canada. His
public quarrels with John Sutherland,
Louis Dudek, and Elspeth Cameron
have been prolonged and bitter, but he
has also been an influential teacher and
personality for many of Canada's
younger poets.

In his foreword to *A Red Carpet for
the Sun* (1959) Layton writes: "I am not
at ease in the world (what poet ever

is?); but neither am I fully at ease in
the world of the imagination. I require
some third realm, as yet undiscovered,
in which to live. My dis-ease has spurred
me on to bridge the two with the stilts
of poetry, or to create inside me an
ironic balance of tensions." In Layton's
best poetry the seething contradictions
of his world are momentarily resolved.
Poetry is for him an extremely necessary activity to act as a stay against the
chaos of the world without, and within
the poet's inner self. The poet is a man
in opposition, but it is from the energy
generated by this opposition that good
poetry comes. He objects strenuously
to the academic approach to poetry of
people such as A. J. M. Smith and
Northrop Frye, for he sees their ele-
gance and balance as antithetical to his
passionate engagement.

Layton has a profound compassion
for those figures like the protagonists
of "The Bull Calf," or "Keine Lazarovitch," or, in his later poetry, Jesus
Christ, who represent a vitality that
transcends our society. This concept
receives one of its fullest expressions
in the remarkable "A Tall Man Exe-
cutes a Jig," where intricate patterns of
imagery are woven together to create
a rich and subtle texture. But the best
creations of our society are continually
endangered, and often the poet finds
him/herself a swimmer, plunged into
depths which are uncomfortable and
dangerous, but a necessary hazard to
transcend the limitations of our culture.

Much of his best poetry is characterized by this meditative, lyric strain.
But Layton is a man of many masks,
who also adopts at times the guise of a
satirist, dionysian lover, or right-wing
activist. A full appreciation of his
achievement requires an ability to keep
these various and sometimes conflicting aspects in balance.

In a number of more recent books, particularly *For My Brother Jesus*, Layton has explored the anti-Semitism which he sees as implicit in Christianity. For him the central twentieth-century event was the Holocaust, which he relates to two thousand years of a Christianity which has institutionalized repression and denial rather than the humanity and creativity of Jesus Christ. Just as much of his early work attacked the sexual repressiveness of Canadian society, so much of his later work denounces "Xians," or pseudo-Christians, whose values he blames for the wars and genocides of the twentieth century.

While a conscientious craftsman, Layton has never been a technical innovator. For a time in the early 1950s he had many personal and literary contacts with Charles Olson and Robert Creeley, but their technical experiments struck no response in him. His is very much a poetry of statement; while his ideas have changed over the years, his manner of presenting them has not changed markedly. Much of his work and his poetic stance is reminiscent of the Old Testament prophets bringing inspired messages to the people. His roots are more in Isaiah and William Blake than in any twentieth-century writer.

•————————•

Layton's works include *The Improved Binoculars* (1956); *A Red Carpet for the Sun* (1959); *Collected Poems* (1965); *The Collected Poems of Irving Layton* (1971); Seymour Mayne, ed., *Engagements: The Prose of Irving Layton* (1972); *A Wild Peculiar Joy* (1982); *The Gucci Bag* (1983); *A Spider Danced a Cozy Jig* (1984); *Waiting for the Messiah* (1985); and *Dance with Desire* (1986).

Works on Layton include Eli Mandel, *Irving Layton* (1969); Seymour Mayne, ed., *Irving Layton: The Poet and His Critics* (1978); Eli Mandel, *The Poetry of Irving Layton: Notes* (1981); Elspeth Cameron, *Irving Layton, a Portrait* (1985); and Wynne Francis, "Irving Layton," *Canadian Writers and their Works*, ed. Robert Lecker, Jack David, and Ellen Quigley (1985), Poetry Series 5: 143–234.

FRANCIS MANSBRIDGE

THE SWIMMER

The afternoon foreclosing, see
The swimmer plunges from his raft,
Opening the spray corollas by his act of war—
The snake heads strike
Quickly and are silent.

Emerging see how for a moment,
A brown weed with marvellous bulbs,
He lies imminent upon the water
While light and sound come with a sharp passion
From the gonad sea around the poles
And break in bright cockle-shells about his ears.

He dives, floats, goes under like a thief
Where his blood sings to the tiger shadows
In the scentless greenery that leads him home,
A male salmon down fretted stairways
Through underwater slums . . . .

Stunned by the memory of lost gills
He frames gestures of self-absorption
Upon the skull-like beach;
Observes with instigated eyes
The sun that empties itself upon the water,
And the last wave romping in
To throw its boyhood on the marble sand.

[1943]

THE COLD GREEN ELEMENT

At the end of the garden walk
the wind and its satellite wait for me;
their meaning I will not know
        until I go there,
but the black-hatted undertaker

who, passing, saw my heart beating in the grass,
is also going there. Hi, I tell him,
a great squall in the Pacific blew a dead poet
  out of the water,
who now hangs from the city's gates.

Crowds depart daily to see it, and return
with grimaces and incomprehension;
if its limbs twitched in the air
  they would sit at its feet
peeling their oranges.

And turning over I embrace like a lover
the trunk of a tree, one of those
for whom the lightning was too much
  and grew a brilliant
hunchback with a crown of leaves.

The ailments escaped from the labels
of medicine bottles are all fled to the wind;
I've seen myself lately in the eyes
  of old women,
spent streams mourning my manhood,

in whose old pupils the sun became
a bloodsmear on broad catalpa leaves
and, hanging from ancient twigs,
  my murdered selves
sparked the air like the muted collisions

of fruit. A black dog howls down my blood,
a black dog with yellow eyes;
he too by someone's inadvertence
  saw the bloodsmear
on the broad catalpa leaves.

But the Furies clear a path for me to the worm
who sang for an hour in the throat of a robin,
and misled by the cries of young boys
  I am again
a breathless swimmer in that cold green element.

[1955]

THE BULL CALF

The thing could barely stand. Yet taken
from his mother and the barn smells
he still impressed with his pride,
with the promise of sovereignty in the way
his head moved to take us in.
The fierce sunlight tugging the maize from the ground
licked at his shapely flanks.
He was too young for all that pride.
I thought of the deposed Richard II.

"No money in bull calves," Freeman had said.
The visiting clergyman rubbed the nostrils
now snuffing pathetically at the windless day.
"A pity," he sighed.
My gaze slipped off his hat toward the empty sky
that circled over the black knot of men,
over us and the calf waiting for the first blow.

Struck,
the bull calf drew in his thin forelegs
as if gathering strength for a mad rush . . .
tottered . . . raised his darkening eyes to us,
and I saw we were at the far end
of his frightened look, growing smaller and smaller
till we were only the ponderous mallet
that flicked his bleeding ear
and pushed him over on his side, stiffly,
like a block of wood.

Below the hill's crest
the river snuffled on the improvised beach.
We dug a deep pit and threw the dead calf into it.
It made a wet sound, a sepulchral gurgle,
as the warm sides bulged and flattened.
Settled, the bull calf lay as if asleep,
one foreleg over the other,
bereft of pride and so beautiful now,
without movement, perfectly still in the cool pit.
I turned away and wept.

[1956]

THE FERTILE MUCK

There are brightest apples on those trees
   but until I, fabulist, have spoken
they do not know their significance
or what other legends are hung like garlands
   on their black boughs twisting
like a rumour. The wind's noise is empty.

Nor are the winged insects better off
   though they wear my crafty eyes
wherever they alight. Stay here, my love;
you will see how delicately they deposit
   me on the leaves of elms
or fold me in the orient dust of summer.

And if in August joiners and bricklayers
   are thick as flies around us
building expensive bungalows for those
who do not need them, unless they release
   me roaring from their moth-proofed cupboards
their buyers will have no joy, no ease.

I could extend their rooms for them without cost
   and give them crazy sundials
to tell the time with, but I have noticed
how my irregular footprint horrifies them
   evenings and Sunday afternoons:
they spray for hours to erase its shadow.

How to dominate reality? Love is one way;
   imagination another. Sit here
beside me, sweet; take my hard hand in yours.
We'll mark the butterflies disappearing over the hedge
   with tiny wristwatches on their wings,
our fingers touching the earth, like two Buddhas.

[1956]

WHATEVER ELSE POETRY IS FREEDOM

Whatever else poetry is freedom.
Forget the rhetoric, the trick of lying
All poets pick up sooner or later. From the river,
Rising like the thin voice of grey castratos—the mist;
Poplars and pines grow straight but oaks are gnarled;
Old codgers must speak of death, boys break windows,
Women lie honestly by their men at last.

And I who gave my Kate a blackened eye
Did to its vivid changing colours
10 Make up an incredible musical scale;
And now I balance on wooden stilts and dance
And thereby sing to the loftiest casements.
See how with polish I bow from the waist.
Space for these stilts! More space or I fail!

And a crown I say for my buffoon's head.
Yet no more fool am I than King Canute,
Lord of our tribe, who scanned and scorned;
Who half-deceived, believed; and, poet, missed
The first white waves come nuzzling at his feet;
20 Then damned the courtiers and the foolish trial
With a most bewildering and unkingly jest.

It was the mist. It lies inside one like a destiny.
A real Jonah it lies rotting like a lung.
And I know myself undone who am a clown
And wear a wreath of mist for a crown;
Mist with the scent of dead apples,
Mist swirling from black oily waters at evening,
Mist from the fraternal graves of cemeteries.

It shall drive me to beg my food and at last
30 Hurl me broken I know and prostrate on the road;
Like a huge toad I saw, entire but dead,
That Time mordantly had blacked; O pressed
To the moist earth it pled for entry.
I shall be I say that stiff toad for sick with mist
And crazed I smell the odour of mortality.

And Time flames like a paraffin stove
And what it burns are the minutes I live.
At certain middays I have watched the cars
Bring me from afar their windshield suns;
40 What lay to my hand were blue fenders,
The suns extinguished, the drivers wearing sunglasses.
And it made me think I had touched a hearse.

So whatever else poetry is freedom. Let
Far off the impatient cadences reveal
A padding for my breathless stilts. Swivel,
O hero, in the fleshy groves, skin and glycerine,
And sing of lust, the sun's accompanying shadow
Like a vampire's wing, the stillness in dead feet—
Your stave brings resurrection, O aggrievèd king.

[1958]

KEINE LAZAROVITCH: 1870–1959

When I saw my mother's head on the cold pillow,
Her white waterfalling hair in the cheeks' hollows,
I thought, quietly circling my grief, of how
She had loved God but cursed extravagantly his creatures.

For her final mouth was not water but a curse,
A small black hole, a black rent in the universe,
Which damned the green earth, stars and trees in its stillness
And the inescapable lousiness of growing old.

And I record she was comfortless, vituperative,
Ignorant, glad, and much else besides; I believe
She endlessly praised her black eyebrows, their thick weave,
Till plagiarizing Death leaned down and took them for his mould.

And spoiled a dignity I shall not again find,
And the fury of her stubborn limited mind;
Now none will shake her amber beads and call God blind,
Or wear them upon a breast so radiantly.

O fierce she was, mean and unaccommodating;
But I think now of the toss of her gold earrings,
Their proud carnal assertion, and her youngest sings
While all the rivers of her red veins move into the sea.

[1961]

· P. K. PAGE ·

1916–

Patricia Kathleen Page was born into the family of a career soldier while he was on a tour of duty in Dorset, England, on 23 November 1916. For the first twenty years of her life she moved around with her parents and her brother to various postings from Calgary, Alberta, to Rothesay, New Brunswick, and eventually to Montreal in 1941 where she joined the *Preview* group of poets and began her career in earnest. She also wrote for Alan Crawley's *Contemporary Verse*, and for John Sutherland's *First Statement* before joining the National Film Board as a script-writer. There she met her husband, Arthur Irwin, who became a diplomat. She continued her travels to postings in Australia, Mexico, the US, and Brazil where she took up drawing and painting. After his retirement in 1964, they settled in Victoria, British Columbia. She stopped publishing poetry between 1956 and 1967, but since then she has more than matched her creative powers of the 1940s and 1950s. She has taught courses and conducted workshops in creative writing, and has received numerous awards, including the Oscar Blumenthal Award for Poetry (1944), the Bertram Warr Memorial Award (1946), the Governor General's Award for Poetry (1954), the Order of Canada (1977), and the National Magazine Medal for Poetry (1984).

For the most part, Page has published her poems in magazines and journals and then selected and arranged them in books. Her early poems of the 1940s reflect the influence of modernists such as T. S. Eliot, W. H. Auden, Stephen Spender, Wilfred Owen, Dylan Thomas, and Rainer Maria Rilke, as well as some of the members of the *Preview* group such as Patrick Anderson, A. M. Klein, and F. R. Scott. Her poems are more psychological than explicitly political in orientation, but they often seem to have a socialist aftertaste in that they tend to focus on socially alienated and repressed individuals. At the same time she weaves complex patterns of imagery to express the fragmentation of human experience in adolescence and adulthood, implying the myth of the lost garden of childhood percipience. "T-Bar," written just after her own honeymoon, describes, in sinister images, the separation of Adam and Eve after the fall, in the context of skiers who are inevitably drawn up the hill of illusory romance only to be thrown apart at the top and to descend separately and alone. The very complex "Stories of Snow" uses a far more baroque set of images to trace essentially the same process, but the last lines suggest a power of seeing, perhaps of discerning truth, which can counteract the disintegrative powers of time.

Page has continued to focus on these themes and to refine her consistent use of colour patterns (especially white and green), imagery (birds, vegetation, eyes, sun, and moon) so that a symbol system amounting to a personal mythology seems to emerge. The poems from the second phase, such as "After Rain," are more introspective and urgent in tone, and concentrate more fully on altered states of consciousness ("keep my heart a size / larger than seeing"), and on the nature and function of the creative process.

More recently, Page's style has tended to open out. The poems are less cluttered with images; the diction is lucid and less demanding; the tone is calmer and more confident of the vision expressed—a vision of paradoxical solidity and mystery. Possibly as a result of her abiding interest in psychology and her renewed interest in Sufism and related theosophies, the poems seem somehow more accessible and yet more intense than anything written earlier. Poems such as "Deaf-Mute in the Pear Tree" contain the characteristic images of vegetation and birds, the slightly strange person and the observing eye, but they seem to stretch higher and achieve more cohesiveness than ever before. There is also a more profound compassion expressed in the latest poems. The pity born of political and psychological observations in the earliest work is now expressed as heartfelt compassion, possibly because the subjects of love and death have joined the dance of mind and art as the source of imaginative synthesis.

. ————— .

Page's works include *As Ten As Twenty* (1946); *The Metal and the Flower* (1954); *Cry Ararat! Poems New and Selected* (1967); *The Sun and the Moon and Other Fictions* (1973); *P. K. Page: Poems Selected and New* (1974); *Evening Dance of the Grey*

Flies (1981); *The Glass Air, Selected Poems* (1985); and *Brazilian Journal* (1987). She has also edited *To Say the Least: Canadian Poets from A to Z* (1979).

Works on Page include John Sutherland, "The Poetry of P. K. Page," *Northern Review* 1 (1946–47): 13–23; A. J. M. Smith, "The Poetry of P. K. Page," *Canadian Literature* 50 (1971): 17–27; Tom Marshall, "Inferno, Paradise and Slapstick," *Canadian Literature* 64 (1975): 104–7; Constance Rooke, "P. K. Page: The Chameleon at the Centre," *Malahat Review* 45 (1978): 169–95; Rosemary Sullivan, "A Size Larger Than Seeing: The Poetry of P. K. Page," *Canadian Literature* 79 (1978): 32–42; Diane Schoemperlen, "Four Themes in the Poetry of P. K. Page," *English Quarterly* 12 (1979): 1–12; Constance Rooke, "Approaching P. K. Page's 'Arras,'" *Canadian Poetry: Studies/Documents/Reviews* 4 (1979): 65–72; and John Orange, "P. K. Page: An Annotated Bibliography," *The Annotated Bibliography of Canada's Major Authors*, ed. Robert Lecker and Jack David (1985), 6: 207–86.

JOHN ORANGE

STORIES OF SNOW

Those in the vegetable rain retain
an area behind their sprouting eyes
held soft and rounded with the dream of snow
precious and reminiscent as those globes—
souvenir of some never-nether land—
which hold their snow-storms circular, complete,
high in a tall and teakwood cabinet.

In countries where the leaves are large as hands
where flowers protrude their fleshy chins
10 and call their colours,

an imaginary snow-storm sometimes falls
among the lilies.
And in the early morning one will waken
to think the glowing linen of his pillow
a northern drift, will find himself mistaken
and lie back weeping.
And there the story shifts from head to head,
of how in Holland, from their feather beds
hunters arise and part the flakes and go
20 forth to the frozen lakes in search of swans—
the snow-light falling white along their guns,
their breath in plumes.
While tethered in the wind like sleeping gulls
ice-boats wait the raising of their wings
to skim the electric ice at such a speed
they leap jet strips of naked water,
and how these flying, sailing hunters feel
air in their mouths as terrible as ether.
And on the story runs that even drinks
30 in that white landscape dare to be no colour;
how flasked and water clear, the liquor slips
silver against the hunters' moving hips.
And of the swan in death these dreamers tell
of its last flight and how it falls, a plummet,
pierced by the freezing bullet
and how three feathers, loosened by the shot,
descend like snow upon it.
While hunters plunge their fingers in its down
deep as a drift, and dive their hands
40 up to the neck of the wrist
in that warm metamorphosis of snow
as gentle as the sort that woodsmen know
who, lost in the white circle, fall at last
and dream their way to death.

And stories of this kind are often told
in countries where great flowers bar the roads
with reds and blues which seal the route to snow—
as if, in telling, raconteurs unlock
the colour with its complement and go
50 through to the area behind the eyes
where silent, unrefractive whiteness lies.

[1945]

T-BAR

Relentless, black on white, the cable runs
through metal arches up the mountain side.
At intervals giant pickaxes are hung
on long hydraulic springs. The skiers ride
propped by the axehead, twin automatons
supported by its handle, one each side.

In twos they move slow motion up the steep
incision in the mountain. Climb. Climb.
Somnambulists, bolt upright in their sleep
their phantom poles swung lazily behind,
while to the right, the empty T-bars keep
in mute descent, slow monstrous jigging time.

Captive the skiers now and innocent,
wards of eternity, each pair alone.
They mount the easy vertical ascent,
pass through successive arches, bride and groom,
as through successive naves, are newly wed
participants in some recurring dream.

So do they move forever. Clocks are broken.
In zones of silence they grow tall and slow,
inanimate dreamers, mild and gentle-spoken
blood-brothers of the haemophilic snow
until the summit breaks and they awaken
imagos from the stricture of the tow.

Jerked from her chrysalis the sleeping bride
suffers too sudden freedom like a pain.
The dreaming bridegroom severed from her side
singles her out, the old wound aches again.
Uncertain, lost, upon a wintry height
these two, not separate, but no longer one.

Now clocks begin to peck and sing. The slow
extended minute like a rubber band
contracts to catapult them through the snow
in tandem trajectory while behind
etching the sky-line, obdurate and slow
the spastic T-bars pivot and descend.

[1954]

AFTER RAIN

The snails have made a garden of green lace:
broderie anglaise from the cabbages,
chantilly from the choux-fleurs, tiny veils—
I see already that I lift the blind
upon a woman's wardrobe of the mind.

Such female whimsy floats about me like
a kind of tulle, a flimsy mesh,
while feet in gum boots pace the rectangles—
garden abstracted, geometry awash—
10 an unknown theorem argued in green ink,
dropped in the bath.
Euclid in glorious chlorophyl, half drunk.

I none too sober slipping in the mud
where rigged with guys of rain
the clothes-reel gauche
as the rangey skeleton of some
gaunt delicate spidery mute
is pitched as if
listening;
20 while hung from one thin rib
a silver web—
its infant, skeletal, diminutive,
now sagged with sequins, pulled ellipsoid,
glistening.

I suffer shame in all these images.
The garden is primeval, Giovanni
in soggy denim squelches by my hub
over his ruin,
shakes a doleful head.
30 But he so beautiful and diademmed,
his long Italian hands so wrung with rain
I find his ache exists beyond my rim
and almost weep to see a broken man
made subject to my whim.

O choir him, birds, and let him come to rest
within this beauty as one rests in love,
till pears upon the bough

encrusted with
small snails as pale as pearls
40 hang golden in
a heart that knows tears are a part of love.

And choir me too to keep my heart a size
larger than seeing, unseduced by each
bright glimpse of beauty striking like a bell,
so that the whole may toll,
its meaning shine
clear of the myriad images that still—
do what I will—encumber its pure line.

[1956]

AFTER READING *ALBINO PHEASANTS*

For Pat Lane

Pale beak . . . pale eye . . . the dark imagination
flares like magnesium. Add but *pale flesh*
and I am lifted to a weightless world:
watered cerulean, chrome-yellow (light)
and green, veronese—if I remember—a soft wash
recalls a summer evening sky.

At Barro de Navidad we watched the sky
fade softly like a bruise. Was it imagination
that showed us Venus phosphorescent in a wash
of air and ozone?—a phosphorescence flesh
wears like a mantle in bright moonlight,
a natural skin-tone in that other world.

Why should I wish to escape this world?
Why should three phrases alter the colour of the sky
the clarity, texture even, of the light?
What is there about the irrepressible imagination
that the adjective *pale* modifying *beak, eye* and *flesh*
can set my sensibilities awash?

If with my thickest brush I were to lay a wash
of thinnest watercolour I could make a world
as unlike my own dense flesh
as the high-noon midsummer sky;
but it would not catch at my imagination
or change the waves or particles of light

yet *pale* can tip the scales, make light
this heavy planet. If I were to wash
everything I own in mercury, would imagination
run rampant in that suddenly silver world—
free me from gravity, set me floating sky-
ward—thistledown—permanently disburdened of my flesh?

Like cygnets hatched by ducks, our minds and flesh
are imprinted early—what to me is light
may be dark to one born under a sunny sky.
And however cool the water my truth won't wash
without shrinking except in its own world
which is one part matter, nine parts imagination.

I fear flesh which blocks imagination,
the light of reason which constricts the world.
Pale beak ... pale eye ... pale flesh ... My sky's awash.

[1978]

DEAF-MUTE IN THE PEAR TREE

His clumsy body is a golden fruit
pendulous in the pear tree

Blunt fingers among the multitudinous buds

Adriatic blue the sky above and through
the forking twigs

Sun ruddying tree's trunk, his trunk
his massive head thick-nobbed with burnished curls
tight-clenched in bud

(Painting by Generalić. Primitive.)

I watch him prune with silent secateurs

Boots in the crotch of branches shift their weight
heavily as oxen in a stall

Hear small inarticulate mews from his locked mouth
a kitten in a box

Pear clippings fall
                    soundlessly on the ground
Spring finches sing
                    soundlessly in the leaves

A stone. A stone in ears and on his tongue

Through palm and fingertip he knows the tree's
quick springtime pulse

Smells in its sap the sweet incipient pears

Pale sunlight's choppy water glistens on
his mutely snipping blades

and flags and scraps of blue
above him make regatta of the day

But when he sees his wife's foreshortened shape
sudden and silent in the grass below
uptilt its face to him

then air is kisses, kisses

stone dissolves

his locked throat finds a little door

and through it feathered joy
flies screaming like a jay

[1984]

· MARGARET AVISON ·

1918–

Born in Galt (now Cambridge), Ontario, in 1918, Margaret Avison grew up in Western Canada until her father, a United Church clergyman, returned east about 1930. Since receiving her B.A. from Victoria College in 1940, she has lived in Toronto and has worked at a wide variety of jobs—including research assistant, textbook editor, teacher, and social worker. She also received her M.A. in 1964. For twenty years she published her poems in a few small Canadian magazines (such as *Contemporary Verse*) as well as in major American periodicals (*Poetry* [Chicago], *Kenyon Review*, *Origin*). In 1956 Avison received a Guggenheim Fellowship, and in 1961 her first collection, *Winter Sun* (1960), won the Governor General's Award for Poetry. More recently, she was made an Officer of the Order of Canada and was presented with an honorary D.Litt. from York University (1985). Her conversion to Christianity in 1963 was sudden and decisive. It has radically altered her life and significantly marked the poetry of her subsequent two collections, *The Dumbfounding* (1966) and *sunblue* (1978).

Avison's poetry impresses readers with its serious, uncompromising, even profound concerns. Its elusive and riddling qualities (generated in part by syntactical complexity and linguistic inventiveness) challenge the reader to enter its labyrinth by an act of imagination. Thus, in her farewell to the sonnet form, "Butterfly Bones," she suggests that critic and reader are not to become "peering boys" anxious to capture meanings for later display as "trophies." And yet, of course, her own self-consciousness as a writer requires that she simultaneously confess her own complicity in the hardening of vision into stiff verbal forms such as sonnets. To enter into vision, to take risks, is

also part of the subject of "The Swimmer's Moment," probably her most anthologized poem. This lyric of implied baptism, with its several levels of meaning regarding moral choice, anticipates the thoroughly religious concerns of Avison's later poetry and, together with "Butterfly Bones," reveals how sometimes her extension of root metaphors endows her poetry with an allegorical or parabolic dimension.

Valuing the revelatory possibilities of the faculty of imagination and opposing to it the constricted, dogmatic methodology of reason is part of Avison's debt to the English Romantics. For example, the experimental empiricism she criticizes in "Voluptuaries and Others" is portrayed as bringing little insight; it is the product of "limited imaginations." Yet readers, despite their best efforts, may feel frustrated when apparently denied the knowledge they crave, as in the enigmatic "Black-White Under Green: May 18, 1965," where the private relevance of the date cannot be established. What Avison seems to stress in the poem is the otherness of the artist; the keening musicality of the verse certainly emphasizes this theme powerfully. In a later poem such as "Stone's Secret," some of the intellectual and defensive posture of the early poems has been relaxed in favour of a new openness to experience. The questions so common in *Winter Sun* are now indented, set off, and then answered (for those with ears to hear) by the word of Christian faith—answers that do not, however, simplify the irreducible mystery of microcosm and macrocosm pointed to by this poem. Furthermore, "Stone's Secret" shows how the reader of Avison's mature poetry must be on the watch for a new kind of allusion—Biblical—as the muted reference to Luke 19:40 in the poem's final line indicates. Indeed, the reader must be prepared for an entirely new poetic, with new priorities and a new decorum. Nevertheless, whatever alterations her Christian imperatives have wrought, Avison's poetry continues to speak with authority. It commands respect, and it rewards the close attention she asks her reader to invest in it.

·————·

Avison's works include *Winter Sun* (1960); *The Dumbfounding* (1966); and *sunblue* (1978).

Works on Avison include Ernest Redekop, *Margaret Avison* (1970);

W. H. New, "The Mind's Eyes (I's), (Ice): The Poetry of Margaret Avison," *Articulating West: Essays on Purpose and Form in Modern Canadian Literature* (1972), 234–58; D. W. Doerkson, "Search and Discovery: Margaret Avison's Poetry," *Canadian Literature* 60 (1974): 7–20; J. M. Kertzer, "Margaret Avison: Power, Knowledge, and the Language of Poetry," *Canadian Poetry: Studies/Documents/Reviews* 4 (1979): 29–44; and Francis Mansbridge, "Margaret Avison: An Annotated Bibliography," *The Annotated Bibliography of Canada's Major Authors*, ed. Robert Lecker and Jack David (1985), 6: 13–66.

DAVID A. KENT

VOLUPTUARIES AND OTHERS

That Eureka of Archimedes out of his bath
Is the kind of story that kills what it conveys;
Yet the banality is right for that story, since it is not a communicable
    one
But just a particular instance of
The kind of lighting up of the terrain
That leaves aside the whole terrain, really,
But signalizes, and compels, an advance in it.
Such an advance through a be-it-what-it-may but
    take-it-not-quite-as-given locale:
Probably that is the core of being alive.
The speculation is not a concession
To limited imaginations. Neither is it
A constrained voiding of the quality of immanent death.
Such near values cannot be measured in values
Just because the measuring
Consists in that other kind of lighting up

That shows the terrain comprehended, as also its containing space,
And wipes out adjectives, and all shadows
          (or, perhaps, all but shadows).

The Russians made a movie of a dog's head
Kept alive by blood controlled by physics, chemistry, equipment,
          and
Russian women scientists in cotton gowns with writing tablets.
The heart lay on a slab midway in the apparatus
And went phluff, phluff.
Like the first kind of illumination, that successful experiment
Cannot be assessed either as conquest or as defeat.
But it is living, creating the chasm of creation,
Contriving to cast only man to brood in it, further.
History makes the spontaneous jubilation at such moments less and
          less likely though,
And that story about Archimedes does get into public school
          textbooks.

[1957]

BUTTERFLY BONES OR SONNET AGAINST SONNETS

The cyanide jar seals life, as sonnets move
Towards final stiffness. Cased in a white glare
These specimens stare for peering boys, to prove
Strange certainties. Plane, dogsled and safari
Assure continuing range. The sweep-net skill,
The patience, learning, leave all living stranger.
Insect—or poem—waits for the fix, the frill
Precision can effect, brilliant with danger.
What law and wonder the museum spectres
Bespeak is cryptic for the shivery wings,
The world cut-diamond-eyed, those eyes' reflectors,
Or herbal grass, sunned motes, fierce listening.
Might sheened and rigid trophies strike men blind
Like Adam's lexicon locked in the mind?

[1959]

THE SWIMMER'S MOMENT

For everyone
The swimmer's moment at the whirlpool comes,
But many at that moment will not say
"This is the whirlpool, then."
By their refusal they are saved
From the black pit, and also from contesting
The deadly rapids, and emerging in
The mysterious, and more ample, further waters.
And so their bland-blank faces turn and turn
Pale and forever on the rim of suction
They will not recognize.
Of those who dare the knowledge
Many are whirled into the ominous centre
That, gaping vertical, seals up
For them an eternal boon of privacy,
So that we turn away from their defeat
With a despair, not from their deaths, but for
Ourselves, who cannot penetrate their secret
Nor even guess at the anonymous breadth
Where one or two have won:
(The silver reaches of the estuary).

[1959]

BLACK-WHITE UNDER GREEN: MAY 18, 1965

This day of the leafing-out
speaks with blue power—
among the buttery grassblades
white, tiny-spraying spokes on the end of a weed-stem
and in the formal beds, tulips
and invisible birds inaudibly hallooing,
enormous, their beaks out wide, throats bulging, aflutter,
eyes weeping with speed

where the ultraviolets play and the scythe of the jets
10 flashes, carrying
    the mind-wounded heartpale person, still a boy, a pianist, dying
        not
    of the mind's wounds (as they read the x-rays) but
    dying, fibres separated, parents ruddy and
    American, strong, sheathed in the cold of
    years of his differentness, clustered by two at
    the nether arc of his flight.

    This day of the leafing-out is one to remember
        how the ice crackled among
            stiff twigs. Glittering strongly
20   the old trees sagged. Boughs
        abruptly unsocketed. Dry, orange gashes
    the dawn's fine snowing discovered and powdered over.

    . . . to remember the leaves ripped loose
    the thudding of the dark sky-beams
    and the pillared plunging sea
    shelterless. Down the centuries
    a flinching speck
        in the white fury found of itself—and another—
    the rich blood spilling, mother to child, threading
30 the perilous combers, marbling
    the surges, flung
    out, and ten-fingered, feeling for
    the lollop, the fine-wired
    music, dying skyhigh
    still between carpets and the
    cabin-pressuring windows
    on the day of the leafing.

    Faces fanned by
    rubberized, cool air
40 are opened; eyes wisely
    smile.
    The tulips, weeds, new leaves
    neither smile nor are scorning to smile nor uncertain,
    dwelling in light.
    A flick of ice, fire, flood,
    far off from
    the day of the leafing-out I knew
    when knee-wagon small, or from my
    father's once at a horse-tail silk-shiny
50 fence-corner or this

day when the runways wait
white in the sun, and a new leaf is
metal, torn out of that blue
afloat in the dayshine.

[1966]

STONE'S SECRET

Otter-smooth boulder
lies under rolling
black river-water
stilled among frozen
hills and the still unbreathed
blizzards aloft;
silently, icily, is probed
stone's secret.

Out there—past trace
of eyes, past these
and those memorial skies
dotting back signals from
men's made mathematics (we
delineators of curves and time who are
                         subject to these)—
out there, inaccessible
to grammar's language the
stones curve vastnesses,
cold or candescent
in the perceived
processional of space.

        The stones out there in the
        violet-black are a part of a
        slow-motion fountain? or of a
        fireworks pin-wheel?
        i.e. breathed in and out
        as in cosmic lungs? or
        one-way as an eye looking?

What mathematicians must,
also the pert,
they will
as the dark river runs.

Word has arrived that
peace will brim up, will come
"like a river and the
glory . . . like a flowing stream."
So.
Some of all people will
wondering wait
until this very stone
utters.

[1978]

· LOUIS DUDEK ·

1918–

Louis Dudek was born 6 February 1918 in Montreal. He completed a B.A. at McGill University and an M.A. and Ph.D. at Columbia University. He taught modern poetry, Canadian literature, and European literature at McGill University for a period of thirty years, until his retirement in 1984. A firm believer in the efficacy of the little magazine and the small press, Dudek has been involved in a number of non-commercial publishing enterprises. In the 1940s he worked with John Sutherland and Irving Layton on the little magazine *First Statement*; in the 1950s he joined with Raymond Souster and Layton in founding and running Contact Press while also participating in the editing of the magazine *CIV/n* (1953–55) and editing his own magazine *Delta* (1957–66). He worked with Glen Siebrasse and Michael Gnarowski in the 1960s, running Delta Canada Press, and ran DC Books with his wife Aileen Collins in the 1970s.

Throughout his career Dudek's work has evinced a constant evolution. Of the poets of his generation, he has been the one who has striven for an epic scope in his work. His poetry represents an important contribution to the theory and practice of the Canadian avant garde.

In his early work (*Unit of Five* [1944], *East of the City* [1946]) Dudek concerned himself with writing a socially realistic poetry that emphasized a Marxist orientation. Having been brought up in a working-class family, he saw social equality as an important stage in the evolution of Western civilization. In an early essay, "Academic Poetry" (1943), he argued against the ivory-tower notion of poetry and called for poetry to be used as an important tool of political and social change.

Dudek's work of the early 1950s registered the influences of Ezra Pound (with whom he carried on an extensive correspondence) and Lionel Trilling (with whom he studied at Columbia University). In *Europe* he began to turn his attention away from human society and towards the world of art, the lasting artefacts that an imperfect and unperfectable society had produced.

In his pioneering long poems— *Europe* (1954), *En Mexico* (1958), and *Atlantis* (1967)—Dudek attempted to formulate epic assessments of human culture and evolution. Although the long poem has been the main focus of his attention over the past thirty years, he has also published a number of collections of lyric poems, a book of epigrams, and a substantial body of literary criticism.

As a critic Dudek has stressed the importance of evaluation in criticism while also never losing sight of the social function of literature. For a number of years Dudek spent much of his critical energy refuting the literary theories of Marshall McLuhan and Northrop Frye. Dudek felt that McLuhan's advocacy of popular culture worked in opposition to the criteria of high art, while Frye's mythic orientation tended to reduce literature to thesis while valuing only works that reinforced Frye's system of archetypes.

· ———— ·

Dudek's works include *East of the City* (1946); *Europe* (1954); *The Transparent Sea* (1956); *Literature and the Press* (1960); *Atlantis* (1967); *Collected Poetry* (1971); *Selected Essays and Criticism* (1978); *Continuation I* (1981); *Louis Dudek: Texts & Essays* (1981); and *Ideas for Poetry* (1983). Works on Dudek include Wynne

Francis, "A Critic of Life: Louis Dudek as a Man of Letters," *Canadian Literature* 22 (1964): 5–23; Dorothy Livesay, "The Sculpture of Poetry: On Louis Dudek," *Canadian Literature* 30 (1966): 26–35; Douglas Barbour, "Poet as Philosopher," *Canadian Literature* 53 (1972): 18–29; Eva Seidner, "Modernism in the Booklength Poems of Louis Dudek," *Open Letter* 3rd ser. 7 (1977): 14–40; Frank Davey, *Louis Dudek and Raymond Souster* (1980); and Susan Stromberg-Stein, *Louis Dudek: A Biographical Introduction to His Poetry* (1983).

KEN NORRIS

THE POMEGRANATE

The jewelled mine of the pomegranate, whose hexagons of honey
The mouth would soon devour but the eyes eat like a poem,
Lay hidden long in its hide, a diamond of dark cells
Nourished by tiny streams which crystallized into gems.

The seeds, nescient of the world outside, or of passionate teeth,
Prepared their passage into light and air, while tender roots
And branches dreaming in the cell-walled hearts of plants
Made silent motions such as recreate both men and fruits.

There, in a place of no light, shone that reddest blood,
And without a word of order, marshalled those grenadiers:
Gleaming without a sun—what art where no eyes were!—
Till broken by my hand, this palace of unbroken tears.

To wedding bells and horns howling down an alley,
Muffled, the married pair in closed caravan ride;
And then, the woman grown in secret, shining white,
Unclothed, mouth to mouth he holds his naked bride.

And there are days, golden days, when the world starts to life,
When streets in the sun, boys, and battlefields of cars,
The colours on a bannister, the vendors' slanting stands
Send the pulse pounding on like the bursting of meteors—

As now, the fruit glistens with a mighty grin,
Conquers the room; and, though in ruin, to its death
Laughs at the light that wounds it, wonderfully red,
So that its awful beauty stops the greedy breath.

And can this fact be made, so big, of the body, then?
And is beauty bounded all in its impatient mesh?
The movement of the stars is that, and all their light
Secretly bathed the world, that now flows out of flesh.

[1950]

FROM *EUROPE*

95

The sea retains such images
        in her ever-unchanging waves;
for all her infinite variety, and the forms,
inexhaustible, of her loves,
she is constant always in beauty,
        which to us need be nothing more
    than a harmony with the wave on which we move.
All ugliness is a distortion
of the lovely lines and curves
        which sincerity makes out of hands
                and bodies moving in air.
Beauty is ordered in nature
        as the wind and sea
shape each other for pleasure; as the just
know, who learn of happiness
        from the report of their own actions.

[1954]

COMING SUDDENLY TO THE SEA

Coming suddenly to the sea in my twenty-eighth year,
to the mother of all things that breathe, of mussels and whales,
I could not see anything but sand at first
and burning bits of mother-of-pearl.
But this was the sea, terrible as a torch
which the winter sun had lit,
flaming in the blue and salt sea-air
under my twenty-eight-year infant eyes.
And then I saw the spray smashing the rocks
and the angry gulls cutting the air,
the heads of fish and the hands of crabs on stones:
the carnivorous sea, sower of life,
battering a granite rock to make it a pebble—
love and pity needless as the ferny froth on its long smooth waves.
The sea, with its border of crinkly weed,
the inverted Atlantic of our unstable planet,
froze me into a circle of marble, sending the icy air out in lukewarm
    waves.
And so I brought home, as an emblem of that day
ending my long blind years, a fistful of blood-red weed in my hand.

[1956]

TAO

(for F.R.S.)

Things that are blown or carried by a stream
seem to be living—not in that they oppose the wind
or oppose the water, but in that they move
                                        lightly blown,
lightly flowing, like things that live.

We who are actually living do best when we do not resist,
do not insist, when winds and water blow,
but go gently with them, being of their kind,
in the secret of wind and water, the thought of flow.

[1980]

· AL PURDY ·

1918–

Al (Alfred Wellington) Purdy was born in 1918, "of degenerate Loyalist stock" as he claims, at Wooler, Ontario. He spent most of his childhood in Trenton and was educated there and at Albert College in Belleville; he never attended a university but his autodidactic erudition is extraordinary. During the 1930s he rode the rods to Vancouver, where he worked in a mattress factory and in other manual occupations, which he later followed in Montreal. In 1957 he settled in Ameliasburg, the small Loyalist community celebrated in his poems, and from that period he has made his living by freelance writing and related tasks, such as editing, poetry-reading, and stints as writer-in-residence at various places. He won the Governor General's Award for poetry in 1965 and 1986, and has received several Canada Council awards.

Purdy has been one of Canada's most prolific poets; up to the present he has published no less than twenty-six volumes of verse (some of them selections or collections) and ten broadsheets. Despite occasional pot-boiling excursions into other genres (represented by the largely anecdotal essays in his single prose volume, *No Other Country* [1977]) Purdy has remained principally dedicated to the poetry he has written restlessly and copiously since boyhood. It has been a poetry closely related to his experience, shaped in many ways by the working-class lifestyle he so long maintained, and fed by the lengthy travels that have taken him far and into many cultural zones: in Canada from Newfoundland west to Vancouver Island and north to Baffin Island; abroad to Cuba and Mexico, to most of Europe, to Turkey, Japan, and Africa.

Purdy first appeared, in *The Enchanted Echo* (1944), as a traditional and derivative poet, influenced largely by Canadian late romantics like Roberts and Carman; the latter's fascination with vagabondage stayed long with Purdy. Not until fifteen years later did a long period of experimentation lead him to the discovery of his own characteristic voice, which first became audible in the collection he published in 1959 with the wryly ironical title, *The Crafte So Longe to Lerne*. It was in this volume that his forms opened out to liberate his relaxed, loping line formations, and to give voice to the gruff and garrulous persona that henceforward haunts his poems and turns them into a philosophic and conversational continuum in which the here-and-now, vividly apprehended, becomes the changing mirror in which his visions and values are reflected.

Purdy is a poet whose experience moves very quickly into his work. Some of his best poems have emerged almost immediately from his travels; others—especially the poems about loyalist Ontario—have come through the long channels of memory and tradition. Purdy has combined a strong sense of place with a deep awareness of the past pressing upon the present to produce a kind of geohistorical poetry which marvellously projects the nature of Canada—and of other places. This has probably been the aspect of his poetry that has most influenced other poets.

Experience has tended to affect the form as well as the content of Purdy's poems. During the 1960s he took part zestfully in the movement that took poets wandering over the country, reading their work to audiences of many kinds, and there seems no doubt, while it would be unjust to dismiss him as an oral poet, that this exercise helped him loosen his rhythms and also fostered the elements of humour and anger which were already present in his work. If *Poems for All the Annettes* (1962) was the first book in which he seemed entirely himself, independent of other poets' styles, it was in *The Cariboo Horses* (1965) that his mature manner—colloquially free without sacrificing the suggestive dimensions of lyrical imagery—was fully revealed. Later collections, and especially *Being Alive* (1978), show how well, once he had established his individuality and found his true voice, Purdy has not only sustained the quality of his writing but has kept it fresh by exploring new aspects of human character and destiny. His *Collected Poems* (1986) establish his status as a major poet, not only in Canada, but in the general tradition of English verse.

• ———— •

Purdy's works include *The Crafte So Longe to Lerne* (1959); *Poems for All the Annettes* (1962); *The Cariboo Horses* (1965); *North of Summer: Poems from Baffin Island* (1967); *Wild Grape Wine* (1968); *In Search of Owen Roblin* (1974); *Being Alive: Poems 1958–1978* (1978); *The Stone Bird* (1981); *Piling Blood* (1984); and *The Collected Poems of Al Purdy* (1986).

Works on Purdy include George Bowering, *Al Purdy* (1970); George Woodcock, "On the Poetry of Al Purdy," in *The World of Canadian Writing* (1980), 261–69; Marianne Micros, "Al Purdy: An Annotated Bibliography," *The Annotated Bibliography of Canada's Major Authors*, ed. Robert Lecker and Jack David (1980), 2: 221–77; and George Woodcock, "Al Purdy," *The Oxford Companion to Canadian Literature*, ed. William Toye (1983).

GEORGE WOODCOCK

THE COUNTRY NORTH OF BELLEVILLE

Bush land scrub land—
      Cashel Township and Wollaston
Elzevir McClure and Dungannon
green lands of Weslemkoon Lake
where a man might have some
      opinion of what beauty
is and none deny him
           for miles—

Yet this is the country of defeat
10 where Sisyphus rolls a big stone
year after year up the ancient hills
picnicking glaciers have left strewn

with centuries' rubble
                    backbreaking days
                    in the sun and rain
when realization seeps slow in the mind
without grandeur or self deception in
                    noble struggle
of being a fool—

20 A country of quiescence and still distance
a lean land
                    not like the fat south
with inches of black soil on
                    earth's round belly—
And where the farms are
                    it's as if a man stuck
both thumbs in the stony earth and pulled

                    it apart
                    to make room
30 enough between the trees
for a wife
                    and maybe some cows and
                    room for some
of the more easily kept illusions—
And where the farms have gone back
to forest
                    are only soft outlines
                    shadowy differences—
Old fences drift vaguely among the trees
40   a pile of moss-covered stones
gathered for some ghost purpose
has lost meaning under the meaningless sky
          —they are like cities under water
and the undulating green waves of time
                    are laid on them—

This is the country of our defeat
          and yet
during the fall plowing a man
might stop and stand in a brown valley of the furrows
50   and shade his eyes to watch for the same
                    red patch mixed with gold
                    that appears on the same
                    spot in the hills
                    year after year
                    and grow old

plowing and plowing a ten-acre field until
the convolutions run parallel with his own brain—

And this is a country where the young
          leave quickly
60 unwilling to know what their fathers know
or think the words their mothers do not say—

Herschel Monteagle and Faraday
lakeland rockland and hill country
a little adjacent to where the world is
a little north of where the cities are and
sometime
we may go back there
                    to the country of our defeat
Wollaston Elzevir and Dungannon
70 and Weslemkoon lake land
where the high townships of Cashel
                McClure and Marmora once were—
But it's been a long time since
and we must enquire the way
        of strangers—

[1965]

THE CARIBOO HORSES

At 100 Mile House the cowboys ride in rolling
stagey cigarettes with one hand reining
half-tame bronco rebels on a morning grey as stone
—so much like riding dangerous women
        with whiskey coloured eyes—
such women as once fell dead with their lovers
with fire in their heads and slippery froth on thighs
—Beaver or Carrier women maybe or
        Blackfoot squaws far past the edge of this valley
10 on the other side of those two toy mountain ranges
        from the sunfierce plains beyond

But only horses
               waiting in stables
hitched at taverns
               standing at dawn
pastured outside the town with
jeeps and fords and chevvys and
busy muttering stake trucks rushing
importantly over roads of man's devising
20 over the safe known roads of the ranchers
families and merchants of the town
               On the high prairie
are only horse and rider
               wind in dry grass
clopping in silence under the toy mountains
dropping sometimes and
               lost in the dry grass
               golden oranges of dung

Only horses
30   no stopwatch memories or palace ancestors
not Kiangs hauling undressed stone in the Nile Valley
and having stubborn Egyptian tantrums or
Onagers racing thru Hither Asia and
the last Quagga screaming in African highlands
               lost relatives of these
               whose hooves were thunder
the ghosts of horses battering thru the wind
whose names were the wind's common usage
whose life was the sun's
40   arriving here at chilly noon
               in the gasoline smell of the
               dust and waiting 15 minutes
               at the grocer's

[1965]

ESKIMO GRAVEYARD

Walking in glacial litter
frost boils and boulder pavements
of an old river delta
where angry living water
changes its mind every half century
and takes a new direction
to the blue fiord
The Public Works guy I'm with
says you always find good gravel
10 for concrete near a graveyard
where digging is easy maybe
a footnote on human character
But wrapped in blankets
above ground a dead old woman
(for the last few weeks I'm told)
without a grave marker
And a hundred yards away
the Anglican missionary's grave
with whitewashed cross
20 that means equally nothing
The river's soft roar
drifts to my ears and changes
tone when the wind changes
ice debris melts at low tide
& the Public Works guy is mildly pleased
with the good gravel we found
for work on the schoolhouse
which won't have to be shipped in
from Montreal
30 and mosquitoes join happily
in our conversation   Then
he stops to consult
with the construction foreman
I walk on
toward the tents of The People
half a mile away
at one corner of the picture
Mothers with children on their backs
in the clean white parkas
40 they take such pride in
buying groceries at H.B.C.

boys lounging under the store
in space where timber stilts
hold it above the permafrost
with two of them arm in arm
in the manner of Eskimo friends
After dinner
I walk down among the tents
and happen to think of the old woman
50 neither wholly among the dead
nor quite gone from the living
and wonder how often
a thought of hers enters the minds
of people she knew before
and what kind of flicker it is
as lights begin to come on
in nightlong twilight
and thoughts of me
occur to the mosquitoes
60 I keep walking
as if something ought to happen
(I don't know what)
with the sun stretching
a yellow band across the water
from headland to black headland
at high tide in the fiord
sealing in the settlement
as if there was no way out
and indeed there isn't
70 until the looping Cansos come
dropping thru the mountain doorway
That old woman?
it occurs to me
I might have been thinking
about human bookkeeping
debits and credits that is
or profit and loss
(and laugh at myself)
among the sealed white tents
80 like glowing swans
hoping
for a most improbable
birth

PANGNIRTUNG [1967]

WILDERNESS GOTHIC

Across Roblin Lake, two shores away,
they are sheathing the church spire
with new metal. Someone hangs in the sky
over there from a piece of rope,
hammering and fitting God's belly-scratcher,
working his way up along the spire
until there's nothing left to nail on—
Perhaps the workman's faith reaches beyond:
touches intangibles, wrestles with Jacob,
replacing rotten timber with pine thews,
pounds hard in the blue cave of the sky,
contends heroically with difficult problems of
gravity, sky navigation and mythopeia,
his volunteer time and labour donated to God,
minus sick benefits of course on a non-union job—

Fields around are yellowing into harvest,
nestling and fingerling are sky and water borne,
death is yodelling quiet in green woodlots,
and bodies of three young birds have disappeared
in the sub-surface of the new county highway—

That picture is incomplete, part left out
that might alter the whole Dürer landscape:
gothic ancestors peer from medieval sky,
dour faces trapped in photograph albums escaping
to clop down iron roads with matched greys:
work-sodden wives groping inside their flesh
for what keeps moving and changing and flashing
beyond and past the long frozen Victorian day.
A sign of fire and brimstone? A two-headed calf
born in the barn last night? A sharp female agony?
An age and a faith moving into transition,
the dinner cold and new-baked bread a failure,
deep woods shiver and water drops hang pendant,
double yolked eggs and the house creaks a little—
Something is about to happen. Leaves are still.
Two shores away, a man hammering in the sky.
Perhaps he will fall.

[1968]

LAMENT FOR THE DORSETS
(Eskimos extinct in the 14th century A.D.)

Animal bones and some mossy tent rings
scrapers and spearheads   carved ivory swans
all that remains of the Dorset giants
who drove the Vikings back to their long ships
talked to spirits of earth and water
—a picture of terrifying old men
so large they broke the backs of bears
so small they lurk behind bone rafters
in the brain of modern hunters
10 among good thoughts and warm things
and come out at night
to spit on the stars

The big men with clever fingers
who had no dogs and hauled their sleds
over the frozen northern oceans
awkward giants
                    killers of seal
they couldn't compete with little men
who came from the west with dogs
Or else in a warm climatic cycle
20 the seals went back to cold waters
and the puzzled Dorsets scratched their heads
with hairy thumbs around 1350 A.D.
—couldn't figure it out
went around saying to each other
plaintively
                "What's wrong? What happened?
                Where are the seals gone?"
And died

30 Twentieth century people
apartment dwellers
executives of neon death
warmakers with things that explode
—they have never imagined us in their future
how could we imagine them in the past
squatting among the moving glaciers
six hundred years ago
with glowing lamps?

As remote or nearly
40 as the trilobites and swamps
   when coal became
   or the last great reptile hissed
   at a mammal the size of a mouse
   that squeaked and fled

   Did they ever realize at all
   what was happening to them?
   Some old hunter with one lame leg
   a bear had chewed
   sitting in a caribou-skin tent
50 —the last Dorset?
   Let's say his name was Kudluk
   and watch him sitting there
   carving 2-inch ivory swans
   for a dead grand-daughter
   taking them out of his mind
   the places in his mind
   where pictures are
   He selects a sharp stone tool
   to gouge a parallel pattern of lines
60 on both sides of the swan
   holding it with his left hand
   bearing down and transmitting
   his body's weight
   from brain to arm and right hand
   and one of his thoughts
   turns to ivory
   The carving is laid aside
   in beginning darkness
   at the end of hunger
70 and after a while wind
   blows down the tent and snow
   begins to cover him.

   After 600 years
   the ivory thought
   is still warm

   [1968]

· RAYMOND SOUSTER ·

1921–

Raymond Holmes Souster was born on 21 January 1921 in Toronto, where he has lived ever since. On his graduation from high school in 1939 he went to work for the Imperial Bank (now the Canadian Imperial Bank of Commerce), and except for the years 1941–45 when he was in the Royal Canadian Air Force, he stayed there until his retirement in the fall of 1984. Souster's involvement in the literary scene began with *Direction* (1943–46), a little magazine which he helped to edit and publish from his Air Force posting in Nova Scotia. In the 1950s he edited *Contact* (1952–54) and *Combustion* (1957–60; 1966), both of which played a key role in introducing American post-modernist poetics into Canada. With Irving Layton and Louis Dudek, Souster started Contact Press (1952–67), certainly the most influential Canadian poetry-publishing house in the post-war period. Souster has been honoured with a Governor General's Award for *The Colour of the Times* (1964) and a City of Toronto Book Award for *Hanging In* (1979).

Souster's early poems, from Ronald Hambleton's anthology *Unit of Five* (1944) to *City Hall Street* (1951), show him working in a style learned in part from the English poets of the 1930s, as well as from such American poets as Kenneth Fearing and Carl Sandburg. The diction is colloquial and the rhythms reflect conversation rather than formal speech or inherited metrics. The subjects of the poems are drawn from the experiences of lower-middle-class urban life and are frequently realistic to the point of bleakness. The city is mostly imagined as an anti-Eden, as in "Yonge Street Saturday Night" (from *Go to Sleep, World* [1947]), where the speaker walks aimlessly, "a little bored, a little lost, a little angry," looking for

something to provide "a strange new happiness, a lost but recovered joy." Yet Souster never loses a residual romantic joy and freshness, and this combination of despair and happiness is characteristic of all of his work.

In the early 1950s Louis Dudek introduced Souster to the work of William Carlos Williams, whose stress on the objectivity of the poetic imagination and the need to allow a subject to insist on its own form were the final formative influences on Souster's work. His poetry of the 1950s and 1960s is technically tighter and more austere than the early poems, and the influence of Williams is especially to be seen in his imagistic concentration on things of the seen world. These are not always objects pure and simple—"Study: The Bath," for example, has to do with a particular domestic moment transformed into a tableau by the poet's apperception—but the poetic language is kept bare and responsive to the subject of the poem. *The Colour of the Times* (1964) collected some twelve years of poetry in this style, and it is the mode which has become identified by readers as Sousterian.

In succeeding years Souster has mostly consolidated and added to an already considerable body of work. *Ten Elephants on Yonge Street* (1965), *As Is* (1967), *Change-Up* (1974), and the other books of new poems since them contain mostly poems in the established manner. Exact perception continues to coexist with a humane moral outlook that Souster usually keeps in reserve until the end of a poem, as he does in "Pigeons on George Street." In the 1970s Souster has experimented with other forms, including found poetry and narrative. His interest in narrative is long-standing (he published two pseudonymous novels), and a series of longish narrative poems based on historical material concerning World War II ("Pictures of a Long-Lost World") led to the publication in 1984 of a book-length narrative poem about the Dieppe raid, *Jubilee of Death* (1984). Souster's narrative line sounds disarmingly artless, but its apparent simplicity arises from a lifetime of poetic devotion to the ideal of allowing the material to speak for itself. The subject of the narratives—World War II—has been a central concern in his work almost from the beginning. It represents for Souster all that is evil—his sphere of Blakean experience—against which is balanced a sphere of innocence inhabited by animals, baseball players, and children.

·————·

Souster's works include *When We Are Young* (1946); *Go to Sleep, World* (1947); *The Winter of Time* (1949); *City Hall Street* (1951); *Cerberus* (1952); *Shake Hands with the Hangman* (1953); *A Dream That Is Dying* (1954); *Walking Death* (1954); *For What Time Slays* (1955); *The Selected Poems* (1956); *Crepe-Hanger's Carnival* (1958); *A Local Pride* (1962); *Place of Meeting* (1962); *The Colour of the Times* (1964); *Ten Elephants on Yonge Street* (1965); *As Is* (1967); *Lost and Found* (1968); *Selected Poems of Raymond Souster* (1972); *On Target* (1972); *Change-Up* (1974); *Extra Innings* (1977); *Hanging In* (1979); *Collected Poems* (1980–84); *Going the Distance* (1983); and *Jubilee of Death* (1984); *It Takes All Kinds* (1986); and *The Eyes of Love* (1987). He has edited *Poets 56* (1956); *New Wave Canada* (1966); *Generation Now* (1970); *Made in Canada* (1970); *Sights and Sounds* (1973); *100 Poems of Nineteenth Century Canada* (1974); *These Loved, These Hated Lands* (1975); *Poems of a Snow-Eyed Country* (1980); and the poems of W. W. E. Ross (1956 and 1968), William Wilfred Campbell (1978), Archibald Lampman (1979), Bliss Carman (1986), and Duncan Campbell Scott (1986).

Works on Souster include Louis Dudek, "Groundhog Among the Stars: The Poetry of Raymond Souster," *Canadian Literature* 22 (1964): 34–49; Hugh Cook, "Development in the Early Poetry of Raymond Souster," *Studies in Canadian Literature* 3 (1978): 113–18; Francis Mansbridge, "A Delicate Balance: Craft in Raymond Souster's Poetry," *Canadian Poetry: Studies/Documents/Reviews* 4 (1979): 45–51; Frank Davey, *Louis Dudek & Raymond Souster* (1980); Bruce Whiteman, *Collected Poems of Raymond Souster: Bibliography* (1984); and "Raymond Souster," *Canadian Writers and Their Works*, ed. Robert Lecker, Jack David, and Ellen Quigley (1985), 5: 237–76.

BRUCE WHITEMAN

YONGE STREET SATURDAY NIGHT

Except when the theatre crowds engulf the sidewalks
at nine, at eleven-thirty,
this street is lonely, and a thousand lights
in a thousand store windows
wouldn't break her lips into a smile.

There are a few bums out,
there are lovers with hands held tightly,
there are also the drunk ones
but they are princes among men, and are few.

And there are some like us,
just walking, making both feet move out ahead of us,
a little bored, a little lost, a little angry,

walking as though we were honestly going somewhere,
walking as if there was really something to see
at Adelaide or maybe on King,
something, no matter how little
that will give us some fair return
on our use of shoe-leather,

something perhaps that will make us smile
with a strange new happiness,
a lost but recovered joy.

[1947]

DOWNTOWN CORNER NEWSSTAND

It will take death to move you from this corner,
for it's become your world and you its unshaved,
bleary-eyed, foot-stamping king.

In winter you curse the cold, huddled in your coat from the wind,
then fry in summer like an egg hopping in a pan,
and always that whining voice, those nervous-flinging arms,
the red face, shifting eyes watching, waiting
under the grimy cap for God knows what to happen.

But nothing ever does; downtown Toronto
goes to sleep and wakes the next morning
always the same, except a little dirtier,
as you stand with your armful of *Stars* and *Telys*,
the peak of your cap well down against the sun,
and all the city's restless, seething river
surges up around you, but never once
do you plunge in its flood to be carried or tossed away—

but reappear always, beard longer than ever, nose running,
to catch the noon editions at King and Bay.

[1953]

STUDY: THE BATH

In the dim light
of the bathroom
a woman steps from white tub,
towel around her shoulders.

Drops of water glisten
on her body
from slight buttocks,
neck, tight belly,
fall at intervals
from the slightly plumed
oval of crotch.

The neck bent forward,
eyes collected,
her attention gathered
at the end of fingers.

lovingly removing
dead, flaked skin
from the twin nipples.

[1954]

TWO DEAD ROBINS

In the driveway, their bodies so small
I almost stepped on them, two baby robins,
enormous mouths, bulging eyes, bodies thin wire
stretched over taut skin frames, bones showing
like aroused veins.
                    It looked as though they'd either
tried to fly from the nest above
or the wind had swept them down. For some reason
I couldn't bear to pick them up in my hands,
so got a spade and buried them quickly
at the back of the garden, thinking as I did it

how many will die today, have much worse burial
than these two my shovel mixes under?

[1956]

PIGEONS ON GEORGE STREET

As I draw abreast of him
the stranger draws from his leather pouch
handfuls of feed-grain which he sprinkles
half on the sidewalk, half at the curb,
next, slices of dried bread which he breaks
and scatters just as carefully:
                      while across
the street and above on the tight-rope wire
of the telephone lines at least a hundred pigeons
burn with the desire to flutter down, attack
the daily handout.
                But no-one moves,
and my new friend says, "There's too much traffic
on the street today for them, they'll all sit tight
until things quiet down."
                And he's right:
when I look down the street
five minutes later, one hundred pigeons
are still up there on the wires, and only half a dozen
braver (hungrier?) sparrows busy eating.

Which for no good reason I can think of
gives me the curious feeling that long, long after
the last pigeon has flapped off the earth,
the sparrows, if they have their way,
will still be with us.

[1979]

· ELI MANDEL ·

1922–

Eli Mandel's early poetry consciously creates an alternative world to that of his actual beginnings, which were on the prairies in Estevan, Saskatchewan, where he was born and grew up. Despite the early attempt to erase his past, the Souris River valley and the prairie geography have been increasingly important to Mandel. His most recent poetry returns to explore what was first set aside, while also courageously confronting the ugly realities of the larger world community. He grew up experiencing the harshness and deprivation of the Depression, being closely attuned to the wild prairie land, and having a profound sense of his Jewish background. His later education at the University of Saskatchewan was interrupted by service in the army medical corps during World War II, but he returned at war's end to complete an M.A. (1949) and then moved on to the University of Toronto for doctoral studies (Ph.D., 1957). He taught in the English Departments of the Collège Militaire Royal de Saint-Jean, Quebec, and the University of Alberta, Edmonton, and has just retired as professor of English and Humanities at York University, Toronto. Mandel has travelled widely (in Europe, South America, India), and this is reflected in his poetry. He was writer-in-residence for the City of Regina (1978–79) and held visiting professorships at the University of Victoria (1979–80) and the University of Rome (1983). He received the Governor General's Award for Poetry for *An Idiot Joy* (1967) and was made a Fellow of the Royal Society of Canada in 1982. As well as being an important poet, Mandel has been influential as a critic and as an editor of poetry and critical essays.

His early poems recall other poems, poets, and artists. There are echoes of and allusions to the whole tradition of myth and literature, and the poems are often obscure and extravagant. They can be labelled metaphysical, mythic, or fantastic. Dream is a recurring image, and reality is often inverted or confused. When Canadian places or experiences are explored, they are explored in terms of Cain, Icarus, or Hamlet. The dimensions of the landscape are mythic rather than historic, and the social aspect of the early poems is the revelation of secrets for the good of society as a whole. In "Notes from the Underground," for instance, Mandel describes his poetic muse as a sibyl-like creature barricaded in a cave with "torn machines," "rusting texts," and dictionaries. The horrors of life seek her out as well, and these are the same horrors that Mandel feels he must reveal in his poetry. He describes as well the liberating force of writing this poetry: "Would you believe how free I have become / with lusting after her?" By revealing his ugly secrets, the poet can, paradoxically, rejuvenate the world and sing "of a free green life."

This is still a very private vision, not political in the public sense of the later poems. Over the years, more political concerns have been creeping into Mandel's poetry. Jewish tradition naturally leads into an awareness of twentieth-century politics and Nazi atrocities, and this awareness is expressed in a concern for the subsequent dehumanization of language and art, a concern for all types of inhumanity and repressive actions, and a concern with silence as a constant alternative. Thus Mandel's more recent poetry deals with concentration camps, the Vietnam War, the meaninglessness of political words, and the atrocities perpetrated in South America by totalitarian regimes. The poem *"Grandfather's Painting* : David Thauberger," for instance, compares

Mandel's urge to write "poems about land" and his prairie roots, with his awareness of "betrayal and South American Nazis." Torture, here and throughout Mandel's poetry, is a powerful image for the betrayal of both men and language.

The later poems are also sharper and more direct than the earlier ones. The images are clearer, and the forms more experimental. Mandel blends poems with photographs and journal entries. There are spare concrete poems and looser prose poems, found poems, lists, lyrics, and elegies. In *Stony Plain* (1973) Mandel returns to his prairies, making myths from the very land which he sees as a form of language. Instead of laying literary or classical myths on the land, Mandel sees the landscape in increasingly environmentally mythic terms. It is seen as the place for which the poet is searching as well as the place from which he first came; it is a beginning as well as an end, both a source and the object of a quest. This duplicitous vision is clearly demonstrated in "the double world," in *Out of Place* (1977). Mandel argues that a sense of place is related to being "out of place," the poet's constant tension. His images are often reflexive: labyrinths, Chinese boxes, mirrors; and his structures are also doubled: parodies, deconstructions, revisions. The poet is the divided man, and his road is the one "between the worlds."

Former traditions and structures no longer hold now; they must be deconstructed, "derealized," in order that the new lines may be written. The new lines in *Life Sentence* involve increasing risks. Mandel exposes his own vulnerability and links it powerfully to the extremities of our times; for instance, in "In My 57th Year," a poem which also suggests another of Mandel's recurrent concerns—the fictive nature of reality. Separations and displacements provide structure and content for Mandel's poems. Questions of politics and linguistics merge. His is a poetry of difficult visions and sensitive awareness.

.———————.

Mandel's works include *Trio* (1954) with Gael Turnbull and Phyllis Webb; *Fuseli Poems* (1960); *Black and Secret Man* (1964); *Criticism: The Silent-Speaking Words* (1966); *An Idiot Joy* (1967); *Irving Layton* (1969, 1981); *Crusoe* (1973); *Stony Plain* (1973); *Out of Place* (1977); *Another Time* (1977); *Dreaming Backwards: Selected Poems* (1981); *Life Sentence* (1981); and *The Family Romance* (1986).

Works on Mandel include John Ower, "Black and Secret Poet, Notes on Eli Mandel," *Canadian Literature* 42 (1969): 14–25; Margery Fee, "An Interview with Eli Mandel," *Essays on Canadian Writing* 1 (1974): 2–13; Dennis Cooley, "Double or Nothing: Eli Mandel's *Out of Place* and *Another Time*," *Essays on Canadian Writing* 10 (1978): 73–81; David Arnason, Dennis Cooley, and Robert Enright, "Interview with Eli Mandel: March 16/78," *Essays on Canadian Writing* 18/19 (1980): 70–89; Peter Stevens, "Poet as Critic as Prairie Poet," *Essays on Canadian Writing*, 18/19 (1980): 54–69; Andrew Suknaski, "borges and i; mandel and me," *Brick* 9 (1980): 16–24; Andrew Suknaski, "Out of *narayan* to *bifrost* / the word," *Brick* 14 (1982): 50–56; Ann Munton, "The Structural Horizons of Prairie Poetics: The Long Poem, Eli Mandel, Andrew Suknaski, and Robert Kroetsch," *The Dalhousie Review* 63 (1983): 69–97; and Smaro Kamboureli, "Locality as Writing: a Preface to the 'Preface' of *Out of Place*," *Open Letter* 6th Ser. 2–3 (1985): 267–77.

ANN MUNTON

NOTES FROM THE UNDERGROUND

A woman built herself a cave
    and furnished it with torn machines
    and tree-shaped trunks and dictionaries.
Out of the town where she sprang
    to her cave of rusting texts and springs
    rushed fables of indifferent rape
    and children slain indifferently
    and daily blood.

Would you believe how free I have become
    with lusting after her?
                That I have become
a melodramatist, my friends ashamed?

I have seen by the light of her burning texts
    how the indifferent blood drips
    from the brass mouths of my friends,
    how at the same table I have supped
    and grown fat.

Her breasts are planets in a reedy slough.
Lie down beside that slough awhile
    and taste the bitter reeds.

Read in the water how a drowning man
    sings of a free green life.

[1960]

THE DOUBLE WORLD:

it is variously believed that this world is the
double of another, as in Plato, Swedenborg,
        Malebranche,
some of Immanuel Kant, Arthur C. Clarke, Isaac
        Asimov,
Stanley Kubrick
                Two clocks set at the same time in
identical universes should stop at the same time.
This clock is a shadow of that real clock. When I
        look at my clock I have no way of knowing
        whether I am in
the first or second universe. It is spring there too:
and the other Ann has grown an avocado exactly
        the same
height, greenness, number of leaves as the one
        Ann grew
here or there. My grandfather Berner weighed the
        same
in both universes, sang sweet Jewish psalms, ate
        sour
curds. In the two graveyards Annie Berner is
        dead.
Nothing on either prairie changes though the
        winds blow
across immensities your heart would shrivel to
        imagine
knowing they pass between the worlds and can be
        heard to do
so on the road to Wood Mountain. That is what
        was written
in the rocks.

[1977]

IN MY 57TH YEAR

This is the year my mother lay dying
knocked down by tiny strokes she claimed
never once hit her though when she lay
crib-like where they laid her there she wept
for shame to be confined so near her death.
This is the year the cancer inside my father's
groin began its growth to knock him down
strong as he was beside his stricken wife.
This is the year I grew, ignorant of politics,
specious with law, careless of poetry.
There were no graves. The prairie rolled on
as if it were the sea. Today my children make
their way alone across those waves.
Do lines between us end as sharply
as lines our artists draw upon the plains?
I cry out. They keep their eye upon
their politics, their myths,
careful of lives as I was careless.

What shall I say? It is too late to tell again
tales we never knew. The legends of ourselves
spill into silence. All we never said, father
to daughter, son to unmanned man, we cannot say
to count the years.
        I no longer know time or age
thinking of parents, their time, their grave of names.
Telling the time, fiction consumes me.

[1980]

"GRANDFATHER'S PAINTING": DAVID THAUBERGER

Under David Thauberger's painting
showing his grandfather's house
and that giant horse standing above it,
the town of Holdfast, wheat fields,

church, elevators, and prairie grass
the TV set turned to a
Saturday Night Movie called "Marathon Man"
looks very small and peculiar,
but the movie is about politics,
10 betrayal and South American Nazis: it has to do
with various kinds of torture,
the use of a dentist's drill,
for example, the tyranny of McCarthy
in America of the fifties, Jews,
their memory, camps, the White Angel,
specialist in teeth, skulls, and diamonds.
    You wouldn't believe how large the horse is
in Thauberger's painting above the TV set
and yet it only portrays a symbol of how his grandfather
20 ruled the land, the power by which the little town
was run, the motor of the little town called Holdfast
while beneath it the real powers that run us,
pictures, say, and how we know how to kill one another,
metaphors of murder, these are played out night
upon night and I watch them and watch the painting,
no longer knowing whether I should write poetry,
especially poems about land, about Estevan,
or about why I came back to Regina, Saskatchewan,
this cold winter of 1979 or what I thought
30 I might find in a city of this kind to write of,
now that my father is dead for many years, and my mother,
and most of my friends are in the arts
                                There are nights
cold enough to kill. They remind me of my boyhood,
how much I loved the winter on the prairies, never
believing it was deadly or that we fought to be alive here
though my fantasies were of war. That powerful animal,
this evening with the Marathon Man running,
running, I suddenly know David was right to paint him,
40 his grandfather. We stand over the land, fathers,
and over our homes and over each other.
We have terrible forces inside us: we can paint them,
green, acrylic, glitter: the form never lies.
The truth is in the long dead winters where we live.

[1981]

· MILTON ACORN ·

1923–1986

Milton Acorn was born in Charlottetown, Prince Edward Island. He worked as a carpenter there, and later in Quebec and Ontario, but abandoned his trade for poetry in the late 1950s. While in Montreal, Acorn met a number of poets who influenced his writings, particularly Al Purdy, who in later years contributed a short but penetrating account of Acorn's early career in an introduction to *I've Tasted My Blood: Poems 1956–1968* (1969). In 1964 he moved to Vancouver, where he was active in politics and poetry, only to return to Toronto in the late 1960s. In 1970, when he did not receive the Governor General's Award for *I've Tasted My Blood*, a number of fellow Toronto poets awarded him the title of "The People's Poet." He later did win the Governor General's Award for *The Island Means Minago* (1975), a book dealing, in part, with Prince Edward Island, to which he eventually returned, and where he died.

When viewed in terms of the development of Canadian poetry, Acorn seems, at first, a striking and isolated individual. His open commitment to politics, in particular, makes him a difficult author to explicate in relation to the mainstream of Canadian writing. Unlike most Canadian poets, Acorn defiantly announced and insisted upon his political views, and he declared that his politics informed his poetry. However, the careful reader soon discovers that this repeatedly self-declared Marxist, Marxist-Leninist, Maoist, and Canadian nationalist had his own private view of a Canadian social ideal, one that did not adhere to any socialist ideology. In other words, despite Acorn's rather vociferous assertions of political allegiance, he is best viewed as having been a spokesman of the oppressed, as an articulator of the out

rage felt when man victimizes either himself or his fellow man. Nevertheless, it is important to note that, like Al Purdy or Irving Layton or Leonard Cohen, Acorn elected to forge an outspoken public persona which was capable of continually shocking its audience in an effort to expand and broaden the dominant senses of the "poetic."

No specific theory of politics or poetics, then, is involved in Acorn's art: it is an eclecticism aimed at voicing everything from personal indignation to private joy. He was, in other words, a social poet, in the largest sense of the term. The public image added the necessary resonance to his works so that they transcend any narrow notion of what a poem should be. What gives force, unity, power, and conviction to his best poems is not theory but an unhesitating sense of lyricism, point of view, imagery, and rhythmic subtlety. In the title poem of *I've Tasted My Blood*, for example, the poet describes his mother's wasted life in the following lines: " . . . I loved her too much to like / how she dragged her days like a sled over gravel." Although the specific political or social causes of the mother's wasted life are never mentioned, the lines suggest a boy's outrage in an image wholly appropriate to a child's sensibility—a sled dragged over gravel. The interplay of consonance and assonance in the words evokes the harshness and bitterness of the feelings involved; the emotion is conveyed with the intensity of verbal precision and evocativeness, not with political theory.

Despite the greatness of Acorn's lyricism, any summary of this poet's work has to emphasize the overall inconsistency of his achievement, for he did vacillate between the brilliant and the mediocre. His themes of love, the lack of love, nature, friendship, work, and the role of the poet in society were at their best when given the focus of direct personal experience. He could create a sense of intimacy or isolation with an economy and conviction that few Canadians approach. His weakest poems border on didacticism and polemic, often resembling vague, undigested political theory riddled with nebulous abstractions. However, if his tenacious determination to describe the worker's world led him, at times, to uncontrolled stridency, the same force seems to inform the most convincing poetry of social protest ever attained by a Canadian writer. The troublesome, if not bellicose, public self image Acorn created places him among the late modernists like Purdy and Layton who have, with equal force, attempted to break down the comfortable and neat division of the private man and the public poet.

·————————·

Acorn's works include *In Love and Anger* (1956); *The Brain's the Target* (1960); *Against a League of Liars* (1961); *Jawbreakers* (1963); *I've Tasted My Blood: Poems 1956–1968* (1969); *I Shout Love and On Shaving off His Beard* (1971); *More Poems for People* (1972); *The Island Means Minago* (1975); *Jackpine Sonnets* (1977); and *The Uncollected Acorn* (1987).

Works on Acorn include a special issue of *Fiddlehead* 56 (1963); M. Gnarowski, "Milton Acorn: A Review in Retrospect," *Culture* 25 (1964): 119–29; and Dorothy Livesay, "Search for a Style: The Poetry of Milton Acorn," *Canadian Literature* 40 (1969): 33–42.

ED JEWINSKI

CHARLOTTETOWN HARBOUR

An old docker with gutted cheeks,
time arrested in the used-up-knuckled hands
crossed on his lap, sits
in a spell of the glinting water.

He dreams of times in the cider sunlight
when masts stood up like stubble;
but now a gull cries, lights,
flounces its wings ornately, folds them,
and the waves slop among the weed-grown piles.

[1960]

I'VE TASTED MY BLOOD

If this brain's over-tempered
consider that the fire was want
and the hammers were fists.
I've tasted my blood too much
to love what I was born to.

But my mother's look
was a field of brown oats, soft-bearded;
her voice rain and air rich with lilacs:
and I loved her too much to like
how she dragged her days like a sled over gravel.

Playmates? I remember where their skulls roll!
One died hungry, gnawing grey perch-planks;
one fell, and landed so hard he splashed;
and many and many
come up atom by atom
in the worm-casts of Europe.

My deep prayer a curse.
My deep prayer the promise that this won't be.
My deep prayer my cunning,
my love, my anger,
and often even my forgiveness
that this won't be and be.
I've tasted my blood too much
to abide what I was born to.

[1963]

THE IDEA

It's events itch the idea
into existence. The clawing
pixilating world lofts
the mind and its wrangling images
as contrary, gusty, circling

winds toss, flaunt the flags
(splendrous as if living) of
old duchies, unforgotten empires.

Then something palpable as voltage,
maybe a grim preacher, maybe
a wild thin man on a soapbox,
or even a character lugging
a pail and whitewash brush
(whitewash or smear it's all
a point of view) takes charge:
something you want in a way
savage or happy, takes charge:
the idea grows flesh with nerves
to feel the pain of dismemberment.

But its life is death, and life's
going back to the chewing
creation obeying just itself;
so the herded clouds, dream-beasts
in the eyes' pasture, are torn
to fall like tears, like blood.
Then the idea's more like blood,
something in time with running feet,
with typewriter, with heartbeat.

[1963]

THE NATURAL HISTORY
OF ELEPHANTS

In the elephant's five-pound brain
The whole world's both table and shithouse
Where he wanders seeking viands, exchanging great farts
For compliments. The rumble of his belly
Is like the contortions of a crumpling planetary system.
Long has he roved, his tongue longing to press the juices
From the ultimate berry, large as
But tenderer and sweeter than a watermelon;
And he leaves such signs in his wake that pygmies have fallen
10 And drowned in his great fragrant marshes of turds.

In the elephant's five-pound brain
The wind is diverted by the draughts of his breath,
Rivers are sweet gulps, and the ocean
After a certain distance is too deep for wading.
The earth is trivial, it has the shakes
And must be severely tested, else
It'll crumble into unsteppable clumps and scatter off
Leaving the great beast bellowing among the stars.

In the elephant's five-pound brain
20 Dwarves have an incredible vicious sincerity,
A persistent will to undo things. The beast cannot grasp
The convolutions of destruction, always his mind
Turns to other things—the vastness of green
And of frangibility of forest. If only once he could descend
To trivialities he'd sweep the whole earth clean of his tormentors
In one sneeze so mighty as to be observed from Mars.

In the elephant's five-pound brain
Sun and moon are the pieces in a delightfully complex ballgame
That have to do with him . . . never does he doubt
30 The sky has opened and rain and thunder descend
For his special ministration. He dreams of mastodons
And mammoths and still his pride beats
Like the heart of the world, he knows he could reach
To the end of space if he stood still and imagined the effort.

In the elephant's five-pound brain
Poems are composed as a silent substitute for laughter,
His thoughts while resting in the shade
Are long and solemn as novels and he knows his companions
By names differing for each quality of morning.
40 Noon and evening are ruminated on and each overlaid
With the taste of night. He loves his horny perambulating hide
As other tribes love their houses, and remembers
He's left flakes of skin and his smell
As a sign and permanent stamp on wherever he has been.

In the elephant's five-pound brain
The entire Oxford dictionary'ld be too small
To contain all the concepts which after all are too weighty
Each individually ever to be mentioned;
Thus of course the beast has no language
50 Only an eternal pondering hesitation.

In the elephant's five-pound brain
The pliable trunk's a continuous diversion
That in his great innocence he never thinks of as perverse,
The pieces of the world are handled with such a thrilling
Tenderness that all his hours
Are consummated and exhausted with love.
Not slow to mate every female bull and baby
Is blessed with a gesture grandly gracious and felt lovely
Down to the sensitive great elephant toenails.

60 And when his more urgent pricking member
Stabs him on its horrifying season he becomes
A blundering mass of bewilderment . . . . No thought
But twenty tons of lust he fishes madly for whales
And spiders for copulation. Sperm falls in great gouts
And the whole forest is sticky, colonies of ants
Are nourished for generations on dried elephant semen.

In the elephant's five-pound brain
Death is accorded no belief and old friends
Are continually expected, patience
70 Is longer than the lives of glaciers and the centuries
Are rattled like toy drums. A life is planned
Like a brushstroke on the canvas of eternity,
And the beginning of a damnation is handled
With great thought as to its middle and its end.

[1969]

· JAMES REANEY ·

1926–

James Reaney was born and raised on a farm near Stratford, in Southwestern Ontario. He was educated in Stratford and at the University of Toronto, which granted his M.A. in 1949. That same year he published his first book, *The Red Heart,* which won the Governor General's Award for poetry. Reaney spent the next seven years teaching English at the University of Manitoba (he married the poet Colleen Thibaudeau in 1951) and returned to Toronto in 1956 to study for his Ph.D. His graduating year, 1958, was once again marked by the publication of a Governor General's Award-winning book of poems, *A Suit of Nettles.* Since 1960, Reaney has taught at the University of Western Ontario, not far from the locale of his youth and a good place from which to explore the body and soul of the region he loves. The explosion of poetry and drama that followed his establishment in London gained Reaney another Governor General's Award, for *Twelve Letters to a Small Town* (1962), a Chalmers Award, a University of Alberta National Award in Letters for his trilogy of plays *The Donnellys,* and an honorary doctorate from Carleton University. Reaney has been elected to the Royal Society of Canada and invested as a Member of the Order of Canada.

Margaret Atwood has said that "Reaney's early world . . . is an unredeemed one," and it is true that *The Red Heart* is the product of a youthful mind which felt stuck in the static round of a backwater existence. Even here, however, there are poems like "Antichrist as a Child" which feature the wisely innocent voice and viewpoint that are Reaney trademarks. From the time of *A Suit of Nettles* on, moreover, the enclosed feeling of *The Red Heart* becomes only one component of a broader anagogic vision that contains it. Anagogy is a name for the expanded consciousness that results when the outer world is absorbed and organized by the imagination. The giant mental state thus produced is what Reaney shows forming in the sound poem he calls "The Alphabet." Reaney has never more charmingly embodied such complex matters than in *A Suit of Nettles,* his long poem modelled on Spenser's *Shepheardes Calender* and concerning a flock of geese in an Ontario farmyard. *A Suit of Nettles* is a satire on various sorts of passivity and narrow-mindedness. Both thematically and technically (in its use of various poetic forms) the volume aims to "box the compass of reality," to use the nautical metaphor Reaney once applied to the mythopoeic poetry of a kindred spirit, Jay Macpherson.

A Suit of Nettles and *Twelve Letters to a Small Town* are the first volumes to show signs of an enduring influence—the criticism of Northrop Frye. Frye offered Reaney an imaginative system (the modal approach to literary theory) that confirmed his own intuitive vision of the total coherence of the literary world. He has spent a good many years exploring that theory, not only in his poetry and plays, but also in his little magazine *Alphabet* (1960–68). *Alphabet* was meant to show how the "secret alphabet or iconography or language of symbols and myths" of the literary world is rooted in—and therefore clarifies—life as it is actually lived. Myth and documentary, the universal and the local: these are the polarities whose interpenetration characterizes Reaney's writing in all forms, including his essays on his own work and on that of others.

Since *Twelve Letters,* the publication of volumes of Reaney's poetry has mainly involved consolidating the early work in various selections, and especially in the collected *Poems*. Increasingly, since the 1960s, Reaney has turned his efforts to the more public genre of drama. And he himself locates a watershed between two stages of his playwriting career. The first encompasses all the plays written up to *Listen to the Wind* (1972), which was first performed in 1966. These works, of which *The Easter Egg* (in *Masks of Childhood* [1972]) is typical, acknowledge a debt to theatrical realism, though their action and characters are inclined to be symbolic. In and after *Listen to the Wind*, Reaney's drama is unapologetically archetypal and technically experimental. In workshops at the Alpha Centre in London during the 1960s, Reaney discovered his own theatrical language, a hybrid of mime, fiction, poetry, song, dance, and all the traditional resources of theatre. This language could be spoken by a few actors playing multiple roles and using simple props and sets. The result, in plays like *The Donnellys*, is a living tapestry of rich visual and aural effects.

Reaney's post-Donnelly plays have often involved the sort of historical research that produced *The Donnellys*. Some of them, like *The Dismissal* (1978) and *King Whistle!* (1980), were centennial project commissions. *Traps*, a mime-play about mind-control, and *Gyroscope* (1980), a comedy on the themes of poetry and marriage, are two exceptions. Possibly the quintessential Reaney work is the autobiographical *Colours in the Dark* (1969). It is a play of the three-ring circus or theatrical-collage phase, about growing up, the archetypal theme that animates so much of Reaney's work in all genres, early and late, for children and adults. And it is an anthology of Reaney's early poems. But *The Donnellys*, his trilogy of plays about the "Black Donnellys" who were massa-

cred in 1880, is Reaney's masterpiece: a local story made convincingly universal because in it the texture of Biddulph Township between 1830 and 1880 is realized in amazing detail, and because it employs Reaney's multi-layered technique so organically.

.———.

Reaney's works include *The Red Heart* (1949); *A Suit of Nettles* (1958); *Twelve Letters to a Small Town* (1962); *The Killdeer and Other Plays* (1962); *The Boy with an Я in His Hand* (1965); *Colours in the Dark* (1969); *Masks of Childhood* (1972); *Listen to the Wind* (1972); *Poems* (1972); *Apple Butter and Other Plays for Children* (1973); *Sticks and Stones: The Donnellys, Part I* (1975); *The St. Nicholas Hotel, Wm. Donnelly, Prop.: The Donnellys, Part II* (1976); *Handcuffs: The Donnellys, Part III* (1977); *Baldoon (1976)* [with C. H. Gervais]; *14 Barrels from Sea to Sea* (1977); *The Dismissal* (1978); *Wacousta!* (1979); *King Whistle!* (1980); and *Gyroscope* (1980).

Works on Reaney include Alvin A. Lee, *James Reaney* (1968); Ross G. Woodman, *James Reaney* (1971); Germaine Warkentin, Introduction, *Poems* (1972); Margaret Atwood, "Reaney Collected," *Canadian Literature* 57 (1973): 113–17; Louis Dudek, "A Problem of Meaning," *Canadian Literature* 59 (1974): 16–29; James Stewart Reaney, *James Reaney* (1977); Stan Dragland, "James Reaney's 'Pulsating Dance in and out of Forms,' " *The Human Elements: Critical Essays*, ed. David Helwig (1978): 112–33; W. J. Keith, "James Reaney's 'Scrutumnus' and the Critics: An Individual Response," *Canadian Poetry: Studies/Documents/Reviews* 6 (1980): 2–34; and Stan Dragland (ed.), *Approaches to the Work of James Reaney* (1983).

STAN DRAGLAND

ANTICHRIST AS A CHILD

When Antichrist was a child
He caught himself tracing
The capital letter A
On a window sill
And wondered why
Because his name contained no A.
And as he crookedly stood
In his mother's flower-garden
He wondered why she looked so sadly
Out of an upstairs window at him.
He wondered why his father stared so
Whenever he saw his little son
Walking in his soot-coloured suit.
He wondered why the flowers
And even the ugliest weeds
Avoided his fingers and his touch.
And when his shoes began to hurt
Because his feet were becoming hooves
He did not let on to anyone
For fear they would shoot him for a monster.
He wondered why he more and more
Dreamed of eclipses of the sun,
Of sunsets, ruined towns and zeppelins,
And especially inverted, upside down churches.

[1946]

THE RED HEART

The only leaf upon its tree of blood,
My red heart hangs heavily
And will never fall loose,
But grow so heavy
After only a certain number of seasons
(Sixty winters, and fifty-nine falls,
Fifty-eight summers, and fifty-seven springs)
That it will bring bough

Tree and the fences of my bones
Down to a grave in the forest
Of my still upright fellows.

So does the sun hang now
From a branch of Time
In this wild fall sunset.
Who shall pick the sun
From the tree of Eternity?
Who shall thresh the ripe sun?
What midwife shall deliver
The Sun's great heir?
It seems that no one can,
And so the sun shall drag
Gods, goddesses and parliament buildings,
Time, Fate, gramophones and Man
To a gray grave
Where all shall be trampled
Beneath the dancing feet of crowds
Of other still-living suns and stars.

[1949]

THE SUNDOGS

I saw the sundogs barking
On either side of the Sun
As he was making his usual will
And last testament
In a glorious vestment.
And the sundogs cried,
"Bow wow!
We'll make a ring
Around the moon
10   And children, seeing it, will say:
Up there they play Farmer in the Dell
And the moon like the cheese stands still.
Bow wow!
We shall drown the crickets,
Set the killdeer birds crying,

Send shingles flying,
And pick all the apples
Ripe or not.
Our barking shall overturn
20 Hencoops and rabbit-hutches,
Shall topple over privies
With people inside them,
And burn with invisible,
Oh, very invisible!
Flames
In each frightened tree.
Whole branches we'll bite off
And for the housewife's sloth
In not taking them in
30 We'll drag her sheets and pillow cases
Off the fence
And dress up in them
And wear them thin.
And people will say
Both in the country
And in the town
It falls in pails
Of iron nails.
We'll blow the curses
40 Right back into the farmer's mouths
As they curse our industry
And shake their fists,
For we will press the oats
Close to the ground,
Lodge the barley,
And rip open the wheat stooks.
We shall make great faces
Of dampness appear on ceilings
And blow down chimneys
50 Till the fire's lame.
With the noise of a thousand typewriters
We shall gallop over the roofs of town.
We are the Sun's animals.
We stand by him in the West
And ready to obey
His most auburn wish
For Rain, Wind and Storm."

[1949]

THE ALPHABET

Where are the fields of dew?
I cannot keep them.
They quip and pun
The rising sun
Who plucks them out of view:
But lay down fire-veined jasper!

For out of my cloudy head
Come Ay Ee I Oh and U,
Five thunders shouted;
10   *Drive in sardonyx!*

And Ull Mm Nn Rr and hisSsings
Proclaim huge wings;
Pour in sea blue sapphires!

Through my bristling hair
Blows Wuh and Yuh
Puh, Buh, Phuh and Vuh,
The humorous air:
Lift up skies of chalcedony!

Huh, Cuh, Guh and Chuh
20   Grunt like pigs in my acorn mind:
Arrange these emeralds in a meadow!

Come down Tuh, Duh and Thuh!
Consonantly rain
On the windowpane
Of the shrunken house of the heart;
Lift up blood red sardius!

Lift up golden chrysolite!
Juh, Quuh, Zuh and X
Scribble heavens with light,
30   Steeples take fright.

In my mouth like bread
Stands the shape of this glory;
Consonants and vowels
Repeat the story:
And sea-green beryl is carried up!

The candle tongue in my dark mouth
Is anguished with its sloth
And stung with self-scoff
As my eyes behold this treasure.
40   *Let them bring up topaz now!*

Dazzling chrysoprase!
Dewdrops tempt dark wick to sparkle.
Growl Spark! you whelp and cur,
Leap out of tongue kennel
And candle sepulchre.

I faint in the hyacinthine quarries!
My words pursue
Through the forest of time
The fading antlers of this dew.

50   A B C D E F G H I J K L M
Take captive the sun
Slay the dew quarry
Adam's Eve is morning rib
Bride and bridegroom marry
Still coffin is rocking crib
Tower and well are one
The stone is the wind, the wind is the stone
New Jerusalem
N O P Q R S T U V W X Y Z!

[1960]

· ROBERT KROETSCH ·

1927–

Robert Kroetsch grew up on a farm near Heisler, Alberta. After he completed his B.A. in English and philosophy at the University of Alberta (1948), his employment included three seasons on the Mackenzie River, an experience that entered into his first novel. He completed his M.A. at Middlebury College, Vermont (1956), and his Ph.D. at Iowa State University (1961). For the next fifteen years, he taught at the State University of New York at Binghamton and was associate editor of the postmodernist journal, *Boundary 2*. During these years he wrote much of *Field Notes* (1981), and his first six novels, winning the Governor General's Award (1969) for *The Studhorse Man*. He returned to Canada in 1978 and continues to write and to teach at the University of Manitoba, where he is Distinguished Professor.

Robert Kroetsch began publishing poetry only after he had established himself as a novelist. In his poems, as in his novels, he writes of the (impossible) quest for origins. His poetry also reveals the fascination with post-structuralist theories evident in his fiction since *The Studhorse Man*. Consistently refusing closure, he describes his poems as part of a longer "continuing poem" he calls *Field Notes*, a title that suggests the fragments of a life, the totality of which can never be recovered. Frequently the poems work against closure by a doubled discourse: we can cite the two columns of "The Ledger," the documentary language of one column of "The Criminal Intensities of Love as Paradise" and the language of dreams and the unconscious of the second column, the narration of a journey across Canada and the surreal poems it gives rise to in "Mile Zero," and Frazer's translation of and commentary on

Pausanias's description of Greece as part of Kroetsch's account of his own visit there. These poems create an intertextual space, either by extensively quoting prior texts ("The Ledger," "Delphi: Commentary," and the sonnets of "Advice to My Friends") or by placing next to one another different linguistic codes to emphasize the indeterminacy of signs.

A self-reflexive and playful use of multiple linguistic codes characterizes Kroetsch's approach to language; the "identity"of signifier and signified continually slides into difference and the deferral of meaning. Clichés and colloquial language, puns and allusions, the rhetoric of guidebooks, airlines, railway timetables, seed catalogues, ledgers, tombstones, mathematics, etymologies, dreams, laments, elegies, epics, epithalamia, letters, and sonnets stand side by side in the poems. Kroetsch uses this intertextual space and these many linguistic codes to emphasize the indeterminacy and plurality of the sign and to situate the reader in the gap between the columns, between the texts and linguistic codes, where s/he must invent or "unhide" the poem.

Increasingly, Robert Kroetsch has come to see the continuing poem "Field Notes" as autobiographical: "I am writing this poem with my life," he tells us in "How I Joined the Seal Herd." We can understand this assertion only by recognizing that his critical and writerly presuppositions set him against the concept of the self dominating Western metaphysics, that the "I" is a coherent, unified (and solipsistic) construct. Kroetsch is committed to a plurality of shifting selves which enter his poetry initially through the multiple discourses of document and memory, then by his speaking through personae, and finally by the languages of the (many times) doubled self we see in the *Doppelgänger* of "The Frankfurt *Hauptbahnhof*," in the diachronic "(1969/ 1981)" and the double-voiced self (traveller/poet) of "Mile Zero," and in the voices of Pausanias, Frazer, and the poet at Delphi. "To say 'I' " in so many voices, becomes "a release" from the unified, solipsistic notion of "I."

. ——————— .

Kroetsch's works include *But We Are Exiles* (1966); *The Words of my Roaring* (1966); *Alberta* (1968); *The Studhorse Man* (1969); *Gone Indian* (1973); *Badlands* (1975); *What the Crow Said* (1978); *Field Notes* (1981); "Essays," *Open Letter* 5th ser. 4 (1983); *Alibi* (1983); *Advice to My Friends* (1985); and *Excerpts from the Real World* (1986). He has co-edited *Creation* (1970) and published a journal, *The "Crow" Journals* (1980).

Works on Kroetsch include Susan Wood, "Reinventing the Word: Kroetsch's Poetry," *Canadian Literature* 77 (1978): 28–39; Peter Thomas, *Robert Kroetsch* (1980); Shirley Neuman and Robert Wilson, *Labyrinths of Voice: Conversations with Robert Kroetsch* (1982); Shirley Neuman, "Allow Self, Portraying Self: Autobiography in *Field Notes*," *Line* 2 (1983): 104–21; "Reflections," a special issue of *Open Letter* 5th series 8–9 (1984); and Robert Lecker, *Robert Kroetsch* (1986).

SHIRLEY NEUMAN

FROM *THE SAD PHOENICIAN*

and even if it's true, that my women all have new lovers, then laugh,
     go ahead
but don't expect me to cry
and believe you me I have a few tricks up my sleeve myself
but I'm honest, I'm nothing if not honest; a friend of mine in Moose
     Jaw who shall remain anonymous tells me he met the girl from
     Swift Current who scorned my offer of sex in a tree house; a
     bird in the hand, he said, joking, of course
and flapped his arms
but she didn't speak, she told him nothing, at least not a particular of
     her need for me
and I didn't let on that I got the message
but I recognized in an instant that I'd been the cause of her
     sweating, her shortness of breath
and true, I'd be off like a shot to see her
but the woman in Montreal is not so evasive, not so given to outright
     lies, deceptions
and when she gets the letter I wrote last night, she'll say
but darling, I was following a fire truck
and quite by accident found the divine, ha, flicker
but if I don't even bother to mail the letter she'll learn what it feels
     like to be ignored
and the girl from Swift Current, the woman, can go climb a tree, I'm
     human too, you know, no slur intended

[1979]

but   even if it's true, that my women all have new lovers, offer no
      pity, remember, the worm turns
and   could it not be argued, the grease gets the squeaking wheel, the
      bridegroom the bride, the knot gets all or nun, ha, the sea sits
      firmly on top of land
but   I live by a kind of resistance
and   that explains why I was not there when she hollered uncle, the
      huntress, she with her glasses strung to her neck, the guide
      concealed in her canvas purse, a Franklin stove for a mouth, a
      rocker her hat or hair, two vinegar bottles under her blouse,
      behind her a round oak table
but   the eye is a liar, the sun does not set
and   any rogue of the first water would know how to wait, time flies,
      there are other fish in the ocean
but   enough: let one be the square root of one
and   lonely is only lonely, it has no other name like hand or hope or
      trust, or pissing against the wind, it has no habit of upside-down,
      it slams no doors, it does not fly south in autumn
but   I love you

[1978–79]

and if the hook fits the eye, madam, whoop-de-doo; the old button-
plucker, neither does she, nor, having done it, say the word; may
her first buttonhole be her last, the worm gets hungry too, love
but I remember the taste of sunset, the cargo all below deck, the
whiff on the sultry air
and no feasting allowed: the ox, the crane, C as in fig, D for door;
hieroglyph to no man, he; the horned asp
but don't be embarrassed, we all wear them; G, in outline, the camel's
head
and neck, carry on; hanky-pank, all hail; aye, the law had the goods
on me from the start; ho, skip it, the wine bowl empty, no
goading at the harried gate
but dear Miss Reading saw it, the owl, a rising out of Montreal; to
wit, the city burning, the city, burned in the snowing night
and here in the west she writes me, please, I carried the torch for
her, ha, could you send one burrowing owl, postpaid, I have
found a hole in the mountain, no more the arctic dream; the
Metro, if you don't mind
but he, a fishy business, that, the hooked eye, snitched from the
nooky night, running his blastfamous poem to halt, who goes
there, speak
and ready to call it quits

[1978–79]

MILE ZERO

". . . hockey is a *transition game:* offence to defence, defence to offence, one team to another. Hundreds of tiny fragments of action, some leading somewhere, most going nowhere. Only one thing is clear. Grand designs don't work."

—Ken Dryden, *The Game*

:   being some account of a journey through
western Canada in the dead of six nights

1

I looked at the dust
on the police car hood.
I looked around the horizon.
(Insert here passage on
nature—

>   *try*: The sun was blight
>   enough for the wild rose.
>   A musky flavor on the milk
>   foretold the cracked earth . . .
>
>   *try*: One crow foresaw my fright,
>   leaned out of the scalding
>   air, and ate a grasshopper's
>   warning . . .
>
>   *try*: A whirlwind of gulls
>   burned the black field white,
>   burned white the dark ploughman
>   and the coming night . . .)

I AM A SIMPLE POET
I wrote in the dust
on the police car hood

"Chateau (A Landing) Frontenac"

crisp, and the wind
the winter bleat

rain and the best
are never mulled

champlain
is green

madonna
the river is hungry

champlain, look in
my window, wait

absurd as undertow
or word

the hurt of lovers
hand in hand

repay the rot
the risk, the rain

madonna
madrona

announce and
enter, adding (end)

champlain is green
has empty eyes

westering is
madrona, west

the wooden shore
to look inland

Where did the virgin come from
on my second night west?

> Let me, prosaically, parenthetically, remark
> from what I observed: the lady in question took
> from the left (or was it right?) pocket of her
> coffee-stained apron a small square pad of lined
> sheets of paper. She bit the wood back from
> the lead of a stub of pencil. And she wrote,

←————————————————

> without once stopping to think, the loveliest
> goddamned (I had gauged her breasts when she
> wiped the table) poem that Christ ever read.

She had a clean mind.

"Driving, Accidental, West"

1

the shaped infinity
to hammer home

help, and the wild geese
heading south

and every way and
which, confuse

the fall of light
the fatal peen

how, and the commonest
crow or sparrow

speak the pale
or sensing moon

2

accelerate, the swan
sing, or eloquent as

antelope, the crisp
rejoinder of the duck's

quack to the deer's
leap, and, even then

even, a static dream
twitter and acquit

the kill, wait, for
and the nasty snow

fall, fall and for
tonight, only, dream

On the third night west
a mountain stopped us.
The mountains were lined up
to dance. I raised my baton:
rooted in earth, the lightning
rod on the roof of the barn,
on my soul's body. A crow
flew over the moon. I raised
my baton, a moon, a mountain.
*

    The crow flew over the mountain

---

*I have removed from this stanza the two lines

    Verily, I insist: I did
    not raise the purple crow

(and I like the ambiguity created by the line break)

partly because the "Verily" intrudes what we might call another language code, and that an unfortunate one in this case, for all the play on *truth*;

partly because the sexual innuendo puts me, as actual poet behind the implied speaker ("I") in a bad light; that is, self-mockery is, so to speak, harder to come by, as one (the poet, the implied speaker, the I or the "I") grows older (RK).

"Descent, as Usual, into Hell"

i've told her now so long
so often and sojourn *salut*

diamond
star or

(*ouest*
or quest or)

worry bead
relinquish

redolent as always
as the heated rose

summer and
a scent

(allot illusion as
is necessary to)

annealing praise
reticulate as tongue

mighty and a mouse
alike a maze

can he her up haul
or over if and may

asylum for her worship
in the night announce

the word of way
widen and weave

the was or is of
story is a story of

* Order, gentlemen. Order

is the ultimate
mountain. I raised my baton.

---

*I have removed from this stanza the single line

  (her breasts were paradigms)

(originally in parenthesis, as indicated) because I am
somewhat offended by the offhand reference to paradigm.
And yet, is not the mother figure the figure at once most
present in and most absent from this poet's work? The
concern with *nostos* is related to a long family history
of losses: *e.g.*, the paternal side of the family landing
in New York in June, 1841, aboard the *Pauline*, and the
mother of the large Kroetsch family, settled in Waterloo
County, Ontario, a few years thereafter widowed, the
early death of the poet's mother in Alberta, a century
after that first un-homing. Both quest and goal become
paradigmatic (RK).

"Awake, Awakening"

inhale, enact
the crappy sun

or face
finagle

far, and the body
wait

(the blackfoot had
no names for days)

the banjo, call
clairvoyant, still

gesticulate
triumphant

strum
and the morning

first, archaic
be, become

wrong or alone
we live, in delay's body

bone, altering
bone

after the word (after
which there can be no after)

cart
and the whipped horse

I lick your nipples
with my hand

The bindertwine of place—
The mansource of the man—
The natural odor of stinkweed—
The ache at the root of
*   the spinal thrust—

(Despair is   not writing the poem
say what you will about despair.)

---

*Surely this is where the original version of the poem
(1969) fails (Ron Smith of Oolichan Books on Vancouver
Island, pointing to the reliance on dashes)—the poet,
come to a crucial moment in the journey, hesitating to
write the longish poem the occasion dictates. The westward
(and return) journey that fascinates Kroetsch is here
turned entirely into implication without adequate substance
(i.e., ground), into, at best, intertext . . . Only later
do three couples suggest themselves, relating the journey to
the poet's equal fascination with the visit to the land of
the dead (in search of?)—

   (interior, the
   dark shore)

   the godfish
   hole

   the bait bait, and
   the hung hook hang

—but it is too late now, too late to weld such post-surreal
niceties into a voice that in the sixties insisted on a
source that was at once oral and local (RK).

"Weather Vane"

muse
I figure

hold us, cock and after
after the hot sun

clydesdale or
and forecast if

under adam's gun
we live

or dithyramb
of sorts, allow

self, portraying
self

think you think
the globe round

the cupola
to deem or dream

trajectory
of ignorance

(the bent pine
resisting west)

wind, swing
the arrow's edge

What I took to be an eagle
turned out to be a gull.
We glimpsed the sea.
The road ended

but it did not end:
the crying gulls turned
on the moon. The moon
was in the sea.
Despair that had sought the moon's
meaning found now the moon.
(Mile Zero is everywhere.)
The roar of the sea was the sea's roar.

the story of the poem
become
the poem of the story
become

"Collected Poem"

Every year is the same:
it's different.

visions of
exactitude

Death is a live
issue.

The world is   always
ending.

When you get to the
beginning   stop.

Green apples make you
shit like a bird, or

once in a while, just over
the next low hill

legs are longer than arms with
few exceptions

why doesn't bogus
rhyme with slump

I want to see one square
cloud.

(tempus
forgets)

The tree is there every morning.
Maybe you noticed that too.

[1982]

· PHYLLIS WEBB ·

1927–

Phyllis Webb was born 8 April 1927 in Victoria, British Columbia, educated in Victoria and Vancouver, and graduated from the University of British Columbia in 1949 with a B.A. in English and philosophy. An important early influence was F. R. Scott, whom she met while campaigning in a provincial election as a candidate for the Co-operative Commonwealth Federation (CCF). From 1950 to 1957, she lived and worked in Montreal. A government Overseas Award enabled her to move to Paris (1957–59). Here she fell under the spell of Adamov, Artaud, Sartre, and others. After teaching English at the University of British Columbia (1959–63), where she met the major Black Mountain poets, and several from San Francisco, she became a program organizer for CBC, Toronto, working mainly on *Ideas* and with such intellectuals as Glenn Gould, Paul Goodman, and R. D. Laing. In 1969 she settled on Saltspring Island, since which time she has taught creative writing at the University of British Columbia and the University of Victoria, and been writer-in-residence at the University of Alberta, Edmonton.

In 1982, because *Wilson's Bowl* (1980) had failed to win even a nomination for the Governor General's Award, a group of poets led by Margaret Atwood, Michael Ondaatje, bpNichol, and P. K. Page, collected $2,300 which they sent to Webb, stating that "this gesture is a response to your whole body of work as well as to your presence as a touchstone of true, good writing in Canada, which we all know is beyond awards and prizes." This gesture is unique in the history of Canadian literature. In 1983, Webb won the Governor General's Award for *The Vision Tree: Selected Poems.*

Her early poetry is characterized by the inward focus common to much seventeenth-century metaphysical poetry. Her subject is often love (and hate) which "all other sights controls, / And makes one little room an everywhere." In conflict with the metaphysics of passion is an existential world view, giving a tense philosophic turn to many poems in *Trio* (1954) and *Even Your Right Eye* (1956). Here, and in the next two volumes, the poet is "in observation of the small event," and the best metaphor for the most powerful aspects of her early style is "a statement, judicious and polite": sound in discernment and wisely critical, the poet expresses herself in words that are polished, refined, and cultivated. But the movement, apparent in *The Sea Is Also a Garden* (1962), is already outwards, to the state and its "guardians," to a political world that still needs bomb shelters and prosecutes war criminals.

Webb's apprenticeship culminates in *Naked Poems* (1965), just as her middle period matures into *Water and Light: Ghazals and Anti Ghazals: Poems* (1984), both volumes are technically innovative (the former more radical than the latter), departing from poetic norms established in the books that precede them. Between 1965 and 1980, while she worked full time, and struggled with revolutionary issues—her own psyche, anarchism, and feminism—Webb's poetic voice was intermittent; but, with the publication of *Wilson's Bowl*, the voice ceases to be uncertain, semi-private, and self-conscious and becomes strong, clearly female, and publicly committed. Great personal dreams "pass on / to the common good." The idea of the poet as "private Man speaking to public men" is, ironically, mastered and replaced by a woman *Talking* (1982): "*I* speak to *you*. Very simple. Very direct."

Resolution and confidence are evident in the outburst of creative energy that produced five new volumes in the first four years of the 1980s. Webb's work is distinguished by the enormous variety of her verse forms, her on-going experiment with poetic line, her wonderfully subtle musical sense, her technical craft, and the vigorous self-criticism that allows her to publish nothing that will diminish the reputation she has established among her peers.

. —————— .

Webb's works include "Falling Glass" in *Trio: First Poems by Gael Turnbull, Phyllis Webb, and E.W. Mandel* (1954); *Even Your Right Eye* (1956); *The Sea Is Also a Garden* (1962); *Naked Poems* (1965); *Selected Poems 1954–1965* (1971); *Wilson's Bowl* (1980); *Talking* (1982); *Sunday Water: Thirteen Anti Ghazals* (1982); *The Vision Tree: Selected Poems*

(1982); and *Water and Light: Ghazals and Anti Ghazals: Poems* (1984).

Works on Webb include Helen W. Sonthoff, "Structures of Loss: The Poetry of Phyllis Webb," *Canadian Literature* 9 (1961): 15–22; John F. Hulcoop, "Phyllis Webb and the Priestess of Motion," *Canadian Literature* 32 (1967): 29–39; John F. Hulcoop, introduction, *Selected Poems, 1954–1965* (1971) 13–45; Jean Mallinson, "Ideology and Poetry: An Examination of Some Recent Trends in Canadian Criticism," *Studies in Canadian Literature* 3.1 (1978): 93–109; Sharon Thesen, introduction, *The Vision Tree* (1982) 9–20; Douglas Barbour, "Lyric/Anti-Lyric: Some Notes About a Concept," *Line* 3 (1984): 45–63; John F. Hulcoop, " 'Birdsong in the Apparatus': Webb's New Selected Poems," *Essays on Canadian Writing* 30 (1984–85): 359–70; and Stephen Scobie, "I and I: Phyllis Webb's 'I Daniel,' " *Open Letter* 2–3 (1985): 61–68.

JOHN F. HULCOOP

MARVELL'S GARDEN

Marvell's garden, that place of solitude,
is not where I'd choose to live
yet is the fixed sundial
that turns me round
unwillingly
in a hot glade
as closer, closer I come to contradiction
to the shade green within the green shade.

The garden where Marvell scorned love's solicitude—
10 that dream—and played instead an arcane solitaire,
shuffling his thoughts like shadowy chance

across the shrubs of ecstasy,
and cast the myths away to flowering hours
as yes, his mind, that sea, caught at green
thoughts shadowing a green infinity.

And yet Marvell's garden was not Plato's
garden—and yet—he did care more for the form
of things than for the thing itself—
ideas and visions,
20 resemblances and echoes,
things seeming and being
not quite what they were.

That was his garden, a kind of attitude
struck out of an earth too carefully attended,
wanting to be left alone.
And I don't blame him for that.
God knows, too many fences fence us out
and his garden closed in on Paradise.

On Paradise! When I think of his hymning
30 Puritans in the Bermudas, the bright oranges
lighting up that night! When I recall
his rustling tinsel hopes
beneath the cold decree of steel,
Oh, I have wept for some new convulsion
to tear together this world and his.

But then I saw his luminous plumèd Wings
prepared for flight,
and then I heard him singing glory
in a green tree,
40 and then I caught the vest he'd laid aside
all blest with fire.

And I have gone walking slowly in
his garden of necessity
leaving brothers, lovers, Christ
outside my walls
where they have wept without
and I within.

[1956]

from THE KROPOTKIN POEMS

Syllables disintegrate ingrate alphabets
               lines decline into futures and limbos
                    intentions and visions fall

and fall like bad ladders.

I shaft my needle again and again
            into hell's veins and heaven's
                 listening for messages pulsing

on whose bloody hopes?

Whose love, tell me, o love's divine airs
                   elaborates the oratorio?

His dream. His exile. His imprisonments. Shadows

of his brother fixed in handiwork, letters, lexicons,

                    lessons, bereavements.

                      Alexander.

And him growing old. Peter. Who loved him before his marriage
at age thirty-six? Who did he lust for or sleep with
and who shifted his decorous sweetness into plain-song
                  pain-song, body to body?

                Peter.

The state of affairs so bad, the sufferings
             power in things awry
                   crooked
and perilous orders, forcing his language.

He cut his own vein
         stateless in grace
              o love words flow

on love whose airs are his own oratorio.

              In Adam's garden

he plants all his blood.

[1980]

MESSAGES

"They are always projecting themselves.
Cats play to cats we cannot see.
This is confidential."
        (Letter from E. D. Blodgett)

The young psychic comes back from halfway down the hall
to tell me to write about the cat on the postcard
tacked to the wall above my typewriter.

There is an understanding between us, and I show her
a photo in the *Journal* where the cat appears behind
my shoulder—

A piece of politics. A creature of state.

Out of Ptolemy's reign, cast in bronze (earrings restored)
far from Egypt now in its northern home.
10 Probable use: to hold the bones of a kitten.
Representative on this earth of the Goddess Bastet.

She prances toward me down the ramp of the poem
sent to me by the young psychic who is writing
an historical novel.
She moves toward me through an aura composed
of new light and the golden dust of Ptolemy.
Halfway down the ramp her high ears turn against
the task of the poem toward allurements
of stockmarket and monopoly.

20 *Cats play to cats we cannot see.*

Now it is night. I have locked her in this pyramid
of my own free will. She toys with the unwinding
sheet of a mummified king, paws at royal jewels
and sighs.
As I sleep at the 5 a.m. poem's edge she sniffs my skin
for news of her old lost world.
She names the Princes as they pass
heading for Bay Street in the winter blight.

They are always projecting themselves.
30 *This is confidential.*

Now it is morning in North Nineteen Hundred and Eighty.
The message clear: price of gold slumps,
war cracks at the border.
The Queen's cold mouth sends warning:

Beware.

How to get out of the poem without a scratch?
Each cast of the line seductive and minimal.
The ramp of the poem folding against
the power of the cat.
40 Possible use: to hold the bones of little ones
who cannot speak for themselves
or the Goddess Bastet.

Possible worth: treasure beyond speech
out of the old tomb, out of the mind's
sarcophagus. Wanting to touch
wanting to stare at her agate eyes
in the dark night of a museum postcard.

Bastet!
She moves toward me. She is here—
50 HISS HISS
With one paw raised
she scratches the final hieroglyphs
at the end of a bronze poem
I cannot see.

[1981]

LEANING

I am half-way up the stairs
of the Leaning Tower of Pisa.

Don't go down. You are in this
with me too.

I am leaning out of the Leaning
Tower heading into the middle distance

where a fur-blue star contracts, becomes
the ice-pond Brueghel's figures are skating on.

North Magnetic pulls me like a flower
out of the perpendicular

angles me into outer space
an inch at a time, the slouch

of the ground, do you hear that?
the hiccup of the sludge about the stone.

(Rodin in Paris, his amanuensis, a torso . . .)
I must change my life or crunch

over in vertigo, hands
bloodying the inside tower walls

lichen and dirt under the fingernails
Parsifal vocalizing in the crazy night

my sick head on the table where I write
slumped one degree from the horizontal

the whole culture leaning . . .

the phalloi of Miës, Columbus returning
stars all shot out—

And now this. Smelly tourists
shuffling around my ears

climbing into the curvature.
They have paid good lira to get in here.

So have I. So did Einstein and Bohr.
Why should we ever come down, ever?

And you, are you still here

tilting in this stranded ark
blind and seeing in the dark.

[1984]

· JAY MACPHERSON ·

1931–

Born in England, Jay Macpherson moved to Newfoundland when she was nine, with her mother and brother. After four years they moved to Ottawa where she studied at Glebe Collegiate and Carleton College (now Carleton University), receiving her B.A. in 1951. She spent a year in London, England, and another at McGill University in Montreal where she attended library school, before entering graduate school at the University of Toronto. She received her M.A. in 1955, with a thesis entitled "Milton and the Pastoral Tradition," and her Ph.D. in 1964, with a dissertation entitled "Narcissus, or the Pastoral of Solitude: Some Conventions of Nineteenth Century Romance." She has remained at the University of Toronto and is now a professor in the English department at Victoria College. She received the Governor General's Award for poetry in 1958 for *The Boatman*, her best-known book.

Although Macpherson's total poetic output has been slight, its quality is high, and its influence on a number of other Canadian poets marked. She is generally described as being part (along with James Reaney and the early Eli Mandel) of the mythopoeic school of poetry centred on the teachings of Northrop Frye. Indeed, Macpherson's poetry is most often dedicated to Frye; *Poems Twice Told* simply acknowledging "For Norrie as always." Macpherson writes suites of intricate, beautiful lyrics, related by both subject and allusion. In these she creates her own world in microcosm, peopled by the beings of myth, religion, and literature: Adam and Eve, Cain, Noah, Odysseus, Eurynome, Narcissus, Isis, Merlin, Ophelia, Prufrock. She rewrites and reworks mythic themes in a contemporary and witty style. Colloquialisms are mixed with literate borrowings: from Anglo-Saxon and Elizabethan lines, the Bible, Blake, Shakespeare, and Milton, and Greek and Babylonian myths. She also includes echoes of Christmas carols, fairy tales, and nursery rhymes; as well as gothic tales and horror movies. She continually experiments with traditional verse forms and returns to the universal and recurring thematic patterns of creation, the fall, the flood, redemption, and apocalypse.

Noah is her "Boatman," symbolic of the artist and artistic experience. He exists in a fallen world suggestive of *Paradise Lost*, in which the sexes are separated. Variously seen as a rival of God and a sleeping shepherd-giant, this poet-creator holds the secret of the lost Edenic world. The ark, with all of creation inside, can also be viewed in psychological terms as a reflection of the collective unconscious of mankind. The poet translates for the reader, marching "beasts" "through his sockets," as in "The Boatman," and then turning the reader inside out "to get his beasts outside him." Macpherson's book, then, can be seen as an ark filled with strange beasts and images which reflect universal archetypes and at the same time challenge our superficial lives. *The Boatman* (1957) is a dark vision of a fallen world with the possibility of redemption through imagination and the creative act. "The Anagogic Man," like several poems in this sequence, is a double of a simpler and freer poem, "The Boatman." Here a sleeping, dreaming Noah "carries, balancing with care," "All us and our worlds," reflecting Frye's anagogic view of poetry, as suggested by Macpherson's title and set out in Frye's *Anatomy of Criticism*. Frye emphasizes the connection between religion and this view of literature in which literature is seen as "containing life and reality in a system of verbal relationships"; he also emphasizes the universality of this vision which is found again and again in all levels of literature from the Bible to Shakespeare to fairy tales, as Macpherson demonstrates.

In *Welcoming Disaster* (1974) Macpherson questions this possible transcendence and posits another dark journey. After a period of actual creative silence in her own life, a period during which she attended horror films to put her back in touch with her dream world, she began to plumb her unconscious depths. This movement into the underworld is both psychological and mythical, the descent to face ("welcome") the darkness ("disaster") that is now necessary for creativity. The poet finds herself adrift, without the usual sureties. Reaching back in time, she takes as her guide for this journey her childhood teddy-bear, Tedward (or Tadwit). Similarly, as in "What Falada Said," childhood stories are rehearsed, but here the original is turned inside out, following Macpherson's pattern. Echoing the Grimms' fairy tale "The Goose Girl," Macpherson describes herself as the misplaced princess "drudging ... in exile." The head of Falada, the executed horse, gives its daily message. But whereas, in the fairy tale, the horse's words lead to the unmasking of the villain, the restoration of position, and a happily-ever-after ending, in Macpherson's poem the horse promises a false surety which is impossible to repossess in the fallen world of disasters. The companion piece from *Welcoming Disaster* printed here, "Umbrella Song," displays Macpherson's playfulness. This concrete poem suggests pictorially a form of "shelter" in the flood. God's handiwork has gone awry, but again a way of surviving the disaster through creativity is suggested. The ark has become but an umbrella, a "wordtree," but there is some company under the deluged cover.

.————.

Macpherson's works include *Nineteen Poems* (1952); *O Earth Return* (1954); *The Boatman* (1957); *Four Ages of Man: The Classical Myths* (1962); *The Boatman and Other Poems* (1968); *Pratt's Romantic Mythology: The Witches' Brew* (1972); *Welcoming Disaster: Poems, 1970–4* (1974); and *The Spirit of Solitude: Conventions and Continuities in Late Romance* (1982).

Works on Macpherson include James Reaney, "The Third Eye—Jay Macpherson's *The Boatman*," *Canadian Literature* 3 (1960): 23–34; sections in D. G. Jones, *Butterfly on Rock* (1970); Northrop Frye, *The Bush Garden* (1971): 70–75; Suniti Namjoshi, "In the Whale's Belly:—Jay Macpherson's Poetry," *Canadian Literature* 79 (1978): 54–59; and Audrey Berner, "The 'Unicorn' Poems of Jay Macpherson," *Journal of Canadian Poetry* 3 (1980): 9–16.

ANN MUNTON

THE ANAGOGIC MAN

Noah walks with head bent down;
For between his nape and crown
He carries, balancing with care,
A golden bubble round and rare.

Its gently shimmering sides surround
All us and our worlds, and bound
Art and life, and wit and sense,
Innocence and experience.

Forbear to startle him, lest some
Poor soul to its destruction come,
Slipped out of mind and past recall
As if it never was at all.

O you that pass, if still he seems
One absent-minded or in dreams,
Consider that your senses keep
A death far deeper than his sleep.

Angel, declare: what sways when Noah nods?
The sun, the stars, the figures of the gods.

[1957]

THE BOATMAN

You might suppose it easy
For a maker not too lazy
To convert the gentle reader to an Ark:
But it takes a willing pupil
To admit both gnat and camel
Quite an eyeful, all the crew that must embark.

After me when comes the deluge
And you're looking round for refuge
From God's anger pouring down in gush and spout,

Then you take the tender creature
—You remember, that's the reader—
And you pull him through his navel inside out.

That's to get his beasts outside him,
For they've got to come aboard him,
As the best directions have it, two by two.
When you've taken all their tickets
And you've marched them through his sockets,
Let the tempest bust Creation: heed not you.

For you're riding high and mighty
In a gale that's pushing ninety
With a solid bottom under you—that's his.
Fellow flesh affords a rampart,
And you've got along for comfort
All the world there ever shall be, was, and is.

[1957]

WHAT FALADA SAID

All I have left from home—the horse that brought me,
Dead, flayed, its head hung up, its power of speaking
Left, like an echo—gives its daily message
    In the dark entry:

'Daughter, betrayed and drudging here in exile,
Those who let these things happen were—believe me—
Foreigners, strangers, none of those who loved you:
    Not your true mother.

She if she knew would send someone to fetch you,
Carry you home, restore the past, again her
Child, joy from pain: at least, if she could know it
    She would be sorry.'

So on my nursery floor my dolls consoled me.
No: there are four, not two: a constellation
Turning: maimed child, barbed mother—torn, rent open
    Womb, bladed baby.

[1974]

UMBRELLA POEM

In the beginning
there was One,
holding the roof up
all alone.

One was clever,
invented Two—
nice—accepting—
joy! calloo!
—found at length it
wouldn't do—
or, more likely,
always knew
time would wear the
plaything through.

One was clumsy:
darling Two
got mislaid or
slipped from view:
haunted forest,
space, ensue.

One was lucky:
God sent Two,
with a note its
name was *You*—
magic word to
make things new!
out of One, be-
hold, *I* grew.

Rooftree—wordtree—
space—time—friend—
make some shelter,
till the end.

[1974]

· ALDEN NOWLAN ·

1933–1983

Alden Nowlan was born in Stanley, near Windsor, Nova Scotia. He dropped formal schooling in Grade Five but continued to read voraciously while working as a pulp-cutter and millhand. In 1952, he took a job in New Brunswick with the *Hartland Observer*. His poems began to appear in little magazines, mainly in the US, and by the time he left for a job with the *Telegraph-Journal* in Saint John in 1963, he had published five collections of verse. After undergoing cancer surgery, Nowlan was appointed writer-in-residence at the University of New Brunswick in Fredericton in 1968, a post he held until his death in June 1983. He won the Governor General's Award for *Bread, Wine and Salt* (1967). He was a Guggenheim fellow (1967–68), and he won the University of Western Ontario's President's Medal for fiction in 1970, the Canadian Authors' Association Silver Medal in 1978, and the Queen's Jubilee Medal in 1979.

As a boy Nowlan created for himself an imaginary world and imaginary roles, which embodied his aspirations to achieve power through language. He began composing verse in his teens. His early poems are generally tightly formal, compact, and charged with irony, often inspired by observing the behaviour of people confronted by conditions of bitter necessity, in rural or small-town settings. As he became aware of what contemporary poets like Raymond Souster were doing, he began to move to more open verse and common speech rhythms. By 1962, when *The Things Which Are* appeared, his style was fully mature, though he continued to move toward greater flexibility. His measure, evident in the way he read his poems, became an instinctive weighting, close to that of William Carlos Williams's movable foot.

As his poetry relaxed in rhythm and tone, irony gave way to closer empathy with his subjects. As he moved from rural to small-town to urban to university settings, the range of his subjects widened, though he retained strong ties, particularly in his fiction, with the region of his childhood. His wide reading of the Bible and European history and literature allowed him even in his early work to see local subjects against wider contexts. He increasingly took as his themes the paradoxes and quirks of human behaviour, viewed wryly and compassionately. He continued throughout his career to see himself as "various persons, including those of saints, monsters and comic-book heroes." Most of his poems, though lyrical in intent, begin as narratives or personal anecdotes.

·————————·

Nowlan's works include *The Things Which Are* (1962); *Bread, Wine and Salt* (1967); *Miracle at Indian River* (1968); *The Mysterious Naked Man* (1969); *Between Tears and Laughter* (1971); *Various Persons Named Kevin O'Brien* (1973); *I'm a Stranger Here Myself* (1974); *Smoked Glass* (1977); *I Might Not Tell Everybody This* (1982); *The Early Poems* (1983); *Will Ye Let the Mummers In* (1984); and *An Exchange of Gifts: Poems New and Selected* (1985). He wrote, with Walter Learning, *The Dollar Woman* (1972), *Frankenstein* (1973), and *The Incredible Murder of Cardinal Tosca* (1978).

Works on Nowlan include Michael Brian Oliver, *Poet's Progress* (1978); "The Alden Nowlan Special Issue" *Fiddlehead* 81 (1969); and Sandra Djwa, "Alden Nowlan 1933–83," *Canadian Literature* 101 (1984): 180–83.

ROBERT GIBBS

THE BULL MOOSE

Down from the purple mist of trees on the mountain,
lurching through forests of white spruce and cedar,
stumbling through tamarack swamps,
came the bull moose
to be stopped at last by a pole-fenced pasture.

Too tired to turn or, perhaps, aware
there was no place left to go, he stood with the cattle.
They, scenting the musk of death, seeing his great head
like the ritual mask of a blood god, moved to the other end
of the field, and waited.

The neighbours heard of it, and by afternoon
cars lined the road. The children teased him
with alder switches and he gazed at them
like an old, tolerant collie. The women asked
if he could have escaped from a Fair.

The oldest man in the parish remembered seeing
a gelded moose yoked with an ox for plowing.
The young men snickered and tried to pour beer
down his throat, while their girl friends took their pictures.

And the bull moose let them stroke his tick-ravaged flanks,
let them pry open his jaws with bottles, let a giggling girl
plant a little purple cap
of thistles on his head.

When the wardens came, everyone agreed it was a shame
to shoot anything so shaggy and cuddlesome.
He looked like the kind of pet
women put to bed with their sons.

So they held their fire. But just as the sun dropped in the river
the bull moose gathered his strength
like a scaffolded king, straightened and lifted his horns
so that even the wardens backed away as they raised their rifles.
When he roared, people ran to their cars. All the young men
leaned on their automobile horns as he toppled.

[1962]

THE EXECUTION

On the night of the execution
a man at the door
mistook me for the coroner.
"Press," I said.

But he didn't understand. He led me
into the wrong room
where the sheriff greeted me:
"You're late, Padre."

"You're wrong," I told him. "I'm Press."
"Yes, of course, Reverend Press."
We went down a stairway.

"Ah, Mr. Ellis," said the Deputy.
"Press!" I shouted. But he shoved me
through a black curtain.
The lights were so bright
I couldn't see the faces
of the men sitting
opposite. But, thank God, I thought
they can see me!

"Look!" I cried. "Look at my face!
Doesn't anybody know me?"

Then a hood covered my head.
"Don't make it harder for us," the hangman whispered.

[1962]

THE MYSTERIOUS NAKED MAN

A mysterious naked man has been reported
on Cranston Avenue. The police are performing
the usual ceremonies with coloured lights and sirens.
Almost everyone is outdoors and strangers are conversing excitedly
as they do during disasters when their involvement is peripheral.
"What did he look like?" the lieutenant is asking.
"I don't know," says the witness. "He was naked."
There is talk of dogs—this is no ordinary case
of indecent exposure, the man has been seen
a dozen times since the milkman spotted him and now
the sky is turning purple and voices
carry a long way and the children
have gone a little crazy as they often do at dusk
and cars are arriving
from other sections of the city.
And the mysterious naked man
is kneeling behind a garbage can or lying on his belly
in somebody's garden
or maybe even hiding in the branches of a tree,
where the wind from the harbour
whips at his naked body,
and by now he's probably done
whatever it was he wanted to do
and wishes he could go to sleep
or die
or take to the air like Superman.

[1969]

THE BROADCASTER'S POEM

I used to broadcast at night
alone in a radio station
but I was never good at it,
partly because my voice wasn't right
but mostly because my peculiar
metaphysical stupidity

made it impossible
for me to keep believing
there was somebody listening
10 when it seemed I was talking
only to myself in a room no bigger
than an ordinary bathroom.
I could believe it for a while
and then I'd get somewhat
the same feeling as when you
start to suspect you're the victim
of a practical joke.
                        So one part of me
was afraid another part
20 might blurt out something
about myself so terrible
that even I had never until
that moment suspected it.
                        This was like the fear
of bridges and other
high places: Will I take off my glasses
and throw them
into the water, although I'm
half-blind without them?
30 Will I sneak up behind
myself and push?
                        Another thing:
as a reporter
I covered an accident in which a train
ran into a car, killing
three young men, one of whom
was beheaded. The bodies looked
boneless, as such bodies do.
More like mounds of rags.
40 And inside the wreckage
where nobody could get at it
the car radio
was still playing.
                        I thought about places
the disc jockey's voice goes
and the things that happen there
and of how impossible it would be for him
to continue if he really knew.

[1974]

· LEONARD COHEN ·

1934–

Born in Montreal in 1934, Leonard Cohen comes from a well-to-do Westmount family. Although he has lived for extended periods in Greece and in California, Montreal is always his spiritual home; it is the city to which he returns in order, as he once said in a widely quoted phrase, "to renew my neurotic affiliations." He attended McGill and Columbia universities, but has largely avoided academic life. In 1969 he turned down a Governor General's Award. Owing mainly to his fame as a singer, he has a wide international reputation, especially in Europe. His works have been translated into many languages, including French, German, Swedish, Portuguese, and Polish.

Although Cohen's major period of creative activity was the mid-1960s, his first book, *Let Us Compare Mythologies*, appeared in 1956; and the atmosphere of the 1950s—the influence of the Beat Poets, the recent memories of the Nazi holocaust, the impending doom of the nuclear bomb—defines much of his work. Even at his most romantic, as in the beautiful love lyrics of *The Spice-Box of Earth* (1961), Cohen's vision is dark and violent. Poetry, religion, sex, death, beauty, and power form an interlocked pattern heightened by the sensuousness of his language, and also emphasized by a wild, outrageous, and black sense of humour. Cohen celebrates the destruction of the self and the abnegation of power: his "losers" are "beautiful" *because* they are losers, not in spite of it.

Flowers for Hitler (1964) represents the first stage of Cohen's continued attempt to undercut his own reputation, to deny his own lyricism. Its harsh and ugly satiric poems portray a nightmare world, which is still defined by the image of the concentration camp. Later, *The Energy of Slaves* (1972) proclaims a similarly anti-poetic stance. The doubts and uncertainties about the validity of his own writing produced much hesitancy, and long periods of silence; in the 1970s they are reflected in the divided and bitterly self-contestatory texts and commentaries of *Death of a Lady's Man* (1978). However, *Book of Mercy* (1984) returns to a much more assured and lyrical, as well as reverential and religious, voice.

The crisis in confidence in poetry per se is also reflected in Cohen's attention to other forms. He has published two novels: the semi-autobiographical *The Favourite Game* (1963), and *Beautiful Losers* (1966), his most important single work. By turns historical and surreal, religious and obscene, comic and ecstatic, it remains the most radical (and beautiful) experimental novel ever published in Canada.

But since the mid-1960s, Cohen's most consistent and rewarding output has been as a songwriter and performer. Although the songs tend to be less dark and more humane than his work in other media, they are still incisive, troubling works of art, filled with a memorable richness of phrasing and lyricism of language and image. The pared-down simplicity of *Songs from a Room* (1969) is perhaps the most impressive achievement, though the popular preference will always be for the earlier "Suzanne." Whereas Cohen faltered in poetry and abandoned the novel during the 1970s, the recordings continue at a very high level, and *Recent Songs* (1979) and *Various Positions* (1984) show him still at the height of his powers.

In many ways Leonard Cohen seems an anachronism, cut off from all such poetic or critical trends as post-modernism and post-structuralism; the scope and themes of his work were defined in the 1950s, and have remained remarkably constant ever since. His voice is utterly individual, and still commands attention.

· ———— ·

Cohen's works include *Let Us Compare Mythologies* (1956); *The Spice-Box of Earth* (1961); *The Favourite Game* (1963); *Flowers for Hitler* (1964); *Beautiful Losers* (1966); *Selected Poems 1956–1968* (1968); *The Energy of Slaves* (1972); *I Am a Hotel* (Video, 1983); and *Book of Mercy* (1984). His recordings include *Songs of Leonard Cohen* (1968); *Songs from a Room* (1969); *New Skin for the Old Ceremony* (1974); *Death of a Lady's Man* (1977); *Recent Songs* (1979); and *Various Positions* (1984).

Works on Cohen include Michael Ondaatje, *Leonard Cohen* (1970); Jacques Vassal, *Leonard Cohen* (1974); Michael Gnarowski, ed., *Leonard Cohen: The Artist and His Critics* (1976); and Stephen Scobie, *Leonard Cohen* (1978).

STEPHEN SCOBIE

I HAVE NOT LINGERED IN EUROPEAN MONASTERIES

I have not lingered in European monasteries
and discovered among the tall grasses tombs of knights
who fell as beautifully as their ballads tell;
I have not parted the grasses
or purposefully left them thatched.

I have not released my mind to wander and wait
in those great distances
between the snowy mountains and the fishermen,
like a moon,
or a shell beneath the moving water.

I have not held my breath
so that I might hear the breathing of God,
or tamed my heartbeat with an exercise,
or starved for visions.
Although I have watched him often
I have not become the heron,
leaving my body on the shore,
and I have not become the luminous trout,
leaving my body in the air.

I have not worshipped wounds and relics,
or combs of iron,
or bodies wrapped and burnt in scrolls.

I have not been unhappy for ten thousand years.
During the day I laugh and during the night I sleep.
My favourite cooks prepare my meals,
my body cleans and repairs itself,
and all my work goes well.

[1961]

FOR E. J. P.

I once believed a single line
    in a Chinese poem could change
        forever how blossoms fell
and that the moon itself climbed on
    the grief of concise weeping men
        to journey over cups of wine
I thought invasions were begun for crows
    to pick at a skeleton
        dynasties sown and spent
to serve the language of a fine lament
    I thought governors ended their lives
        as sweetly drunken monks
telling time by rain and candles
    instructed by an insect's pilgrimage
        across the page—all this
so one might send an exile's perfect letter
to an ancient home-town friend

I chose a lonely country
    broke from love
        scorned the fraternity of war
I polished my tongue against the pumice moon
    floated my soul in cherry wine
        a perfumed barge for Lords of Memory
to languish on to drink to whisper out
    their store of strength
        as if beyond the mist along the shore
their girls their power still obeyed
    like clocks wound for a thousand years
I waited until my tongue was sore

Brown petals wind like fire around my poems
    I aimed them at the stars but
        like rainbows they were bent
before they sawed the world in half
    Who can trace the canyoned paths
        cattle have carved out of time
wandering from meadowlands to feasts
    Layer after layer of autumn leaves
        are swept away
Something forgets us perfectly

[1964]

WHAT I'M DOING HERE

I do not know if the world has lied
I have lied
I do not know if the world has conspired against love
I have conspired against love
The atmosphere of torture is no comfort
I have tortured
Even without the mushroom cloud
still I would have hated
Listen
I would have done the same things
even if there were no death
I will not be held like a drunkard
under the cold tap of facts
I refuse the universal alibi

Like an empty telephone booth passed at night
and remembered
like mirrors in a movie palace lobby consulted
only on the way out
like a nymphomaniac who binds a thousand
into strange brotherhood
I wait
for each one of you to confess

[1964]

TWO WENT TO SLEEP

Two went to sleep
almost every night
one dreamed of mud
one dreamed of Asia
visiting a zeppelin
visiting Nijinsky
Two went to sleep
one dreamed of ribs
one dreamed of senators
10 Two went to sleep
two travellers
The long marriage
in the dark
The sleep was old
the travellers were old
one dreamed of oranges
one dreamed of Carthage
Two friends asleep
years locked in travel
20 Good night my darling
as the dreams waved goodbye
one travelled lightly
one walked through water
visiting a chess game
visiting a booth
always returning
to wait out the day
One carried matches
one climbed a beehive
30 one sold an earphone
one shot a German
Two went to sleep
every sleep went together
wandering away
from an operating table
one dreamed of grass
one dreamed of spokes
one bargained nicely
one was a snowman
40 one counted medicine
one tasted pencils
one was a child
one was a traitor

visiting heavy industry
visiting the family
Two went to sleep
none could foretell
one went with baskets
one took a ledger
50 one night happy
one night in terror
Love could not bind them
Fear could not either
they went unconnected
they never knew where
always returning
to wait out the day
parting with kissing
parting with yawns
60 visiting Death till
they wore out their welcome
visiting Death till
the right disguise worked

[1966]

[UNTITLED POEM]

Welcome to these lines
There is a war on
but I'll try to make you comfortable
Don't follow my conversation
it's just nervousness
Didn't I make love to you
when we were students of the East
Yes the house is different
the village will be taken soon
I've removed whatever
might give comfort to the enemy
We are alone
until the times change
and those who have been betrayed
come back like pilgrims to this moment
when we did not yield
and call the darkness poetry

[1972]

· GEORGE BOWERING ·

1935–

George Bowering was born in Penticton, British Columbia, in 1935. He is the author of more than a dozen books and chap-books of poetry, plus three novels and three collections of short stories. He has won the Governor General's Award for both poetry (1969) and fiction (1980). Bowering has been involved in the publication of influential magazines such as the poetry newsletters *Tish, Imago,* and *Open Letter.* He earned a B.A. and an M.A. at the University of British Columbia. Bowering now lives in Vancouver and teaches at Simon Fraser University.

Having been heavily influenced by Black Mountain poetic theory during the first five years of his public writing life, Bowering produced several volumes of adept open-form lyrics. Poems like "Grandfather" and "Inside the Tulip" illustrate the use of the breathline and a fleet movement from one perception to another that Charles Olson advocated in his seminal essay "Projective Verse."

In the mid-1960s Bowering became interested in longer poem structures, in the book as a unit of composition, and in the interface between author and personal/social history. In *Autobiology* (1972) Bowering wrote: "Consciousness is how it is composed," and his work since that time has served as a record of his personal consciousness and attendant self-consciousness.

Bowering's early serial poem *Baseball: A Poem in the Magic Number 9* (1967) and the poem suite *Rocky Mountain Foot* (1968), for which he won the Governor General's Award, employed standard forms of poetic extension, using narrative and collage techniques pioneered by the early modernists. Later works like *Curious* (1973) and *Autobiol-*ogy are much more interesting and imaginative poems. In *Curious* Bowering offers forty-eight portraits of other poets filtered through his own consciousness, while in *Autobiology* he focuses upon moments in his physiological development that altered his consciousness and his way of perceiving the world.

In his introduction to the short-story anthology *Fiction of Contemporary Canada*, Bowering uses the analogy of a man watching television, while at the same time seeing his own reflection in the screen, to describe the condition of post-modernism. Bowering's own poetry has reflected a gradual realization of just such a condition; rarely in his recent work are we unaware of the presence of the author and of our own participation in the formulation of the aesthetic experience.

· ———— ·

Bowering's works include *Points on the Grid* (1964); *The Silver Wire* (1966); *Rocky Mountain Foot* (1968); *The Gangs of Kosmos* (1969); *Touch: Selected Poems 1960-1970* (1971); *In the Flesh* (1974); *A Short Sad Book* (1977); *Burning Water* (1980); *Particular Accidents* (1980); *West Window* (1982); *Kerrisdale Elegies* (1984); and *Delayed Mercy* (1987).

Works on Bowering include Ken Norris, "The Poetry of George Bowering," *Brave New Wave,* ed. Jack David (1978): 83–107; Allan Brown, "Beyond the Crenel: A View of George Bowering," *Brick* 6 (1979): 36–39; Robin Blaser, "George Bowering's Plain Song," introduction, *Particular Accidents* (1980); and Ellen Quigley, "*Tish*: Bowering's Infield Position," *Studies in Canadian Literature* 5 (1980): 23–46.

KEN NORRIS

GRANDFATHER

Grandfather
          Jabez Harry Bowering
strode across the Canadian prairie
hacking down trees
                    and building churches
delivering personal baptist sermons in them
leading Holy holy holy lord god almighty songs in them
red haired man squared off in the pulpit
reading Saul on the road to Damascus at them

Left home
          big walled Bristol town
at age eight
              to make a living
buried his stubby fingers in root snarled earth
for a suit of clothes and seven hundred gruelly meals a year
taking an anabaptist cane across the back every day
for four years till he was whipped out of England

Twelve years old
                  and across the ocean alone
to apocalyptic Canada
                      Ontario of bone bending child labor
six years on the road to Damascus till his eyes were blinded
with the blast of Christ and he wandered west
to Brandon among wheat kings and heathen Saturday nights
young red haired Bristol boy shoveling coal
in the basement of Brandon college five in the morning

Then built his first wooden church and married
a sick girl who bore two live children and died
leaving several pitiful letters and the Manitoba night

He moved west with another wife and built children and churches
Saskatchewan Alberta British Columbia Holy holy holy
lord god almighty
                    struck his labored bones with pain
and left him a postmaster prodding grandchildren with crutches
another dead wife and a glass bowl of photographs
and holy books unopened save the bible by the bed

Till he died the day before his eighty fifth birthday
in a Catholic hospital of sheets white as his hair

[1962]

AGAINST DESCRIPTION

I went to the blackberries
on the vine.

They were blackberries
on the vine.

They were
blackberries.

Black
berries.

[1965]

THE HOUSE

1.

If I describe my house
I may at last describe myself

but I will surely lie
about the house.

For there is the first lie.
It is not a house at all

but a fragment, a share
of a house, instinct drives me

to one door. As certain as
10 one hair lies beside another.

As certain as these rows of books
carry me from house to house,

arrange me to their will. I
squat for an hour, eye level

to those books, saying I will
read this, or I will read this,

& this way never succeed
in reading my self, no time

left in the hour between
20 the news & the pants on the floor.

2.

In the morning the window
is bamboo & behind that

snow. (But here I am trying
to go outside the house, remember

what I said.) My bare feet
find no wood, the water

runs warm from the tap,
the coffee in the white cup

on which is painted a green
30 tree. There is a newspaper

on the floor inside the door,
& a woman in the chiffon

of the bed. A salt shaker
of glass & an aluminum

pepper shaker, & in the
farthest room, papers, orderly.

Those are the reason for the house
& its enemy. I am the fisher

who lays his fish side by side
40 in the pan. The noise of the pen

on paper is the drift of
cigarette smoke in the window's light.

3.

The house has a refrigerator
& a stove, a painting & a

husband, & the husband
has fingers from which words

fall as the wine glass falls
unbroken on the rug.

The key fits into the door
50 as my feet step in snow, cutting

precise patterns & the silence
of wind, & from outside

the windows are glass, &
behind that the house is not empty.

[1966]

THRU

She says it makes her mad
I wake her up
laughing in my sleep.

I dont remember that happiness
wrapt with her & the sheets,
& if it is the edge of

what? where is that place,
maybe for ease we call it eternity,
what was funny there?

Dont wake the sleep-
walker they say, how about
the man giggling with his eyes closed?

He may be left in the place
we court so solemnly
in our poems—he may

have been laughing
to enrich his courage, faced
with unspeakable horror.

Or one time I will
catch myself laughing among friends,
& a glimpse of it,

in the moment their faces
melt away, that instant's
springtime, the monster

under the grass, that I return to,
the mystery best forgotten
in the springtime of waking

to the alarm, the alarm.

[1969]

SUMMER SOLSTICE

I

The cool Pacific spring has gone without
my notice, now summer lies around us
once again. How long life is, how many
more of these seasons must I see, hydrangea
& the fat rhododendron sullen on the
neighbour's lawn. & I must rise, stick
fluid in mouth, stick beaten vegetables
into my living daughter's mouth, shit, it comes
& goes, it goes, thru us pretending we are
10 not some more, shit, the wearisome sun
& the sad motes in its visitations envelop
my mind even when it is thinking action
& when it thinks offers impatience with this
boring reappearance of the grass.

II

          Must I
live longer year by year, watching from this
small mountain the heavier pall of sludge
residing over this city & the yet discernible
waterways of bygone sea manoeuvres, my baby
breathing under that? Every midnight, every
20 winter, removing familiar clothes & taking
others more familiar to my bed of habit?

III

What nature gave me at my birth no more
than this, a prospectus of recurring faces, old
leaves appear above ground, old words grow
to surround them, old fingers join to pull
them & cast them to their home.

IV

The grass needs cutting, part of it
is yellow, it is dying of starvation, hell
it will be back next year, somewhere
30 else, & so will we, will we? Will

we endure that? The Pacific winter remembered more fondly than it is, some
unconvincing refuge of the life-giving
horror felt in the knives of Quebec December.
We congratulate each other for the snowy
re-emergence of the mountains, our mountains
we say with fancy dinners at the top
& hydroelectric sticks poking up the
slopes, our mountains re-emerging from our
40 papermaking smoke, our mountains showing up
each year with their peaks capt, silent
& gentle, the air restful over them, the sea
content to lie beneath them, not looking
for any entrance to that stilled heart.

V

It is slowly dying, but so slowly, the
earthquake belt is forty miles west, the sea
deterred by that long island. Every summer's
pollen mixt with more haze. We come
back here to partake of slow death, the dying
50 ocean so lifelike, harder to beat down than some
great lake. The mountains once promist me
a rapid death, fall is a fall, to the
rocks below—but the mountains are somebody's back yard, hydrangea bushes all round.

VI

I haven't heard a timely utterance for a
long time, there we are, hung on those
hands, watching & watching, & will they
never move? We seek out ways of death,
but slowly, or given minimal expectation, why
60 do I climb those stairs every morning?
To visit her, lift her eighteen pounds, &
clean her, more of it she'll pass & never
recall, to bring her downstairs for more,
of the same. Some will say that is reason
enough. Few will say enough of reason. It's
not reason I seek upstairs, we ought to be
past that, it's legs take us up there, legs
more tired every season. She makes utterances
we measure her time by.

VII

70 Sunday, I & Thea were there when Angela
woke up. So I'm back, she said, &
reacht to touch her baby's fuzzy head. Why,
where you been, I ask her.

I went on a car ride with a Fairie,
name of Mab.

What did she tell you?

She said things are going to get better.

VIII

I am slowly dying, water evaporating
from a saucer. I saw my daughter this
80 morning, trying to walk, & it fell like a vial
of melted lead into my heart, my heart so
deep in my chest. She will have to do it now,
we have presented her with a world,
whose spectres take shapes before her eyes
have fully focust, poor voyager! For joy
she brings us every morning we exchange
an accelerating series of shocks. We are together
cannibals of her spirit, we feast to nurture
our tired bodies, turning music to shit, a shock
90 felt numbly here & radiating to collisions
at the rim of space. You dont believe me?
See her eyes when first she wakes. A visible
tyrant of light yanks their traces, demanding
they stride apace.

IX

                    Then cannibal I will be—
her father. & I cant even teach her love,
but loose the horses, let a ghost ride &
call him loving, turn her away finally &
soothe her with a merry-go-round. That music
100 will disgust her in time, it rings & rings,
& I will instruct her of gold & gold
bedevillings, I will toil to win her trust,
& we will fall where we will rust
& watch the golden horses prancing by.

X

So fall will come
& winter too,
& she will wear
her first tight shoe

& she will wear
110 the seasons round
& watch the summers
wear me down.

XI

Thea, never read my lines, love your mother,
love your father, distrust circles, reach
this way & that. Remember how you can
the afternoon a bird came to sit at your shoulder
& let me remember how I dropt my game
to fly to your side, protecting your eyes.
Accept no promise from the mountains.
120 I have never seen your face before, & when
I leave you I will leave you time.
Forgive me the light that fades not fast away,
forgive me the continuous feast
we make from your remembered day.

[1976]

· JOHN NEWLOVE ·

1938–

Born in Regina, John Herbert New-love was raised in a number of farming communities in eastern Saskatchewan where his mother was employed as a schoolteacher. He left the Prairies in 1960 and held a variety of jobs from Vancouver to the Maritimes, including positions as senior editor at McClelland and Stewart (1970–74) and writer-in-residence at various institutions. He returned to Regina to become the city's writer-in-residence in 1979–80 and lived there until he moved in 1983 to his current residence in Nelson, British Columbia. Newlove has published widely internationally and was the recipient of a Governor General's Award for his *Lies* (1972).

One of a group of young poets, including Margaret Atwood, George Bowering, Dennis Lee, and Alden Nowlan, who first came into prominence in the 1960s, Newlove is distinguished by his compassion for the sufferings of everyday people and by his highly individualistic and meticulously crafted style. Since his first book, *Grave Sirs* (1962), his central concern has been the conflict between desire and reality, a preoccupation that has often led to the polarities of love/hate, hope/despair, triumph/loss, and national identity/personal alienation in his work. In any such confrontation, a disillusioning reality is inevitably the victor, but the poetry is saved from unmitigated gloom by Newlove's startling use of direct statement, sharp irony, and elegant prosody, even in the face of absolute darkness or desolation.

The bulk of Newlove's poetry is personal and immediate, effects achieved through his manipulation of the first person and his rejection of simile and ornate description. As a result the reader feels as if he or she is there, or has been there, and for this reason it is difficult to leave a Newlove poem without feeling in some way touched or disturbed. Misled by the apparent simplicity of statement, early commentators assumed that the poetry was strictly autobiographical: that is to say, lacking entirely in metaphor or symbol. Although the poems are no doubt rooted in Newlove's own personal experience, his first-person poet is also a persona of modern humankind. The road, for instance, in "The Flowers" may be taken as a metaphor of life; the young man in "The Hitchhiker" might be seen as a symbol of twentieth-century rootlessness. The richness of Newlove's simplicity lies in his ability to reflect what it is like to be human in a rapidly changing society which has been cut off from both its past and its contact with the land.

From the beginning reviewers and anthologists fixed on the "dark strain" in Newlove's poetry in spite of his broad range and mastery of different techniques. Newlove has now come to be accepted as the first important prairie poet, a poet interested in integrating the moral meaning and the history of the land into the Canadian psyche in an attempt to heal such twentieth-century diseases as alienation and despair. Newlove would have us become indigenous through an acceptance of our native people's past rather than continue as listless immigrants in a cold, impersonal present; in "The Pride" and "Samuel Hearne in Wintertime" he reminds us of these heroic roots. Newlove's range also includes sensitive, probing love lyrics; poems such as "That There Is No Relaxation" about the difficulty of writing poetry; and free-wheeling, humorous poetic letters, usually written in a longer form—a characteristic of his more optimistic verse—and with a looser line than the sparely written, terse poems that are his trademark. When Newlove's imagination is unfettered by a harsh reality, the poetry sometimes takes on a surreal quality, as in some of his dream poems, and an ethereal texture, as in *The Green Plain* (first published with John Metcalf's "Girl in Gingham" in *Dreams Surround Us*, 1977; then reprinted by itself in 1981). *The Green Plain* marks a departure for Newlove in its wholesome celebration of the beauty of life; it is as though the poet has finally made it out of the hell of experience to an Eden-like paradise—not an innocence that has been lost, but rather one that has been regained (as Newlove would have us regain the roots of a native past). The liberal use of white space in this long poem focuses our attention on the highly visual as well as the aural qualities of Newlove's work.

·——————·

Newlove's works include *Grave Sirs* (1962); *Elephants, Mothers & Others* (1963); *Moving in Alone* (1965); *Notebook Pages* (1966); *What They Say* (1967);

Black Night Window (1968); *The Cave* (1970); *7 Disasters, 3 Theses, and Welcome Home. Click.* (1971); *Lies* (1972); *The Fat Man: Selected Poems 1962–1972* (1977); *Dreams Surround Us* [with John Metcalf] (1977); *The Green Plain* (1981); and *The Night the Dog Smiled* (1986). Newlove has edited *Dream Craters* [by Joe Rosenblatt] (1974); *The Collected Poems of Earle Birney* (1975); *Canadian Poetry: The Modern Era* (1977); and *The Collected Poems of F. R. Scott* (1981).

Works on Newlove include Jan Bartley, "Something in Which to Believe for Once: The Poetry of John Newlove," *Brave New Wave*, ed. Jack David (1978) 196–208; Douglas Barbour, "John Newlove: More Than Just Honest Despair; Some Further Approaches," *RePlacing*, ed. Dennis Cooley (1980) 256–80; Jan Bartley, "An Interview with John Newlove," *Essays on Canadian Writing* 23 (1982): 135–56; and Robert Lecker and David O'Rourke, "John Newlove: An Annotated Bibliography," *The Annotated Bibliography of Canada's Major Authors*, ed. Robert Lecker and Jack David (1985), 6: 67–128.

DAVID O'ROURKE

THE FLOWERS

It is raining, rain
streaks down the window to my left,
cars sluice water in the gutters
in the night, the round
neon clock-containing sign
hanging outside beside my window
sways in the wind and buzzes.

The flowers sprout everywhere,
in pots and boxes, on lawns

10 and trees, in gardens and ditches
the flowers are growing; the wet
wind will nourish them, cut
some down but feed the rest.

The sign crackles
and swings on its bar,
iron bar; the cars go by
all the night. They cut
a momentary trail and mark,
disappearing, on the wet
20 black pavement. The cars go by,
the police in their cars
prowl restlessly
up and down the rainy avenue
looking for interlopers, anyone
afoot at night in the rain,
the blue and dangerous
gun-hipped cops.

The car came smashing
and wrecking his face, his head,
30 poor hit hurt head
bleeding on the roadway
and in the cool hospital
night in bandages
and glued-on tape.

His eyes, they said,
were soft and easy
years ago. Now
he wears them cleverly
like some secret
40 coupled badge,
twin and original, dark
ice eyes that watch and assess
slowly what they have
fixed
on; his head does not move.

In the hospitals
with antiseptic nurses
stripping him, knife-
fisted surgeons bending down,

50 they cut, irony,
   to save his life; and he stayed
   days and years filled
   with tantalizing drugs, interminable
   dreams, tangled in bandages and
   shocks, suspicions, a nonchalant
   profusion of hopes and cures,
   surrounded by the tears
   of his rainy crazy peers.

   Rain, wind, and spring, all things
60 drove him crazy and grow
   flowers, flowers
   that dance in the rain,
   the bulging flowers that grew
   in his head, plants
   of evil or god, some
   holy epileptic angel, bloated
   inhuman flowers shining
   their bright colours
   insistently, turning
70 slowly in the wind
   and spring, tortuous
   creaking growths, thick
   cancerous things
   in the rain, stems
   like the barrels of rifles,
   fat lead bullet roots
   gripping the damp earth.

   And the cars
   pass up and down
80 the streets, disappearing
   trails, the blue police
   pass, coughing
   behind their leathery fists,
   guns dangling
   from their hips, eyes
   watching. My flowery clock
   buzzes and mutters,
   typewriter taps
   like the rain. I breathe
90 as harshly as the wind.

   [1965]

SAMUEL HEARNE IN WINTERTIME

1.

In this cold room
I remember the smell of manure
on men's heavy clothes as good,
the smell of horses.

It is a romantic world
to readers of journeys
to the Northern Ocean—

especially if their houses are heated
to some degree, Samuel.

10 Hearne, your camp must have smelled
like hell whenever you settled down
for a few days of rest and journal-work:

hell smeared with human manure,
hell half-full of raw hides,
hell of sweat, Indians, stale fat,
meat-hell, fear-hell, hell of cold.

2.

One child is back from the doctor's while
the other one wanders about in dirty pants
and I think of Samuel Hearne and the land—

20 puffy children coughing as I think,
crying, sick-faced,
vomit stirring in grey blankets
from room to room.

It is Christmastime—
the cold flesh shines.
No praise in merely enduring.

3.

Samuel Hearne did more
in the land (like all the rest

full of rocks and hilly country,
30 many very extensive tracts of land,
tittimeg, pike and barble,

and the islands:
the islands, many
of them abound

as well as the main
land does
with dwarf woods,

chiefly pine
in some parts intermixed
40 with larch and birch) than endure.

The Indians killed twelve deer.
It was impossible to describe
the intenseness of the cold.

4.

And, Samuel Hearne,
I have almost begun to talk

as if you wanted to be
gallant, as if you went
through that land for a book—

as if you were not SAM, wanting
50 to know, to do a job.

5.

There was that Eskimo girl
at Bloody Falls, at your feet,

Samuel Hearne, with two spears in her,
you helpless before your helpers,

and she twisted about them like
an eel, dying, never to know.

[1966]

CRAZY RIEL

Time to write a poem
or something.
Fill up a page.
The creature noise.
Huge massed forces of men
hating each other.
What young men do not know.
To keep quiet,
contemporaneously.
10 Contempt. The robin diligently
on the lawn sucks up worms,
hopping from one to another.
Youthfully. Sixteen miles
from my boyhood home
the frogs sit in the grassy marsh
that looks like a golf course
by the lake. Green frogs.
Boys catch them for bait or sale.
Or caught them. Time.
20 To fill up a page.
To fill up a hole.
To make things feel better. Noise.
The noise of the images
that are people I will never understand.
Admire them though I may.

Poundmaker. Big Bear. Wandering Spirit,
those miserable men.
Riel. Crazy Riel. Riel hanged.
Politics must have its way.

30 The way of noise. To fill up.
The definitions bullets make,
and field guns.

The noise your dying makes,
to which you are the only listener.
The noise the frogs hesitate
to make as the metal hook
breaks through the skin
and slides smoothly into place
in the jaw. The noise
40 the fish makes caught in the jaw,
which is only an operation
of the body and the element,
which a stone would make
thrown in the same water, thrashing,
not its voice.
The lake is not displaced
with one less jackfish body.
In the slough that looks like a golf course
the family of frogs sings. Metal throats.
50 The images of death hang upside-down.
Grey music.
It is only the listening for death,
fingering the paraphernalia,
the noise of the men you admire.
And cannot understand.
Knowing little enough about them.
The knowledge waxing.
The wax that paves hell's road,
slippery as the road to heaven.
60 So that as a man slips
he might as easily slide
into being a saint as destroyer.
In his ears the noise magnifies.
He forgets men.

[1968]

DRIVING

You never say anything in your letters. You say,
I drove all night long through the snow
in someone else's car
and the heater wouldn't work and I nearly froze.
But I know that. I live in this country too.
I know how beautiful it is at night
with the white snow banked in the moonlight.

Around black trees and tangled bushes,
how lonely and lovely that driving is,
how deadly. You become the country.
You are by yourself in that channel of snow
and pines and pines,
whether the pines and snow flow backwards smoothly,
whether you drive or you stop or you walk or you sit.

This land waits. It watches. How beautifully desolate
our country is, out of the snug cities,
and how it fits a human. You say you drove.
It doesn't matter to me.
All I can see is the silent cold car gliding,
walled in, your face smooth, your mind empty,
cold foot on the pedal, cold hands on the wheel.

[1977]

THE GREEN PLAIN

Small human figures and fanciful monsters
abound. Dreams surround us,
preserve us. We praise constancy as brave,
but variation's lovelier.

Rain surrounds us, arguments and dreams, there are
forests between us, there are
too many of us for comfort, always were.

                                        Is civilization
        only a lack of room, only
10   an ant-heap at last?—the strutting cities
        of the East, battered gold,
        the crammed walls of India,
        humanity swarming, indistinguishable
                                from the earth?

        Even the nomads roaming the green plain, for them
        at last no land was ever enough.

        Spreading—but now we can go anywhere
                                and we are afraid
        and talk of small farms instead of the stars
20   and all the places we go
        space is distorted.

        How shall we save the symmetry of the universe?—
        or our own symmetry, which is the same.

                                Which myths
        should capture us, since we do not wish
        to be opened, to be complete?—
        or are they all the same, all of them?

        Now a dream involves me, of a giant sprawled among stars,
        face to the dark, his eyes closed.
30   Common.

        Only he is not breathing, he does not heave.
        Is it Gulliver?—huge, image of us, tied, webbed in,
        and never learning anything,

                                always ignorant,
        always amazed, always capable of delight,
        and giving it, though ending in hatred, but
        an image only. Of disaster. But there is no disaster.
        It is just that we lose joy and die.

        But is there a symmetry?
40   Is there reason
        in the galaxies—Or is this all glass,
        a block bubbled in a fire, accident only,
        prettiness fused without care, pettiness,
        though some logic, alien but understandable,
        in the ruined crystal?

The forests, the forests, swaying,
there is no reason why they should be beautiful.
They live for their own reasons, not ours.
But they are.

50 It is not time that flows but the world.

And the world flows,
still flows. Even in these worn-out days,
worn-out terms,
once in a while our poets
must
speak

of Spring! Of all things! The flowers
blow in their faces too, and they smell perfumes,
and they are seduced
60 by colour—rural as the hairy crocus or urban as a waxy tulip.

But confusion. The world
flows past. It is hard to remember age. Does
this always world flow? Does it? Please say it does,
not time.
Do not say time flows.
Say: We do. Say: We live.

Fly-speck, fly-speck. In this ever island Earth
we are the tiny giants, swaggering
behind the dinosaurs, lovely,
70 tame brontosaurus, sweet cows lumbering
among the coal trees, fronds offering
shade and future fuel.

And the land around us green and happy,
waiting as you wait for a killer to spring,
a full-sized blur,
waiting like a tree in southern Saskatchewan,
remarked on, lonely and famous as a saint.

The mechanisms by which the stars generate invention
live all over and around us
80 and yet we refine machines, defer
to tricks as discovery. Everything is always here,
and burning.

There are no surprises, there is only
what is left. We live
inside the stars,

burning, burning,

the mechanisms.

Stars, rain, forests.
Stars rain forests.
90 Sew up the lives together. There is
this only world. Thank God: this World
and its wrapped variations
spreading around and happy, flowing,
flowing through the climate of intelligence,
beautiful confusion looking around,
seeing the mechanics and the clouds
and marvelling, O Memory...

[1977]

THE PERMANENT TOURIST
COMES HOME

1.

To the oppressed
nothing is left but song,
which the rich will adopt in a more melodious form.
Even your voice will be stolen from you
and the rhythm of your chains will be modulated
by choirs of celestial beings—which is necessary:
okay, okay, obey,
since your only function is to die.

2.

Speak.
Speak. But be careful of making moulds
which the spiritually illiterate
can fill up with gumbo.

3.

Guarded and guided,
the fact before hypothesis: early morning,
somewhere in the time
that I was, this simple apparition—
my small mother, orange flannel nightgown,
early light. Wee Willie Winkie, her finger
to her lips, walks in slow motion
on her delicate ankles,
sibilant, saying Shh, shh,
Father's dead.

4.

I wake up
and sit on the edge of the bed.
You sparrow, mother, you beautiful sparrow.

5.

I love you. Father is not dead.
Time is dead. There is a scoop in time
whatever self my self is
returns to every time, my grey sweet mother.

6.

Well, to die in the Spring
and be buried in the muck
seems reasonable. Enough
of this. The mountains are bright tonight
outside my window, and passing by.
Awkwardly, I am in love again.

[1983]

· MARGARET ATWOOD ·

1939–

Margaret Eleanor Atwood was born on 18 November 1939, in Ottawa, to Carl Edmund Atwood, a professional entomologist, and Margaret (Killam) Atwood. She received her B.A. from Victoria College, University of Toronto, in 1961. In the same year her first collection of poems, *Double Perse-phone*, was published and was awarded the E. J. Pratt medal. She received her M.A. from Radcliffe College, Harvard, in 1962. In 1967 her first full-length book of poems, *The Circle Game*, won a Governor General's Award. She received a D.Litt. from Trent University in 1973, and an LL.D. from Queen's University in 1974. She was awarded the Bess Hopkins Prize by Poetry (Chicago) in 1974, the City of Toronto Book Award in 1976, and the Radcliffe Medal in 1980. She is an active member of the Writers' Union of Canada, of Amnesty International, and of the Canadian Civil Liberties Association. She lives in Toronto with novelist Graeme Gibson and a daughter, Jess, born to them in 1976.

Margaret Atwood is one of the first generation of Canadian poets who learned how to write poetry not only from British classics, traditional and modern, and from American models, but also from an established body of Canadian poetry. The poets writing in Canada immediately before her and around her had produced and were producing a poetry of virtuoso skill and variety. The precocious speed with which she found her own poetic voice and range is attributable in part to the fact that she began to write in an already flourishing community of poets.

The genre in which she habitually writes is the reflective lyric, sometimes extended to a series, as in "Trainride, Vienna-Bonn," sometimes dramatized in a sequence of mask lyrics, as in *The Journals of Susanna Moodie* (1970),

sometimes focused in a lyric of crisis or predicament with a slight narrative base, as in "Progressive Insanities of a Pioneer." In choosing this genre, she places herself centrally in the modernist tradition stemming from T. S. Eliot, whose influence is pervasive in her early work, rather than in the American imagist tradition.

Her early poems are often sinister and Gothic in their fictions, though her interest in classical mythology—often treated ironically, as in "The Sybil"—is apparent as early as in *Double Persephone*, her first brief collection. She also had at hand two new sources of narrative and imagery: documentary Canadian literature, brilliantly exploited in the Susanna Moodie poems, from which "Departure from the Bush" is taken; and North American Indian myths and motifs, used, for example, in "Totems," from the brief series "Some Objects of Wood and Stone." She shares with her contemporaries a concern with language and its conventions, and an uneasiness about its ability to render the real; an interest in the coercive power of fictions; and a preoccupation with the moral question of how to live in a world in which the history of human occupation has been overwhelmingly destructive. "Progressive Insanities of a Pioneer" is a brilliant expression of a wide range of attitudes toward the imposition of human conventions on the natural world, expressed in a fiction which is vividly present to Margaret Atwood, as a poet in a land as newly settled as Canada. Her apprehension of the catastrophic, if piecemeal, transformation of the wilderness by human settlement is modified by her strong sense of the closeness of the archaic, and the omnipresence of wild nature. This double sense is finely balanced in "Departure from the Bush," from the Susanna Moodie poems. The poet's uneasiness, pervasive in her poetry, about her own complicity in the destructiveness of the human presence, is poignantly expressed in the poem series "Trainride, Vienna-Bonn." She is contemporary, too, in her preference for irony over lyrical intensity. "There is Only One of Everything," with its nuances of praise and its tenuous sense of wonder, is as close as her poems come to lyrical affirmation.

Margaret Atwood's poetic works include *Double Persephone* (1961); *The Circle Game* (1966); *The Animals in That Country* (1968); *The Journals of Susanna Moodie* (1970); *Procedures for Underground* (1970); *Power Politics* (1971); *You Are Happy* (1974); *Selected Poems* (1976); *Two-Headed Poems* (1978); *True Stories* (1981); and *Interlunar* (1984).

Margaret Atwood's fiction includes *The Edible Woman* (1969); *Surfacing* (1972); *Lady Oracle* (1976); *Life Before Man* (1979); *Dancing Girls* (1977); *Bodily Harm* (1981); *Bluebeard's Egg* (1983); and *The Handmaid's Tale* (1985).

Works on Atwood include Gloria Onley, "Power Politics in Bluebeard's Castle," *Canadian Literature* 60 (1974): 21–42; Frank Davey, "Atwood's Gorgon Touch," *Studies in Canadian Literature* 2 (1977): 146–63; Eli Mandel, "Atwood Gothic," *Another Time* (1977); 137–45; Alan J. Horne, "Margaret Atwood: An Annotated Bibliography," *The Annotated Bibliography of Canada's Major Authors*, ed. Robert Lecker and Jack David (1980) 2: 13–54; Arnold E. Davidson and Cathy E. Davidson (ed.), *The Art of Margaret Atwood: Essays in Criticism* (1981); Frank Davey, *Margaret Atwood: A Feminist Poetics* (1984); and Jean Mallinson, "Margaret Atwood," *Canadian Writers and Their Works*, ed. Robert Lecker, Jack David, and Ellen Quigley (1985), Poetry Series 9: 17–81.

JEAN MALLINSON

THIS IS A PHOTOGRAPH OF ME

It was taken some time ago.
At first it seems to be
a smeared
print: blurred lines and grey flecks
blended with the paper;

then, as you scan
it, you see in the left-hand corner
a thing that is like a branch: part of a tree
(balsam or spruce) emerging
and, to the right, halfway up
what ought to be a gentle
slope, a small frame house.

In the background there is a lake,
and beyond that, some low hills.

(The photograph was taken
the day after I drowned.

I am in the lake, in the center
of the picture, just under the surface.

It is difficult to say where
precisely, or to say
how large or small I am:
the effect of water
on light is a distortion

but if you look long enough,
eventually
you will be able to see me.)

[1965]

THE ANIMALS IN THAT COUNTRY

In that country the animals
have the faces of people:

the ceremonial
cats possessing the streets

the fox run
politely to earth, the huntsmen
standing around him, fixed
in their tapestry of manners

the bull, embroidered
with blood and given
an elegant death, trumpets, his name
stamped on him, heraldic brand
because

(when he rolled
on the sand, sword in his heart, the teeth
in his blue mouth were human)

he is really a man

even the wolves, holding resonant
conversations in their
forests thickened with legend.

> In this country the animals
> have the faces of
> animals.
>
> Their eyes
> flash once in car headlights
> and are gone.
>
> Their deaths are not elegant.
>
> They have the faces of
> no-one.

[1967]

PROGRESSIVE INSANITIES OF A PIONEER

i

He stood, a point
on a sheet of green paper
proclaiming himself the centre,

with no walls, no borders
anywhere; the sky no height
above him, totally un-
enclosed
and shouted:

Let me out!

ii

10 He dug the soil in rows,
   imposed himself with shovels
   He asserted
   into the furrows, I
   am not random.

   The ground
   replied with aphorisms:

   a tree-sprout, a nameless
   weed, words
   he couldn't understand.

iii

20 The house pitched
   the plot staked
   in the middle of nowhere.

   At night the mind
   inside, in the middle
   of nowhere.

   The idea of an animal
   patters across the roof.

   In the darkness the fields
   defend themselves with fences
30 in vain:
         everything
         is getting in.

iv

   By daylight he resisted.
   He said, disgusted
   with the swamp's clamourings and the outbursts
   of rocks,
         This is not order
   but the absence
   of order.

40 He was wrong, the unanswering
   forest implied:

      It was
      an ordered absence

  v

    For many years
    he fished for a great vision,
    dangling the hooks of sown
    roots under the surface
    of the shallow earth.

    It was like
50 enticing whales with a bent
    pin. Besides he thought

    in that country
    only the worms were biting.

  vi

    If he had known unstructured
    space is a deluge
    and stocked his log house-
    boat with all the animals

    even the wolves,

    he might have floated.

60 But obstinate he
    stated, The land is solid
    and stamped,

    watching his foot sink
    down through stone
    up to the knee.

vii

Things
refused to name themselves; refused
to let him name them.

The wolves hunted
70 outside.

On his beaches, his clearings,
by the surf of under-
growth breaking
at his feet, he foresaw
disintegration
              and in the end
through eyes
made ragged by his
effort, the tension
80 between subject and object,

the green
vision, the unnamed
whale invaded.

[1967]

DEPARTURE FROM THE BUSH

I, who had been erased
by fire, was crept in
upon by green
          (how
lucid a season)

      In time the animals
arrived to inhabit me,

first one
  by one, stealthily
(their habitual traces
burnt); then
having marked new boundaries
returning, more
confident, year
by year, two
by two

but restless: I was not ready
altogether to be moved into

They could tell I was
too heavy: I might
capsize;

I was frightened
by their eyes (green or
amber) glowing out from inside me

I was not completed; at night
I could not see without lanterns.

He wrote, We are leaving. I said
I have no clothes
left I can wear

The snow came. The sleigh was a relief;
its track lengthened behind,
pushing me towards the city

and rounding the first hill, I was
(instantaneous)
unlived in: they had gone.

There was something they almost taught me
I came away not having learned.

[1970]

THERE IS ONLY ONE OF
EVERYTHING

Not a tree but the tree
we saw, it will never exist, split by the wind
             and bending down
like that again. What will push out of the earth

later, making it summer, will not be
grass, leaves, repetition, there will
have to be other words. When my

eyes close language vanishes. The cat
with the divided face, half black half orange
nests in my scruffy fur coat, I drink tea,

fingers curved around the cup, impossible
to duplicate these flavours. The table
and freak plates glow softly, consuming themselves,

I look out at you and you occur
in this winter kitchen, random as trees or sentences,
entering me, fading like them, in time you will disappear

but the way you dance by yourself
on the tile floor to a worn song, flat and mournful,
so delighted, spoon waved in one hand, wisps of
             roughened hair

sticking up from your head, it's your surprised
body, pleasure I like. I can even say it,
though only once and it won't

last: I want this. I want
this.

[1973]

TRAINRIDE, VIENNA-BONN

i

It's those helmets we remember,
the shape of a splayed cranium,
and the faces under them,
ruthless & uniform

But these sit on the train
clean & sane, in their neutral
beige & cream: this girl smiles,
she wears a plastic butterfly, and the waiter gives
a purple egg to my child
10 for fun. Kindness abounds.

ii

Outside the windows the trees flow
past in a tender mist,
lightgreen & moist with buds

What I see though is the black trunks,
a detail from Breughel:
the backs of three men returning
from the hunt, their hounds following,
stark lines against the snow.

iii

The forest is no darker
20 than any forests, my own
included, the fields we pass
could be my fields; except
for what the eye puts there.

In this field there is a man
running, and three others, chasing,
their brown coats
flapping against their boots.

Among the tree roots the running man
stumbles and is thrown
30 face down and stays there.

iv

What holds me
in the story we've all heard
so many times before:

the few who resisted,
who did not do what they were told.

This is the old fear:
not what can be done to you
but what you might do
yourself, or fail to.

40 This is the old torture.

v

Three men in dark archaic
coats, their backs to me, returning
home to food and a good fire,
joking together, their hounds following.

This forest is alien
to me, closer than skin,
unknown, something early
as caves and buried, hard,

a chipped stone knife, the
50 long bone lying in darkness
inside my right arm: not
innocent but latent.

[1981]

· DAPHNE MARLATT ·

1942–

Born in Australia, Daphne Buckle Marlatt spent her childhood in Malaysia and then travelled through England on her way to Vancouver, where her family immigrated in 1951. She entered the University of British Columbia in 1960; here her poetics developed in association with the West Coast "Tish" group. She studied with the influential critic Warren Tallman, with the US poet Robert Creeley, and, during the 1963 Vancouver Poetry Conference, with another Black Mountain poet, Charles Olson. Robert Duncan was another formative influence. In a fiction-writing class with Earle Birney, she wrote her first work to be published, a novella, "The Sea Haven." During the early sixties, Marlatt received both the Brissenden and the Macmillan Award for writing.

In 1964 Marlatt moved to Bloomington, Indiana, where she completed her master's thesis, a translation of the French writer Francis Ponge's *Le Parti pris des choses*. Here she wrote *Frames* (1968), a return in poetry and prose to one of "her own sources," the Hans Christian Andersen fairy tale "The Snow Queen." This was followed by the spare, short-line poems like "so cocksure" collected in *leaf leaf's*, her "poetic apprenticeship." These books initiated Marlatt's attentiveness to language, and her interest in problems of narrative. While her early writing moved between short- and long-lined compositions, increasingly her lines expanded into poetic prose.

Reviews of and interviews with Marlatt point to her association with Olson's phenomenological poetics of "proprioception" where bodily perception is central. Her work emphasizes sexual difference in writing, and insists on the gender-specific nature of consciousness within a patriarchal culture.

Marlatt's interest in the work of women writers is reflected in her early reviews of Anais Nin and H.D., and her delight in Gertrude Stein.

Throughout the 1970s Marlatt reveals a growing interest in feminist politics and poetics. *What Matters: Writings 1968–70* (1980) uses the journal, a traditionally female narrative form, as well as poems, to explore the consciousness of a young woman writer and mother in lines "as tense, as double-edged, as being felt." A serial, long-line poem, "Rings," included in the current collection, re-enacts in writing the experiences of pregnancy and birth. In "broke," one of the sections of *our lives* (1975), Marlatt juxtaposes the experience of "breaking" childhood with the deprivation of the unemployed. Of women's oppression, she writes: "since we do half the dying, we ought to do half the living, some woman said." *The Story, She Said* (1977) is a collaborative twin narrative which documents a trip she took with seven other writers. The title insists on the voice of the writer as gendered; the structure of the narrative implies a split subject. "Seeing your world from the outside" suggests how woman is marginalized and made invisible in both public space and popular discourse. By appropriating and subverting song lyrics and street graffiti, Marlatt celebrates the chorus of women writers who "refuse to keep in all that silence."

A number of Marlatt's books on travel or immigration focus on what it means to be "other." Her own immigrant experience created "a perfect seedbed for the writing sensibility. If you don't belong, you can *imagine* you belong and you can construct in writing a world where you do belong." "Imagine: a town" opens her long poem *Steveston* (1974) and invites the reader into a textual landscape where "a language rush imitates a river in flood moving out to sea," giving voice to the everyday lives of Vancouver's Japanese-Canadian fishing community. *Zocalo* (1977), her first long prose book, is a fictional retelling of a Mexican trip she took with a lover, written in an associative embodied language which explores cultural and gender difference. The series of letters and poems in *In the Month of Hungry Ghosts* (1979) chronicles her return to the place of her childhood as "princess" in Malaysian colonial society. She writes of the contradictions she experienced: "Mostly it's a struggle, an old old resistance against the colonial empire of the mind. . . . How can I write of all this? What language, or what *structures* of language can carry this being here?" A trip to England documented in *How Hug a Stone* (1983) maps out a militarized "Thatcherized" landscape where a picturesque language runs parallel to a catalogue of nuclear double-talk in "delphiniums blue and geraniums red."

A meeting with Quebec's Nicole Brossard in 1981 introduced Marlatt to French feminist theorizing about feminine narrative, woman's relation to language, female subjectivity, and female desire in writing. Her poetics and writing begin a dialogue with this theory. *Mauve* (1985), an interpretative translation and "reading" of a text by Nicole Brossard, illustrates this fruitful exchange. The reader can trace the development of Marlatt's interest in desire in "from somewhere," published in *here & there*. It alludes to the classical female storyteller, the weaver Minerva, who spins the text (from *texere*, to weave) embedding the etymological origin of "desire," ("to shine,") within the telling. With *Touch to My Tongue* (1984), a series of erotic lesbian love poems, Marlatt increasingly returns to etymology, an area explored years before in an undergraduate paper for Charles Olson. In the transformations and roots

of language she finds echoes and resonances through which a female voice can sound. "Hidden ground" reproduces in writing the erotic rhythms of the female body.

The female narrator in her *Ana Historic* awakes from a dream and asks the reader: "Who's there?" With her ear intelligent to the sensual detail of language, Marlatt pushes her reading of feminine narrative into history and examines "the cultural labyrinth of our inheritance, mother to daughter to mother. . . ."

· ———— ·

Marlatt's works include *Frames of a Story* (1968); *leaf leaf/s* (1969); *Rings* (1971); *Vancouver Poems* (1972); *Steveston* [with Robert Minden], (1974); *Our Lives* (1975, 1980); *Zocalo* (1977); *The Story, She Said* (1977); "In the Month of Hungry Ghosts," *The Capilano Review* (1979); *Net Work: Selected Writing* (1980); *What Matters: Writing 1968–1970* (1980): *here & there* (1981); *How Hug a Stone* (1983); *Touch to My Tongue* (1984); *Mauve* (1985); and *Ana Historic* (1988).

Works on Marlatt include Douglas Barbour, "The Phenomenological I: Daphne Marlatt's *Steveston*," "*Figures in a Ground: Canadian Essays on Modern Literature Collected in Honor of Sheila Watson*, ed. Diane Bessai and David Jackel (1978): 174–88; Robert Lecker, "Perceiving It as It Stands: Daphne Marlatt's Poetry," *Canadian Literature* 76 (1978): 56–67; George Bowering, "Given This Body: An Interview with Daphne Marlatt," *Open Letter* 4th ser. 3 (1979): 32–88; Fred Wah, introduction, *Net Work: Selected Writing* (1980); Christina Cole, "Daphne Marlatt as Penelope, Weaver of Words: A Feminist Reading of *Steveston*," *Open Letter* 6th ser. 1 (1985): 5–19; and Janice Williamson, "Speaking in and of Each Other: An Interview with Daphne Marlatt and Betsy Warland," *Fuse* 8.5 (1985): 25–29.

JANICE WILLIAMSON

SO COCKSURE

i

momentum

eventually of stars
runs down
hill,
      the shingle

back't us slippery
feet collide with dry
sky

ii

as simply
spoken out as even
its tongue
licks lights lightens its
hunger hole in
visible over

black water, branches

lie under
lined our
laughter his
half-expected
emergence from

iii

warm to
touch

iv

unspoken his
head of
stars stares
a head

that lie that eyes
suffice

that we shd kiss & make
up he sd before
driving to
sleep.

[1968]

IMAGINE: A TOWN

Imagine a town running
                (smoothly?
a town running before a fire
canneries burning
                (do you see the shadow of charred stilts
on cool water? do you see enigmatic chance standing
just under the beam?
                He said they were playing cards in the
Chinese mess hall, he said it was dark (a hall? a shack.
they were all, crowded together on top of each other.
He said somebody accidentally knocked the oil lamp over, off
the edge
        where stilts are standing, Over the edge of the
dyke a river pours, uncalled for, unending:
                                where chance lurks
fishlike, shadows the underside of pilings, calling up his hall
the bodies of men & fish corpse piled on top of each other (residue
time is, the delta) rot, an endless waste the trucks of production

grind to juice, driving thru
                smears, blood smears in the dark
dirt) this marshland silt no graveyard can exist in but water swills,
endlessly out of itself to the mouth
                                ringed with residue, where
chance flicks his tail & swims, thru

[1974]

SEEING YOUR WORLD FROM THE OUTSIDE

outside night, light
absence is whirling down. down the order of night, not upside, out—
alleyways, all ways the walls say no.

standing inside your world is
full of holes floating doors: "a scream is an appraisal," you.
apprised of what we see are messages off walls.

& let me read
the black tint under your eyes from banging your head all night,
against the wall of your own want. "salud! ladies of the night." who do
not win (*Express yourself*)

Do Not phone. Do Not move on to Go.

this game is rigged, because somebody has to be at the bottom, lottery
system, lots have to be at the bottom so somebody else comes out on
top. because everybody wants. & chance is the midnight bus with the
winning number: will it stop where you stop? is this the right spot? is
this a stop at all? stop.

the night is full of losers & empty buses, palisades of light adrift.
nosed in to the curb, some slight collision, lights still on, sits under
neon, nothing left to lose. black are the scrawls of want on the walls
that do not see us ("annie was here") to be lost ("take me home") in
want, o baby, "will you still feed me? will you still need me?"

black & white. & you. standing inside your world are photographing
doors or holes in the wall night pours thru. "a scream is an appraisal."
you. a scream is a refusal. we. refuse to keep in all that silence
pressing thru the walls o women, women who write

"because the night belongs to us"

[1980]

FROM SOMEWHERE

from somewhere downhill trumpet notes rise on the rustling air, up, in the scale of a story. river rushes out to view, out of the corner of an eye, not ever leaving. proceeding is how we go onward in the increasing movement of this current's push, off, push away from limits (instant definition of a riverbank), move meant or implied . . .

than what keeps this wasp returning to my typewriter, my hand's sweat here, some other type of meat, my yellow top some other flower? what draws, what moves us one way to return against the procession?

   crows, scare off the curious osprey. i scare her off her nest by swimming below, delight in the way she banks, she soars, tail feathers spread, screaming alarm at my insistent, my circling head.

   light desire, from shine we are caught by. every longing an attempt on the stars. starlike spread, 8 legs missing I, i can see the stump on her head, who suddenly insists herself upon this page: spider, spinner, finding a place to live, she spins it out of her, thru tiny passages secretes the silky thread she slings along air currents, floating herself to rest. her there here

          i would make here, as the sound of a trumpet announces his presence on the lake, his moving in music his boat takes him thru a circling body of water, as the sentence moves running in a returning body of language to rest.

   i cannot rest, visited by messengers who beat upstream against the rest. you particular, you moving by. i catch a glint, a flash of, the impossible re-run, return, as you slip by.

[1981]

DELPHINIUMS BLUE &
GERANIUMS RED

rose light in the blue, at eye level (where is the dormouse
curled?) their kitchen looks out on where it suffuses hayfield,
appletree, vegetable-garden hedge—day's amber, stilled &
stilling. watch fresh lettuce leaves, curled, disappear in the
spinner, watch a child, curled up in himself for comfort,
dreaming of blue. roselight makes of their kitchen unearthly
hue, seraphic even, in our vision blue, is a healing colour
even a bird will spring toward.

but i was blue with cold on the Didcot Platform in a wind
10 the intercity diesels roar on through. torn holes in attention.
out of nowhere we are near the source. a shallow brook
ripples by a few crosses at fords, a few stone walls for leaning
up against—the Thames, really? not that one. wellspring.
dayspring. home—when the walls come down, what kind
of source?

that was Old Bernie, she said, on his last legs waiting outside
surgery with his stick, "they're all full up in there"–refused
the chair she offered to fetch from the grocer's. no relief from
the blinking exit sign: alone & knowing it.

20 despite all this pulling together. Taunton, Weirfield. running
out on the hockey team blue with cold, "you can't be cold."
grown older, painting the open wound with iodine, "it
doesn't hurt, it's for your own good really." slogans on the
road to selfless, sightless in the guise of ought-to-be—
chrysanthemums, say, on the unclipped village graves. when
five-year-olds (are) *looting burned-out shops* "these days of career
marchers & young punks tearing up the streets. it's all me-me,
no sense of the common good, now have they?"

& if The Common Good, pointing its nineteenth century
30 hand, has tyrannized all sense of me, small voice essential
to life? so that we falls apart, gone mad at the mask of Reason
which still is quoting Good in the face of annihilation: tactical
advantage, counterforce capability, stockpiling. *the first few
weapons arriving do almost all the damage conceivable to the
fabric of the country.* have done so, without ever arriving, the
nest we live in full of holes these days.

& still: *i suppose all these people know better than i*—doubtful,
paws to eyes, small creature at the heart of dreaming some
blue otherwhere. *& that is the reason*, the story continues,
40 circling back to its source, the dormouse curls, imagining
delphiniums blue, o blue/black hole at centre, folding in on
itself.

[1983]

· MICHAEL ONDAATJE ·

1943–

Philip Michael Ondaatje was born on 12 September 1943 in Colombo, Sri Lanka. At the age of eleven he moved to London, England, then to Canada at the age of nineteen, where he enrolled in Bishop's University. He received his B.A. from the University of Toronto and his M.A. from Queen's University. (His thesis explored the mythical patterns in Edwin Muir's poetry.) He taught at the University of Western Ontario from 1967 to 1971, and at Glendon College, York University, since 1971. He has twice received the Governor General's Award for poetry: for *The Collected Works of Billy the Kid* (1970), and for *There's a Trick with a Knife I'm Learning to Do* (1979).

One cannot separate Michael Ondaatje the poet from Michael Ondaatje the novelist, photographer, and filmmaker; each of these roles invigorates and inspires the others. Even his earliest lyrics from *The Dainty Monsters* (1967) reveal the sensitivity to the physical world, the almost painfully clear imagery which we often find in film and still photography.

This overlapping of his interest in visual and linguistic forms of expression makes Ondaatje especially sensitive to the ability of the word and the camera alike to fix and capture experience. Many of his most powerful lyrics from *Rat Jelly* (1973) address precisely this tension—"Spider Blues," "King Kong Meets Wallace Stevens," and especially "The Gate in His Head." Others, such as "White Dwarfs," explore the relationship between words and silence. Both of these tensions—fixity and flux, the word and silence—are peculiarly post-modernist obsessions, and Ondaatje examines them at greater length in *The Collected Works of Billy the Kid* (a mélange of prose and poetry) and his imagistic novel *Coming Through Slaughter* (1976). The latter work is especially concerned with expression and silence; it is a fictionalized portrait of the early jazz master Buddy Bolden—an artist who was, significantly, never recorded. The conflict between chaos and order invades Buddy's story as well; his music is fluid, he breaks through windows (literally and metaphorically), and yet he is also "tormented by order."

These works, taken together, reveal Ondaatje's growing obsession with his art; images such as spiders' webs, stars, fences, and photographic frames all bespeak a fascination with the limitations that words impose upon experience by giving it a name and a form. Often, Ondaatje has even felt the need to abandon words altogether; he once commented that making his film about bpNichol, *Sons of Captain Poetry* (1970), provided him with a needed escape from the printed word after the completion of *The Collected Works of Billy the Kid*. Appropriately, Ondaatje chose a visual form in order to capture the essence of a primarily visual poet. Ondaatje has claimed that even in writing *The Collected Works of Billy the Kid* he was "trying to make the film I couldn't afford to shoot, in the form of a book."

Recently, Ondaatje's obsession with words and experience has led him to consider the ways we retell and thus reshape past experience. The later lyrics in *There's a Trick with a Knife I'm Learning to Do*, such as "Light," and "Uswetakeiyawa," signal Ondaatje's growing fascination with the world of his past—a fascination that was strengthened by his first trip back to Sri Lanka in 1978. In *Running in the Family*, a fictionalized memoir of his family, all of these obsessions converge. Instead of historical figures (Buddy Bolden, Billy the Kid), Ondaatje himself and his past become the material; fact is abandoned for truer fiction and words themselves are revealed as the precious and sometimes inadequate means by which we tell our own private fictions.

·———————·

Ondaatje's works include *The Dainty Monsters* (1967); *The Man with Seven Toes* (1969); *The Collected Works of Billy the Kid* (1970); *Sons of Captain Poetry* (film, 1970); *Rat Jelly* (1973); *The Clinton Special* (film, 1974); *Coming Through Slaughter* (1976); *Elimination Dance* (1978); *There's a Trick with a Knife I'm Learning to Do* (1979); *Tin Roof* (1982); *Running in the Family* (1982); *Secular Love* (1984); and *In the Skin of a Lion* (1987).

Works on Ondaatje include Sam Solecki, "Making and Destroying: Michael Ondaatje's *Coming Through Slaughter* and Extremist Art," *Essays on Canadian Writing* 12 (1978): 24–47; and "Nets and Chaos: The Poetry of Michael Ondaatje," *Brave New Wave*, ed. Jack David (1978); 24–50; Stephen Scobie, "*Coming Through Slaughter*: Fictional Magnets and Spider's Webbs," *Essays on Canadian Writing* 12 (1978): 5–23; and "His Legend a Jungle Sleep: Michael Ondaatje and Henri Rousseau," *Canadian Literature* 76 (1978): 6–21; Judith Brady, "Michael Ondaatje: An Annotated Bibliography," *The Annotated Bibliography of Canada's Major Authors*, ed. Robert Lecker and Jack David (1985), 6: 129–206; and Sam Solecki, ed., *Spider Blues* (1986).

LORRAINE YORK

KING KONG MEETS WALLACE STEVENS

Take two photographs—
Wallace Stevens and King Kong
(Is it significant that I eat bananas as I write this?)

Stevens is portly, benign, a white brush cut
striped tie. Businessman but
for the dark thick hands, the naked brain
the thought in him.

Kong is staggering
lost in New York streets again
a spawn of annoyed cars at his toes.
The mind is nowhere.
Fingers are plastic, electric under the skin.
He's at the call of Metro-Goldwyn-Mayer.

Meanwhile W.S. in his suit
is thinking chaos is thinking fences.
In his head—the seeds of fresh pain
his exorcising,
the bellow of locked blood.

The hands drain from his jacket,
pose in the murderer's shadow.

[1970]

WHITE DWARFS

This is for people who disappear
for those who descend into the code
and make their room a fridge for Superman
—who exhaust costume and bones that could perform flight,
who shave their moral so raw
they can tear themselves through the eye of a needle
this is for those people
that hover and hover
and die in the ether peripheries

10 There is my fear
of no words of
falling without words
over and over of
mouthing the silence
Why do I love most
among my heroes those
who sail to that perfect edge
where there is no social fuel
Release of sandbags
20 to understand their altitude—

            that silence of the third cross
3rd man hung so high and lonely
we don't hear him say
say his pain, say his unbrotherhood
What has he to do with the smell of ladies
can they eat off his skeleton of pain?

The Gurkhas in Malaya
cut the tongues of mules
so they were silent beasts of burden
30 in enemy territories
after such cruelty what could they speak of anyway
And Dashiell Hammett in success
suffered conversation and moved
to the perfect white between the words

This white that can grow
is fridge, bed,
is an egg—most beautiful
when unbroken, where
what we cannot see is growing
40 in all the colours we cannot see

there are those burned out stars
who implode into silence
after parading in the sky
after such choreography what would they wish to speak of   anyway

[1971]

THE GATE IN HIS HEAD
(for Victor Coleman)

Victor, the shy mind
revealing the faint scars
coloured strata of the brain,
not clarity but the sense of shift

a few lines, the tracks of thought

Landscape of busted trees
the melted tires in the sun
Stan's fishbowl
with a book inside
turning its pages
like some sea animal
camouflaging itself
the typeface clarity
going slow blonde in the sun full water

My mind is pouring chaos
in nets onto the page.
A blind lover, dont know
what I love till I write it out.
And then from Gibson's your letter
with a blurred photograph of a gull.
Caught vision. The stunning white bird
an unclear stir.

And that is all this writing should be then.
The beautiful formed things caught at the wrong moment
so they are shapeless, awkward
moving to the clear.

[1973]

THE CINNAMON PEELER

If I were a cinnamon peeler
I would ride your bed
and leave the yellow bark dust
on your pillow.

Your breasts and shoulders would reek
you could never walk through markets
without the profession of my fingers
floating over you. The blind would
stumble certain of whom they approached
10 though you might bathe
under rain gutters, monsoon.

Here on the upper thigh
at this smooth pasture
neighbour to your hair
or the crease
that cuts your back. This ankle.
You will be known among strangers
as the cinnamon peeler's wife.

I could hardly glance at you
20 before marriage
never touch you
—your keen nosed mother, your rough brothers.
I buried my hands
in saffron, disguised them
over smoking tar,
helped the honey gatherers. . .

*

When we swam once
I touched you in water
and our bodies remained free,
30 you could hold me and be blind of smell.
You climbed the bank and said

          this is how you touch other women
the grass cutter's wife, the lime burner's daughter.
And you searched your arms
for the missing perfume
             and knew

          what good is it
to be the lime burner's daughter
left with no trace
40 as if not spoken to in the act of love
as if wounded without the pleasure of a scar.

        You touched
        your belly to my hands
        in the dry air and said
        I am the cinnamon
        peeler's wife. Smell me.

[1981]

· bpNichol ·

1944–

Barrie Phillip Nichol was born in Vancouver; his early life was spent there, and also in Winnipeg and Port Arthur. His father worked on the railway, and the trans-Canada rail journey is a recurring motif in Nichol's work. Since the mid-1960s, however, he has lived in Toronto. He worked for several years for the therapeutic community Therafields, and he also taught at York University. He won a Governor General's Award in 1971, and the Three-Day-Novel Award in 1982. In addition to his solo work as poet, novelist, critic, translator, and editor he has since 1970 been part of the performance group the Four Horsemen. He is a member of the editorial boards of *Open Letter* and Coach House Press.

Nichol is best known as an "experimental" poet, though he himself is unhappy with that word, preferring to speak of himself as doing "research," or as being an "apprentice to language." The avant-garde quality of his writing is most evident in his work as a concrete poet, both in visual and in sound poetry; but more fundamental is the very range and pervasiveness of his writing—which includes "trad" poetry, typewriter- or computer-generated visual poems, drawings, solo or group sound poems, short stories, novels, speculative or critical essays, collaborations with other poets, musicians, or visual artists, and conventional or "homolinguistic" translations. There is scarcely a conceivable form of literary activity that bpNichol has not touched, tried, and transformed.

Yet at the centre of this diversity is a firm commitment to the ideal of a human community, and the role of language in shaping and embodying that community. In the final sentence of "Two Words: A Wedding," Nichol says that "we are words and our mean-

ings change." To say that "we are words" is to insist on a deeply humanist identification between ourselves and the language that is our medium, and in which we are "wedded." At the same time, to say that "our meanings change" is to throw into doubt any certainty or assurance that we might have felt, to enter the flux and indeterminacy of language as it is conceived in contemporary theory. Nichol is deeply aware of post-structuralism (especially of Jacques Lacan's insistence that "the unconscious is structured as a language"), and much of his work is a stunning dramatization of such abstract concepts as free play and dissemination.

Nichol's visual work stems from the international concrete poetry movement of the 1960s, when he acquired an international reputation; his early visual poems are elegant, witty, and concise. In the 1970s, partly as a result of his collaboration with the other members of the Four Horsemen (Steve McCaffery, Paul Dutton, and Rafael Barreto-Rivera), he concentrated more on sound, working in a wide range between "abstract" vocal noise and complex multi-voiced texts. His great interest in and debt to Gertrude Stein is perhaps most visible in his prose fiction, especially in the intense, repetitive, and psychoanalytically obsessive *Journal* (1978).

At the centre of all Nichol's writing, however, is *The Martyrology*, a long "continuing" poem, sections of which have been published in 1972, 1976, 1977, 1982, and 1987. Starting from a simple word-game (the "canonization" of all words beginning with the letters st), *The Martyrology* has evolved an all-embracing structure, ranging from world mythology to Toronto streetnames; from the narrative of Nichol's personal life to the theoretical celebration of language. Not the least important aspect of the poem is the fact that it simply *does* go on: that it resists closure, that it projects a continuous, open-ended, metonymic accumulation, rather than a closed and perfected object.

· ———————— ·

Nichol's works include *Journeying & the returns* (1967); *Two Novels* (1969); *Still Water* (1970); *The Martyrology* (1971, 1976, 1977, 1982, 1987); *love: a book of remembrances* (1974); *Craft Dinner* (1978); *Journal* (1978); *Translating Translating Apollinaire* (1979); *As Elected: Selected Writing 1962-1979* (1980); *Still* (1983);

and *Zygal: A Book of Mysteries and Translations* (1985). Records by the Four Horsemen include *CaNADAda* (1972); and *Live in the West* (1977). Their performance scores were published as *The Prose Tattoo* (1982).

Works on Nichol include Jack David, "Writing Writing: bpNichol at 30," *Essays on Canadian Writing* 1 (1974): 37–48; Douglas Barbour, "bpNichol: The Life of Letters and the Letters of Life," *Essays on Canadian Writing* 9 (1977–78): 97–108; Brian Henderson, "Radical Poetics: Dada, bpNichol and the Horsemen," dissertation, York University, 1982; and Stephen Scobie, *bpNichol: What History Teaches* (1984).

STEPHEN SCOBIE

1335 COMOX AVENUE

in fall
we lose ourselves
in new rooms, gaze
from windows grown old
in that season

we choose
new beds
to love in, cover our bodies
in confusions
10 of all
that should be left
behind

bury our faces in each other
tasting flesh in mouth
gathering warmth
possessing each other
as a way of loving

we are too near the sea
we hear the gulls cry
20 cars pass
the horns of ships
and cry
to see the moss grown

throw windows open
to night   to kneel   to pray
hands on each other
pressing body into body
some sort of liturgy

hear the sea   the bells
30 the sound of people passing
voices drifting up
and cold winds come
to chill our naked hearts

love is some sort of fire
come to warm us
fill our bodies
all in these motions
flowing into each other
in despair   the room
40 one narrow world
that might be anywhere

[1963]

DADA LAMA

(to the memory of Hugo Ball)
1

hweeeee
hweeeee
hyonnnn
hyonnnn

hweeeee
hweeeee
hyonnnn
hyonnnn

tubadididdo
10 tubadididdo
hyon
hyon

tubadididdo
tubadididdo
hyon
hyon

ffffffffffffffffffffffftsssssssss
fffffffffffffffffffffffitsssssssss
ffffffffffffffffffffffflitsssssssss

hyonnnnnn
        unh

hyonnnnnn
20 unh

2

eeeeeeeeeeeeeeeeeeeeeeeeeee
EEEEEEEEEEEEEEEEEEEEEEEEEEE
eeeeeeeeeeeeeeeeeeeeeeeeeeee

EEEEEEEEEEEEEEEEEEEEEEEEEEE
eeeeeeeeeeeeeeeeeeeeeeeeeeee
EEEEEEEEEEEEEEEEEEEEEEEEEEEE

30 eeeeeeeeeeeeeeeeeeeeeeeeeee
EEEEEEEEEEEEEEEEEEEEEEEEEEEE
eeeeeeeeeeeeeeeeeeeeeeeeeeee

3

oudoo doan doanna
tinna limn limn
la leen
untloo lima
limna doo doo

dee du deena
deena dee du
40 deena deena
dee du deena

ah-ooo runtroo
lintle leave lipf
lat lina tanta
tlalum cheena
ran tron tra troo
deena dee du
deena deena
dee du deena
50 deena dee du

da dee di do du
deena
      deena

4

AAAAAAAAAAAAAAAAAAAAA
aaaaaaaaaaaaaaaaaaaaaaaaaa
AAAAAAAAAAAAAAAAAAAAA

aaaaaaaaaaaaaaaaaaaaaaaaaa
AAAAAAAAAAAAAAAAAAAAA
aaaaaaaaaaaaaaaaaaaaaaaaaa

60 AAAAAAAAAAAAAAAAAAAAA
aaaaaaaaaaaaaaaaaaaaaaaaaa
AAAAAAAAAAAAAAAAAAAAA

5

tlic
tloc

tlic tloc
tlic tloc

tlic tloc tlic
tloc tlic tloc

tlic tloc tlic tloc
70 tlic tloc tlic tloc

tlic tloc tlic tloc tlic
tloc tlic tloc tlic tloc

tlic tloc tlic tloc tlic tloc
tlic tloc tlic tloc tlic tloc

tlic tloc tlic tloc tlic
tloc tlic tloc tlic tloc

tlic tloc tlic tloc
tlic tloc tlic tloc

tlic tloc tlic
80 tloc tlic tloc

tlic tloc
tlic tloc

tlic
tloc

6

wwwwwwwwwwwwwwwwwwwwwwwww
mmmmmmmmmmmmmmmmmmmmmmmm
wwwwwwwwwwwwwwwwwwwwwwwww
mmmmmmmmmmmmmmmmmmmmmmmm

Wwwwwwwwwwwwwwwwwwwwwwww
90 Mmmmmmmmmmmmmmmmmmmmmmmm
Wwwwwwwwwwwwwwwwwwwwwwww
Mmmmmmmmmmmmmmmmmmmmmmmm

WWWWWWWWWWWWWWWWWWWWWWWWW
MMMMMMMMMMMMMMMMMMMMMMMM
WWWWWWWWWWWWWWWWWWWWWWWWW

OUOOOOOOOOOOOOOOOOOOOOOOOH
MMMMMMMMMMMMMMMMMMMMMMMM
OUOOOOOOOOOOOOOOOOOOOOOOOH
MMMMMMMMMMMMMMMMMMMMMMMM

100 FREEEEEEEEEEEEEEEEEEEEEEEE
EEEAAAAAAAAAAAAAAAAAAAAAAH
FREEEEEEEEEEEEEEEEEEEEEEEE
EEEAAAAAAAAAAAAAAAAAAAAAAH

FREEEEEEEEEEEEEEEEEEEEEEEE
DUMMMMMMMMMMMMMMMMMMMMMM
FREEEEEEEEEEEEEEEEEEEEEEEE
DUMMMMMMMMMMMMMMMMMMMMMM

[1965–66]

BLUES

[1967]

A SMALL SONG THAT IS HIS

adore adore
adore adore
an opening an o
an h a leg a table or
a window & a w
a sky that is d
a lake that is f
e

d e f
f f f f
d d
   e e e
d f f e f e
f e f e

me
you or me or
i h & d
m e
e f d
o

d f h e w

f

f e w h d

o

w d

f

[1974]

TWO WORDS: A WEDDING

for Rob & Sheron

There are things you have words for, things you do not
have words for. There are words that encompass all your
feelings & words that encompass none. There are feelings
you have that are like things to you, picked up &
placed in the pocket, worn like the cloth the pocket is
attached to, like a skin you live inside of. There is a body
of feeling, of language, of friends; the body politic, the
body we are carried inside of till birth, the body we carry
our self inside of till death, a body of knowledge that tells
of an afterlife, a heaven, an unknown everything we
have many words for but cannot encompass. There are
relationships between words & concepts, between
things, between life & death, between friends & family,
between each other & some other other. We wed words
to things, people to feelings, speak of a true wedding of
the mind & heart, intuition & intellect, & out of this form
our realities. Our realities are wedded one to another,
concepts & people are joined, new people conceived
within that mesh of flesh & realities, are carried forward
in the body of the mother, the family, the bodily love we
have for one another. They are creating their own reality
each step of the way, daily, another kind of reality is
born, each new word, person, expanding our vocabulary,
our concepts, new realities are conceived, our old reality
changes, the 'real' grows realer every day. We are
marrying the flesh to the flesh, the word to the daily flux
of lives we know & don't know, our friends grow older &
marry, raise children as you once were children with
mothers & fathers of your own, grow older, so many
things you still lack words for, struggle to wed the inner &
outer worlds, the self to some other self or selves, confess
your love & struggle with one another, together, conscious
there is this word is you, your name, & that you
are yet another thing or things you will never encompass,
never exhaust the possibilities of, because you are
wedded to the flux of life, because we are words and our
meanings change.

[1978]

· MARY DI MICHELE ·

1949–

Born in Italy, Mary di Michele immigrated to Canada with her family in 1955. She is a graduate of the University of Toronto, and the graduate program in English and creative writing at the University of Windsor, where she studied with Joyce Carol Oates. She has won several major awards, including the first prize for poetry in the CBC Literary Competition in 1980, and an Air Canada Writing Award in 1983. In addition to the books that she has written or edited, she has also worked as poetry editor for the magazines *Toronto Life* and *Poetry Toronto*. She was the writer-in-residence at the University of Toronto in 1985–86.

In "Born in August," one of the important early poems from her first book *Tree of August* (1978), di Michele traces elements of her biography and her personal understanding of history: "born Maria Luisa di Michele, / baptized at Santa Lucia / in an ancient town, Lanciano, the Abruzzi, / scarred by cruel claws / of war, the fangs of tyranny: / Austerlitz, Auschwitz, Hiroshima...." Many of her poems deal with her Italian heritage and her desire to resist certain elements, and embrace other elements, of the immigrant imagination. Di Michele often writes of love— of the various ways love is subverted by history, and the way love can at times transcend the barbarity of history. On the back of *Tree of August* she is described as a "would-be feminist, often self-dubbed a romantic-existentialist, really a victim and carrier of the disease of objectivity..." These concerns are also seen in her second collection, *Bread and Chocolate: Poems by Mary di Michele and Bronwen Wallace* (1980), where in several poems she confronts questions of sexual power and politics. "The Disgrace" is a particularly disquieting poem, full of ominous and sometimes violent images, as though the poet is attempting to exorcize a variety of personal demons.

Di Michele's poetic sensibilities are perhaps nowhere better seen than in the long poem "Mimosa." Like much of her other work, this poem is about the contrast between the Old World and the New World, and about the voices that compose these worlds. It is an attempt to fashion a sensitive understanding of the world in the midst of contradictory perspectives. Family, memory, poetry, guilt, the "geography of hearts"—these are the elements of this poem and of the other shorter poems in this volume. At times, di Michele's poems are emotional and almost unconscious responses to images or memories that seem to have troubled her for a long time. In other poems there is a sense of quietness and patience.

In her most recent poems, di Michele sharpens her understanding of relationships—between herself and various men, various women, and, perhaps most importantly, between herself and her daughter Emily. In the title poem from *Necessary Sugar* (1983), she talks about the difference between men, who build "cathedrals in an attempt / to sculpt light" and Emily, who is "the firefly / I collected between my legs." Di Michele is attentive to both the transience and the permanence of love, and the desire to hold on to some semblance of genuine passion and intelligence. She counsels Emily to "know yourself" and to try to live "intelligently"—statements that echo lines from an earlier poem where she says: "The problem of how to love intelligently / perplexes us." These are the things that di Michele tells herself in other poems in order to try to understand some of the arguments and questions that prey on the individual imagination. Di Michele does not search for definitive answers in her poems. Instead she tries to confront the misunderstanding and strangeness of the world. Love obsesses her, yet she says in several poems that she doesn't understand it, or what she can say about it. Robert Billings has said that di Michele's poems demonstrate a "persistent and sympathetic exploration of feeling." As she matures as a poet, she becomes more comfortable with questions than answers, with what she refers to as "intrigue" and "incongruity." Di Michele mixes meditation and anger in a way that is unique in contemporary poetry.

Di Michele's works include *Tree of August* (1978); *Bread and Chocolate: Poems by Mary di Michele and Bronwen Wallace* (1980); *Mimosa and Other Poems* (1981); *Necessary Sugar: Poems* (1983); and *Immune to Gravity* (1986). She has edited *Anything Is Possible: A Selection of Eleven Women Poets* (1984).

Works on di Michele include Rosemary Sullivan, "A Fine Anguish," *Waves* 10.1–2 (1981): 116–17; and Robert Billings, "Discovering the Sizes of the Heart: The Poems of Mary di Michele," *Essays on Canadian Writing* 27 (1983–84): 95–115.

PETER O'BRIEN

THE DISGRACE

But there's one disgrace we've never known:
we've never been women, we've never been nobodies
Cesare Pavese

A skinned rabbit sits in a bowl of blood.
In the foetal position, it dreams its own death,
I swell quietly by the warmth of the kitchen,
like the yolk that is the hidden sun of the egg.

The old wives and the new wives
are blabbering their gossip,
the intimate news of an idle moment.
Their children are blowing like seedclocks
in the yard. They are safe for now.
10 The girls are ready to be caught by the first
breeze and nestle in the grass.
Some of the boys will surely jump the fence.

On the first day I forget to play.
I am cramped in the corner like a snail
climbing the wall by the stove,
trying to sip camomile tea
with a blanket wrapped around my middle
to ease the first labour of blood.

My mother and aunts are eating
20 the unwritten stories of their lives
which they wipe away without a thought
and the crumbs on the table.

They all dine on the rabbit stew
together, good wives, good women, with an inch
of red wine in a glass and a carafe
brimming with secret desire.

This blood is anonymous and at times
gives off such a strong odour
that lettuce wilts in the hand,
30 and the new wine turns sour,
and onions cry in their sleeves.

My blood is knotted into worry beads.
Deliver me, if you can, from the cup
that I am, the spilling cup.

The ladies, *le signore*, are ready to tell their stories
as my mother serves coffee and cake.
When they crack the whip, out of their closet
mouths come dancing familiar skeletons:

uncle Gianni, who made his wife suffer (poor saint),
40 bringing in his mistress to live with the family,
her own room, for the slut, and the wife to play
the servant; he sent the children to school
with extra money for lunch, such a treat,
when their mouths were so tightly shut
they could not open them to bite,

Maria Luisa, my father's youngest sister,
went mad in her sleep,
she tried to kill the elder, Chiarina,
with a knife, she cut her own throat
50 in a hospital a week later

and I'm named for her,
the consequences to be revealed by my stars,

while Giuliano was named in the spirit
of a good joke by my father
after a Sicilian bandit
hung on the day he was born;
my mother didn't laugh then, but she smiles now
as she tells the anecdote,
cutting another piece of cake,
60 pouring another cup of coffee.

Filomena, whose husband was sent to Ethiopia
to provide a repast for crocodiles;
she married his death,
then pined a long unrequited love for her own tragic dust,

and finally, of most recent interest, Anna's wedding night,
viewing for the first time the mysteries of a man's primordial appetite
for the blood he must claim as his own
and on the next day she had to study
the art of walking.

I am marking the day of my first bleeding
in red pencil in my work book.
70 I am ten years old.
Already they are plotting
a new and disquieting role for me.

Here is my initiation into the confessional of the kitchen
(will they stop my thinking?).
The men are in another room drinking grappa, smoking cigarettes,
while the hockey game minds its own business on the TV screen.

The men check the scores often, remembering their bets,
80 postulating the outcome of the series from a sophisticated knowledge
of the history and statistics of the league

Through the open doorway I can just see
a shadow school of the men's heads
bobbing like buoys in the white wash.
They think they are creating life in the living-room
while the dust of the outside world still clings to their shoes,
but even men, when they are common,
men of the trades: barber, plumber, electrician,

who make the real world because they lay
90 bricks for it, do not write their own histories.
They tell similar stories as the women
but with authority, with the weight of the fist
and the cry of the accordion.
However you will not read in books
the exploits of these family
men.

[1980]

POEM FOR MY DAUGHTER

Toys, the blue rhinoceros with the spidery lashes,
the monkey coyly seeing no evil,
hands taped over his eyes,
a truth barrier, his long sad tail
like a phallus soft with spent love,
the flower rattle, the pink squeeze-toy
and an Indian doll whose black braid you use
to tug her along,
such are the objects you have so far
to know yourself.

Emily, these baubles that people your world
have no desires of their own,
baby woman, what can I tell you to try to be
without being wrong?

Try to live intelligently and be happy
as you are
as your mother read too many books
thinking she could not be pretty.

A single season may strike campfires in a man's blood.
Keep what you feel underground.
Only the lead in your pencil
as you note these things
need poison your reflection
wanting the power that can make an old bone
rise.
Few men may come back from the dead for you.

I can tell you this because I have found a man's duty
a cold bed to sleep in
and his lust a fast train,
because you are not unique,
you who have so soon discovered your hands and feet,
because even Sartre betrayed Simone de Beauvoir
for every half-baked dish in Paris,
I advise you to steel yourself
although there's no escape from pain
you can burnish with it
like an iron in the fire.

[1983]

AS IN THE BEGINNING

A man has two hands and when one
gets caught on the belt and his fingers
are amputated and then patched
he cannot work. His hands are insured
however so he gets some money
for the work his hands have done before.
If he loses a finger he gets a flat sum
of $250 for each digit &/or $100 for a joint
missing for the rest of his stay on earth,
like an empty stool at a beggar's banquet.
When the hands are my father's hands
it makes me cry although my pen must keep scratching
its head across the page of another night.
To you my father is a stranger
and perhaps you think the insurance paid is enough.

Give me my father's hands when they are not broken
and swollen,
give me my father's hands, young again,
and holding the hands of my mother,
give me my father's hands still brown and uncallused,
beautiful hands that broke bread for us at table,
hands as smooth as marble and naked as the morning,
give me hands without a number tattooed at the wrist,
without the copper sweat of clinging change,
give my father's hands as they were in the beginning,
whole,
open,
warm
and without fear.

[1983]

· ROO BORSON ·

1952–

Roo Borson was born in Berkeley, California. She received a B.A. in English from Goddard College, Vermont, and an M.F.A. in creative writing from the University of British Columbia. She has also worked in various non-literary jobs, among them as a physics technician. In 1982 she won first prize in the CBC Literary Competition. Her most recent collection of poems, *The Whole Night, Coming Home* (1984), was nominated for the Governor General's Award.

Borson's early poetry, collected in *Landfall* (1977) and *In the Smoky Light of the Fields* (1980), is steeped in images from the natural world, and explores the way romance and sensuality influence our daily lives. The poems are mostly imagistic and quite short—even "Migrations," the longest poem in *Landfall*, is not so much a long poem as it is a grouping of fifteen brief, lyrical passages. In *Rain* (1980) Borson begins to expand her forms: the poems become longer and the words are more likely to meander around on the page. These poems explore the world of shadows and greyness, and the corresponding mysteries of memory and creation. At times, Borson's explorations uncover tactile images, at other times they uncover dream-like fantasies.

With *A Sad Device* (1981) Borson began to acquire an enthusiastic audience. The book prompted Mark Abley to speculate that Borson "may well be the first major poet to emerge in Canada in the '80s." It is a book of personal and often private lyrics, full of romantic longing and discomfort. Borson has always managed to use common devices such as simile and metaphor in startlingly new ways, and in *A Sad Device* this talent is particularly evident. In the poem "Shapes" she describes "A man lying in the snow like a broken bag of groceries"; and "Gray Glove" begins: "Among branches / a bird lands fluttering, a soft gray glove / with a heart." These images give the reader a sense of Borson's rich, sometimes contemplative, sometimes disturbing, private landscape. In other poems, such as "At Night You Can Almost See the Corona of Bodies," she is able to compassionately embrace a world of contradictions. In this poem she talks of the earth as being "speakably lovely, its confetti / of snow, jungles of costumed birds, / lapis, seas, pyrite, / every kind of weather fused / into this planet." It is this clash of disparate associations that makes Borson's poetry continually fascinating.

The Whole Night, Coming Home (1984), Borson's most ambitious book to date, is divided into two sections: the first is composed of what she calls "traditional line-length poems" and the second is composed of prose poems. In an interview with Bruce Meyer and Brian O'Riordan, Borson talks about these "two totally different media." She explains: "Prose poems are not short stories, but they aren't poems either. There's something different in terms of rhythmic flow. Instead of having thought or idea-breaks at the end of lines, you have something less compact but more dramatic." One can almost see this collection as two quite distinct books wedded together. In the first section we get a sense of Borson's "Whole Night": the moon, the planets, the streetlights, and stars pulsing against the consuming blackness of the night sky. This darkness and its various permutations is most evident in such poems as "By Flashlight": "The taste of coffee, deep at night, when nobody could care. / The bat that sweeps at eye-level through the twilit house. / The hidden inhabitants, the unknown guests." In the second section we get a sense of

Borson "Coming Home": of her childhood mysteries, her remembrance of favourite trees, forts, and tunnels; and her understanding of the folklore of familial relations, such as in "The Watermelon," where she talks about how "a single act becomes a legend, the way a child's first mispronunciation of a word becomes a family intimacy, referencing that one instant forever." Borson's poetry is based on continual exploration and discovery. In each of her books she examines the sense of "home" that one carries around inside oneself, and attempts to map this place through private images and observations.

Borson's works include *Landfall* (1977); *In the Smoky Light of the Fields*, (1980); *A Sad Device* (1981); *The Whole Night, Coming Home* (1984); and with Kim Maltman, *The Transparence of November/Snow* (1985).

Works on Borson include Anita Hurwitz, "It's Dry Between the Raindrops," *Waves* 10.3 (1982): 85–88; Don McKay, "sunsets like an armful of dying flamingoes," *Brick* 15 (1982): 5–6; and David Manicom, "An Interview with Roo Borson," *Rubicon* 8 (1987): 52–85.

PETER O'BRIEN

AT NIGHT
YOU CAN ALMOST SEE
THE CORONA OF BODIES

In the twilit grasses: beasts
like a billion implications.
Through impeccable air they look up
but their eyes are not tools.

Past this planet and moon chasing each other
lurk the huge spaces
we're about to break loose into,
and the stars seep out
like those unfelt tears that gather
10 at the edges of the eyes in a big wind.

Turning back to our lovers
for a final look that will last perhaps
another fifty years
before our eyes are irrevocably altered,
what can we do or say?
The conflicting scale of things.

At rush hour
there are a billion people walking away forever.
They come at me
20 with the face of a herd
bound for extinction.

II

Men walk around, dressed
from the neck up in memories.
If you look in their eyes
sometimes their lives are showing.
Sometimes the imploded faces
of dead men.

At times a word can amplify the twilight,
but in talking the tongue moves
30 like a puppet or a shadow.

Placing yourself in that slight peril,
like a hero, an athlete of existence,
will not save you.

Everywhere you go: the incurable beauty
of the earth. The sunsets like an armful
of dying flamingoes.

III

Ocean of failed wings,
cypresses that grope into shapes of wind:
girls homely enough to have secrets
40 lean here and there in every landscape
as quietly as brooms.

Over the mills
strands of smoke test their wingspread
and are pulled apart in the beaks of wind.

How is it possible that young girls
sit by the firelight and daydream of dying?
Not yet fearing anything.

The wharves lean like dark waterbirds, ankleted with light.
The invisible outer planets sit in the palm trees;

50 grief, the bird, flies to and fro in the great
shadowy combs. Between rows of crates
sealed for trade, the moon, a frozen heartbeat.
Laughter dispersing like smoke.

Dusty men spend night along the docks, smoking,
looking out to sea, which is full of answers.
On the grassy promenade
dark-clothed men lead women sheathed in twilight,
who offer only
open, frightened faces.

IV

60 Snow that sparkles like fresh-laid concrete,
pines exhaling an odor of mint and sweat,
I wake up every day, not even knowing where the earth is.
Why should I speak?

The animals' eyes are full of nuance,
but that is only the look of being alive.

Men injected with this restlessness, to them
the cool hills knotted with trees,
the animals and plants smell of a thousand repetitive processes.
The chasm between stars, godless,
70 neither night nor day nor point of view,
a place where light travels
invisibly until it hits, dreamless,
a deep sleep among the movements of bodies.

V

The white rain of oncoming cars
slides down the pane of this continent, this hour.
History we make up to go to sleep by. That way
the hugeness of space
does not damage us.

In the twilit air where men lie
80 side by side with spirits,
beasts alternately hunt and sleep.
It is hard to know the depths of things,
even of our own eyes, but the earth
is speakably lovely, its confetti

of snow, jungles of costumed birds,
lapis, seas, pyrite,
every kind of weather fused
into this planet, over whose night horizon
the moon lifts like the face of a man coming to in battle,
90 the earth at his cheek,
seeing nothing but the open sky.

[1981]

NOW AND AGAIN

Night should be fuller than this.
Lying on our backs in scratchy twigs,
there aren't enough stars in this place,
the brightest lights are the distant buildings
in a circle around us. Two people
without a thing to say to one another, or things
that can't be said. Right beside us:
whole societies of frogs and insects,
and we in ours.
I don't want to be made of words and feelings.
I don't want to be a body that craves.
We get up and stumble through bushes,
back toward civilization. Who are we
to be holding hands? The pond gives back
the reflections of two creatures a little startled
at being brought up to date
on their own existence.
How old can a person get?
Now and again it seems like it's time
to pass the baton and let somebody else
run their little way into the future.

[1981]

JACARANDA

Old earth, how she sulks,
dark spin-off
wielding wings and swords,
mountain ranges, centuries,
our eyes with their impurities.

Dusk. Planets like spilled mercury
and the stars exuding
loneliness, the old battle
for which there are no medals.

Often I look in that mirror
in which things happen over again.
Useless. Or I look
to the teasing water full of days
and clouds that drift like smoke,
and hours when the head sleeps,
an inn for strange guests. If only
we were easier creatures.

But the jacaranda reclines
like a wise thing,
stars crystallizing
beyond its dusky plumes.
Here in the amethyst air of early autumn,
the dryness a talisman,
the moon the egg of a luminous bird,
the jacaranda's wand-like branches
command each thing to be.
The jacaranda with its feathery leaves
blooms clusters of amethysts,
and its winged boxes
lilt toward the green plains bearing
an imploded formula
for jacarandas.

This is the endless catechism of beasts,
each a question and an answer,
on which time
in luminous drops
is raining down.

[1981]

GRAY GLOVE

Among branches
a bird lands fluttering,
a soft gray glove
with a heart.

The land at twilight.
Swamp of black mist.
A first planet. A swordtip.
The bird chanting
in a jail of darkness.

This is the last unclassified bird,
the one one never sees,
but hears when alone, walking.

You can see how far I've gone
not to speak of you.
Birds have made a simple bargain
with the land.

The only song I know
is the one I see with my eyes,
the one I'd give up my eyes
in order for you to hear.

[1981]

•SHORT FICTION•

· CHARLES G. D. ROBERTS ·

1860–1943

Note: A biography of Charles G. D. Roberts appears in the poetry section.

DO SEEK THEIR MEAT FROM GOD

One side of the ravine was in darkness. The darkness was soft and rich, suggesting thick foliage. Along the crest of the slope tree-tops came into view—great pines and hemlocks of the ancient unviolated forest—revealed against the orange disk of a full moon just rising. The low rays slanting through the moveless tops lit strangely the upper portion of the opposite steep—the western wall of the ravine, barren, unlike its fellow, bossed with great rocky projections and harsh with stunted junipers. Out of the sluggish dark that lay along the ravine as in a trough rose the brawl of a swollen, obstructed stream.

Out of a shadowy hollow behind a long white rock, on the lower edge of that part of the steep which lay in the moonlight, came softly a great panther. In common daylight his coat would have shown a warm fulvous hue, but in the elvish decolorizing rays of that half-hidden moon he seemed to wear a sort of spectral gray. He lifted his smooth round head to gaze on the increasing flame, which presently he greeted with a shrill cry. That terrible cry, at once plaintive and menacing, with an undertone like the fierce protestations of a saw beneath the file, was a summons to his mate, telling her that the hour had come when they should seek their prey. From the lair behind the rock, where the cubs were being suckled by their dam, came no immediate answer. Only a pair of crows, that had their nest in a giant firtree across the gulf, woke up and croaked harshly their indignation. These three summers past they had built in the same spot, and had been nightly awakened to vent the same rasping complaints.

The panther walked restlessly up and down, half a score of paces each way, along the edge of the shadow, keeping his wide-open green eyes upon the rising light. His short, muscular tail twitched impatiently, but he made no sound. Soon the breadth of confused brightness had spread itself farther down the steep, disclosing the foot of the white rock, and the bones and antlers of a deer which had been dragged thither and devoured.

By this time the cubs had made their meal, and their dam was ready for such enterprise as must be accomplished ere her own hunger, now grown savage, could hope to be assuaged. She glided supplely forth into the glimmer, raised her head, and screamed at the moon in a voice as terrible as her mate's. Again the crows stirred, croaking harshly; and the two beasts, noiselessly mounting the steep, stole into the shadows of the forest that clothed the high plateau.

The panthers were fierce with hunger. These two days past their hunting had been wellnigh fruitless. What scant prey they had slain had for the most part been devoured by the female; for had she not those small blind cubs at home to nourish, who soon must suffer at any lack of hers? The settlements of late had been making great inroads on the world of ancient forest, driving before them the deer and smaller game. Hence the sharp hunger of the panther parents, and hence it came that on this night they hunted together. They purposed to steal upon the settlements in their sleep, and take tribute of the enemies' flocks. Through the dark of the thick woods, here and there pierced by the moonlight, they moved swiftly and silently. Now and again a dry twig would snap beneath the discreet and padded footfalls. Now and again, as they rustled some low tree, a pewee or a nuthatch would give a startled chirp. For an hour the noiseless journeying continued, and ever and anon the two gray, sinuous shapes would come for a moment into the view of the now well-risen moon. Suddenly there fell upon their ears, far off and faint, but clearly defined against the vast stillness of the Northern forest, a sound which made those stealthy hunters pause and lift their heads. It was the voice of a child crying—crying long and loud, hopelessly, as if there were no one by to comfort it. The panthers turned aside from their former course and glided toward the sound. They were not yet come to the outskirts of the settlement, but they knew of a solitary cabin lying in the thick of the woods a mile and more from the nearest neighbour. Thither they bent their way, fired with fierce hope. Soon would they break their bitter fast.

Up to noon of the previous day the lonely cabin had been occupied. Then its owner, a shiftless fellow, who spent his days for the most part at the corner tavern three miles distant, had suddenly grown disgusted with a land wherein one must work to live, and had betaken himself with his seven-year-old boy to seek some more indolent clime. During the long lonely days when his father was away at the tavern the little boy had been wont to visit the house of the next neighbour, to play with a child of some five summers, who had no other playmate. The next neighbour was a prosperous pioneer, being master of a substantial frame-house in the midst of a large and well-tilled clearing. At times, though rarely, because it was forbidden, the younger child would make his way by a rough wood road to visit his poor little disreputable playmate. At length it had appeared that the five-year-old was learning unsavoury language from the elder boy, who rarely had an opportunity of hearing speech more desirable. To the bitter grief of both children, the companionship had at length been stopped by unalterable decree of the master of the frame-house.

Hence it had come to pass that the little boy was unaware of his comrade's departure. Yielding at last to an eager longing for that comrade, he had stolen away late in the afternoon, traversed with endless misgivings the lonely stretch of wood road, and reached the cabin, only to find it empty. The door, on its leathern hinges, swung idly open. The one room had been stripped of its few poor furnishings. After looking in the rickety shed, whence darted two wild and hawklike chickens, the child had seated himself on the hacked threshold, and sobbed passionately with a grief that he did not fully comprehend. Then seeing the shadows lengthen across the tiny clearing, he had grown afraid to start for home. As the dusk gathered, he had crept trembling into the cabin, whose door would not stay shut. When it grew quite dark, he crouched in the inmost corner of the room, desperate with fear and loneliness, and lifted up his voice piteously. From time to time his lamentations would be choked by sobs or he would grow breathless, and in the terrifying silence would listen hard to hear if anyone or anything were coming. Then again would the shrill childish wailings arise, startling the unexpectant night and piercing the forest depths, even to the ears of those great beasts which had set forth to seek their meat from God.

The lonely cabin stood some distance, perhaps a quarter of a mile, back from the highway connecting the settlements. Along this main road a man was plodding wearily. All day he had been walking, and now as he neared home his steps began to quicken with anticipation of rest. Over his shoulder projected a double-barrelled fowling-piece, from which was slung a bundle of such necessities as he had purchased in town that morning. It was the prosperous settler, the master of the frame-house. His mare being with foal, he had chosen to make the tedious journey on foot.

The settler passed the mouth of the wood road leading to the cabin. He had gone perhaps a furlong beyond, when his ears were startled by the sound of a child crying in the woods. He stopped, lowered his burden to the road, and stood straining ears and eyes in the direction of the sound. It was just at this time that the two panthers also stopped and lifted their heads to listen. Their ears were keener than those of the man, and the sound had reached them at a greater distance.

Presently the settler realized whence the cries were coming. He called to mind the cabin, but he did not know the cabin's owner had departed. He cherished a hearty contempt for the drunken squatter; and on the drunken squatter's child he looked with small favour, especially as a playmate for his own boy. Nevertheless, he hesitated before resuming his journey.

"Poor little devil!" he muttered, half in wrath. "I reckon his precious father's drunk down at 'the Corners,' and him crying for loneliness?" Then he reshouldered his burden and strode on doggedly.

But louder, shriller, more hopeless and more appealing, arose the childish voice, and the settler paused again, irresolute and with deepening indignation. In his fancy he saw the steaming supper his wife would have awaiting him. He loathed the thought of retracing his steps, and then stumbling a quarter of a mile through the stumps and bog of the wood road. He was foot-sore as well as hungry, and he cursed the vagabond squatter with serious emphasis; but in that wailing was a terror which would not let him go on. He thought of his own little one left in such a position, and straightway his heart melted. He turned, dropped his bundle behind some bushes, grasped his gun, and made speed back for the cabin.

"Who knows," he said to himself, "but that drunken idiot has left his youngster without a bite to eat in the whole miserable shanty? Or maybe he's locked out, and the poor little beggar's half scared to death. *Sounds* as if he was scared"; and at this thought the settler quickened his pace.

As the hungry panthers drew near the cabin and the cries of the lonely child grew clearer, they hastened their steps, and their eyes opened to a wider circle, flaming with a greener fire. It would be thoughtless superstition to say the beasts were cruel. They were simply keen with hunger and alive with the eager passion of the chase. They were not ferocious with any anticipation of battle, for they knew the voice was the voice of a child, and something in the voice told them the child was solitary. Theirs was no hideous or unnatural rage, as it is the custom to describe it. They were but seeking with the strength, the cunning, the deadly swiftness given them to that end, the food convenient for them. On their success in accomplishing that for which nature had so exquisitely designed them depended not only their own but the lives of their blind and helpless young, now whimpering in the cave on the slope of the moonlit ravine. They crept through a wet alder thicket, bounded lightly over the ragged brush fence, and paused to reconnoitre on the edge of the clearing in the full glare of the moon. At the same moment the settler emerged from the darkness of the wood-road on the opposite side of the clearing. He saw the two great beasts, heads down and snouts thrust forward, gliding toward the open cabin door.

For a few moments the child had been silent. Now his voice rose again in pitiful appeal, a very ecstasy of loneliness and terror. There was a note in the cry that shook the settler's soul. He had a vision of his own boy, at home with his mother, safeguarded from even the thought of peril. And here was this little one left to the wild beasts! "Thank God! Thank God I came!" murmured the settler, as he dropped on one knee to take a surer aim. There was a loud report (not like the sharp crack of a rifle), and the female panther, shot through the loins, fell in a heap, snarling furiously and striking with her forepaws.

The male walked around her in fierce and anxious amazement. As the smoke lifted he discerned the settler kneeling for a second shot. With a high screech of fury, the lithe brute sprang upon his enemy, taking a bullet full in his chest without seeming to know he was hit. Ere the man could slip in another cartridge the beast was upon him, bearing him to the ground and fixing keen fangs in his shoulder. Without a word, the man set his strong fingers desperately into the brute's throat, wrenched himself partly free, and was struggling to rise when the panther's body collapsed upon him all at once, a dead weight which he easily flung aside. The bullet had done its work just in time.

Quivering from the swift and dreadful contest, bleeding profusely from his mangled shoulder, the settler stepped up to the cabin door and peered in. He heard sobs in the darkness.

"Don't be scared, sonny," he said in a reassuring voice. "I'm going to take you home along with me. Poor little lad, *I'll* look after you if folks that ought to don't."

Out of the dark corner came a shout of delight, in a voice which made the settler's heart stand still. "Daddy, daddy," it said, "I knew you'd come. I was so frightened when it got dark!" And a little figure launched itself into the settler's arms and clung to him trembling. The man sat down on the threshold and strained the child to his breast. He remembered how near he had been to disregarding the far-off cries, and great beads of sweat broke out upon his forehead.

Not many weeks afterwards the settler was following the fresh trail of a bear which had killed his sheep. The trail led him at last along the slope of a deep ravine, from whose bottom came the brawl of a swollen and obstructed stream. In the ravine he found a shallow cave, behind a great white rock. The cave was plainly a wild beast's lair, and he entered circumspectly. There were bones scattered about, and on some dry herbage in the deepest corner of the den he found the dead bodies, now rapidly decaying, of two small panther cubs.

[1892]

· ETHEL WILSON ·

1888–1980

Ethel Wilson was an extraordinary example of the literary late starter. She came to Vancouver in 1898, in her own and the city's childhood, both of which she described in her longest and most nearly autobiographical novel, *The Innocent Traveller* (1949). But she did not publish her first story until 1937, when she was forty-nine and "I Just Love Dogs" appeared in the *New Statesman*. Her first novel, *Hetty Dorval*, appeared in 1947, when she was fifty-nine, after which she had a brief but productive writing history. The last of her six books, the collection entitled *Mrs. Golightly and Other Stories*, from which "From Flores" is taken, appeared in 1961, and the last of her contributions to literary periodicals in 1964. She lived long afterwards, until 1980, but in her later years she withdrew into the silence of sickness and bereavement.

Thus she belonged by age to the same generation as D. H. Lawrence (who was three years older) and Aldous Huxley (who was six years younger) and was considerably senior to the novelists, like Morley Callaghan, Hugh MacLennan, and Sinclair Ross, with whom the Canadian novel in its modern form emerged during the 1930s and the early 1940s. She came, in fact, to public attention with the post-war generation and in that sense was the contemporary of much younger writers like Margaret Laurence.

This resulted in what turned out a fruitful overlapping of loyalties, for Ethel Wilson, who had been a young woman of 26 when World War I began, had roots in a past remote from the time in which her creativity flowered. As I remarked in *The World of Canadian Writing*: "she had retained . . . an Edwardian sensibility, but she had developed a contemporary ironic intelligence, and it was the interplay of the two that gave her books their special quality."

Character and place are the most important elements in Wilson's fiction. She claimed that character came first: that a phrase overheard or some trivial incident would give her a clue out of which she could build a character in her mind, how he or she spoke and looked, and that the character would be living beside her in her imagination before she even began. Perhaps that is why the leading characters in her novels, from *Hetty Dorval* down to *Love and Salt Water* (1956), were women; she could imagine them with a surer eye. Yet, as "From Flores" shows, her insight into human motives and her observation of human character also enabled her to create thoroughly believable male characters.

Virtually all Ethel Wilson's fiction is set in British Columbia. She admired Proust greatly, but while most people think of him as the great novelist of time, she valued him most for his presentation of place. And when one reads her novels and stories, and recognizes how much the landscape becomes interwoven with the action, and how the characters' connections with where they live reflect their ways of thinking, one understands why place has seemed to Ethel Wilson so important an element in her appraisal of other novelists. In "From Flores" the human wilfulness of Ed the crewman, and the natural forces of wind and water at work on the Pacific Coast, show the remarkable complicity of character and place which brings about the disastrous ending whose consequences ripple out to affect many lives.

Ethel Wilson always thought of herself as a straightforward narrative writer, and distrusted symbolic explanations of her works. Yet she evokes such patterns of echoes between the inner landscapes of people's minds and the outer landscapes of their settings, that her descriptions of the natural world often create clusters of images that are potent with associative suggestion and take on the power of potent archetypal symbols. Her writing, simple and innocent at first reading, is rather like the surface of one of the lakes she loved, clear and pellucid but falling away into darkening depths of implication.

. ——————— .

Works by Ethel Wilson include *Hetty Dorval* (1947); *The Innocent Traveller* (1949); *The Equations of Love: Tuesday and Wednesday: Lilly's Story* (1952); *Swamp Angel* (1954); *Love and Salt Water* (1956);

and *Mrs. Golightly and Other Stories* (1961).

Works on Ethel Wilson include Dorothy Livesay, "Ethel Wilson: West Coast Novelist," *Saturday Night* 67 (26 July 1952): 20, 36; Desmond Pacey, *Ethel Wilson* (1967); Beverly J. Mitchell, "In Defence of Hetty Dorval," *Studies in Canadian Literature* 1 (1976): 26–48; David Stouck, "Ethel Wilson's Novels," *Canadian Literature* 7 (1977): 74–88; *The Ethel Wilson Symposium*, ed. and intro. Lorraine McMullen (1981); W. J. Keith, "Ethel Wilson," *The Oxford Companion to Canadian Literature*, ed. William Toye (1983); and Bonnie Martyn McComb, "Ethel Wilson: An Annotated Bibliography," *The Annotated Bibliography of Canada's Major Authors*, ed. Robert Lecker and Jack David (1984), 5: 415–80.

GEORGE WOODCOCK

FROM FLORES

Up at Flores Island, Captain Findlay Crabbe readied his fishboat the *Effie Cee* for the journey home and set out in good spirits while the weather was fair. But even by the time he saw the red shirt flapping like mad from the rocky point just north of the Indian's place the wind had freshened. Nevertheless Fin Crabbe told the big man at the wheel to turn in to shore because there must be some trouble there and that Indian family was pretty isolated. As the man at the wheel turned the nose of the boat towards the shore, the skipper listened to the radio. The weather report was good, and so he went out on the small deck well satisfied and stood there with his hands on his hips, looking at the shore where the red flag was.

The third man on the fishboat was just a young fellow. Up at Flores Island he had come down to the float with his gear all stowed in a duffel bag and asked the skipper to take him down to Port Alberni. He was an anxious kid, tall, dark, and thin-faced. He said he'd pay money for the ride and he spoke of bad news which with a young man sounds like parents or a girl and with an older young man sounds like a wife or children or a girl. Fin Crabbe said shortly that the boy could come, although the little *Effie Cee* was not geared for passengers. He didn't need to pay.

Captain Crabbe was small. He had come as an undersized boy to the west coast of Vancouver Island and there he had stayed. He had been fairish and was now bald. His eyes were sad like a little bloodhound's eyes and pink under, but he was not sad. He was a contented man and rejoiced always to be joined again with his wife and his gangling son and daughter. Mrs. Crabbe's name was Effie but she was called Mrs. Crabbe or Mom and her name had come to be used only for the *Effie Cee* which was by this time more Effie than Mrs. Crabbe was. "I'm taking home an Indian basket for Mrs. Crabbe," the skipper might say. "Mrs. Crabbe sure is an authority on Indian baskets." Fin Crabbe was his name up and down the coast but at home he was the Captain or Pop, and so Mrs. Crabbe would say, "The Captain plans to be home for Christmas. The Captain's a great family man. I said to him 'Pop, if you're not home for Christmas, I'll . . .!' " Thus they daily elevated each other in esteem and loved each other with simple mutual gratification. In bed no names were needed by Mrs. Crabbe and the Captain. (When they shall be dead, as they will be, what will avail this happy self-satisfaction. But now they are not dead, and the Captain's wife as often before awaits the Captain who is on his way down the coast from Flores Island, coming home for Christmas.)

Fin Crabbe had planned for some time to reach Port Alberni early in Christmas week and that suited Ed, the big crewman, too. Ed was not a family man although he had a wife somewhere; but what strong upspringing black curly hair he had and what gambling eyes. He was powerful, not to be governed, and a heller when he drank. He was quick to laugh, quick to hit out, quick to take a girl, quick to leave her, a difficult wilful volatile enjoying man of poor judgement, but he got along all right with little Fin Crabbe. He did not want to spend Christmas in Flores Island when there was so much doing in Alberni and Port Alberni.

Captain Crabbe's family lived in Alberni proper, which to the dweller in a city seems like a fairly raw small town at the end of a long arm through the forest to nowhere, and to the dweller up the coast or in the Queen Charlottes seems like a small city with every comfort, every luxury, motor cars speeding in and out by the long road that leads through the forest to the fine Island Highway, lighted streets, plumbing, beer parlours, a hospital, churches, schools, lumber mills, wharves. It lives for and on trees and salt water. Behind it is a huge hinterland of giant forests. Before it lies the long tortuous salt-water arm of the open sea.

Captain Crabbe, as the bow of the *Effie Cee* turned towards the pine-clad but desolate and rocky shore, cutting across the tricky undulations of the ocean, again gave his habitual look at the sky, north and west.

The sky was overclouded but so it usually is in these parts at this time of year. Since these rocky shores are not protected as are the rocky shores of the British Columbia mainland by the long stretches of sweet liveable gulf islands and by the high barrier of mountainous Vancouver Island itself, the west coast of the island lies naked to the Pacific Ocean, which rolls in all the way from Asia and breaks upon the reefs and rocks and hard sands, and the continuous brewing of weather up in an air cauldron in the north seethes and spills over and rushes out of the Gulf of Alaska, often moderating before it reaches lower latitudes; but sometimes it roars down and attacks like all hell. The fishboat and tugboat men know this weather well and govern themselves accordingly. Next morning, perhaps the ocean smiles like a dissolute angel. The fishboat and tugboat men know that, too, and are not deceived. So that although Fin Crabbe knew all this as well as he knew his own thumb, he did not hesitate to turn the *Effie Cee* towards the shore when he saw the red shirt flapping at the end of the rock point but he had no intention of stopping there nor of spending any time at all unless his judgement warranted it, for on this trip his mind was closely set to home.

The turning aside of the fishboat in her journey irked the young passenger very much. Since the weather report on the radio was fairly good and anyway he was used to poor weather, he felt no concern about that. But here was delay and how much of it. He did not know how often he had read the letter, which he again took out of his pocket, not looking at Big Ed nor at little Captain Crabbe but frowning at the letter and at some memory. He was possessed entirely, usurped, by impatience for contact, by letter, by wire or—best of all—by speech and sight and touch with the writer of this letter. Now that he had started on the journey towards her, now that he had started, now that he was on his way, his confusion seemed to clear. He read again in the letter: "Dear Jason I am very unhappy I dont know I should tell you Ive thought and thought before I wrote you and then what kind of a letter because I could say awful things and say you must come to Vancouver right away and marry me or believe me I could just cry and cry or I could write and say plain to you O Jason do I beseech you think if we couldnt get married right away. I could say I love you and I do."

The young man folded the letter again. He looked with distaste at the red flag that signified an Indian's trouble and his own delay and his mind ran backwards again. The letter had found him at last and only two days ago. He had left the camp and had crossed to Flores and there an old man with a beard had told him that Fin Crabbe was all set to go to Alberni the next morning, and he had enquired for Captain Crabbe. As he had walked up and down the float pushing time forward, sometimes a violence of joy rose in him and surprised him. This was succeeded by a real fear that something would happen to prevent the fishboat from leaving, would prevent them reaching Alberni very soon, while all the time Josie did not even know whether he had received the letter. Many feelings were induced in him by what Josie had written, and now he thought ceaselessly about her to whom, only three days before, he had barely given a thought. He unfolded the letter again.

"I gess I dont know too much about love like in the pictures but I do love you Jason and I wouldnt ever ever be a person who would throw this up at you. I dont sleep very good and some nights I threton to myself to kill myself and tho I am awful scared of that maybe that would be better and easier for us all and the next night I say no. Lots of girls go through with this but what do they do with the Baby and no real home for it and then I am bafled again and the time is going."

Jason, looking out to the ocean but not seeing it, was aware of a different Josie. If a person had told me, he thought, that I'd want to get married and that I'd be crazy for this baby I'd say they were crazy, I'd say they were nuts, and impatience against delay surged over him again. The boat neared the mouth of the bay.

"One thing I do know I couldnt go back to the prairies with the Baby," (no, that's right, you couldn't go back) "so where would the Baby and me go. Mother would let me feel it every day even if she didnt mean to tho she would take us but Father no never. Then I think its the best thing for the Baby I should drown myself its quite easy in Vancouver its not like the prairies I do mean that."

The skipper was talking back and forth to the crewman at the wheel and the *Effie Cee* slowed down. There were beams of sunshine that came and went.

"I cant believe its me and I do pitty any poor girl but not begging you Jason because you must decide for yourself. Some people would pay no attention to this letter but I kind of feel youre not like some people but O please Jason get me a word soon and then I can know what. Josie."

From the pages arose the helpless and lonely anguish of little Josie and this anguish entered and consumed him too and it was all part of one storm of anxiety and anger that she was alone and she so quiet, and not her fault (he said), and impatience rose within him to reach a place where he could say to her Don't you worry kid, I'm coming! He thought with surprise Maybe I'm a real bad guy and I never knew it, maybe we're all bad and we don't know it. He read once more: "I am bafled again and the time is going . . . I do love you Jason." He put his head in his hands with dumb anger that she should be driven to this, but as soon as he reached a telephone in Alberni everything would be all right. As he suddenly looked up he thought he would go mad at this turning off course for any sick guy, or any kid who'd been crazy enough to break an arm. In his frustration and impatience there was an infusion of being a hero and rushing to save someone. Some hero, he said very sourly to himself, some hero.

The *Effie Cee* slowed to a stop and a black volley of cormorants, disturbed, flew away in a dark line. There was an Indian and an Indian woman and a little boy in a rowboat almost alongside the fishboat. The little boy was half lying down in an uncomfortable way and two rough sticks were tied to his leg. Three smaller children stood solemnly on the rocky shore looking at the two boats. Then they turned to play in a clumsy ceremonial fashion among the barnacled rocks. They did not laugh as they played.

Jason put the letter in his pocket and stood up. The rowboat jiggled on the water and Captain Crabbe was bending down and talking to the Indian. He listened and talked and explained. The Indian's voice was slow and muffled, but not much talk was needed. Anyone could see. "Okay," said the skipper and then he straightened himself and turned to look at Ed and Jason as much as to say . . . and Jason said, 'Better I got into the rowboat and helped him lift the kid up,' and the skipper said 'Okay.'

All this time the woman did not say anything. She kept her hands wrapped in her stuff dress and looked away or at the child. Jason slipped over the side and the rowboat at once became overcrowded, which made it difficult for him and the Indian to lift the child up carefully without hurting him and without separating the boats. The Indian child made no sound and no expression appeared on his face so no one knew how much pain he suffered or whether he suffered at all. His eyes were brown and without meaning like the dusky opaque eyes of a fawn. The Indian spoke to his wife and she reached out her hands and held on to the fishboat so that the two craft would not be parted. Jason and the father succeeded in slipping their arms—"This way," said Jason, "see? do it this way"—under the child and raised him gradually up to where Ed and the skipper were kneeling. Everyone leaned too much to one side of the rowboat and Jason tried to steady it so that they would not fall with the child into the sea. All this time the woman had not spoken but had accepted whatever other people did as if she had no rights in the matter. When the child was safely on board, Jason sprang onto the deck and at once, at once, the *Effie Cee* turned and tore away with a white bone of spume in her mouth and a white wake of foam behind, leaving the Indians in the rowboat and the children on the shore looking after her.

"Best lay him on the floor, he'd maybe roll off of the bunk," said Fin Crabbe when they had lifted the child inside. "Mustn't let you get cold, Sonny," he said, and took down a coat that swung from a hook. The child regarded him in silence and with fear in his heart. One two another white man taking him to some place he did not know.

"Make supper Ed, and I'll take the wheel," said skipper. The boat went faster ahead, rising and plunging as there was now a small sea running.

What'd I better do, thought Fin Crabbe and did not consult the crewman who hadn't much judgement. There were good reasons for going on through and trying to make Alberni late in the night or in early morning. That would surprise Mrs. Crabbe and she would be pleased, and the young fella seemed desperate to get to Alberni on account of this bad news; but here was this boy he'd taken aboard and the sooner they got him into hospital the better. I think it's his hip (he thought), I could turn back to Tofino but it'd be dark then and would he be any better off landing him in the dark and likely no doctor. Anyway I can make Ucluelet easy and spend the night. I don't like to take no chances but all in all I think we'll go on. And they went on.

Evening came and black night. It was winter cold outside and Jason crowded into the wheelhouse and looked out at the dark. The coming of night brought him nearer the telephone, so near he could all but touch it, but he could not touch it.

The *Effie Cee* could not make much speed now and ploughed slowly for hours never ending, it seemed to Jason, through water that had become stormy and in the dark she followed a sideways course so that she could cut a little across the waves that were now high and deep. Ed had the wheel and Captain Crabbe stood beside him. The storm increased. The boat's nose plunged into the waves and rose with the waves and the water streamed over. There was a wallowing, a sideways wallowing. The little fishboat became a world of noise and motion, a plunging, a rising, a plunging again. Jason wedged the child against the base of the bunk. The child cried out, and vomited with seasickness and fear. "Now now," said Jason, patting him. "Try the radio again," said Captain Crabbe.

Jason fiddled with the radio. "Can't seem to get anything," he said.

"Let me," said the skipper.

"Bust," he said.

But now the storm rapidly accelerated and the waves, innocent and savage as tigers, leaped at the *Effie Cee* and the oncoming rollers struck broadside and continuously. The little boy made sounds like an animal and Jason, in whom for the first time fear of what might come had struck down all elation and expectation, took the child's hand and held it. The little plunging boat was now the whole world and fate to Jason and to Fin Crabbe and to the Indian boy but not to Ed who had no fear. Perhaps because he had no love he had no fear. Standing over the wheel and peering into the dark, he seemed like a great black bull and it was to Jason as though he filled the cabin.

Ed turned the boat's nose towards shore to get away from the broadside of the waves. Fin Crabbe shouted at him to be heard above the storm. The boat had been shipping water and Jason, crouching beside the shaking child in a wash of water heard the words "Ucluelet" and "lighthouse" and "rocks" but Ed would not listen. The skipper went on shouting at him and then he seized the wheel. He pushed the big man with all his strength, turning the wheel to starboard. Jason and the Indian child saw the big man and the little man fighting in the small space, in the din of the ocean, the howl of the wind, for possession of the wheel. As quick as a cat Ed drew off and hit the older man a great blow. Fin

Crabbe crumpled and fell. He lay in the wash of water at Ed's feet and Ed had his way, so the fishboat drove inshore, hurled by the waves onto the reefs, or onto the hard sand, or onto the place that Ed knew that he knew, whichever the dark should disclose, but not to the open sea. Captain Crabbe tried to raise himself and Jason crawled over towards him.

The skipper could not stand in the pitching boat. He looked up at Ed who was his executioner, the avenger of all that he had ever done, driving on against death for sure.

The thought of the abandonment of Josie (for now a belief was formed terribly in him that she was to be abandoned) pierced Jason through and through and then in the immediate danger the thought of Josie was no longer real but fled away on the wind and water, and there was nothing but fear. Without knowing what he did, he seized and held the child. Never could a man feel greater despair than Jason in the walnut shell of a reeling boat soon to be cracked between land and water. Ed, bent over the wheel, knowing everything, knowing just where they were, but not knowing, looked only forward into the blackness and drove on. The sea poured into the boat and at the same minute the lights went out and they were no longer together. Then the *Effie Cee* rose on a great wave, was hurled upwards and downwards, struck the barnacled reef, and split, and the following seas washed over.

A few days later the newspaper stated that in the recent storm on the west coast of Vancouver Island the fishboat *Effie Cee* was missing with two men aboard. These men were Findlay Crabbe aged fifty-six and Edward Morgan aged thirty-five, both of Alberni. Planes were continuing the search.

A day or two afterwards the newspapers stated that it was thought that there might have been a third man aboard the *Effie Cee*. He was identified as Jason Black aged twenty-two, employed as a logger up the coast near Flores Island.

On the second morning after the wreck of the *Effie Cee* the skies were a cold blue and the ocean lay sparkling and lazy beneath the sun. Up the Alberni Canal the sea and air were chilly and brilliant but still. Mrs. Crabbe spent the day waiting on the wharf in the cold sunshine. She stood or walked or sat, accompanied by two friends or by the gangling son and daughter, and next day it was the same, and the next. People said to her "But he didn't set a day? When did he *say* he'd be back?"

"He never said what day," she said. "The Captain couldn't ever say what day. He just said the beginning of the week, maybe Monday was what he said." She said "he said, he said, he said" because it seemed to establish him as living. People had to stop asking because they could not bear to speak to Mrs. Crabbe standing and waiting on the busy wharf, paying the exorbitant price of love. They wished she would not wait there because it made them uncomfortable and unhappy to see her.

Because Josie did not read the papers, she did not know that Jason was dead. Days had passed and continued to pass. Distraught, alone, deprived of hope and faith (two sovereign remedies) and without the consolation of love, she took secretly and with terror what she deemed to be the appropriate path.

The Indian, who had fully trusted the man who took his son away, heard nothing more. He waited until steady fine weather came and then took his family in his small boat to Tofino. From there he made his way to Alberni. Here he walked slowly up and down the docks and at last asked someone where the hospital was; but at the hospital no one seemed to know anything about his only son.

[1961]

· MORLEY CALLAGHAN ·

1903–

Born in Toronto on 22 February 1903, Morley Edward Callaghan graduated from Saint Michael's College, University of Toronto, in 1925, and then attended Osgoode Hall law school. In 1928, the year of the publication of his first novel, he was called to the bar. Fiction writing, however, commanded his complete attention and he never practised law. While at college he took a summer position at the *Toronto Daily Star* where his fellow reporters included Ernest Hemingway. He worked at the *Star* for four summers. In April 1929, he travelled with his wife to Paris, where their literary circle of friends included Hemingway, F. Scott Fitzgerald, and James Joyce. The following autumn he returned to Toronto, which always has been and remains his physical and literary home. Among his many honours are the Governor General's Award for *The Loved and the Lost* (1951), the Lorne Pierce Medal of the Royal Society of Canada (1960), the Canada Council Medal (1966), the Molson Prize, the Royal Bank Award (1970), and investiture as a Companion of the Order of Canada (1982).

The author of thirteen novels and more than a hundred shorter pieces of fiction, Callaghan is Canada's first professional writer, the first artist to devote his life to the vocation of writing fiction. "For me, he was the best example of a professional writer," the experimental novelist Graeme Gibson notes, "he was the best example that it was possible to be a professional writer in Canada."

Callaghan takes episodes of ordinary life and shapes them into a novel or a short story. The purpose of the writer, he maintains, is to capture the drama of the ordinary: "The writer's problem is somehow or other to catch the tempo, the stream, the way people live, think, and feel in their time, quite aside from any intellectual attitude to the matter." To achieve this, his writing is direct, frank, almost starkly realistic. He believes that fiction should present the object or reality and not seek to transform it into something it is not. "I'd be damned if the glory of literature was in the metaphor. Besides, it was not a time for the decorative Renaissance flight into simile. Tell the truth cleanly," he wrote in *That Summer in Paris*. "Strip the language, and make the style, the method, all the psychological ramifications, the ambience of the relationships, all the one thing, so the reader couldn't make separations," he continued. In such a direct mode of presentation, Callaghan creates fiction that is totally naturalistic, where the moods and tensions of individual lives are captured through a sensitive recording of the most telling details.

Although Callaghan's fiction depicts the lives of ordinary people, trapped and even victimized by the tyranny of social institutions as well as by human insensitivities, it offers no external remedies to social ills. Callaghan finds people's inner strength and moral being the only avenue possible for overcoming and even transcending the pains and injustices of this world. His novels and short stories often become spare moral parables on the human condition.

"Now That April's Here," originally published in 1929, depicts the folly and loneliness of two American homosexuals in the Paris of the twenties. "Congratulations on getting those two nitwits down perfectly," Ezra Pound wrote to Callaghan after reading the story. "My suggestion to you is that you go to Washington and get some of those senators down in exactly the same way."

· ———— ·

Callaghan's works include *Strange Fugitive* (1928); *A Native Argosy* (1929); *It's Never Over* (1930); *No Man's Meat* (1931); *A Broken Journey* (1932); *Such Is My Beloved* (1934); *They Shall Inherit the Earth* (1935); *Now That April's Here and Other Stories* (1936); *More Joy in Heaven* (1937); *Luke Baldwin's Vow* (1948); *The Varsity Story* (1948); *The Loved and the Lost* (1951); *Morley Callaghan's Stories* (1959); *The Many Colored Coat* (1960); *A Passion in Rome* (1961); *That Summer in Paris: Memories of Tangled Friendships with Hemingway, Fitzgerald and Some Others* (1963); *A Fine and Private Place* (1975); *Season of the Witch* (1976); *Close to the Sun Again* (1977); *No Man's Meat* and *The Enchanted Pimp* (1978); *A Time for Judas* (1983); *Our Lady of the Snows* (1985); and *The Lost and Found Stories of Morley Callaghan* (1985).

Works on Callaghan include Brandon Conron, *Morley Callaghan* (1966); Victor Hoar, *Morley Callaghan* (1969); Brandon Conron, ed., *Morley Callaghan* (1969); Patricia Morley, *Morley Callaghan* (1978); David Staines, ed., *The Callaghan Symposium* (1981); and Judith Kendle, "Morley Callaghan: An Annotated Bibliography," *The Annotated Bibliography of Canada's Major Authors*, ed. Robert Lecker and Jack David (1984), 5: 13–177.

DAVID STAINES

NOW THAT APRIL'S HERE

As soon as they got the money they bought two large black hats and left America to live permanently in Paris. They were bored in their native city in the Middle West and convinced that the American continent had nothing to offer them. Charles Milford, who was four years older than Johnny Hill, had a large round head that ought to have belonged to a Presbyterian minister. Johnny had a rather chinless faun's head. When they walked down the street the heads together seemed more interesting. They came to Paris in the late autumn.

They got on very quickly in Montparnasse. In the afternoons they wandered around the streets, looking in art gallery windows at the prints of the delicate clever unsubstantial line work of Foujita. Pressing his nose against the window Johnny said, "Quite a sound technique, don't you think, Charles?"

"Oh sound, quite sound."

They never went to the Louvre or the museum in the Luxembourg Gardens, thinking it would be in the fashion of tourists, when they intended really to settle in Paris. In the evenings they sat together at a table on the terrace of the café, and clients, noticing them, began thinking of them as "the two boys". One night, Fanny Lee, a blonde, fat American girl who had been an entertainer at Zelli's until she lost her shape, but not her hilarity, stepped over to the boys' table and yelled, "Oh, gee, look what I've found." They were discovered. Fanny, liking them for their quiet, well-mannered behaviour, insisted on introducing them to everybody at the bar. They bowed together at the same angle, smiling so cheerfully, so obviously willing to be obliging, that Fanny was anxious to have them follow her from one bar to another, hoping they would pay for her drinks.

They felt much better after the evening with Fanny. Johnny, the younger one, who had a small income of $100 a month, was supporting Charles, who, he was sure, would one day become a famous writer. Johnny did not take his own talent very seriously; he had been writing his memoirs of their adventures since they were fifteen, after reading George Moore's *Confessions of a Young Man.* George Moore's book had been mainly responsible for their visit to Paris. Johnny's memoirs, written in a snobbishly aristocratic manner, had been brought up to the present and now he was waiting for something to happen to them. They were much happier the day they got a cheaper room on Boulevard Arago near the tennis court.

They were happy at the cafés in the evenings but liked best being at home together in their own studio, five minutes away from the cafés. They lay awake in bed together a long time talking about everything that happened during the day, consoling each other by saying the weather would be finer later on and anyway they could always look forward to the spring days next April. Fanny Lee, who really liked them, was extraordinarily friendly and only cost them nine or ten drinks an evening. They lay awake in bed talking about her, sometimes laughing so hard the bed springs squeaked. Charles, his large round head buried in the pillow, snickered gleefully listening to Johnny making fun of Fanny Lee.

Soon they knew everybody in the Quarter, though no one knew either of them very intimately. People sitting at the café in the evening when the lights were on, saw them crossing the road together under the street lamp, their bodies leaning forward at the same angle, and walking on tiptoe. No one knew where they were going. Really they weren't going anywhere in particular. They had been sitting at the café, nibbling pieces of sugar they had dipped in coffee, till Johnny said, "We're being seen here too much, don't you think, Charles?" And Charles said, "I think we ought to be seen at all the bars. We ought to go more often to the new bar." So they had paid for their coffee and walked over to a side-street bar panelled in the old English style, with a good-natured English bartender, and sat together at a table listening to the careless talk of five customers at the bar, occasionally snickering out loud when a sentence overheard seemed incredibly funny. Stan Mason, an ingenuous heavy drinker, who had cultivated a very worldly feeling sitting at the same bars every night, explaining the depth of his sophistication to the same people, saw the boys holding their heads together and yelled, "What are you two little goats snickering at?" The boys stood up, bowing to him

᠌o politely and seriously he was ashamed of himself and asked them to ᠌ave a drink with him. The rest of the evening they laughed so charmingly at his jokes he was fully convinced they were the brightest youngsters who had come to the Quarter in years. He asked the boys if they liked Paris, and smiling at each other and raising their glasses together they said that architecturally it was a great improvement over America. They had never been in New York or any other large American city but had no use for American buildings. There was no purpose in arguing directly with them. Charles would simply have raised his eyebrows and glanced slyly at Johnny, who would have snickered with his fingers over his mouth. Mason, who was irritated, and anxious to make an explanation, began talking slowly about the early block-like houses of the Taos Indians and the geometrical block style of the New York skyscrapers. For ten minutes he talked steadily about the Indians and a development of the American spirit. The boys listened politely, never moving their heads at all. Watching them, while he talked, Mason began to feel uncomfortable. He began to feel that anything he had to say was utterly unimportant because the two boys were listening to him so politely. But he finished strongly and said, "What do you think?"

"Do you really believe all that's important?" Charles said.

"I don't know, maybe it's not."

"Well, as long as you don't think it important," Johnny said.

At home the boys sat on the edge of the bed, talking about Stan Mason and snickered so long they were up half the night.

They had their first minor disagreement in the Quarter one evening in November with Milton Simpson, a prosperous, bright and effeminate young American business man who was living in Paris because he felt vaguely that the best approach to life was through all the arts together. He was secretly trying to write, paint and compose pieces for the piano. The boys were at a small bar with a floor for dancing and an American jazz artist at the piano, and Simpson and his wife came in. Passing, Simpson brushed against Charles, who, without any provocation at all, suddenly pushed him away. Simpson pushed too and they stood there pushing each other. Simpson began waving his arms in circles, and the man at the piano threw his arms around Charles, dragging him away. Neither one of them could have hurt each other seriously and everybody in the room was laughing at them. Finally Simpson sat down and Charles, standing alone, began to tremble so much he had to put his head down on the table and cry. His shoulders were moving jerkily. Then everybody in the room was sorry for Charles. Johnny, putting his arm around him, led him outside. Simpson, whose thin straight lips were moving nervously, was so impressed by Charles's tears, that he and his wife followed them outside and over to the corner café where they insisted on sitting down with them at one of the brown oblong tables inside. Simpson bought the boys a brandy and his wife, who was interested in the new psychology, began to talk eagerly with Charles, evidently expecting some kind of an emotional revelation. The boys finished their brandies and Simpson quickly ordered another for them. For an hour the boys drank brandies and listened patiently and seriously to Simpson, who was talking ecstatically because he thought they were sensitive, sympathetic boys. They only smiled at him when he excitedly called them "sensitive organisms". Charles, listening wide-eyed, was nervously scratching his cheek with the nail of his right forefinger till the flesh was torn and raw.

Afterwards, undressing slowly at home, Johnny said, "Simpson is such a bore, don't you think so, Charles?"

"I know, but the brandies were very good." They never mentioned the fight at the bar.

"It was so funny when you looked at him with that blue-eyed Danish stare of yours," Johnny said, chuckling.

"People think I expect them to do tricks like little animals when I look at them like that," Charles explained.

Naked, they sat on the edge of the bed, laughing at Simpson's eagerness to buy them brandies, and they made so many witty sallies they tired themselves out and fell asleep.

For two weeks they weren't seen around the cafés. Charles was writing another book and Johnny was typing it for him. It was a literary two weeks for both of them. They talked about all the modern authors and Johnny suggested that not one of them since Henry James had half Charles's perception or subtle delicacy. Actually Charles did write creditably enough and everything he did had three or four good paragraphs in it. The winter was coming on and when this literary work was finished they wanted to go south.

No one ever knew how they got the money to go to the Riviera for the winter. No one knew how they were able to drink so much when they had only Johnny's hundred dollars a month. At Nice, where Stan Mason was living, they were very cheerful and Mason, admiring their optimism because he thought they had no money, let them have a room in his apartment. They lived with him till the evening he put his ear against the thin wall and heard them snickering, sitting on the edge of the bed. They were talking about him and having a good laugh. Stan Mason was hurt because he had thought them bright boys and really liked them. He merely suggested next morning that they would have to move since he needed the room.

The boys were mainly happy in Nice because they were looking forward to returning to Paris in April. The leaves would be on all the trees and people would be sitting outside on the terraces at the cafés. Everybody they met in Nice told them how beautiful it was in Paris in the early spring, so they counted upon having the happiest time they had ever had together. When they did leave Nice they owed many thousand francs for an hotel bill, payment of which they had avoided by tossing their bags out of the window at two o'clock in the morning. They even had a little extra money at the time, almost twenty dollars they had received from an elderly English gentleman, who had suggested, after talking to them all one morning, he would pay well to see the boys make a "tableau" for him. The old fellow was enthusiastic about the "tableau" and the boys had something to amuse them for almost two weeks.

They returned to Paris the first week in April. Now that April was here they had expected to have so much fun, but the weather was disagreeable and cold. This year the leaves were hardly on the trees and there was always rain in the dull skies. They assured each other that the dull days could not last because it was April and Paris was the loveliest city in the world in the early spring.

Johnny's father had been writing many irritable letters from England, where he was for a few months, and the boys decided it was an opportune time for Johnny to go and see him for a week. When he returned they would be together for the good days at the end of the month.

People were not very interested in Charles while Johnny was away. They liked him better when he was with Johnny. All week he walked around on tiptoe or sat alone at a corner table in the café. The two boys together seemed well mannered and bright, but Charles, alone, looked rather insignificant. Without thinking much about it he knew the feeling people had for him and avoided company, waiting impatiently for the days to pass, worrying about Johnny. He said to Stan Mason late one night, "I hope Johnny has enough sense not to pick up with a girl over in England."

"Why worry? Do it yourself now."

"Oh I do, too, only I don't take them as seriously as Johnny does. Not that I mind Johnny having a girl," he said, "only I don't want him to have a complicated affair with one."

The night Johnny returned to Paris they went around to all the bars and people, smiling, said, "There go the two boys." They were happy, nervously happy, and Charles was scratching his cheek with his nail. Later on they wanted to be entirely alone and left the café district and the crowds to walk down the narrow side streets to the Seine while Johnny, chuckling, related the disagreeable circumstances of his visit to his father. His father had contended that he was a wastrel who ought to be earning his own living, and Johnny had jeeringly pointed out that the old man had inherited his money without having to work for it. They were angry with each other, and the father had slapped Johnny, who retaliated by poking him in the jaw. That was the most amusing part of the story the boys talked about, walking along the left bank of the Seine opposite the Louvre. Casually Johnny told about a few affairs he had had with cheap women in London, and Charles understood that these affairs had not touched him at all. It was a warm clean evening, the beginning of the real spring days in April, and the boys were happy walking by the river in the moonlight, the polished water surface reflecting the red and white lights on the bridges.

Near the end of the month Constance Foy, whom the boys had known at Nice, came to Paris, and they asked her to live with them. She was a simple-minded fat-faced girl with a boy's body and short hair dyed red, who had hardly a franc left and was eager to live with anybody who would keep her. For a week the three of them were happy in the big studio. The boys were proud of their girl and took her around to all the bars, buying drinks for her, actually managing to do it on the hundred dollars a month. In the night-time they were impartial and fair about Constance, who appeared to have all her enthusiasm for the one who, at the moment, was making love to her. But she said to Stan Mason one evening, "I don't know whether or not I ought to be there messing up that relationship."

"Aren't the three of you having a good time?"

"Good enough, but funny things are happening."

The boys were satisfied till Charles began to feel that Johnny was making love to Constance too seriously. It was disappointing, for he had never objected to having her in the studio, and now Johnny was so obvious in his appreciation of her. Charles, having this feeling, was now unable to touch her at all, and resented Johnny's unabated eagerness for her. It was all the same to Constance.

Before the end of the month the two boys were hardly speaking to each other, though always together at the cafés in the evening. It was too bad, for the days were bright and clear, the best of the April weather, and Paris was gay and lively. The boys were sad and hurt and sorry but determined to be fair with each other. The evening they were at the English bar, sitting at one of the table beer barrels, Charles had a hard time preventing himself crying. He was very much in love with Johnny and felt him slipping away. Johnny, his fingers over his mouth, sometimes shook his head but didn't know what to say.

Finally they left the bar to walk home. They were going down the short, quiet street leading to the Boulevard.

"What are you going to do about Constance?" Charles said.

"If it's all the same to you I'll have her to myself."

"But what are you going to do with her?"

"I don't know."

"You'd let a little tart like that smash things," Charles said, shaking his hand at Johnny.

"Don't you dare call her a tart."

"Please, Johnny, don't strike at me."

But Johnny who was nearly crying with rage swung his palm at Charles, hitting him across the face. Stan Mason had just turned the corner at the Boulevard, coming up to the bar to have a drink, and saw the two of them standing there.

"What's wrong?" he said.

"I begged him, I implored him not to hit me," Charles said.

"Oh, I hit him, I hit him, I hit him, what'll I do?" Johnny said, tears running down his cheeks.

They stood there crying and shaking their heads, but would not go home together. Finally Charles consented to go with Stan to his hotel and Johnny went home to Constance.

Charles stayed with Mason all week. He would not eat at all and didn't care what he was drinking. The night Mason told him Johnny was going back to America, taking Constance with him, he shook his head helplessly and said, "How could he hit me, how could he hit me, and he knew I loved him so much."

"But what are you going to do?"

"I don't know."

"How are you going to live?"

"I'll make enough to have a drink occasionally."

At the time, he was having a glass of Scotch, his arm trembling so weakly he could hardly lift the glass.

The day Johnny left Paris it rained and it was cold again, sitting at the café in the evening. There had been only one really good week in April. The boys always used to sit at the cafés without their hats on, their hair brushed nicely. This evening Charles had to go home and get his overcoat and the big black hat he had bought in America. Sitting alone at his table in the cool evening, his overcoat wrapped around him, and the black hat on, he did not look the same at all. It was the first time he had worn the hat in France.

[1929]

· SINCLAIR ROSS ·

1908–

Born on a homestead near Shellbrook, Saskatchewan, James Sinclair Ross witnessed daily the desperation of the generation whose lives he explores in his fiction. Raised by his mother, who worked on farms as a housekeeper, Ross left school at sixteen for full-time work as a bank clerk. After several small-town Prairie branches, he was transferred to Winnipeg in 1933 and then did military service in England with the Canadian Ordnance Corps. He was transferred to the Montreal head office of the bank in 1946. Since retiring in 1968, he has lived in Greece, Spain, Montreal, and now Vancouver. Though his first short story won third prize in a 1934 international contest in London, his first novel attracted little attention. Not until its reprinting in 1957 did *As for Me and My House* (1941) become recognized as a classic and Ross as among the country's finest authors.

Ross's best fiction deals with the victims of isolation on farms or alienation in false-fronted towns scattered across the weather-beaten Prairies during the drought and depression of the 1930s. Succeeding the naturalists who considered nature as a malevolent force and man as a victim of compulsion and circumstance, Ross portrays the environment as a psychological projection of the mind. Nature may actually be alien to man or it may only seem that way to a lonely wife, as in the following passage from "The Painted Door":

> *In the clear, bitter light the long white miles of prairie landscape seemed a region alien to life. Even the distant farmsteads she could see served only to intensify a sense of isolation. Scattered across the face of so vast and bleak a wilderness it was difficult to conceive them as a testimony of human hardihood and endurance. Rather they seemed futile, lost, to cower before the implacability of snow-swept earth and clear pale sun-chilled sky.*

The environment is difficult to *conceive* as anything more than it *seems* to be. Conception and appearance belong to the realm of subjective perception rather than objective reality.

Many of Ross's short stories lead towards a traumatic change made all the more powerful by his denial of the conventional cathartic conclusion. The reader is left to imagine the full consequences that would follow if the story were to continue. "One's a Heifer" depicts a boy's loss of innocence as a fall from faith to doubt, leaving him to question his comprehension of a stranger's guilt. "The Lamp at Noon" ends with a woman, still unaware that she has smothered her baby in her arms during a dust storm, assuring her husband that the clearing sky "means tomorrow will be fine." "The Painted Door" ends with a woman discovering that her husband's death was a suicidal reaction to her adultery. Torn between fire and frost, passion and repression, dream and reality, her brief lapse leaves us to imagine the lasting reality of the guilt she will now suffer.

This pattern of transferring unvented emotion to the reader is perfected in *As for Me and My House.* Continuing his interest in documenting the unbearable tension of strained marital relations, Ross presents the diary of a woman whose husband is a faithless preacher. By withholding Philip Bentley's thoughts and feelings from the reader, Mrs. Bentley's limited viewpoint creates a semblance of the unarticulated tension of Philip's restrained life. The emotional restraint of each sentence, so often stifled to a fragment or phrase dense with meaning, contributes to the sense of claustrophobia that felt by those under constant observation.

Whether nature is considered hostile, indifferent, or redemptive remains an important key to Ross's fiction. While nature is redemptive to Philip, it reflects Mrs. Bentley's sterility. Their vacation in the wilderness revitalizes Philip but further isolates his wife. Thus their move from the rural parish to the city might not renew their marriage. Having demonstrated that relationships are inevitably subverted by incompatible individuals, Ross moves on to explore how the subjective viewpoint reduces truth to relativity, facts to feelings. Determining where to lay the blame for the Bentleys' unbearable relationship is thus beside the point. His explorations of the criminal mind in his next two novels contain analogies with the incompatible Bentleys. Nature is the redemptive force for the protagonist in *The Well* (1958), who overcomes his obsession with material progress by learning the traditions of the past, a time when heroic toil earned man a harmonious relationship with the land. In *Whir of Gold* (1970), Mad replaces Mrs. Bentley's type of self-defeating domination with sacrificial self-control. Mad abandons her attempt to marry and thus renew a self-absorbed musician, because she loves him too much to continue directing him.

Sawbones Memorial (1974) marks a return to the Prairie community of his earlier fiction but provides a release of tension through the same ironic humour as that revealed by the Chautauqua musician who recalls a farmer's comment during the Depression: "The wife's in an insane asylum, and I don't know how she caught that—she hasn't been off the farm in twenty years." Recording the conversations, memories, and thoughts that occur at the retirement party for a town's first doctor, Ross depicts the whole town of Upward looking back at Horizon with apprehension about its progress. Doc Hunter is not as proud of the town's spontaneously co-operative heroism in times of crisis as he is dismayed over its lapses. He asks why "the enormous amount of sympathy and goodwill that springs up the moment someone is in trouble" is afterwards so quickly thrown away. Yet this shaman-like doctor represents the artist as a man of action who has not entirely failed in his attempt to introduce changes to a narrow-minded community. With his son to succeed him in April, there is hope for renewal: "I only hope that he'll look back and say, as I do: "They were not wasted years.""

·————·

Ross's works include *As for Me and My House* (1941); *The Well* (1958); *The Lamp at Noon and Other Stories* (1968); *Whir of Gold* (1970); *Sawbones Memorial* (1974); and *The Race and Other Stories* (1982).

Works on Ross include Robert D. Chambers, *Sinclair Ross and Ernest Buckler* (1975); Lorraine McMullen, *Sinclair Ross* (1979); David Latham, "Sinclair Ross: An Annotated Bibliography," *The Annotated Bibliography of Canada's Major Authors*, ed. Robert Lecker and Jack David (1981), 3: 365–95; and Ken Mitchell, *Sinclair Ross, A Reader's Guide* (1981).

DAVID LATHAM

THE PAINTED DOOR

Straight across the hills it was five miles from John's farm to his father's. But in winter, with the roads impassable, a team had to make a wide detour and skirt the hills, so that from five the distance was more than trebled to seventeen.

"I think I'll walk," John said at breakfast to his wife. "The drifts in the hills wouldn't hold a horse, but they'll carry me all right. If I leave early I can spend a few hours helping him with his chores, and still be back by suppertime."

She went to the window, and thawing a clear place in the frost with her breath, stood looking across the snowswept farmyard to the huddle of stables and sheds. "There was a double wheel around the moon last night," she countered presently. "You said yourself we could expect a storm. It isn't right to leave me here alone. Surely I'm as important as your father."

He glanced up uneasily, then drinking off his coffee tried to reassure her. "But there's nothing to be afraid of—even supposing it does start to storm. You won't need to go near the stable. Everything's fed and watered now to last till night. I'll be back at the latest by seven or eight."

She went on blowing against the frosted pane, carefully elongating the clear place until it was oval-shaped and symmetrical. He watched her a moment or two longer, then more insistently repeated, "I say you won't need to go near the stable. Everything's fed and watered, and I'll see that there's plenty of wood in. That will be all right, won't it?"

"Yes—of course—I heard you—" It was a curiously cold voice now, as if the words were chilled by their contact with the frosted pane. "Plenty to eat—plenty of wood to keep me warm—what more could a woman ask for?"

"But he's an old man—living there all alone. What is it, Ann? You're not like yourself this morning."

She shook her head without turning. "Pay no attention to me. Seven years a farmer's wife—it's time I was used to staying alone."

Slowly the clear place on the glass enlarged: oval, then round, then oval again. The sun was risen above the frost mists now, so keen and hard a glitter on the snow that instead of warmth its rays seemed shedding cold. One of the two-year-old colts that had cantered away when John turned the horses out for water stood covered with rime at the stable door again, head down and body hunched, each breath a little plume of steam against the frosty air. She shivered, but did not turn. In the clear, bitter light the long white miles of prairie landscape seemed a region alien to life. Even the distant farmsteads she could see served only to intensify a sense of isolation. Scattered across the face of so vast and bleak a wilderness it was difficult to conceive them as a testimony of human hardihood and endurance. Rather they seemed futile, lost, to cower before the implacability of snow-swept earth and clear pale sun-chilled sky.

And when at last she turned from the window there was a brooding stillness in her face as if she had recognized this mastery of snow and cold. It troubled John. "If you're really afraid," he yielded, "I won't go today. Lately it's been so cold, that's all. I just wanted to make sure he's all right in case we do have a storm."

"I know—I'm not really afraid." She was putting in a fire now, and he could no longer see her face. "Pay no attention. It's ten miles there and back, so you'd better get started."

"You ought to know by now I wouldn't stay away," he tried to brighten her. "No matter how it stormed. Before we were married—remember? Twice a week I never missed and we had some bad blizzards that winter too."

He was a slow, unambitious man, content with his farm and cattle, naïvely proud of Ann. He had been bewildered by it once, her caring for a dull-witted fellow like him; then assured at last of her affection he had relaxed against it gratefully, unsuspecting it might ever be less constant than his own. Even now, listening to the restless brooding in her voice, he felt only a quick, unformulated kind of pride that after seven years his absence for a day should still concern her. While she, his trust and earnestness controlling her again:

"I know. It's just that sometimes when you're away I get lonely. . . . There's a long cold tramp in front of you. You'll let me fix a scarf around your face."

He nodded. "And on my way I'll drop in at Steven's place. Maybe he'll come over tonight for a game of cards. You haven't seen anybody but me for the last two weeks."

She glanced up sharply, then busied herself clearing the table. "It will mean another two miles if you do. You're going to be cold and tired enough as it is. When you're gone I think I'll paint the kitchen woodwork. White this time—you remember we got the paint last fall. It's going to make the room a lot lighter. I'll be too busy to find the day long."

"I will though," he insisted, "and if a storm gets up you'll feel safer, knowing that he's coming. That's what you need, maybe—someone to talk to besides me."

She stood at the stove motionless a moment, then turned to him uneasily. "Will you shave then, John—now—before you go?"

He glanced at her questioningly, and avoiding his eyes she tried to explain, "I mean—he may be here before you're back—and you won't have a chance then."

"But it's only Steven—we're not going anywhere."

"He'll be shaved, though—that's what I mean—and I'd like you too to spend a little time on yourself."

He stood up, stroking the heavy stubble on his chin. "Maybe I should—

only it softens up the skin too much. Especially when I've got to face the wind."

She nodded and began to help him dress, bringing heavy socks and a big woollen sweater from the bedroom, wrapping a scarf around his face and forehead. "I'll tell Steven to come early," he said, as he went out. "In time for supper. Likely there'll be chores for me to do, so if I'm not back by six don't wait."

From the bedroom window she watched him nearly a mile along the road. The fire had gone down when at last she turned away, and already through the house there was an encroaching chill. A blaze sprang up again when the draughts were opened, but as she went on clearing the table her movements were furtive and constrained. It was the silence weighing upon her—the frozen silence of the bitter fields and sun-chilled sky—lurking outside as if alive, relentlessly in wait, mile-deep between her now and John. She listened to it, suddenly tense, motionless. The fire crackled and the clock ticked. Always it was there. "I'm a fool," she whispered, rattling the dishes in defiance, going back to the stove to put in another fire. "Warm and safe—I'm a fool. It's a good chance when he's away to paint. The day will go quickly. I won't have time to brood."

Since November now the paint had been waiting warmer weather. The frost in the walls on a day like this would crack and peel it as it dried, but she needed something to keep her hands occupied, something to stave off the gathering cold and loneliness. "First of all," she said aloud, opening the paint and mixing it with a little turpentine, "I must get the house warmer. Fill up the stove and open the oven door so that all the heat comes out. Wad something along the window sills to keep out the draughts. Then I'll feel brighter. It's the cold that depresses."

She moved briskly, performing each little task with careful and exaggerated absorption, binding her thoughts to it, making it a screen between herself and the surrounding snow and silence. But when the stove was filled and the windows sealed it was more difficult again. Above the quiet, steady swishing of her brush against the bedroom door the clock began to tick. Suddenly her movements became precise, deliberate, her posture self-conscious, as if someone had entered the room and were watching her. It was the silence again, aggressive, hovering. The fire spit and crackled at it. Still it was there. "I'm a fool," she repeated. "All farmers' wives have to stay alone. I mustn't give in this way. I mustn't brood. A few hours now and they'll be here."

The sound of her voice reassured her. She went on: "I'll get them a good supper—and for coffee after cards bake some of the little cakes with raisins that he likes. . . . Just three of us, so I'll watch, and let John play. It's better with four, but at least we can talk. That's all I need—someone to talk to. John never talks. He's stronger—doesn't need to. But he likes Steven—no matter what the neighbours say. Maybe he'll have him come again, and some other young people too. It's what we need, both of us, to help keep young ourselves. . . . And then before we know it we'll be into March. It's cold still in March sometimes, but you never mind the same. At least you're beginning to think about spring."

She began to think about it now. Thoughts that outstripped her words, that left her alone again with herself and the ever-lurking silence. Eager and hopeful first, then clenched, rebellious, lonely. Windows open, sun and thawing earth again, the urge of growing, living things. Then the days that began in the morning at half-past four and lasted till ten at night; the meals at which John gulped his food and scarcely spoke a word; the brute-tired stupid eyes he turned on her if ever she mentioned town or visiting.

For spring was drudgery again. John never hired a man to help him. He wanted a mortgage-free farm; then a new house and pretty clothes for her. Sometimes, because with the best of crops it was going to take so long to pay off anyway, she wondered whether they mightn't better let the mortgage wait a little. Before they were worn out, before their best years were gone. It was something of life she wanted, not just a house and furniture; something of John, not pretty clothes when she would be too old to wear them. But John of course couldn't understand. To him it seemed only right that she should have the clothes—only right that he, fit for nothing else, should slave away fifteen hours a day to give them to her. There was in his devotion a baffling, insurmountable humility that made him feel the need of sacrifice. And when his muscles ached, when his feet dragged stolidly with weariness, then it seemed that in some measure at least he was making amends for his big hulking body and simple mind. Year after year their lives went on in the same little groove. He drove his horses in the field; she milked the cows and hoed potatoes. By dint of his drudgery he saved a few months' wages, added a few dollars more each fall to his payments on the mortgage; but the only real difference that it all made was to deprive her of his companionship, to make him a little duller, older, uglier than he might otherwise have been. He never saw their lives objectively. To him it was not what he actually accomplished by means of the sacrifice that mattered, but the sacrifice itself, the gesture—something done for her sake.

And she, understanding, kept her silence. In such a gesture, however futile, there was a graciousness not to be shattered lightly. "John," she would begin sometimes, "you're doing too much. Get a man to help you—just for a month—" but smiling down at her he would answer simply, "I don't mind. Look at the hands on me. They're made for work." While in his voice there would be a stalwart ring to tell her that by her thoughtfulness she had made him only the more resolved to serve her, to prove his devotion and fidelity.

They were useless, such thoughts. She knew. It was his very devotion that made them useless, that forbade her to rebel. Yet over and over, sometimes hunched still before their bleakness, sometimes her brush making swift sharp strokes to pace the chafe and rancour that they brought, she persisted in them.

This now, the winter, was their slack season. She could sleep sometimes till eight, and John till seven. They could linger over their meals a little, read, play cards, go visiting the neighbours. It was the time to relax, to indulge and enjoy themselves; but instead, fretful and impatient, they kept on waiting for the spring. They were compelled now, not by labour, but by the spirit of labour. A spirit that pervaded their lives and brought with idleness a sense of guilt. Sometimes they did sleep late, sometimes they did play cards, but always uneasily, always reproached by the thought of more important things that might be done. When John got up at five to attend to the fire he wanted to stay up and go out to the stable. When he sat down to a meal he hurried his food and pushed his chair away again, from habit, from sheer work-instinct, even though it was only to put more wood in the stove, or go down cellar to cut up beets and turnips for the cows.

And anyway, sometimes she asked herself, why sit trying to talk with a man who never talked? Why talk when there was nothing to talk about but crops and cattle, the weather and the neighbours? The neighbours, too—why go visiting them when still it was the same—crops and cattle, the weather and the other neighbours? Why go to the dances in the schoolhouse to sit among the older women, one of them now, married seven years, or to waltz with the work-bent, tired old farmers to a squeaky fiddle tune? Once she had danced with Steven six or seven times in the evening, and they had talked about it for as many months. It was easier to stay at home. John never danced or enjoyed himself. He was always uncomfortable in his good suit and shoes. He didn't like shaving in the cold weather oftener than once or twice a week. It was easier to stay at home, to stand at the window staring out across the bitter fields, to count the days and look forward to another spring.

But now, alone with herself in the winter silence, she saw the spring for what it really was. This spring—next spring—all the springs and summers still to come. While they grew old, while their bodies warped, while their minds kept shrivelling dry and empty like their lives. "I mustn't," she said aloud again. "I married him—and he's a good man. I mustn't keep on this way. It will be noon before long, and then time to think about supper. . . . Maybe he'll come early—and as soon as John is finished at the stable we can all play cards."

It was getting cold again, and she left her painting to put in more wood. But this time the warmth spread slowly. She pushed a mat up to the outside door, and went back to the window to pat down the woollen shirt that was wadded along the sill. Then she paced a few times round the room, then poked the fire and rattled the stove lids, then paced again. The fire crackled, the clock ticked. The silence now seemed more intense than ever, seemed to have reached a pitch where it faintly moaned. She began to pace on tiptoe, listening, her shoulders drawn together, not realising for a while that it was the wind she heard, thin-strained and whimpering through the eaves.

Then she wheeled to the window, and with quick short breaths thawed the frost to see again. The glitter was gone. Across the drifts sped swift and snakelike little tongues of snow. She could not follow them, where they sprang from, or where they disappeared. It was as if all across the yard the snow were shivering awake—roused by the warnings of the wind to hold itself in readiness for the impending storm. The sky had become a sombre, whitish grey. It, too, as if in readiness, had shifted and lay close to earth. Before her as she watched a mane of powdery snow reared up breast-high against the darker background of the stable, tossed for a moment angrily, and then subsided again as if whipped down to obedience and restraint. But another followed, more reckless and impatient than the first. Another reeled and dashed itself against the window where she watched. Then ominously for a while there were only the angry little snakes of snow. The wind rose, creaking the troughs that were wired beneath the eaves. In the distance, sky and prairie now were merged into one another linelessly. All round her it was gathering; already in its press and whimpering there strummed a boding of eventual fury. Again she saw a mane of snow spring up, so dense and high this time that all the sheds and stables were obscured. Then others followed, whirling fiercely out of hand; and, when at last they cleared, the stables seemed in dimmer outline than before. It was the snow beginning, long lancet shafts of it, straight from the north, borne almost level by the straining wind. "He'll be there soon," she whispered, "and coming home it will be in his back. He'll leave again right away. He saw the double wheel—he knows the kind of storm there'll be."

She went back to her painting. For a while it was easier, all her thoughts half-anxious ones of John in the blizzard, struggling his way across the hills; but petulantly again she soon began, "I knew we were going to have a storm—I told him so—but it doesn't matter what I say. Big stubborn fool—he goes his own way anyway. It doesn't matter what becomes of me. In a storm like this he'll never get home. He won't even try. And while he sits keeping his father company I can look after his stable for him, go ploughing through snowdrifts up to my knees—nearly frozen—"

Not that she meant or believed her words. It was just an effort to convince herself that she did have a grievance, to justify her rebellious thoughts, to prove John responsible for her unhappiness. She was young still, eager for excitement and distractions; and John's steadfastness rebuked her vanity, made her complaints seem weak and trivial. She went on, fretfully, "If he'd listen to me sometimes and not be so stubborn we wouldn't still be living in a house like this. Seven years in two rooms—seven years and never a new stick of furniture. . . . There—as if another coat of paint could make it different anyway."

She cleaned her brush, filled up the stove again, and went back to the window. There was a void white moment that she thought must be frost formed on the window pane; then, like a fitful shadow through the whirling snow, she recognized the stable roof. It was incredible. The sudden, maniac raging of the storm struck from her face all its pettishness. Her eyes glazed with fear a little; her lips blanched. "If he starts for home now," she whispered silently—"But he won't—he knows I'm safe—he knows Steven's coming. Across the hills he would never dare."

She turned to the stove, holding out her hands to the warmth. Around her now there seemed a constant sway and tremor, as if the air were vibrating with the shudderings of the walls. She stood quite still, listening. Sometimes the wind struck with sharp, savage blows. Sometimes it bore down in a sustained, minute-long blast, silent with effort and intensity; then with a foiled shriek of threat wheeled away to gather and assault again. Always the eave-troughs creaked and sawed. She stared towards the window again, then detecting the morbid trend of her thoughts, prepared fresh coffee and forced herself to drink a few mouthfuls. "He would never dare," she whispered again. "He wouldn't leave the old man anyway in such a storm. Safe in here—there's nothing for me to keep worrying about. It's after one already. I'll do my baking now, and then it will be time to get supper ready for Steven."

Soon, however, she began to doubt whether Steven would come. In such a storm even a mile was enough to make a man hesitate. Especially Steven, who was hardly the one to face a blizzard for the sake of someone else's chores. He had a stable of his own to look after anyway. It would be only natural for him to think that when the storm blew up John had turned again for home. Another man would have—would have put his wife first.

But she felt little dread or uneasiness at the prospect of spending the night alone. It was the first time she had been left like this on her own resources, and her reaction, now that she could face and appraise her situation calmly, was gradually to feel it a kind of adventure and responsibility. It stimulated her. Before nightfall she must go to the stable and feed everything. Wrap up in some of John's clothes—take a ball of string in her hand, one end tied to the door, so that no matter how blinding the storm she could at least find her way back to the house. She had heard of people having to do that. It appealed to her now because suddenly it made life dramatic. She had not felt the storm yet, only watched it for a minute through the window.

It took nearly an hour to find enough string, to choose the right socks and sweaters. Long before it was time to start out she tried on John's clothes, changing and rechanging, striding around the room to make sure there would be play enough for pitching hay and struggling over snowdrifts; then she took them off again, and for a while busied herself baking the little cakes with raisins that he liked.

Night came early. Just for a moment on the doorstep she shrank back, uncertain. The slow dimming of the light clutched her with an illogical sense of abandonment. It was like the covert withdrawal of an ally, leaving the alien miles unleashed and unrestrained. Watching the hurricane of writhing snow rage past the little house she forced herself, "They'll never stand the night unless I get them fed. It's nearly dark already, and I've work to last an hour."

Timidly, unwinding a little of the string, she crept out from the shelter of the doorway. A gust of wind spun her forward a few yards, then plunged her headlong against a drift that in the dense white whirl lay invisible across her path. For nearly a minute she huddled still, breathless and dazed. The snow was in her mouth and nostrils, inside her scarf and up her sleeves. As she tried to straighten a smothering scud flung itself against her face, cutting off her breath a second time. The wind struck from all sides, blustering and furious. It was as if the storm had discovered her, as if all its forces were concentrated upon her extinction. Seized with panic suddenly she threshed out a moment with her arms, then stumbled back and sprawled her length across the drift.

But this time she regained her feet quickly, roused by the whip and batter of the storm to retaliative anger. For a moment her impulse was to face the wind and strike back blow for blow; then, as suddenly as it had come, her frantic strength gave way to limpness and exhaustion. Suddenly, a comprehension so clear and terrifying that it struck all thoughts of the stable from her mind, she realized in such a storm her puniness. And the realization gave her new strength, stilled this time to a desperate persistence. Just for a moment the wind held her, numb and swaying in its vise; then slowly, buckled far forward, she groped her way again towards the house.

Inside, leaning against the door, she stood tense and still a while. It was almost dark now. The top of the stove glowed a deep, dull red. Heedless of the storm, self-absorbed and self-satisfied, the clock ticked on like a glib little idiot. "He shouldn't have gone," she whispered silently. "He saw the double wheel—he knew. He shouldn't have left me here alone."

For so fierce now, so insane and dominant did the blizzard seem, that she could not credit the safety of the house. The warmth and lull around her was not real yet, not to be relied upon. She was still at the mercy of the storm. Only her body pressing hard like this against the door was staving it off. She didn't dare move. She didn't dare ease the ache and strain. "He shouldn't have gone," she repeated, thinking of the stable again, reproached by her helplessness. "They'll freeze in their stalls— and I can't reach them. He'll say it's all my fault. He won't believe I tried."

Then Steven came. Quickly, startled to quietness and control, she let him in and lit the lamp. He stared at her a moment, then flinging off his cap crossed to where she stood by the table and seized her arms. "You're so white—what's wrong? Look at me—" It was like him in such little situations to be masterful. "You should have known better—for a while I thought I wasn't going to make it here myself—"

"I was afraid you wouldn't come—John left early, and there was the stable—"

But the storm had unnerved her, and suddenly at the assurance of his touch and voice the fear that had been gripping her gave way to an hysteria of relief. Scarcely aware of herself she seized his arm and sobbed against it. He remained still a moment unyielding, then slipped his other arm around her shoulder. It was comforting and she relaxed against it, hushed by a sudden sense of lull and safety. Her shoulders trembled with the easing of the strain, then fell limp and still. "You're shivering,"—he drew her gently towards the stove. "It's all right—nothing to be afraid of. I'm going to see to the stable."

It was a quiet, sympathetic voice, yet with an undertone of insolence, a kind of mockery even, that made her draw away quickly and busy herself putting in a fire. With his lips drawn in a little smile he watched her till she looked at him again. The smile too was insolent, but at the same time companionable; Steven's smile, and therefore difficult to reprove. It lit up his lean, still-boyish face with a peculiar kind of arrogance: features and smile that were different from John's, from other men's—wilful and derisive, yet naïvely so—as if it were less the difference itself he was conscious of, than the long-accustomed privilege that thereby fell his due. He was erect, tall, square-shouldered. His hair was dark and trim, his lips curved soft and full. While John, she made the comparison swiftly, was thickset, heavy-jowled, and stooped. He always stood before her helpless, a kind of humility and wonderment in his attitude. And Steven now smiled on her appraisingly with the worldly-wise assurance of one for whom a woman holds neither mystery nor illusion.

"It was good of you to come, Steven," she responded, the words running into a sudden, empty laugh. "Such a storm to face—I suppose I should feel flattered."

For his presumption, his misunderstanding of what had been only a momentary weakness, instead of angering quickened her, roused from latency and long disuse all the instincts and resources of her femininity. She felt eager, challenged. Something was at hand that hitherto had always eluded her, even in the early days with John, something vital, beckoning, meaningful. She didn't understand, but she knew. The texture of the moment was satisfyingly dreamlike: an incredibility perceived as such, yet acquiesced in. She was John's wife—she knew—but also she knew that Steven standing here was different from John. There was no thought or motive, no understanding of herself as the knowledge persisted. Wary and poised round a sudden little core of blind excitement she evaded him, "But it's nearly dark—hadn't you better hurry if you're going to do the chores? Don't trouble—I can get them off myself—"

An hour later when he returned from the stable she was in another dress, hair rearranged, a little flush of colour in her face. Pouring warm water for him from the kettle into the basin she said evenly, "By the time you're washed supper will be ready. John said we weren't to wait for him."

He looked at her a moment, "You don't mean you're expecting John tonight? The way it's blowing—"

"Of course." As she spoke she could feel the colour deepening in her face. "We're going to play cards. He was the one that suggested it."

He went on washing, and then as they took their places at the table, resumed, "So John's coming. When are you expecting him?"

"He said it might be seven o'clock—or a little later." Conversation with Steven at other times had always been brisk and natural, but now all at once she found it strained. "He may have work to do for his father. That's what he said when he left. Why do you ask, Steven?"

"I was just wondering—it's a rough night."

"You don't know John. It would take more than a storm to stop him."

She glanced up again and he was smiling at her. The same insolence, the same little twist of mockery and appraisal. It made her flinch, and ask herself why she was pretending to expect John—why there should be this instinct of defence to force her. This time, instead of poise and excitement, it brought a reminder that she had changed her dress and rearranged her hair. It crushed in a sudden silence, through which she heard the whistling wind again, and the creaking saw of the eaves. Neither spoke now. There was something strange, almost frightening, about this Steven and his quiet, unrelenting smile; but strangest of all was the familiarity: the Steven she had never seen or encountered, and yet had always known, always expected, always waited for. It was less Steven himself that she felt than his inevitability. Just as she had felt the snow, the silence and the storm. She kept her eyes lowered, on the window past his shoulder, on the stove, but his smile now seemed to exist apart from him, to merge and hover with the silence. She clinked a cup— listened to the whistle of the storm—always it was there. He began to speak, but her mind missed the meaning of his words. Swiftly she was making comparisons again; his face so different to John's, so handsome and young and clean-shaven. Swiftly, helplessly, feeling the imperceptible and relentless ascendancy that thereby he was gaining over her, sensing sudden menace in this new, more vital life, even as she felt drawn towards it.

The lamp between them flickered as an onslaught of the storm sent shudderings through the room. She rose to build up the fire again and he followed her. For a long time they stood close to the stove, their arms almost touching. Once as the blizzard creaked the house she spun around sharply, fancying it was John at the door; but quietly he intercepted her. "Not tonight—you might as well make up your mind to it. Across the hills in a storm like this—it would be suicide to try."

Her lips trembled suddenly in an effort to answer, to parry the certainty in his voice, then set thin and bloodless. She was afraid now. Afraid of his face so different from John's—of his smile, of her own helplessness to rebuke it. Afraid of the storm, isolating her here alone with him. They tried to play cards, but she kept starting up at every creak and shiver of the walls. "It's too rough a night," he repeated. "Even for John. Just relax a few minutes—stop worrying and pay a little attention to me."

But in his tone there was a contradiction to his words. For it implied that she was not worrying—that her only concern was lest it really might be John at the door.

And the implication persisted. He filled up the stove for her, shuffled the cards—won—shuffled—still it was there. She tried to respond to his conversation, to think of the game, but helplessly into her cards instead she began to ask, Was he right? Was that why he smiled? Why he seemed to wait, expectant and assured?

The clock ticked, the fire crackled. Always it was there. Furtively for a moment she watched him as he deliberated over his hand. John, even in the days before they were married, had never looked like that. Only this morning she had asked him to shave. Because Steven was coming—because she had been afraid to see them side by side—because deep within herself she had known even then. The same knowledge, furtive and forbidden, that was flaunted now in Steven's smile. "You look cold," he said at last, dropping his cards and rising from the table. "We're not playing, anyway. Come over to the stove for a few minutes and get warm."

"But first I think we'll hang blankets over the door. When there's a blizzard like this we always do." It seemed that in sane, commonplace activity there might be release, a moment or two in which to recover herself. "John has nails to put them on. They keep out a little of the draught."

He stood on a chair for her, and hung the blankets that she carried from the bedroom. Then for a moment they stood silent, watching the blankets sway and tremble before the blade of wind that spurted around the jamb. "I forgot," she said at last, "that I painted the bedroom door. At the top there, see—I've smeared the blankets."

He glanced at her curiously, and went back to the stove. She followed him, trying to imagine the hills in such a storm, wondering whether John would come. "A man couldn't live in it," suddenly he answered her thoughts, lowering the oven door and drawing up their chairs one on each side of it. "He knows you're safe. It isn't likely that he'd leave his father, anyway."

"The wind will be on his back," she persisted. "The winter before we were married—all the blizzards that we had that year—and he never missed—"

"Blizzards like this one? Up in the hills he wouldn't be able to keep his direction for a hundred yards. Listen to it a minute and ask yourself."

His voice seemed softer, kindlier now. She met his smile a moment, its assured little twist of appraisal, then for a long time sat silent, tense, careful again to avoid his eyes.

Everything now seemed to depend on this. It was the same as a few hours ago when she braced the door against the storm. He was watching her, smiling. She dared not move, unclench her hands, or raise her eyes. The flames crackled, the clock ticked. The storm wrenched the walls as if to make them buckle in. So rigid and desperate were all her muscles set, withstanding, that the room around her seemed to swim and reel. So rigid and strained that for relief at last, despite herself, she raised her head and met his eyes again.

Intending that it should be for only an instant, just to breathe again, to ease the tension that had grown unbearable—but in his smile now, instead of the insolent appraisal that she feared, there seemed a kind of warmth and sympathy. An understanding that quickened and encouraged her—that made her wonder why but a moment ago she had been afraid. It was as if the storm had lulled, as if she had suddenly found calm and shelter.

Or perhaps, the thought seized her, perhaps instead of his smile it was she who had changed. She who, in the long, wind-creaked silence, had emerged from the increment of codes and loyalties to her real, unfettered self. She who now felt his air of appraisal as nothing more than an understanding of the unfulfilled woman that until this moment had lain within her brooding and unadmitted, reproved out of consciousness by the insistence of an outgrown, routine fidelity.

For there had always been Steven. She understood now. Seven years—almost as long as John—ever since the night they first danced together.

The lamp was burning dry, and through the dimming light, isolated in the fastness of silence and storm, they watched each other. Her face was white and struggling still. His was handsome, clean-shaven, young. Her eyes were fanatic, believing desperately, fixed upon him as if to exclude all else, as if to find justification. His were cool, bland, drooped a little with expectancy. The light kept dimming, gathering the shadows round them, hushed, conspiratorial. He was smiling still. Her hands again were clenched up white and hard.

"But he always came," she persisted. "the wildest, coldest nights—even such a night as this. There was never a storm—"

"Never a storm like this one." There was a quietness in his smile now, a kind of simplicity almost, as if to reassure her. "You were out in it yourself for a few minutes. He'd have it for five miles, across the hills. . . . I'd think twice myself, on such a night before risking even one."

Long after he was asleep she lay listening to the storm. As a check on the draught up the chimney they had left one of the stovelids partly off, and through the open bedroom door she could see the flickerings of flame and shadow on the kitchen wall. They leaped and sank fantastically. The longer she watched the more alive they seemed to be. There was one great shadow that struggled towards her threateningly, massive and black and engulfing all the room. Again and again it advanced, about to spring, but each time a little whip of light subdued it to its place among the others on the wall. Yet though it never reached her still she cowered, feeling that gathered there was all the frozen wilderness, its heart of terror and invincibility.

Then she dozed a while, and the shadow was John. Interminably he advanced. The whips of light still flickered and coiled, but now suddenly they were the swift little snakes that this afternoon she had watched twist and shiver across the snow. And they too were advancing. They writhed and vanished and came again. She lay still, paralysed. He was over her now, so close that she could have touched him. Already it seemed that a deadly tightening hand was on her throat. She tried to scream but her lips were locked. Steven beside her slept on heedlessly.

Until suddenly as she lay staring up at him a gleam of light revealed his face. And in it was not a trace of threat or anger—only calm, and stonelike hopelessness.

That was like John. He began to withdraw, and frantically she tried to call him back. "It isn't true—not really true—listen, John—" but the words clung frozen to her lips. Already there was only the shriek of wind again, the sawing eaves, the leap and twist of shadow on the wall.

She sat up, startled now and awake. And so real had he seemed there, standing close to her, so vivid the sudden age and sorrow in his face, that at first she could not make herself understand she had been only dreaming. Against the conviction of his presence in the room it was necessary to insist over and over that he must still be with his father on the other side of the hills. Watching the shadows she had fallen asleep. It was only her mind, her imagination, distorted to a nightmare by the illogical and unadmitted dread of his return. But he wouldn't come. Steven was right. In such a storm he would never try. They were safe, alone. No one would ever know. It was only fear, morbid and irrational; only the sense of guilt that even her new-found and challenged womanhood could not entirely quell.

She knew now. She had not let herself understand or acknowledge it as guilt before, but gradually through the wind-torn silence of the night his face compelled her. The face that had watched her from the darkness with its stonelike sorrow—the face that was really John—John more than his features of mere flesh and bone could ever be.

She wept silently. The fitful gleam of light began to sink. On the ceiling and wall at last there was only a faint dull flickering glow. The little house shuddered and quailed, and a chill crept in again. Without wakening Steven she slipped out to build up the fire. It was burned to a few spent embers now, and the wood she put on seemed a long time catching light. The wind swirled through the blankets they had hung around the door, and then, hollow and moaning, roared up the chimney again, as if against its will drawn back to serve still longer with the onrush of the storm.

For a long time she crouched over the stove, listening. Earlier in the evening, with the lamp lit and the fire crackling, the house had seemed a stand against the wilderness, a refuge of feeble walls wherein persisted the elements of human meaning and survival. Now, in the cold, creaking darkness, it was strangely extinct, looted by the storm and abandoned again. She lifted the stove lid and fanned the embers till at last a swift little tongue of flame began to lick around the wood. Then she replaced the lid, extended her hands, and as if frozen in that attitude stood waiting.

It was not long now. After a few minutes she closed the draughts, and as the flames whirled back upon each other, beating against the top of the stove and sending out flickers of light again, a warmth surged up to relax her stiffened limbs. But shivering and numb it had been easier. The bodily well-being that the warmth induced gave play again to an ever more insistent mental suffering. She remembered the shadow that was John. She saw him bent towards her, then retreating, his features pale and overcast with unaccusing grief. She re-lived their seven years together and, in retrospect, found them to be years of worth and dignity. Until crushed by it all at last, seized by a sudden need to suffer and atone, she crossed to where the draught was bitter, and for a long time stood unflinching on the icy floor.

The storm was close here. Even through the blankets she could feel a sift of snow against her face. The eaves sawed, the walls creaked, and the wind was like a wolf in howling flight.

And yet, suddenly she asked herself, hadn't there been other storms, other blizzards? And through the worst of them hadn't he always reached her?

Clutched by the thought she stood rooted a minute. It was hard now to understand how she could have so deceived herself—how a moment of passion could have quieted within her not only conscience, but reason and discretion too. John always came. There could never be a storm to stop him. He was strong, inured to the cold. He had crossed the hills since his boyhood, knew every creek-bed and gully. It was madness to go on like this—to wait. While there was still time she must waken Steven, and hurry him away.

But in the bedroom again, standing at Steven's side, she hesitated. In his detachment from it all, in his quiet, even breathing, there was such sanity, such realism. For him nothing had happened; nothing would. If she wakened him he would only laugh and tell her to listen to the storm. Already it was long past midnight; either John had lost his way or not set out at all. And she knew that in his devotion there was nothing foolhardy. He would never risk a storm beyond his endurance, never permit himself a sacrifice likely to endanger her lot or future. They were both safe. No one would ever know. She must control herself— be sane like Steven.

For comfort she let her hand rest a while on Steven's shoulder. It would be easier were he awake now, with her, sharing her guilt; but gradually as she watched his handsome face in the glimmering light she came to understand that for him no guilt existed. Just as there had been no passion, no conflict. Nothing but the sane appraisal of their situation, nothing but the expectant little smile, and the arrogance of features that were different from John's. She winced deeply, remembering how she had fixed her eyes on those features, how she had tried to believe that so handsome and young, so different from John's, they must in themselves be her justification.

In the flickering light they were still young, still handsome. No longer her justification—she knew now—John was the man—but wistfully still, wondering sharply at their power and tyranny, she touched them a moment with her fingertips again.

She could not blame him. There had been no passion, no guilt; therefore there could be no responsibility. Looking down at him as he slept, half-smiling still, his lips relaxed in the conscienceless complacency of his achievement, she understood that thus he was revealed in his entirety—all there ever was or ever could be. John was the man. With him lay all the future. For tonight, slowly and contritely through the day and years to come, she would try to make amends.

Then she stole back to the kitchen, and without thought, impelled by overwhelming need again, returned to the door where the draught was bitter still. Gradually towards morning the storm began to spend itself. Its terror blast became a feeble, worn-out moan. The leap of light and shadow sank, and a chill crept in again. Always the eaves creaked, tortured with wordless prophecy. Heedless of it all the clock ticked on in idiot content.

They found him the next day, less than a mile from home. Drifting with the storm he had run against his own pasture fence and overcome had frozen there, erect still, both hands clasping fast the wire.

"He was south of here," they said wonderingly when she told them how he had come across the hills. "Straight south—you'd wonder how he could have missed the buildings. It was the wind last night, coming every way at once. He shouldn't have tried. There was a double wheel around the moon."

She looked past them a moment, then as if to herself said simply, "If you knew him, though—John would try."

It was later, when they had left her a while to be alone with him, that she knelt and touched his hand. Her eyes dimmed, it was still such a strong and patient hand; then, transfixed, they suddenly grew wide and clear. On the palm, white even against its frozen whiteness, was a little smear of paint.

[1939]

· MAVIS GALLANT ·

1922–

Mavis Gallant (née Young) was born 11 August 1922 in Montreal to Anglo-Scottish parents. When she was four, her parents took the unusual step of sending her to a strict Jansenist convent school where she was the only English-speaking Protestant child. On the positive side, she learned French almost as early as English. Her father, who was a painter, died tragically when she was ten, and Gallant found herself moved from place to place, school to school. She completed her schooling in New York, and then returned to Montreal where she was married for a brief period. At the age of twenty-one she became a reporter with the Montreal *Standard*. In 1950 she left the *Standard* to earn her living as a fiction writer. She travelled to Europe, and lived in many different countries; spending her winters high above the Mediterranean near the border between France and Italy. In 1961 she began living semi-permanently on the Left Bank in Paris. Shortly after Gallant arrived in Europe, the *New Yorker* published "Madeline's Birthday," the beginning of a long and fruitful relationship which has allowed her to earn a living as a fiction writer. Gallant returns frequently to Canada, both privately and for reading tours. In the academic year 1983–84, she was writer-in-residence at the University of Toronto. *Home Truths: Selected Canadian Stories* won the Governor General's Award for Fiction in 1981; in the same year she was invested as an Officer of the Order of Canada.

Gallant's fiction follows in the realist tradition of Chekhov, Mansfield, and Joyce to create the illusion of people living in authentic settings untransformed by language. Yet her fiction also evokes the mystery surrounding individual lives. Her paragraphs often develop as prose poems, the tone and

accent of a person's voice serving as the main indicators of attitudes and beliefs. Many of her characters seem suspended between memory and expectation, leading in *Green Water, Green Sky* (1959) to a condition of generalized insanity. Typically, Gallant's characters find themselves far from family and country, a situation corresponding to spiritual homelessness. As children these people often enjoy a freedom which becomes increasingly disconcerting, causing them to turn to family, profession, and nationality as the conventional adult means of constraining reality. In later life her characters occasionally break free of their mental blinkers to take charge of their lives, even to develop a fresh sense of their individual relationships to time and history, but more frequently they remain in limbo, waiting.

Gallant's manner of setting up and then dissolving the hard-edged substance of everyday life becomes particularly apparent in "The Accident" where a newly married couple wanders between childhood and "real life" in the adult world. "The Accident" also appears as a flashback section of the novel *A Fairly Good Time* (1970), which offers a madcap account of Shirley Higgins, lost amid the supposed rationality of the French. Gallant has explained that she wrote the novel over a number of years. At one point, while rereading the unfinished manuscript, she discovered that the section about the accident stood on its own, and she decided to publish it as a story.

Gallant's more recent fiction delineates the individual within history. The stories in *The Pegnitz Junction* (1973) examine the plight of Germans in the wake of World War II. *Home Truths* (1981) offers a reconstruction of the Montreal of Gallant's youth, from the 1920s to the 1940s, describing Linnet Muir's struggle to achieve independence in a man's world. Her latest collection, *Overhead in a Balloon: Stories of Paris* (1985), depicts Paris in the post-war years where the loss of individual integrity threatens to create a frivolous media-based society, duplicating past Fascist patterns.

·————·

Gallant's works include *The Other Paris* (1956); *Green Water, Green Sky* (1959); *My Heart is Broken: Eight Stories and a Short Novel* (1964); *A Fairly Good Time* (1970); *The Pegnitz Junction: A Novella and Five Short Stories* (1973); *The End of the World and Other Stories* (1974); *From the Fifteenth District: A Novella and Eight Short Stories* (1979); *Home Truths: Selected Canadian Stories* (1981); *What Is to Be Done?* (1983); *Overhead in a Balloon: Stories of Paris* (1985); and *Paris Notebooks: Essays and Reviews* (1986).

Works on Gallant include Peter Stevens, "Perils of Compassion," *The Canadian Novel in the Twentieth Century: Essays from* Canadian Literature, ed. George Woodcock (1975): 202–11; Geoff Hancock, ed., special issue of *Canadian Fiction Magazine* 28 (1978); Grazia Merler, *Mavis Gallant: Narrative Patterns and Devices* (1978); Ronald Hatch, "Mavis Gallant: Returning Home," *Atlantis* 4 (1978): 95–102; "Mavis Gallant and the Expatriate Character," *Zeitschrift der Gesellschaft für Kanada-Studien* 1 (1981): 133–42; David O'Rourke, "Exiles in Time: Gallant's 'My Heart is Broken,'" *Canadian Literature* 93 (1982): 98–107; Debra Martens, "An Interview with Mavis Gallant," *Rubicon* 4 (1984–85): 150–82; Judith Skelton Grant and Douglas Malcolm, "Mavis Gallant: An Annotated Bibliography," *The Annotated Bibliography of Canada's Major Authors*, ed. Robert Lecker and Jack David (1984), 5: 179–230; and Ronald Hatch, "Mavis Gallant and the Creation of Consciousness," *Present Tense*, ed. John Moss (1985): 45-71.

RONALD HATCH

THE ACCIDENT

I was tired and did not always understand what they were asking me. I borrowed a pencil and wrote:

PETER HIGGINS
CALGARY 1935–ITALY 1956

But there was room for more on the stone, and the English clergyman in this Italian town who was doing all he could for me said, "Is there nothing else, child?" Hadn't Pete been my husband, somebody's son? That was what he was asking. It seemed enough. Pete had renounced us, left us behind. His life-span might matter, if anyone cared, but I must have sensed even then that no one would ever ask me what he had been like. His father once asked me to write down what I remembered. He wanted to compose a memorial booklet and distribute it at Christmas, but then his wife died, too, and he became prudent about recollections. Even if I had wanted to, I couldn't have told much—just one or two things about the way Pete died. His mother had some information about him, and I had some, but never enough to describe a life. She had the complete knowledge that puts parents at a loss, finally: she knew all about him except his opinion of her and how he was with me. They were never equals. She was a grown person with part of a life lived and the habit of secrets before he was conscious of her. She said, later, that she and Pete had been friends. How can you be someone's friend if you have had twenty years' authority over him and he has never had one second's authority over you?

He didn't look like his mother. He looked like me. In Italy, on our wedding trip, we were often taken for brother and sister. Our height, our glasses, our soft myopic stares, our assurance, our sloppy comfortable clothes made us seem to the Italians related and somehow unplaceable. Only a North American could have guessed what our families were, what our education amounted to, and where we had got the money to spend on travelling. Most of the time we were just pie-faces, like the tourists in ads—though we were not as clean as those couples, and not quite as grown-up. We didn't seem to be married: the honeymoon in hotels, in strange beds, the meals we shared in cheap, bright little restaurants, prolonged the clandestine quality of love before. It was still a game, but now we had infinite time. I became bold, and I dismissed the universe: "It was a rotten little experiment," I said, "and we were given up long ago." I had been brought up by a forcible, pessimistic, widowed mother, and to be able to say aloud "we were given up" shows how far I had come. Pete's assurance was natural, but mine was fragile, and recent, and had grown out of love. Travelling from another direction, he was much more interested in his parents than in God. There was a glorious treason in all our conversations now. Pete wondered about his parents, but I felt safer belittling Creation. My mother had let me know about the strength of the righteous; I still thought the skies would fall if I said too much.

What struck me about these secret exchanges was how we judged our parents from a distance now, as if they were people we had known on a visit. The idea that he and I could be natural siblings crossed my mind. What if I, or Pete, or both, had been adopted? We had been raised in different parts of Canada, but we were only children, and neither of us resembled our supposed parents. Watching him, trapping him almost in mannerisms I could claim, I saw my habit of sprawling, of spreading maps and newspapers on the ground. He had a vast appetite for bread and pastries and sweet desserts. He was easily drunk and easily sick. Yes, we were alike. We talked in hotel rooms, while we drank the drink of the place, the *grappa* or wine or whatever we were given, prone across the bed, the bottle and glasses and the ashtray on the floor. We agreed to live openly, without secrets, though neither of us knew what a secret was. I admired him as I could never have admired myself. I remembered how my mother, the keeper of the castle until now, had said that one day—one treeless, sunless day—real life would overtake me, and then I would realize how spoiled and silly I had always been.

The longest time he and I spent together in one place was three days, in a village up behind the Ligurian coast. I thought that the only success of my life, my sole achievement, would be this marriage. In a dream he came to me with the plans for a house. I saw the white lines on the blue paper, and he showed me the sunny Italian-style loggia that would be built. "It is not quite what we want," he said, "but better than anything we have now." "But we can't afford it, we haven't got the capital," I cried, and I panicked, and woke: woke safe, in a room of which the details were dawn, window, sky, first birds of morning, and Pete still sleeping, still in the dark.

The last Italian town of our journey was nothing—just a black beach with sand like soot, and houses shut and dormant because it was the middle of the afternoon. We had come here from our village only to change trains. We were on our way to Nice, then Paris, then home. We left our luggage at the station, with a porter looking after it, and we drifted through empty, baking streets, using up the rest of a roll of film. By now we must have had hundreds of pictures of each other in market squares, next to oleanders, cut in two by broomstick shade, or backed up, squinting, against scaly noonday shutters. Pete now chose to photograph a hotel with a cat on the step, a policeman, and a souvenir stand, as if he had never seen such things in Canada—as if they were monuments. I never once heard him say anything was ugly or dull; for if it was, what were we doing with it? We were often stared at, for we were out of our own background and did not fit into the new. That day, I was eyed more than he was. I was watched by men talking in dark doorways, leaning against the façades of inhospitable shops. I was travelling in shorts and a shirt and rope-soled shoes. I know now that this costume was resented, but I don't know why. There was nothing indecent about my clothes. They were very like Pete's.

He may not have noticed the men. He was always on the lookout for something to photograph, or something to do, and sometimes he missed people's faces. On the steep street that led back to the railway station, he took a careful picture of a bakery, and he bought crescent-shaped bread with a soft, pale crust, and ate it there, on the street. He wasn't hungry; it was a question of using time. Now the closed shutters broke out in the afternoon, and girls appeared—girls with thick hair, smelling of jasmine and honeysuckle. They strolled hand in hand, in light stockings and clean white shoes. Their dresses—blue, lemon, the palest peach—bloomed over rustling petticoats. At home I'd have called them cheap, and made a face at their cheap perfume, but here, in their own place, they were enravishing, and I thought Pete would look at them and at me and compare; but all he remarked was "How do they stand those clothes on a day like this?" So real life, the grey noon with no limits, had not yet begun. I distrusted real life, for I knew nothing about it. It was the middle-aged world without feeling, where no one was loved.

Bored with his bread, he tossed it away and laid his hands on a white Lambretta propped against the curb. He pulled it upright, examining it. He committed two crimes in a second: wasted bread and touched an adored mechanical object belonging to someone else. I knew these were crimes later, when it was no use knowing, no good to either of us. The steering of the Lambretta was locked. He saw a bicycle then, belonging, he thought, to an old man who was sitting in a kitchen chair out on the pavement. "This all right with you?" Pete pointed to the bike, then himself, then down the hill. With a swoop of his hand he tried to show he would come straight back. His pantomime also meant that there was still time before we had to be on the train, that up at the station there was nothing to do, that eating bread, taking pictures of shops, riding a bike downhill and walking it back were all doing, using up your life; yes, it was a matter of living.

The idling old man Pete had spoken to bared his gums. Pete must have taken this for a smile. Later, the old man, who was not the owner of the bike or of anything except the fat sick dog at his feet, said he had cried "Thief!" but I never heard him. Pete tossed me his camera and I saw him glide, then rush away, past the girls who smelled of jasmine, past the bakery, down to the corner, where a policeman in white, under a parasol, spread out one arm and flexed the other and blew hard on a whistle. Pete was standing, as if he were trying to coast to a stop. I saw things meaningless now—for instance that the sun was sifted through leaves. There were trees we hadn't noticed. Under the leaves he seemed under water. A black car, a submarine with Belgian plates, parked at an angle, stirred to life. I saw sunlight deflected from six points on the paint. My view became discomposed, as if the sea were suddenly black and opaque and had splashed up over the policeman and the road, and I screamed, "He's going to open the door!" Everyone said later that I was mistaken, for why would the Belgian have started the motor, pulled out, and *then* flung open the door? He had stopped near a change office; perhaps he had forgotten his sunglasses, or a receipt. He started, stopped abruptly, hurled back the door. I saw that, and then I saw him driving away. No one had taken his number.

Strangers made Pete kneel and then stand, and they dusted the bicycle. They forced him to walk—where? Nobody wanted him. Into a pharmacy, finally. In a parrot's voice he said to the policeman, "Don't touch my elbow." The pharmacist said, "He can't stay here," for Pete was vomiting, but weakly—a weak coughing, like an infant's. I was in a crowd of about twenty people, a spectator with two cameras round my neck. In kind somebody's living room, Pete was placed on a couch with a cushion under his head and another under his dangling arm. The toothless old man turned up now, panting, with his waddling dog, and cried that we had a common thief there before us, and everyone listened and marvelled until the old man spat on the carpet and was turned out.

When I timidly touched Pete, trying to wipe his face with a crumpled Kleenex (all I had), he thought I was one of the strangers. His mouth was a purple color, as if he had been in icy water. His eyes looked at me, but he was not looking out.

"Ambulance," said a doctor who had been fetched by the policeman. He spoke loudly and slowly, dealing with idiots.

"Yes," I heard, in English. "We must have an ambulance."

Everyone now inspected me. I was, plainly, responsible for something. For walking around the streets in shorts? Wasting bread? Conscious of my sweaty hair, my bare legs, my lack of Italian—my nakedness—I began explaining the true error of the day: "The train has gone, and all our things are on it. Our luggage. We've been staying up in that village— oh, what's the name of it, now? Where they make the white wine. I can't remember, no, I can't remember where we've been. I could find it, I could take you there; I've just forgotten what it's called. We were down here waiting for the train. To Nice. We had lots of time. The porter took our things and said he'd put them on the train for us. He said the train would wait here, at the border, that it waited a long time. He was supposed to meet us at the place where you show your ticket. I guess for an extra tip. The train must have gone now. My purse is in the duffelbag up at the . . . I'll look in my husband's wallet. Of course that is my husband! Our passports must be on the train, too. Our traveller's checks are in our luggage, his and mine. We were just walking round taking pictures instead of sitting up there in the station. Anyway, there was no place to sit—only the bar, and it was smelly and dark."

No one believed a word of this, of course. Would you give your clothes, your passport, your traveller's checks to a porter? A man you had never seen in your life before? A bandit disguised as a porter, with a stolen cap on his head?

"You could not have taken that train without showing your passport," a careful foreign voice objected.

"What are you two, anyway?" said the man from the change office. His was a tough, old-fashioned movie-American accent. He was puffy-eyed and small, but he seemed superior to us, for he wore an impeccable shirt. Pete, on the sofa, looked as if he had been poisoned, or stepped on. "What are you?" the man from the change office said again. "Students? Americans? No? What, then? Swedes?"

I saw what the doctor had been trying to screen from me: a statue's marble eye.

The tourist who spoke the careful foreign English said, "Be careful of the pillows."

"What? What?" screamed the put-upon person who owned them.

"Blood is coming out of his ears," said the tourist, halting between words. "That is a bad sign." He seemed to search his memory for a better English word. "An *unfortunate* sign," he said, and put his hand over his mouth.

Pete's father and mother flew from Calgary when they had my cable. They made flawless arrangements by telephone, and knew exactly what to bring. They had a sunny room looking onto rusty palms and a strip of beach about a mile from where the accident had been. I sat against one of the windows and told them what I thought I remembered. I looked at the white walls, the white satin bedspreads, at Mrs. Higgins' spotless dressing case, and finally down at my hands.

His parents had not understood, until now, that ten days had gone by since Pete's death.

"What have you been doing, dear, all alone?" said Mrs. Higgins, gently.

"Just waiting, after I cabled you." They seemed to be expecting more. "I've been to the movies," I said.

From this room we could hear the shrieks of children playing on the sand.

"Are they orphans?" asked Mrs. Higgins, for they were little girls, dressed alike, with soft pink sun hats covering their heads.

"It seems to be a kind of summer camp," I said. "I was wondering about them, too."

"It would make an attractive picture," said Pete's mother, after a pause. "The blue sea, and the nuns, and all those bright hats. It would look nice in a dining room."

They were too sick to reproach me. My excuse for not having told them sooner was that I hadn't been thinking and they didn't ask me for it. I could only repeat what seemed important now. "I don't want to go back home just yet" was an example. I was already in the future, which must have hurt them. "I have a girl friend in the Embassy in Paris. I can stay with her." I scarcely moved my lips. They had to strain to hear. I held still, looking down at my fingers. I was very brown, sun streaks in my hair, more graceful than at my wedding, where I knew they had found me maladroit—a great lump of a Camp Fire Girl. That was how I had seen myself in my father-in-law's eyes. Extremes of shock had brought me near some ideal they had of prettiness. I appeared now much more the kind of girl they'd have wanted as Pete's wife.

So they had come for nothing. They were not to see him, or bury him, or fetch home his bride. All I had to show them was a still unlabelled grave.

When I dared look at them, I saw their way of being was not Pete's. Neither had his soft selective stare. Mr. Higgins' eyes were a fanatic blue.

He was thin and sunburned and unused to nonsense. Summer and winter he travelled with his wife in climates that were bad for her skin. She had the fair, papery coloring that requires constant vigilance. All this I knew because of Pete.

They saw his grave at the best time of day, in the late afternoon, with the light at a slant. The cemetery was in a valley between two plaster towns. A flash of the sea was visible, a corner of ultramarine. They saw a stone wall covered with roses, pink and white and near-white, open, without secrets. The hiss of traffic on the road came to us, softer than rain; then true rain came down, and we ran to our waiting taxi through a summer storm. Later they saw the station where Pete had left our luggage but never come back. Like Pete—as Pete had intended to—they were travelling to Nice. Under a glass shelter before the station I paused and said, "That was where it happened, down there." I pointed with my white glove. I was not as elegant as Mrs. Higgins, but I was not a source of embarrassment. I wore gloves, stockings, shoes.

The steep street under rain was black as oil. Everything was reflected upside down. The neon signs of the change office and the pharmacy swam deeply in the pavement.

"I'd like to thank the people who were so kind," said Mrs. Higgins. "Is there time? Shirley, I suppose you got their names?"

"Nobody was kind," I said.

"Shirley! We've met the doctor, and the minister, but you said there was a policeman, and a Dutch gentleman, and a lady—you were in this lady's living room."

"They were all there, but no one was kind."

"The bike's paid for?" asked Mr. Higgins suddenly.

"Yes, I paid. And I paid for having the sofa cushions cleaned."

What sofa cushions? What was I talking about? They seemed petrified, under the glass shelter, out of the rain. They could not take their eyes away from the place I had said was *there*. They never blamed me, never by a word or a hidden meaning. I had explained, more than once, how the porter that day had not put our bags on the train after all but had stood waiting at the customs barrier, wondering what had become of us. I told them how I had found everything intact—passports and checks and maps and sweaters and shoes . . . They could not grasp the importance of it. They knew that Pete had chosen me, and gone away with me, and they never saw him again. An unreliable guide had taken them to a foreign graveyard and told them, without evidence, that now he was there.

"I still don't see how anyone could have thought Pete was stealing," said his mother. "What would Pete have wanted with someone's old bike?"

They were flying home from Nice. They loathed Italy now, and they had a special aversion to the sunny room where I had described Pete's death. We three sat in the restaurant at the airport, and they spoke quietly, considerately, because the people at the table next to ours were listening to a football match on a portable radio.

I closed my hand into a fist and let it rest on the table. I imagined myself at home, saying to my mother, "All right, real life has begun. What's your next prophecy?"

I was not flying with them. I was seeing them off. Mrs. Higgins sat poised and prepared in her linen coat, with her large handbag, and her cosmetics and airsickness tablets in her dressing case, and her diamond maple leaf so she wouldn't be mistaken for an American, and her passport ready to be shown to anyone. Pale gloves lay folded over the clasp of the dressing case. "You'll want to go to your own people, I know," she said. "But you have a home with us. You mustn't forget it." She paused. I said nothing, and so she continued, "What are you going to do, dear? I mean, after you have visited your friend. You mustn't be lonely."

I muttered whatever seemed sensible. "I'll have to get a job. I've never had one and I don't know anything much. I can't even type—not properly." Again they gave me this queer impression of expecting something more. What did they want? "Pete said it was no good learning anything if you couldn't type. He said it was the only useful thing he could do."

In the eyes of his parents was the same wound. I had told them something about him they hadn't known.

"Well, I understand," said his mother, presently. "At least, I think I do."

They imagine I want to be near the grave, I supposed. They think that's why I'm staying on the same side of the world. Pete and I had been waiting for a train; now I had taken it without him. I was waiting again. Even if I were to visit the cemetery every day, he would never speak. His last words had not been for me but to a policeman. He would have said something to me, surely, if everyone hadn't been in such a hurry to get him out of the way. His mind was quenched, and his body out of sight. "You don't love with your soul," I had cried to the old clergyman at the funeral—an offensive remark, judging from the look on his face as he turned it aside. Now I was careful. The destination of a soul was of no interest. The death of a voice—now, that was real. The Dutchman suddenly covering his mouth was horror, and a broken elbow was true pain. But I was careful; I kept this to myself.

"You're our daughter now," Pete's father said. "I don't think I want you to have to worry about a job. Not yet." Mr. Higgins happened to know my family's exact status. My father had not left us well off, and my mother had given everything she owned to a sect that did not believe in blood transfusions. She expected the end of the world, and would not eat an egg unless she had first met the hen. That was Mr. Higgins' view. "Shirley must work if that's what she wants to do," Mrs. Higgins said softly.

"I do want to!" I imagined myself, that day, in a river of people pouring into subways.

"I'm fixing something up for you, just the same," said Mr. Higgins hurriedly, as if he would not be interrupted by women.

Mrs. Higgins allowed her pale forehead to wrinkle, under her beige veil. Was it not better to struggle and to work, she asked. Wasn't that real life? Would it not keep Shirley busy, take her mind off her loss, her disappointment, her tragedy, if you like (though "tragedy" was not an acceptable way of looking at fate), if she had to think about her daily bread?

"The allowance I'm going to make her won't stop her from working," he said. "I was going to set something up for the kids anyway."

She seemed to approve; she had questioned him only out of some prudent system of ethics.

He said to me, "I always have to remember I could go any minute, just like that. I've got a heart." He tapped it—tapped his light suit. "Meantime you better start with this." He gave me the envelope that had been close to his heart until now. He seemed diffident, made ashamed by money, and by death, but it was he and not his wife who had asked if there was a hope that Pete had left a child. No, I had told him. I had wondered, too, but now I was sure. "Then Shirley is all we've got left," he had said to his wife, and I thought they seemed bankrupt, having nothing but me.

"If that's a check on a bank at home, it might take too long to clear," said his wife. "After all Shirley's been through, she needs a fair-sized sum right away."

"She's had that, Betty," said Mr. Higgins, smiling.

I had lived this: three round a table, the smiling parents. Pete had said, "They smile, they go on talking. You wonder what goes on."

"How you manage everything you do without a secretary with you all the time I just don't know," said his wife, all at once admiring him.

"You've been saying that for twenty-two years," he said.

"Twenty-three, now."

With this the conversation came to an end and they sat staring, puzzled, not overcome by life but suddenly lost to it, out of touch. The photograph Pete carried of his mother, that was in his wallet when he died, had been taken before her marriage, with a felt hat all to one side, and an organdie collar, and Ginger Rogers hair. It was easier to imagine Mr. Higgins young—a young Gary Cooper. My father-in-law's blue gaze rested on me now. Never in a million years would he have picked me as a daughter-in-law. I knew that; I understood. Pete was part of him, and Pete, with all the girls he had to choose from, had chosen me. When Mr. Higgins met my mother at the wedding, he thanked God, and was overheard being thankful, that the wedding was not in Calgary. Remembering my mother that day, with her glasses on her nose and a strange borrowed hat on her head, and recalling Mr. Higgins' face, I thought of words that would keep me from laughing. I found, at random, "threesome," "smother," "gambling," "habeas corpus," "sibling." . . .

"How is your mother, Shirley?" said Mrs. Higgins.

"I had a letter . . . She's working with a pendulum now."

"A pendulum?"

"Yes. A weight on a string, sort of. It makes a diagnosis—whether you've got something wrong with your stomach, if it's an ulcer, or what. She can use it to tell when you're pregnant and if the baby will be a girl or a boy. It depends whether it swings north-south or east-west."

"Can the pendulum tell who the father is?" said Mr. Higgins.

"They are useful for people who are afraid of doctors," said Mrs. Higgins, and she fingered her neat gloves, and smiled to herself. "Someone who won't hear the truth from a doctor will listen to any story from a woman with a pendulum or a piece of crystal."

"Or a stone that changes color," I said. "My mother had one of those. When our spaniel had mastoids it turned violet."

She glanced at me then, and caught in her breath, but her husband, by a certain amount of angry fidgeting, made us change the subject. That was the one moment she and I were close to each other—something to do with quirky female humor.

Mr. Higgins did not die of a heart attack, as he had confidently expected, but a few months after this Mrs. Higgins said to her maid in the kitchen, "I've got a terrible pain in my head. I'd better lie down." Pete's father wrote, "She knew what the matter was, but she never said. Typical." I inherited a legacy and some jewelry from her, and wondered why. I had been careless about writing. I could not write the kind of letters she seemed to want. How could I write to someone I hardly knew about someone else who did not exist? Mr. Higgins married the widow of one of his closest friends—a woman six years older than he. They travelled to Europe for their wedding trip. I had a temporary job as an interpreter in a department store. When my father-in-law saw me in a neat suit, with his name, HIGGINS, fastened to my jacket, he seemed to approve. He was the only person then who did not say that I was wasting my life and my youth and ought to go home. The new Mrs. Higgins asked to be taken to an English-speaking hairdresser, and there, under the roaring dryer, she yelled that Mr. Higgins may not have been Pete's father. Perhaps he had been, perhaps he hadn't, but one thing he was, and that was a saint. She came out from under the helmet and said in a normal voice, "Martin doesn't know I dye my hair." I wondered if he had always wanted this short, fox-colored woman. The new marriage might for years have been in the maquis of his mind, and of Mrs. Higgins' life. She may have known it as she sat in the airport that day, smiling to herself, touching her unstained gloves. Mr. Higgins had drawn up a new way of life, like a clean will with everyone he loved cut out. I was trying to draw up a will, too, but I was patient, waiting, waiting for someone to tell me what to write. He spoke of Pete conventionally, in a sentimental way that forbade any feeling. Talking that way was easier for both of us. We were both responsible for something—for surviving, perhaps. Once he turned to me and said defiantly, "Well, she and Pete are together now, aren't they? And didn't they leave us here?"

[1967]

· MARGARET LAURENCE ·

1926–1987

Jean Margaret Wemyss was born in Neepawa, Manitoba, 18 July 1926, to parents of Scottish and Irish descent. She was educated in Neepawa and at United College in Winnipeg, graduating in 1947. In 1948 she married Jack Laurence, a civil engineering graduate of the University of Manitoba, moving to England with him in 1949, and then the following year to Somaliland, where he was in charge of a dam-building project for the British Ministry of Overseas Development. In 1952 the Laurences moved to the Gold Coast, now Ghana, where they lived until their return to Canada in 1957. Their daughter Jocelyn was born in 1952; their son David in 1955. The Laurences separated in 1962; Margaret and the children moved to England. In 1974 Margaret Laurence moved back to Canada, settling in Lakefield, Ontario, where she lived until her death in 1987. She wrote novels, short stories, children's books, and a travel book, as well as a volume of reminiscences, one of literary criticism of contemporary Nigerian writers, and a translation of Somali poetry and folk-tales. She was a Companion of the Order of Canada and a Fellow of the Royal Society, and received numerous honorary degrees, the Governor General's Award for *A Jest of God* (1966) and *The Diviners* (1974), and the Molson Prize. She was a constant, active participant in causes promoting world peace.

Though Laurence had been writing stories since she was a child, her seven years in Africa proved to be the decisive catalyst for her talent. Intrigued by the extensive oral literature of the Somali people, she sought out and translated their folk-tales and poems, published as *A Tree for Poverty* (1954). Later, back in Canada, she wrote *The Prophet's Camel Bell* (1963), a retrospective account of her Somaliland experiences. It was there that she first became aware that the themes which were to inform all her writing—freedom, individual liberty and dignity, responsibility and survival—were universal, and that they were applicable to her Canadian as well as to her African experience. Her first novel, *This Side Jordan* (1960), and the short stories later collected in *The Tomorrow-Tamer* (1963), are set in Ghana just before its independence. She wrote about African people with tact and empathy, so much so that she has been repeatedly praised by Chinua Achebe, the senior Nigerian novelist, for her portrayal of Africans and their dilemmas.

Five works set in the fictional Canadian prairie town of Manawaka constitute the main body of Laurence's *oeuvre*. In these novels, through the voices of five memorable women, she has recreated the Canadian experience in all its facets, through four generations. In *The Stone Angel* (1964) Hagar Shipley tells her story of pride and pain and of learning the meaning of love just before it is too late. Through the crucial events of one summer, Rachel Cameron of *A Jest of God* (1966), a spinster schoolteacher, trapped in Manawaka by her own fears and self-distrust, comes to a degree of self-knowledge and a limited freedom. Her sister, Stacey MacAindra of *The Fire-Dwellers* (1969), living in Vancouver with her husband and four children, is battered from all sides by an urban environment that seems monstrously threatening and by the multiple demands on her as wife, mother, and friend. Far stronger than she believes herself to be, in the weeks before her fortieth birthday Stacey lives through a series of shocks that brings her an increased acceptance of herself and of the irreversible processes of life. The collection of short stories, *A Bird in the House* (1970), centres on the young Vanessa Macleod, her initiation into the mysteries of love and death, and her gradual acceptance and understanding of Grandfather Connor. As a child she feared and resented him and his tyranny; maturity brings her to respect him for his strengths and to pity him for his self-imposed isolation. Morag Gunn of *The Diviners* (1974) is a novelist. On one level the story unfolds the process of Morag's life, from the time of the death of her parents when she was very young, to the novel's present, where, at forty-seven, she is struggling to understand her own life and tormented by concern for her daughter Pique. In its deepest and broadest meaning *The Diviners* is the story of a profoundly religious pilgrimage, the affirmation of faith and the finding of grace.

Laurence's works include *A Tree for Poverty: Somali Poetry and Prose* (1954); *This Side Jordan* (1960); *The Tomorrow-Tamer* (1963); *The Prophet's Camel Bell* (1963); *The Stone Angel* (1964); *A Jest of God* (1966); *Long Drums and Cannons: Nigerian Novelists and Dramatists 1952–1966* (1968); *The Fire-Dwellers* (1969); *A Bird in the House: Stories* (1970); *Jason's Quest* (1970); *The Diviners* (1974); *Heart of a Stranger* (1976); *The Olden Days Coat* (1979); *Six Darn Cows* (1979); and *A Christmas Birthday Story* (1980).

Works on Laurence include Clara Thomas, *Margaret Laurence* (1969); *The Manawaka World of Margaret Laurence* (1975); William H. New, ed., *Margaret Laurence: the Writer and Her Critics* (1977); Susan J. Warwick, "Margaret Laurence: An Annotated Bibliography," *The Annotated Bibliography of Canada's Major Authors*, ed. Robert Lecker and Jack David (1979), 1: 47–101; Patricia Morley, *Margaret Laurence* (1981); and George Woodcock, ed., *A Place to Stand On: Essays By and About Margaret Laurence* (1983).

CLARA THOMAS

A BIRD IN THE HOUSE

The parade would be almost over by now, and I had not gone. My mother had said in a resigned voice, "All right, Vanessa, if that's the way you feel," making me suffer twice as many jabs of guilt as I would have done if she had lost her temper. She and Grandmother MacLeod had gone off, my mother pulling the low box-sleigh with Roddie all dolled up in his new red snow-suit, just the sort of little kid anyone would want people to see. I sat on the lowest branch of the birch tree in our yard, not minding the snowy wind, even welcoming its punishment. I went over my reasons for not going, trying to believe they were good and sufficient, but in my heart I felt I was betraying my father. This was the first time I had stayed away from the Remembrance Day parade. I wondered if he would notice that I was not there, standing on the sidewalk at the corner of River and Main while the parade passed, and then following to the Court House grounds where the service was held.

I could see the whole thing in my mind. It was the same every year. The Manawaka Civic Band always led the way. They had never been able to afford full uniforms, but they had peaked navy-blue caps and sky-blue chest ribbons. They were joined on Remembrance Day by the Salvation Army band, whose uniforms seemed too ordinary for a parade, for they were the same ones the bandsmen wore every Saturday night when they played "Nearer My God to Thee" at the foot of River Street. The two bands never managed to practise quite enough together, so they did not keep in time too well. The Salvation Army band invariably played faster, and afterwards my father would say irritably, "They play those marches just like they do hymns, blast them, as though they wouldn't get to heaven if they didn't hustle up." And my mother, who had great respect for the Salvation Army because of the good work they did, would respond childingly, "Now, now, Ewen—" I vowed I would never say "Now, now" to my husband or children, not that I ever intended having the latter, for I had been put off by my brother Roderick, who was now two years old with wavy hair, and everyone said what a beautiful child. I was twelve, and no one in their right mind would have said what a beautiful child, for I was big-boned like my Grandfather Connor and had straight lanky black hair like a Blackfoot or Cree.

After the bands would come the veterans. Even thinking of them at this distance, in the white and withdrawn quiet of the birch tree, gave me a sense of painful embarrassment. I might not have minded so much if my father had not been among them. How could he go? How could he not see how they all looked? It must have been a long time since they were soldiers, for they had forgotten how to march in step. They were old—that was the thing. My father was bad enough, being almost forty, but he wasn't a patch on Howard Tully from the drugstore, who was completely grey-haired and also fat, or Stewart MacMurchie, who was bald at the back of his head. They looked to me like impostors, plump or spindly caricatures of past warriors. I almost hated them for walking in that limping column down Main. At the Court House, everyone would sing *Lord God of Hosts, be with us yet, lest we forget, lest we forget.* Will Masterson would pick up his old Army bugle and blow the Last Post. Then it would be over and everyone could start gabbling once more and go home.

I jumped down from the birch bough and ran to the house, yelling, making as much noise as I could.

I'm a poor lonesome cowboy
An' a long way from home—

I stepped inside the front hall and kicked off my snow boots. I slammed the door behind me, making the dark ruby and emerald glass shake in the small leaded panes. I slid purposely on the hall rug, causing it to bunch and crinkle on the slippery polished oak of the floor. I seized the newel post, round as a head, and spun myself to and fro on the bottom stair.

I ain't got no father
To buy the clothes I wear.
I'm a poor lonesome—

At this moment my shoulders were firmly seized and shaken by a pair of hands, white and delicate and old, but strong as talons.

"Just what do you think you're doing, young lady?" Grandmother MacLeod enquired, in a voice like frost on a windowpane, infinitely cold and clearly etched.

I went limp and in a moment she took her hands away. If you struggled, she would always hold on longer.

"Gee, I never knew you were home yet."

"I would have thought that on a day like this you might have shown a little respect and consideration," Grandmother Macleod said, "even if you couldn't make the effort to get cleaned up enough to go to the parade."

I realised with surprise that she imagined this to be my reason for not going. I did not try to correct her impression. My real reason would have been even less acceptable.

"I'm sorry," I said quickly.

In some families, *please* is described as the magic word. In our house, however, it was *sorry*.

"This isn't an easy day for any of us," she said.

Her younger son, my Uncle Roderick, had been killed in the Great War. When my father marched, and when the hymn was sung, and when that unbearably lonely tune was sounded by the one bugle and everyone forced themselves to keep absolutely still, it would be that boy of whom she was thinking. I felt the enormity of my own offence.

"Grandmother—I'm sorry."

"So you said."

I could not tell her I had not really said it before at all. I went into the den and found my father there. He was sitting in the leather-cushioned armchair beside the fireplace. He was not doing anything, just sitting and smoking. I stood beside him, wanting to touch the light-brown hairs on his forearm, but thinking he might laugh at me or pull his arm away if I did.

"I'm sorry," I said, meaning it.

"What for, honey?"

"For not going."

"Oh—that. What was the matter?"

I did not want him to know, and yet I had to tell him, make him see. "They look silly," I blurted. "Marching like that."

For a minute I thought he was going to be angry. It would have been a relief to me if he had been. Instead, he drew his eyes away from mine and fixed them above the mantelpiece where the sword hung, the handsome and evil-looking crescent in its carved bronze sheath that some ancestor had once brought from the Northern Frontier of India.

"Is that the way it looks to you?" he said.

I felt in his voice some hurt, something that was my fault. I wanted to make everything all right between us, to convince him that I understood, even if I did not. I prayed that Grandmother MacLeod would stay put in her room, and that my mother would take a long time in the kitchen, giving Roddie his lunch. I wanted my father to myself, so I could prove to him that I cared more about him than any of the others did. I wanted to speak in some way that would be more poignant and comprehending than anything of which my mother could possibly be capable. But I did not know how.

"You were right there when Uncle Roderick got killed, weren't you?" I began uncertainly.

"Yes."

"How old was he, Dad?"

"Eighteen," my father said.

Unexpectedly, that day came into intense being for me. He had had to watch his own brother die, not in the antiseptic calm of some hospital, but out in the open, the stretches of mud I had seen in his snapshots. He would not have known what to do. He would just have had to stand there and look at it, whatever that might mean. I looked at my father with a kind of horrified awe, and then I began to cry. I had forgotten about impressing him with my perception. Now I needed him to console me for this unwanted glimpse of the pain he had once known.

"Hey, cut it out, honey," he said, embarrassed. "It was bad, but it wasn't all as bad as that part. There were a few other things."

"Like what?" I said, not believing him.

"Oh—I don't know," he replied evasively. "Most of us were pretty young, you know, I and the boys I joined up with. None of us had ever been away from Manawaka before. Those of us who came back mostly came back here, or else went no further away from town than Winnipeg. So when we were overseas—that was the only time most of us were ever a long way from home."

"Did you want to be?" I asked, shocked.

"Oh well—" my father said uncomfortably. "It was kind of interesting to see a few other places for a change, that's all."

Grandmother MacLeod was standing in the doorway.

"Beth's called you twice for lunch, Ewen. Are you deaf, you and Vanessa?"

"Sorry," my father and I said simultaneously.

Then we went upstairs to wash our hands.

That winter my mother returned to her old job as nurse in my father's medical practice. She was able to do this only because of Noreen.

"Grandmother MacLeod says we're getting a maid," I said to my father, accusingly, one morning. "We're not, are we?"

"Believe you me, on what I'm going to be paying her," my father growled, "she couldn't be called anything as classy as a maid. Hired girl would be more like it."

"Now, now, Ewen," my mother put in. "it's not as if we were cheating her or anything. You know she wants to live in town, and I can certainly see why, stuck out there on the farm, and her father hardly ever letting her come in. What kind of life is that for a girl?"

"I don't like the idea of your going back to work, Beth," my father said. "I know you're fine now, but you're not exactly the robust type."

"You can't afford to hire a nurse any longer. It's all very well to say the Depression won't last forever—probably it won't, but what else can we do for now?"

"I'm damned if I know," my father admitted. "Beth—"

"Yes?"

They both seemed to have forgotten about me. It was at breakfast, which we always ate in the kitchen, and I sat rigidly on my chair, pretending to ignore and thus snub their withdrawal from me. I glared at the window, but it was so thickly plumed and scrolled with frost that I could not see out. I glanced back to my parents. My father had not replied, and my mother was looking at him in that anxious and half-frowning way she had recently developed.

"What is it, Ewen?" Her voice had the same nervous sharpness it bore sometimes when she would say to me, "For mercy's sake, Vanessa, what is it *now*?" as though whatever was the matter, it was bound to be the last straw.

My father spun his sterling silver serviette ring, engraved with his initials, slowly around on the table.

"I never thought things would turn out like this, did you?"

"Please—" my mother said in a low strained voice, "please, Ewen, let's not start all this again. I can't take it."

"All right," my father said. "Only—"

"The MacLeods used to have money and now they don't," my mother cried. "Well, they're not alone. Do you think all that matters to me, Ewen? What I can't bear is to see you forever reproaching yourself. As if it were your fault."

"I don't think it's the comedown," my father said. "If I were somewhere else, I don't suppose it would matter to me, either, except where you're concerned. But I suppose you'd work too hard wherever you were—it's bred into you. If you haven't got anything to slave away at, you'll sure as hell invent something."

"What do you think I should do, let the house go to wrack and ruin? That would go over well with your mother, wouldn't it?"

"That's just it," my father said. "It's the damned house all the time. I haven't only taken on my father's house, I've taken on everything that goes with it, apparently. Sometimes I really wonder—"

"Well, it's a good thing I've inherited some practicality even if you haven't," my mother said. "I'll say that for the Connors—they aren't given to brooding, thank the Lord. Do you want your egg poached or scrambled?"

"Scrambled," my father said. "All I hope is that this Noreen doesn't get married straightaway, that's all."

"She won't," my mother said. "Who's she going to meet who could afford to marry?"

"I marvel at you, Beth," my father said. "You look as though a puff of wind would below you away. But underneath, by God, you're all hardwood."

"Don't talk stupidly," my mother said. "All I hope is that she won't object to taking your mother's breakfast up on a tray."

"That's right," my father said angrily. "Rub it in."

"Oh Ewen, I'm sorry!" my mother cried, her face suddenly stricken. "I don't know why I say these things. I didn't mean to."

"I know," my father said. "Here, cut it out, honey. Just for God's sake please don't cry."

"I'm sorry," my mother repeated, blowing her nose.

"We're both sorry," my father said. "Not that that changes anything."

After my father had gone, I got down from my chair and went to my mother.

"I don't want you to go back to the office. I don't want a hired girl here. I'll hate her."

My mother sighed, making me feel that I was placing an intolerable burden on her, and yet making me resent having to feel this weight. She looked tired, as she often did these days. Her tiredness bored me, made me want to attack her for it.

"Catch me getting along with a dumb old hired girl," I threatened.

"Do what you like," my mother said abruptly. "What can I do about it?"

And then, of course, I felt bereft, not knowing which way to turn.

My father need not have worried about Noreen getting married. She was, as it turned out, interested not in boys but in God. My mother was relieved about the boys but alarmed about God.

"It isn't natural," she said, "for a girl of seventeen. Do you think she's all right mentally, Ewen?"

When my parents, along with Grandmother MacLeod, went to the United Church every Sunday, I was made to go to Sunday school in the church basement, where there were small red chairs which humiliatingly resembled kindergarten furniture, and pictures of Jesus wearing a white sheet and surrounded by a whole lot of well-dressed kids whose mothers obviously had not suffered them to come unto Him until every face and ear was properly scrubbed. Our religious observances also included grace at meals, when my father would mumble "For what we are about to receive the Lord make us truly thankful Amen," running the words together as though they were one long word. My mother approved of these rituals, which seemed decent and moderate to her. Noreen's religion, however, was a different matter. Noreen belonged to the Tabernacle of the Risen and Reborn, and she had got up to testify no less than seven times in the past two years, she told us. My mother, who could not imagine anyone's voluntarily making a public spectacle of themselves, was profoundly shocked by this revelation.

"Don't worry," my father soothed her. "She's all right. She's just had kind of a dull life, that's all."

My mother shrugged and went on worrrying and trying to help Noreen without hurting her feelings, by tactful remarks about the advisability of modulating one's voice when singing hymns, and the fact that there was plenty of hot water so Noreen really didn't need to hesitate about taking a bath. She even bought a razor and a packet of blades and whispered to Noreen that any girl who wore transparent blouses so much would probably like to shave under her arms. None of these suggestions had the slightest effect on Noreen. She did not cease belting out hymns at the top of her voice, she bathed once a fortnight, and the sorrel-coloured hair continued to bloom like a thicket of Indian paintbrush in her armpits.

Grandmother MacLeod refused to speak to Noreen. This caused Noreen a certain amount of bewilderment until she finally hit on an answer.

"Your poor grandma," she said. "She is deaf as a post. These things are sent to try us here on earth, Vanessa. But if she makes it into Heaven, I'll bet you anything she will hear clear as a bell."

Noreen and I talked about Heaven quite a lot, and also Hell. Noreen had an intimate and detailed knowledge of both places. She not only knew what they looked like—she even knew how big they were. Heaven was seventy-seven thousand miles square and it had four gates, each one made out of a different kind of precious jewel. The Pearl Gate, the Topaz Gate, the Amethyst Gate, the Ruby Gate—Noreen would reel them off, all the gates of Heaven. I told Noreen they sounded like poetry, but she was puzzled by my reaction and said I shouldn't talk that way. If you said poetry, it sounded like it was just made up and not really so, Noreen said.

Hell was larger than Heaven, and when I asked why, thinking of it as something of a comedown for God, Noreen said naturally it had to be bigger because there were a darn sight more people there than in Heaven. Hell was one hundred and ninety milllion miles deep and was in perpetual darkness, like a cave or under the sea. Even the flames (this was the awful thing) *did not give off any light.*

I did not actually believe in Noreen's doctrines, but the images which they conjured up began to inhabit my imagination. Noreen's fund of exotic knowledge was not limited to religion, although in a way it all seemed related. She could do many things which had a spooky tinge to them. Once when she was making a cake, she found we had run out of eggs. She went outside and gathered a bowl of fresh snow and used it instead. The cake rose like a charm, and I stared at Noreen as though she were a sorceress. In fact, I began to think of her as a sorceress, someone not quite of this earth. There was nothing unearthly about her broad shoulders and hips and her forest of dark red hair, but even these features took on a slightly sinister significance to me. I no longer saw her through the eyes or the expressed opinions of my mother and father, as a girl who had quit school at grade eight and whose life on the farm had been endlessly drab. I knew the truth—Noreen's life had not been drab at all, for she dwelt in a world of violent splendours, a world filled with angels whose wings of delicate light bore real feathers, and saints shining like the dawn, and prophets who spoke in ancient tongues, and the ecstatic souls of the saved, as well as denizens of the lower regions— mean-eyed imps and crooked cloven-hoofed monsters and beasts with the bodies of swine and the human heads of murderers, and lovely depraved jezebels torn by dogs through all eternity. The middle layer of Creation, our earth, was equally full of grotesque presences, for No- reen believed strongly in the visitation of ghosts and the communication with spirits. She could prove this with her Ouija board. We would both place our fingers lightly on the indicator, and it would skim across the board and spell out answers to our questions. I did not believe whole- heartedly in the Ouija board, either, but I was cautious about the kind of question I asked, in case the answer would turn out unfavourable and I would be unable to forget it.

One day Noreen told me she could also make a table talk. We used the small table in my bedroom, and sure enough, it lifted very slightly under our fingertips and tapped once for *Yes*, twice for *No*. Noreen asked if her Aunt Ruthie would get better from the kidney operation, and the table replied *No*. I withdrew my hands.

"I don't want to do it any more."

"Gee, what's the matter, Vanessa?" Noreen's plain placid face creased in a frown. "We only just begun."

"I have to do my homework."

My heart lurched as I said this. I was certain Noreen would know I was lying, and that she would know not by any ordinary perception, either. But her attention had been caught by something else, and I was thankful, at least until I saw what it was.

My bedroom window was not opened in the coldest weather. The storm window, which was fitted outside as an extra wall against the winter, had three small circular holes in its frame so that some fresh air could seep into the house. The sparrow must have been floundering in the new snow on the roof, for it had crawled in through one of these holes and was now caught between the two layers of glass. I could not bear the panic of the trapped bird, and before I realised what I was doing, I had thrown open the bedroom window. I was not releasing the sparrow into any better a situation, I soon saw, for instead of remaining quiet and allowing us to catch it in order to free it, it began flying blindly around the room, hitting the lampshade, brushing against the walls, its wings seeming to spin faster and faster.

I was petrified. I thought I would pass out if those palpitating wings touched me. There was something in the bird's senseless movements that revolted me. I also thought it was going to damage itself, break one of those thin wing-bones, perhaps, and then it would be lying on the floor, dying, like the pimpled and horribly featherless baby birds we saw sometimes on the sidewalks in the spring when they had fallen out of their nests. I was not any longer worried about the sparrow. I wanted only to avoid the slight of it lying broken on the floor. Viciously, I thought that if Noreen said, *God sees the little sparrow fall,* I would kick her in the shins. She did not, however, say this.

"A bird in the house means a death in the house," Noreen remarked.

Shaken, I pulled my glance away from the whirling wings and looked at Noreen.

"What?"

"That's what I've heard said, anyhow."

The sparrow had exhausted itself. It lay on the floor, spent and trembling. I could not bring myself to touch it. Noreen bent and picked it up. She cradled it with great gentleness between her cupped hands. Then we took it downstairs, and when I had opened the back door, Noreen set the bird free.

"Poor little scrap," she said, and I felt struck to the heart, knowing she had been concerned all along about the sparrow, while I, perfidiously, in the chaos of the moment, had been concerned only about myself.

"Wanna do some with the Ouija board, Vanessa?" Noreen asked.

I shivered a little, perhaps only because of the blast of cold air which had come into the kitchen when the door was opened.

"No thanks, Noreen. Like I said, I got my homework to do. But thanks all the same."

"That's okay," Noreen said in her guileless voice. "Any time."

But whenever she mentioned the Ouija board or the talking table, after that, I always found some excuse not to consult these oracles.

"Do you want to come to church with me this evening, Vanessa?" my father asked.

"How come you're going to the evening service?" I enquired.

"Well, we didn't go this morning. We went snowshoeing instead, remember? I think your grandmother was a little bit put out about it. She went alone this morning. I guess it wouldn't hurt you and me, to go now."

We walked through the dark, along the white streets, the snow squeaking dryly under our feet. The streetlights were placed at long intervals along the sidewalks, and around each pole the circle of flimsy light created glistening points of blue and crystal on the crusted snow. I would have liked to take my father's hand, as I used to do, but I was too old for that now. I walked beside him, taking long steps so he would not have to walk more slowly on my account.

The sermon bored me, and I began leafing through the Hymnary for entertainment. I must have drowsed, for the next thing I knew, my father was prodding me and we were on our feet for the closing hymn.

Near the Cross, near the Cross,
Be my glory ever,
Till my ransomed soul shall find
Rest beyond the river.

I knew the tune well, so I sang loudly for the first verse. But the music to that hymn is sombre, and all at once the words themselves seemed too dreadful to be sung. I stopped singing, my throat knotted. I thought I was going to cry, but I did not know why, except that the song recalled to me my Grandmother Connor, who had been dead only a year now. I wondered why her soul needed to be ransomed. If God did not think she was good enough just as she was, then I did not have much use for His opinion. *Rest beyond the river*—was that what had happened to her? She had believed in Heaven, but I did not think that rest beyond the river was quite what she had in mind. To think of her in Noreen's flashy Heaven, though—that was even worse. Someplace where nobody ever got annoyed or had to be smoothed down and placated, someplace where there were never any family scenes—that would have suited my Grandmother Connor. Maybe she wouldn't have minded a certain amount of rest beyond the river, at that.

When we had the silent prayer, I looked at my father. He sat with his head bowed and his eyes closed. He was frowning deeply, and I could see the pulse in his temple. I wondered then what he believed. I did not have any real idea what it might be. When he raised his head, he did not look uplifted or anything like that. He merely looked tired. Then Reverend McKee pronounced the benediction, and we could go home.

"What do you think about all that stuff, Dad?" I asked hesitantly, as we walked.

"What stuff, honey?"

"Oh, Heaven and Hell, and like that."

My father laughed. "Have you been listening to Noreen too much? Well, I don't know. I don't think they're actual places. Maybe they stand for something that happens all the time here, or else doesn't happen. It's kind of hard to explain. I guess I'm not so good at explanations."

Nothing seemed to have been made any clearer to me. I reached out and took his hand, not caring that he might think this a babyish gesture.

"I hate that hymn!"

"Good Lord," my father said in astonishment. "Why, Vanessa?"

But I did not know and so could not tell him.

Many people in Manawaka had flu that winter, so my father and Dr. Cates were kept extremely busy. I had flu myself, and spent a week in bed, vomiting only the first day and after that enjoying poor health, as my mother put it, with Noreen bringing me ginger ale and orange juice, and each evening my father putting a wooden tongue-depressor into my mouth and peering down my throat, then smiling and saying he thought I might live after all.

Then my father got sick himself, and had to stay at home and go to bed. This was such an unusual occurrence that it amused me.

"Doctors shouldn't get sick," I told him.

"You're right," he said. "That was pretty bad management."

"Run along now, dear," my mother said.

That night I woke and heard voices in the upstairs hall. When I went out, I found my mother and Grandmother MacLeod, both in their dressing-gowns. With them was Dr. Cates. I did not go immediately to my mother, as I would have done only a year before. I stood in the doorway of my room, squinting against the sudden light.

"Mother—what is it?"

She turned, and momentarily I saw the look on her face before she erased it and put on a contrived calm.

"It's all right," she said. "Dr. Cates has just come to have a look at Daddy. You go on back to sleep."

The wind was high that night, and I lay and listened to it rattling the storm windows and making the dry and winter-stiffened vines of the Virginia creeper scratch like small persistent claws against the red brick. In the morning, my mother told me that my father had developed pneumonia.

Dr. Cates did not think it would be safe to move my father to the hospital. My mother began sleeping in the spare bedroom, and after she had been there for a few nights, I asked if I could sleep in there too. I thought she would be bound to ask me why, and I did not know what I would say, but she did not ask. She nodded, and in some way her easy agreement upset me.

That night Dr. Cates came again, bringing with him one of the nurses from the hospital. My mother stayed upstairs with them. I sat with Grandmother MacLeod in the living room. That was the last place in the world I wanted to be, but I thought she would be offended if I went off. She sat as straight and rigid as a totem pole, and embroidered away at the needlepoint cushion cover she was doing. I perched on the edge of the chesterfield and kept my eyes fixed on *The White Company* by Conan Doyle, and from time to time I turned a page. I had already read it three times before, but luckily Grandmother MacLeod did not know that. At nine o'clock she looked at her gold brooch watch, which she always wore pinned to her dress, and told me to go to bed, so I did that.

I wakened in darkness. At first, it seemed to me that I was in my own bed, and everything was as usual, with my parents in their room, and Roddie curled up in the crib in his room, and Grandmother MacLeod sleeping with her mouth open in her enormous spool bed, surrounded by half a dozen framed photos of Uncle Roderick and only one of my father, and Noreen snoring fitfully in the room next to mine, with the dark flames of her hair spreading out across the pillow, and the pink and silver motto cards from the Tabernacle stuck with adhesive tape onto the wall beside her bed—*Lean on Him, Emmanuel Is My Refuge, Rock of Ages Cleft for Me*.

Then in the total night around me, I heard a sound. It was my mother, and she was crying, not loudly at all, but from somewhere very deep inside her. I sat up in bed. Everything seemed to have stopped, not only time but my own heart and blood as well. Then my mother noticed that I was awake.

I did not ask her, and she did not tell me anything. There was no need. She held me in her arms, or I held her, I am not certain which. And after a while the first mourning stopped, too, as everything does sooner or later, for when the limits of endurance have been reached, then people must sleep.

In the days following my father's death, I stayed close beside my mother, and this was only partly for my own consoling. I also had the feeling that she needed my protection. I did not know from what, nor what I could possibly do, but something held me there. Reverend McKee called, and I sat with my grandmother and my mother in the living room. My mother told me I did not need to stay unless I wanted to, but I refused to go. What I thought chiefly was that he would speak of the healing power of prayer, and all that, and it would be bound to make my mother cry again. And in fact, it happened in just that way, but when it actually came, I could not protect her from this assault. I could only sit there and pray my own prayer, which was that he would go away quickly.

My mother tried not to cry unless she was alone or with me. I also tried, but neither of us was entirely successful. Grandmother MacLeod, on the other hand, was never seen crying, not even the day of my father's funeral. But that day, when we had returned to the house and she had taken off her black velvet overshoes and her heavy sealskin coat with its black fur that was the softest thing I had ever touched, she stood in the hallway and for the first time she looked unsteady. When I reached out instinctively towards her, she sighed.

"That's right," she said. "You might just take my arm while I go upstairs, Vanessa."

That was the most my Grandmother MacLeod ever gave in, to anyone's sight. I left her in her bedroom, sitting on the straight chair beside her bed and looking at the picture of my father that had been taken when he graduated from medical college. Maybe she was sorry now that she had only the one photograph of him, but whatever she felt, she did not say.

I went down into the kitchen. I had scarcely spoken to Noreen since my father's death. This had not been done on purpose. I simply had not seen her. I had not really seen anyone except my mother. Looking at Noreen now, I suddenly recalled the sparrow. I felt physically sick, remembering the fearful darting and plunging of those wings, and the fact that it was I who had opened the window and let it in. Then an inexplicable fury took hold of me, some terrifying need to hurt, burn, destroy. Absolutely without warning, either to her or to myself, I hit Noreen as hard as I could. When she swung around, appalled, I hit out at her once more, my arms and legs flailing. Her hands snatched at my wrists, and she held me, but still I continued to struggle, fighting blindly, my eyes tightly closed, as though she were a prison all around me and I was battling to get out. Finally, too shocked at myself to go on, I went limp in her grasp and she let me drop to the floor.

"Vanessa! I never done one single solitary thing to you, and here you go hitting and scratching me like that! What in the world has got into you?"

I began to say I was sorry, which was certainly true, but I did not say it. I could not say anything.

"You're not yourself, what with your dad and everything," she excused me. "I been praying every night that your dad is with God, Vanessa. I know he wasn't actually saved in the regular way, but still and all—"

"Shut up," I said.

Something in my voice made her stop talking. I rose from the floor and stood in the kitchen doorway.

"He didn't need to be saved," I went on coldly, distinctly. "And he is not in Heaven, because there is no Heaven. And it doesn't matter, see? *It doesn't matter!*"

Noreen's face looked peculiarly vulnerable now, her high wide cheekbones and puzzled childish eyes, and the thick russet tangle of her hair. I had not hurt her much before, when I hit her. But I had hurt her now, hurt her in some inexcusable way. Yet I sensed, too, that already she was gaining some satisfaction out of feeling sorrowful about my disbelief.

I went upstairs to my room. Momentarily I felt a sense of calm, almost of acceptance. *Rest beyond the river.* I knew now what that meant. It meant Nothing. It meant only silence, forever.

Then I lay down on my bed and spent the last of my tears, or what seemed then to be the last. Because, despite what I had said to Noreen, it did matter. It mattered, but there was no help for it.

Everything changed after my father's death. The MacLeod house could not be kept up any longer. My mother sold it to a local merchant who subsequently covered the deep red of the brick over with yellow stucco. Something about the house had always made me uneasy—that tower room where Grandmother MacLeod's potted plants drooped in a lethargic and lime-green confusion, those long stairways and hidden places, the attic which I had always imagined to be dwelt in by the spirits of the family dead, that gigantic portrait of the Duke of Wellington at the top of the stairs. It was never an endearing house. And yet when it was no longer ours, and when the Virginia creeper had been torn down and the dark walls turned to a light marigold, I went out of my way to avoid walking past, for it seemed to me that the house had lost the stern dignity that was its very heart.

Noreen went back to the farm. My mother and brother and myself moved into Grandfather Connor's house. Grandmother MacLeod went to live with Aunt Morag in Winnipeg. It was harder for her than for anyone, because so much of her life was bound up with the MacLeod house. She was fond of Aunt Morag, but that hardly counted. Her men were gone, her husband and her sons, and a family whose men are gone is no family at all. The day she left, my mother and I did not know what to say. Grandmother MacLeod looked even smaller than usual in her fur coat and her black velvet toque. She became extremely agitated about trivialities, and fussed about the possibility of the taxi not arriving on time. She had forbidden us to accompany her to the station. About my father, or the house, or anything important, she did not say a word. Then, when the taxi had finally arrived, she turned to my mother.

"Roddie will have Ewen's seal ring, of course, with the MacLeod crest on it," she said. "But there is another seal as well, don't forget, the larger one with the crest and motto. It's meant to be worn on a watch chain. I keep it in my jewel-box. It was Roderick's. Roddie's to have that, too, when I die. Don't let Morag talk you out of it."

During the Second World War, when I was seventeen and in love with an airman who did not love me, and desperately anxious to get away from Manawaka and from my grandfather's house, I happened one day to be going through the old mahogany desk that had belonged to my father. It had a number of small drawers inside, and I accidentally pulled one of these all the way out. Behind it there was another drawer, one I had not known about. Curiously, I opened it. Inside there was a letter written on almost transparent paper in a cramped angular handwriting. It began—*Cher Monsieur Ewen*— That was all I could make out, for the writing was nearly impossible to read and my French was not good. It was dated 1919. With it, there was a picture of a girl, looking absurdly old-fashioned to my eyes, like the faces on long-discarded calendars or chocolate boxes. But beneath the dated quality of the photograph, she seemed neither expensive nor cheap. She looked like what she probably had been—an ordinary middle-class girl, but in another country. She wore her hair in long ringlets, and her mouth was shaped into a sweetly sad posed smile like Mary Pickford's. That was all. There was nothing else in the drawer.

I looked for a long time at the girl, and hoped she had meant some momentary and unexpected freedom. I remembered what he had said to me, after I hadn't gone to the Remembrance Day parade.

"What are you doing, Vanessa?" my mother called from the kitchen.

"Nothing," I replied.

I took the letter and picture outside and burned them. That was all I could do for him. Now that we might have talked together, it was many years too late. Perhaps it would not have been possible anyway. I did not know.

As I watched the smile of the girl turn into scorched paper, I grieved for my father as though he had just died now.

[1964]

· HUGH HOOD ·

1928–

Hugh John Blagdon Hood was born 30 April 1928 in Toronto, Ontario. The son of an English-Canadian father and a French-Canadian mother, he is completely bilingual. Hood received his early education in Toronto's Roman Catholic school system, and later attended the University of Toronto, where he earned his doctorate in English literature in 1955. His dissertation, "Theories of Imagination in English Thinkers 1650–1790," which examines the structure of the romantic imagination, anticipates the way his own fiction dramatizes how the imagination shapes experience into a meaningful unity. In 1961, after teaching for six years at St. Joseph's College, Hartford, Connecticut, Hood joined the English department of the Université de Montréal, where he has remained. His awards include the Canada Council Arts Award, 1970–71, and the Province of Ontario Council for the Arts Award (shared with Alice Munro, 1974); in 1979, a symposium was held in his honour at Stong College, York University.

Central to Hood's *oeuvre* is a deeply moral vision that seeks to align secular and sacred experience. Hood describes his work as moral realism; this refers to the way his allegorical concerns are expressed through a style that documents, and often catalogues, the details of physical reality. This literary method is most evident in the twelve-volume epic series, *The New Age / Le nouveau siècle* (1975-   ), whose main character, Matthew Goderich, envisages and describes the daily rituals of Canadian life in terms of a universal, timeless drama. Hood's affinity to romantic theories of imagination is also represented in this *roman fleuve* in the way Goderich, a self-professed Wordsworthian, synthesizes diverse times, places, and perspectives into a coherent explanation of human experience.

Apart from *The New Age*, Hood is best known for his collections of short stories, each of which is arranged in relation to a guiding theme. A red kite, whose string symbolically joins earth and heaven, provides the unifying emblem for his first collection, *Flying a Red Kite* (1962), whose eleven stories deal with a type of perception that connects the daily to the divine. Documentary and visionary are fused in Hood's second collection, *Around the Mountain: Scenes from Montreal Life* (1967), where twelve richly detailed city scenes provide the allegorical backdrop for the universal struggle between salvation and damnation. Hood alerts the reader to the formal and thematic unity of his third and fourth collections in their epigraphs. "Human art and love are models of immortality," states the epigraph to *The Fruit Man, The Meat Man and the Manager* (1971)—fifteen stories which are arranged to show how art and love, linking agents of community, are the secular counterparts of devotion, or communion. *Dark Glasses* (1976) is titled after its epigraph; a passage from 1 Corinthians, it is a directive to understanding these stories that contrast situations of moral dimness, darkness, and enlightenment.

"Ghosts at Jarry" is from *None Genuine Without This Signature* (1980), a mélange of contemporary signatures found in commerce, popular music, and, as in this story, sport. For Hood, the divine signature is impressed on all things, and he punctuates this collection with epiphanies into the genuine. This is the case in "Ghosts at Jarry," where Mario and his fellow baseball fans, haunting the deserted Jarry Park, resurrect its communal spirit—and its signature.

·————·

Hood's works include *Flying a Red Kite* (1962); *White Figure, White Ground* (1964); *The Camera Always Lies* (1967); *Around the Mountain: Scenes from Montreal Life* (1967); *A Game of Touch* (1970); *Strength Down Centre: The Jean Béliveau Story* (1970); *The Fruit Man, The Meat Man and the Manager* (1971); *You Can't Get There from Here* (1972); *The Governor's Bridge Is Closed* (1973); six volumes of *The New Age/Le nouveau siècle: The Swing in the Garden* (1975); *A New Athens* (1977); *Reservoir Ravine* (1979); *Black and White Keys* (1982); *The Scenic Art* (1984); and *The Motor Boys in Ottawa* (1986); *None Genuine Without This Signature* (1980); *August Nights* (1985); and *Five New Facts About Giorgione* (1987).

Works on Hugh Hood include Dennis Duffy, "Grace: The Novels of Hugh Hood," *Canadian Literature* 47 (1971): 10–25; J.R. (Tim) Struthers, ed., *Before the Flood* (1979); Anthony John Harding, "Field of Vision: Hugh Hood and the Tradition of Wordsworth," *Canadian Literature* 94 (1982): 85–94; Keith Garebian, *Hugh Hood* (1983); J.R. (Tim) Struthers, "Hugh Hood: An Annotated Bibliography," *The Annotated Bibliography of Canada's Major Authors*, ed. Robert Lecker and Jack David (1984), 5: 231–353; and Susan Copoloff-Mechanic, *Pilgrim's Progress* (1987).

Susan Copoloff-Mechanic

GHOSTS AT JARRY

Mario at the big O, a man who likes company. Squeezed into the 400 level up and in and remote from the *voltigeur de gauche,* not too many people near him in the four dollar seats, filling for a cement sandwich, like being on a slab. Cold concrete. The 400 level is indeterminate space, neither a good seat nor a bad, too far away to hear the cries of the infielders like lonely birds swooping over green, too near to shave the price. That April afternoon he saw *les boucaniers de Pittsburgh* take the Expos as the home forces booted the ball repeatedly. Fresh from Florida the unmeshed infield found the home weather too cold for fumbling fingers, baseballs rolling hither and yon, none penetrating the 400 level. No *fausse balle* enlivened the narrow precinct. Mario decided not to sit there again; it would have to be *le niveau 200, Section 18, Section 20,* or nothing, and it would cost.

He looked for friends, found none, though they were there for sure. They had told him they were coming, Ti-cul, Kurt, Silvo, present but invisible. After the fourth inning he went in search of Silvo, who used to sit out past third base at field level, but there was nobody in his seat, only vast stretches of unoccupied metal pigeonholes, roomy, chilly, in their thousands. He couldn't find his way back upstairs; the arrows and signs confused him, and he watched the rest of the game from a vacant seat downstairs, not having paid the full price. He felt nervous and guilty but no cheerful attendant asked to see his stub; nobody banished him from the third base line. Mario never got away with anything because he never tried to. Nobody came around selling peanuts; the vendors seemed lost in the empty reaches. Parched at the seventh-inning stretch he quit his usurped bench and found a nearby kiosk where nobody stood in line. He was served immediately, then had to find a lavatory, luckily next door. Mario blessed the *Régie des Installations Olympiques* for wise care of their *concitoyens,* but found the lavatory a maze of reverse-swinging doors. He had a hard time escaping, a belated rally in progress along the basepaths. Cash scored, the home forces appeared ready to carry the day. Mario fought his way to freedom in time to see the *Devinez l'assistance* figures flashed on the big board: 21,063, 19,750, 18,322, 20,004.

He thought: those are mistaken. There can't be twenty thousand people here, or eighteen thousand. I would guess maybe seven, he thought, maybe eight thousand. There is nobody buying beer, nobody helped me when I called. I might have perished in there. The board flashed the official figure: *Assistance d'aujourd'hui, 19,750.* He peered around incredulously. Had they counted sold empty seats perhaps? At Jarry such a throng would have stretched services beyond capacity. He'd never have been able to walk straight to the counter and demand a beer, not even after the game was over. Here there was infinite space, and it unsettled him. The long eighth inning continued; extra innings impended; afternoon stretched into early evening; people began to leave; the big O emptied; Mario got frightened.

He wondered if he would come back. It was so close to home, that was the thing. For his whole life, he and Ti-cul and Silvo and Kurt had been hoping for something in the east-end besides the Angus shops. Now here it was, five minutes from Rosemont, and it gave him vertigo. He looked out, squinting through the late shadows, at what-the-hell-was-it, sward? Turf? He wasn't sure of the word. *Gazon? Domtarturf?* It wasn't anything like grass, being a bright emerald, a colour never seen in the natural world, out of a laboratory, bottled. Such green as might be seen in a film about the distant future. He could see where the individual rolls had been zippered together and laughed when a tenth-inning ground ball, out past Parrish, suddenly bounded into the air as it hit one of the zippered seams in the gleaming surface and assumed a long incredible arc, hurtling past the amazed left-fielder towards the warning track. Two runs scored. Expos failed to even the count in their half of the tenth, and the game ended that way, towards six o'clock.

The players vanished like wraiths; never had Mario seen them disappear so fast. He used to stand close to the field after the final out, to watch the inept homesters make their exposed way out to the foul pole in left and into the clubhouse, exchanging discontented repartee with certain regular fans. Once that disgusting, off-speed-pitch-specialist, Howie Reed, had flipped a baseball into *les estrades populaires* as he sauntered, cursing freely and indecently in words Mario failed to recognise, into the sheltering clubhouse. There had been a scramble. Children had injured themselves. Such a thing would be impossible under the new dispensation, contact irretrievably lost. Mario felt specks and points tickling the curling hairs on his neck and looked up. Unbelievably a warm spring rain was finding its way to him from on high, hardly a rain, more a mist, spitting. Nobody was visible but a non-lingual youth who scuttled past turning seats up, mute arguably from birth; nobody could have decided on the evidence. He would have to look for Kurt and the others at the tavern; he was sure to find them there. He moved up the steps and in out of the rain; spring night enveloped him. In the dark, strange patterns defined themselves on the concrete walls as wetness slid down pocked textures.

Roofless, open, the giant structure admitted natural flow of water, perhaps its most grateful feature. He pondered this matter as he made for the main gates, wondering whether he should go home or go downtown to eat. What would the stadium be like in heavy rain, in snow, roofless or roofed? He had heard from a friend in the air-conditioning business that huge conduits, giant circulating pumps, were being installed in the building, which would in time be completed as an all-weather sports palace. But here imagination failed. How heat it in winter? Who would sit in caverns of ice to watch what? Should Expos ever make it into *la série mondiale* they would have to play night games in mid-October; his Mediterranean blood roiled and thickened at the thought. A roof would inhibit free circulation of air. How dank, how chilled it would be, pressed up against that cold stone in late autumn! What could be done about it? And he thought, as he thought most days about the way things went on, how fix?

His feet had decided for him, leading him down the tunnel towards the Métro station. Nobody on the first flight. Nobody on the second flight. Silence along the terraces, solitude beside the newsagents' stands. Inside a sandwich again, he thought, eaten by a giant. One solitary man in a glass booth opening a vacuum bottle. Steam escaped from its top, making him think of the roofless big O. In this rain, in these temperatures, there would be puffs of steam from the hole in the top, possibly even rings of vapour as if expelled from the cancered lungs of a colossal cigarette-smoker. He passed onto an almost silent train; a solitary passenger wasn't anybody he knew.

When he rose up out of the Métro at the Berri-De Montigny station, he found the same spring rain falling into the lights of evening. He thought of the plastic emerald rug; this rain would not promote its growth, false surface. He had heard that the players preferred true grass which grew long, sometimes giving them a break on a hot grounder. Long growth might then be cut to surprise visiting teams with porous infields, a bit of baseball larceny less and less available to canny groundskeepers. Too bright. Too green.

And there there was the look and feeling of the oddly-shaped hole in the roof, a shape that made him peculiarly uncomfortable, something wrong about it. He wasn't a poet; he wasn't an architect; he had a labouring job and didn't want to know about art, but he knew that the hole in the sky was quietly askew, wrong. It shouldn't curve that way because there was nothing in the curve to remind him of women's bodies. If something curved, thought Mario, it ought to curve in a useful or encouraging way.

He wouldn't go back in there; it wasn't like the old park, which had been like a village, close, warming, with the usual run of village characters. There had been a man who brought his goat to twenty games a season, and the club management connived at the smelly invasion, to court press photographers. At the opening game of the 1971 season, Mario's children had carried a huge homemade sign into the bleachers: BIENVENUE A NOS AMOURS LES EXPOS. At two in the afternoon a pressman took a picture, which appeared in the final edition of the *Star* that same afternoon; neighbours phoned excitedly during dinner to tell the family about it. The children had remembered it ever since and there was a copy of the picture still pinned to his bedroom door.

There had been that man who sprang up in the middle of rallies and danced like a dervish up and down the steps of the grandstand, executing unheard-of jigs and reels to an accompaniment of handclapping from thousands of enthusiasts around him, a lean man, crazy-looking, known around the National League as "the Dancer." His steps could not have been danced at the *Stade Olympique*. The pitch of the seats was too gradual, the stairs insufficiently raked. Some sort of classical pavanne would suit them, not the gyrations of the native Québecker.

In the twentieth row of the bleachers, right behind the third base foul pole, had sat night after night an unspeaking man in a short-sleeved shirt, grey-headed, immobile, stumpy cigar always in place, not a word to say for himself but always there. No cheer escaped this man, no violation of the careful probabilities of baseball by fledgling expansion team could make him wince. Mario missed him terribly, searched for him during intense moments at the big O, realising finally that the man had gone forever. He might just possibly be seated somewhere in the new building in his perpetual Buddhist posture but this seemed against all odds, the betting prohibitive. What is to be done, Mario wondered, how can this be restored?

Ballplayers—on the whole an ungenerous group of men—had hated Jarry Park for sound professional reasons as well as from personal pique. Not really great and good ballplayers, most early Expos wished to avoid the inspection of nearby fans, disliked the trudge along the track to the clubhouse, finally prevailed upon management to erect a cement-block tunnel from dugout to clubhouse, rendering themselves unobservable, incorrigible. A very few who for reasons of their own wished to court public favour continued to take the outside walk; but these were popular players apt to be fringe performers, a Ronnie Brand, a Marv Staehle, José Herrera.

The old park had the world's crappiest outfield, frost-humped, deceptively grassy, stippled with rabbit holes, hell to run on. It had no foul area; the bullpens were in the laps of the fans. Visiting relief pitchers endured coarse taunts during rare Expos rallies. Expos firemen grew accustomed to the stagey resignation of the home supporters.

"Attention, Attention. Le numéro vingt-cinq, Dan McGinn, lance maintenant pour les Expos."

At this ominous declaration, Ti-cul, Kurt, Silvo, and Mario would groan, make retching noises. The Buddha of the bleachers might shift one buttock's width to right or left, or he might not.

I will go back and look at Jarry Park, Mario decided. He had clipped a panoramic view of the old place from some special issue of *Le Dimanche*, park packed beyond capacity for some extraordinary occasion. Taken from an altitude of seven hundred and fifty feet, probably from a helicopter hovering above the parking lot to the northeast of the playing field, the photo emphasised the ramshackle, spurious, ad hoc, temporary, incredible cheapness of the silly building. It had cost three million dollars. But no public facility of the contemporary scene could possibly cost three million dollars, the thing was unheard-of. It was eight hundred million or zilch—there is no other way. When Jarry had been built, not all that long ago, Mario recollected, hardly a decade, there had been no cranes sitting idle on the site over weekends, at overtime rates approaching sixty thousand an hour. Overtime for idling cranes alone had cost more at the Olympic site than the entire cost of Jarry Park, three million. How fix?

The players hated it, and it made sense: two strikes. He thought he'd go and have a final look before they started to tear it down; there was no conceivable use for the facility. All he did was work. It looked horrible. The metal flooring of the stands had leaked copiously. If you stood under it during a rain-delay, the precipitation poured down your neck and into the dank bun of your hotdog. Those hotdogs had always been dung-like, inert, without form and void. Soggy, they constituted an offence against nature. No. There was nothing to be said for the former home of the Montréal National League Baseball Club Limited.

Somewhere around the house there was a portable radio, useable on house current or batteries, a discarded Christmas gift with exhausted power pack. Mario located it, dusted it off, supplied the requisite D batteries, and took it with him across town on an indifferent, coolish, Sunday afternoon with the Cards in town.

At fifteen hundred feet a familiar Cessna 150 banked, trailing a long streamer which delivered the Gospel according to Parkside. ALWAYS A BETTER DEAL AT PARKSIDE MOTORS. The plane hastened away as Mario squinted aloft. Perhaps the pilot had forgotten himself, returned to his old flyway mistaking the open space below for the true ballgame, then found it empty. The drone of the engine faded. Jarry was really desert.

He sidled towards the exiguous metal structure. One thing about it, though lonely, deserted, vacant, boarded over, it hadn't corroded. The metal façade shone dully, white in the uncertain atmosphere. It was an afternoon of ill-defined light, little sun, light overcast, a genuine Montréal uncertainty of observation. There was nobody in the park. He passed along the chain-link fencing looking for entry. Surely some boy or dog or vandal had effected the necessary hole—and there it was, back along the third base side near the rickety ticket booths and the press gate, a gaping tear, edges bent backwards, big enough to drive a Jeep through. Somebody had been at work with a pair of wire-cutters. The edges of the severed strands were shiny-fresh and could hurt you. He passed inside.

What is quieter than an abandoned ballpark, unless the tomb? He shuddered to think where all the voices had gone. Once this place had shaken and resounded with the shrieks of fifteen thousand maddened kiddies on Bat Day, fifteen thousand miniature Louisville Sluggers pounding in unison on the metal flooring; it had been a hellish event. Householders for blocks around had complained to the authorities but the promotion had become a recurrent event. Bat Day at Jarry Park was like the Last Judgement, sounding, deeply impressive.

But unlike the judgement in this, that it was not still impending. He stole across the flat paved open area between the fence and the refreshment counters. A blue souvenir stand leaned ready to collapse, doors locked. From between the doors a feather protruded electric blue. Mario tugged at the feather end, and the whole article slid noiselessly from between the locked doors, a celebratory feather dyed red, white, and blue. The other end stuck in the door, perhaps attached to a hat inside, too big to fit through the crack. He could do nothing to release it and left it floating solemnly in the faint breeze, passed up a ramp and into the deserted third-base seats, once the best place in the city to see a game. He idled along towards the foul pole, clutching his radio. The day around him grew imperceptibly warmer, the grey lightened. Vacancy. The seats were all before him and he was at the extreme outfield end of the park, immediately over the gateway to the abandoned clubhouse. He sprawled in one seat, then stood up, chose another, put his legs out in front of him, and switched on the radio.

". . .and after the pre-game show we'll have all the action for you right here at Radio 600, the voice of Montréal Expos baseball. I'm Dave Van Horne and I'll be right here with Duke Snider to keep you up-to-date on the out-of-town scores and the other developments around the majors, right after this message. . ."

The sun came out. Mario drowsed and listened. He saw that this was life as it ought to be lived. The game came to him with perfect clarity and form over the radio. With his eyes shut he could fancy the whole place alive around him. Nothing was gone. The Gautama of the bleachers would be right over there twenty rows up, if he happened to glance in that direction. If the Expos happened to get something going—as they did almost immediately that afternoon—the dancer would get his legs going too. The air would be filled with flying bags of peanuts. People would be passing hotdogs along the rows in a fine comradeship. All he had to do was listen, and keep his eyes shut tight.

". . .opened the inning with a single, went to second on Cromartie's roller to the right side. Valentine homered, his sixth home run of the season and his nineteenth and twentieth RBIs. Perez reached on an error. . ."

Expos won that first game in Mario's resurrected Jarry, a shutout victory for Rogers, and after that there could be no question of viewing the games in the flesh. He started to come to the old park all the time, nights and Saturdays as well as on the Sabbath. He felt in control, as though the whole happening was invented by him. The conviction grew on him that he could influence the course of the games by wishing, commanding in imagination. He knew that this was not strictly so, but all the same the home club seemed to rally more often when he really willed them to—balls found holes in infields, defensive replacements offered models of anticipation. Rookies blossomed—three of them, almost a miracle—all through closed eyes. He now began to think about bringing his portable SANYO along. If the atmospherics were right and the power pack strong, he might be able to watch the games on TV, listen to the expert radio commentary, have his eyes opened. Would the TV picture be an adequate surrogate for all he could imagine?

Night games would tell; they were the best of all because the tall poles no longer supported myriads of hot arcs. All was still, but not dark. Those night games in May and June at Jarry, the longest evenings of the year, had always been vexed by the slow disappearance of the sun behind the bleachers to the northwest. He remembered Ron Fairly refusing to scamper onto the playing area when the umpire called "Play Ball!" because of that late sun, dead in the eyes of the first baseman. Fairly, always an intransigent ballplayer, had been able to persuade Dick Stello to delay the game until the sun disappeared, an unlikely twenty minutes. At Midsummer Day it didn't get dark in the park until the sixth inning or even later, while across town the actual play would be shadowed in shrouding concrete, no illumination relieving the cavernous gloom. Night games were best.

Just about Midsummer Day, with a long brilliant evening light promised, he brought the SANYO along and sneaked into his usual spot. For a while he contented himself with the radio and the fading summer sun on his tight eyelids, but as the light waned he grew curious, and when darkness descended very late, past nine-thirty, he turned on the TV and focussed his gaze on the small picture, like some mystic concentrating on his mandala:

CARTER. 11 HR. 29 RBI. .268

The emission of light from the small screen was the only sparkle in the park, thought Mario. He leaned forward, the sounds of the city in the night drifting almost inaudibly overhead. He watched the final three innings, willing them to win, and they did. And as he switched to the post-game show on the radio, just as he turned his TV off, he caught a gleam of light almost the mirror image of his own at the extreme other end of the stands, over by the first-base foul pole. A line drawn from where he was sitting through centre-field to the distant glimmer would form the base of an isosceles triangle whose equal sides would extend through first and third to home. He had no intention of launching himself into the deep well of darkness in centre. But he felt drawn along the shining metal gangway which ran the length of the grandstand.

The main bank of seats in Jarry was formed in the shape of an enormous letter L, the two equal sides of an isosceles triangle with its apex behind home plate. A fan sitting in Mario's position sensed this shape as a long line extending away towards home, with the other leg of the L running out of the corner of his eye in the direction of the visitors' dressing room under the first-base stands. The whole mass had something the look of an opened penknife, as used in the boy's game of "baseball" early in the century.

The distant figure on the other side of the park now followed Mario's lead and extinguished whatever light had been showing. The whole park lay under the night sky empty, glowing with night-shine off the aluminum seatbacks. A breeze moved quietly in the grass. Mario inched his way silently towards home in the darkness, and peering through the dark he had the sense that somebody else was coming in from right-field. A faint metallic sound drifted above the pitcher's mound, shoes on metal plating. Small shoes, by the sound.

He eased forward along the runway, which stretched out in front of him like a white dusty road in the country under starlight. The towers of extinct arc-lights stood up around the park like sentinels. There was the billboard advertising cigarettes, unreadable in the dark. Out to his left the old scoreboard, which had never worked properly, loomed with comforting familiarity. Clink of shoes on metal. He strained his eyes to see across the narrowing infield. Somebody was there. He caught a glimpse of a pale face in dim reflection. Then he heard swift footsteps and saw a slender form move in the dark like the ghost of a batboy. He ran along the third-base line, reaching home at the same moment as the ghostly figure. A girl in a dark blue halter and a pair of jeans threw herself unresistingly into his arms. This terrified him. Mario had held no girl but his wife in his arms at any time these twenty years. He drew back and tried to see her. Like himself, she carried a small portable TV and a radio.

"I thought you were a ghost," exclaimed this stranger. "Heavens, how you scared me."

"I thought so too," said Mario.

"That you were a ghost? How could you think that?"

"No. That *you* were."

"That's silly," said the girl scornfully. "Anybody can see that I'm not a ghost. I'm a very popular girl."

"I'm sure you are, Miss, but I can't see you very well in the dark."

"Why are you here?"

"I like it better here."

"Oh, so do I, so do I. I hate that other place with a passion."

"And so you started to come back here, just like me, to listen to the games and watch them on your TV. How long have you been coming?"

"This is my first time."

"I hope it won't be your last," said Mario with a gallantry which astounded himself. It would have astonished his wife too.

"But we're . . . all alone in here?"

"There's certainly nobody here now, not even a security guard."

"Would I be safe with you?"

"Would one Expos fan insult another? And besides, now that there are two of us, others will come. I'm certain of it."

"Oh, I hope you're right," said the girl in a beseeching tone.

"I know I'm right," said Mario. "This is exactly how a house gets to be haunted." Afterwards, when he recognised the supreme justice of this observation he wondered how he'd hit on it. He considered himself habitually, by a kind of unthinking reflex, to be a stupid unfeeling person, but in this adventure he had shown, he saw, powerful imagination.

Many came after that first encounter; they came by ones and twos, then in troops, finally in hundreds. The abandoned park sprang back to a loony bootleg life all the sunny summer. People would bring their own hotdogs and beer, their radios. Somehow a cap and souvenir vendor found out about the secret congregation, and he came too one July evening with a trayful of hats and dolls and pennants. Nobody bought anything from him; they were afraid he'd disappear. Obviously the Montréal National League Baseball Club Limited knew nothing about him, a phantom souvenir salesman with phantom goods.

None of them revisited the big O. Not ever. And in the earliest hints of autumn they would laugh, and people in neighbourhood apartment blocks would wonder where the laughing was coming from, as the plangent tones of the Duke of Fallbrook oozed from the radios collected at Jarry.

". . . now we know, Dave and I know, that the club is playing a bit off the pace, but really you know folks that doesn't explain the dropoff in attendance. There has to be a big audience for Expos baseball out there somewhere, and I'm appealing to you—it's the old Duker talking . . ."

"That's right, Duke," said the voice of Dave Van Horne, "we've got a great home stand going here, so come on out to the Olympic Stadium and watch the Expos try to play the role of spoilers in this season's tight race in the National League East. Hope to see you real soon, right, Duke?"

"Right, Dave!"

But the ghosts of Jarry merely guffawed, an immense throng they were by now. And the first of them looked again at the wide heavens. No, he would never go back. He would spend no second afternoon in mental trouble excited by that crater in the air, gazing through the gaping enormous ellipse—was it an ellipse?—in the sky.

[1978]

· ALICE MUNRO ·

1931–

Alice Laidlaw Munro was born in 1931 on what she once called "the untidy, impoverished, wayward edge" of a southwestern Ontario farming town, Wingham. She studied journalism at the University of Western Ontario for two years, then married and moved to Vancouver, then Victoria, where she raised children, founded with her husband a successful bookstore, and struggled to find time and energy to write. *Dance of the Happy Shades* (1968), her first collection of short stories, won the Governor General's Award. She returned to Ontario in 1972, eventually settling in Clinton, where she still lives. Other honours include the Govenor General's Award for *Who Do You Think You Are?* (1978) and *The Progress of Love* (1986, a runner-up for the Booker Prize), and the Canada-Australia Literary Prize.

Munro's early works are largely concerned with what one of her interviewers once called "the ghosts of childhood." In *Dance of the Happy Shades* and *Lives of Girls and Women* (1971), she explores the growing consciousness of the child, whose development is often fraught with shameful humiliations and sudden revelations. Sometimes, as in "Boys and Girls," from *Dance of the Happy Shades,* the nature of these revelations is shadowy, only half understood by the child. Letting the horse Flora run free is a necessary and impulsive act for the young narrator—an act whose affirmative and rebellious nature she does not yet comprehend. Often, too, these early stories like "Boys and Girls," are stories of betrayal and guilt. "The Peace of Utrecht," referred to by Munro as "the first real story I ever wrote," remains one of her most powerful explorations of the "ghosts of childhood."

One development in Munro's writ-ing which is very often ignored is her growing self-consciousness as a writer, as a maker of fictions. One sees early hints of this concern with fictionalizing in "The Office" from *Dance of the Happy Shades,* and in "Epilogue: The Photographer" from *Lives of Girls and Women,* but it reaches a climax in her third work, *Something I've Been Meaning to Tell You* (1974). Here, in stories such as "Tell Me Yes or No" and "Material," Munro explores the frustrating, fascinating dialectic between fiction and reality. In a more recent work, *The Moons of Jupiter* (1982), this motif of fictionality becomes more implicit, embedded in the texture of seemingly conventional realist tales such as "Hard Luck Stories" or "Visitors"—tales which feature a plethora of storytellers.

Accompanying this greater self-consciousness has been a greater willingness on Munro's part to experiment with the traditional short story form. Most of the stories in *Dance of the Happy Shades,* for example, feature a linear, chronological sequence of events, often narrated from a first-person point of view. In stories such as "The Spanish Lady" and "Something I've Been Meaning to Tell You," from *Something I've Been Meaning to Tell You,* Munro brilliantly exploits time sequences in order to capture the texture of non-linear psychological experience. In *Who Do You Think You Are?* Munro attempts her first full-length experiment with a "hybrid" point of view: a third-person perspective which has all of the immediacy and limited insight of a first-person point of view ("Rose gets lonely in new places; she wishes she had invitations. . . .").

This willingness to explore the limitations of the short story and of realism itself seems appropriate to a writer who also explores the traditional limitations placed on female experience. Throughout her career, Munro has sensitively probed the freedom and constraints involved in being female. ("Boys and Girls," for instance, is a study of both constraint and freedom.) Just as Munro is poised between the realist and postmodernist modes of storytelling, so too are her women—Del, Rose—delicately poised between dependence on traditional stereotypes and the painful road to independence.

Munro's fiction, then, combines traditional realism and experimentation. Like Jack Hodgins, Christopher Pratt, and Ken Danby, Munro reveals that the marvellous and exotic often masquerade in the sheep's clothing of the real.

· ———— ·

Munro's works include *Dance of the Happy Shades* (1968); *Lives of Girls and Women* (1971); *Something I've Been Meaning to Tell You* (1974); *Who Do You Think You Are?* (1978); *The Moons of Jupiter: Stories* (1982); and *The Progress of Love* (1986).

Works on Munro include Helen Hoy, " 'Dull, Simple, Amazing and Unfathomable': Paradox and Double Vision in Alice Munro's Fiction," *Studies in Canadian Literature* 5 (1980): 1–15; Louis K. MacKendrick, ed., *Probable Fictions: Alice Munro's Narrative Acts* (1983); Robert Thacker, "Alice Munro: An Annotated Bibliography," *An Annotated Bibliography of Canada's Major Authors*, ed. Robert Lecker and Jack David (1984), 5: 354–414; Hallvard Dahlie, "Alice Munro," *Canadian Writers and Their Works*, ed. Robert Lecker, Jack David, and Ellen Quigley (1985), Fiction Series 7: 215–56; and W. R. Martin, *Alice Munro: Paradox and Parallel* (1987).

LORRAINE YORK

BOYS AND GIRLS

My father was a fox farmer. That is, he raised silver foxes, in pens; and in the fall and early winter, when their fur was prime, he killed them and skinned them and sold their pelts to the Hudson's Bay Company or the Montreal Fur Traders. These companies supplied us with heroic calendars to hang, one on each side of the kitchen door. Against a background of cold blue sky and black pine forests and treacherous northern rivers, plumed adventurers planted the flags of England or of France; magnificent savages bent their backs to the portage.

For several weeks before Christmas, my father worked after supper in the cellar of our house. The cellar was whitewashed, and lit by a hundred-watt bulb over the worktable. My brother Laird and I sat on the top step and watched. My father removed the pelt inside-out from the body of the fox, which looked surprisingly small, mean and rat-like, deprived of its arrogant weight of fur. The naked, slippery bodies were collected in a sack and buried at the dump. One time the hired man, Henry Bailey, had taken a swipe at me with this sack, saying, "Christmas present!" My mother thought that was not funny. In fact she disliked the whole pelting operation—that was what the killing, skinning, and preparation of the furs was called—and wished it did not have to take place in the house. There was the smell. After the pelt had been stretched inside-out on a long board my father scraped away delicately, removing the little clotted webs of blood vessels, the bubbles of fat; the smell of blood and animal fat, with the strong primitive odour of the fox itself, penetrated all parts of the house. I found it reassuringly seasonal, like the smell of oranges and pine needles.

Henry Bailey suffered from bronchial troubles. He would cough and cough until his narrow face turned scarlet, and his light blue, derisive eyes filled up with tears; then he took the lid off the stove, and, standing well back, shot out a great clot of phlegm—hsss—straight into the heart of the flames. We admired him for this performance and for his ability to make his stomach growl at will, and for his laughter, which was full of high whistlings and gurglings and involved the whole faulty machinery of his chest. It was sometimes hard to tell what he was laughing at, and always possible that it might be us.

After we had been sent to bed we could still smell fox and still hear Henry's laugh, but these things, reminders of the warm, safe, brightly lit downstairs world, seemed lost and diminished, floating on the stale cold air upstairs. We were afraid at night in the winter. We were not afraid of *outside* though this was the time of year when snowdrifts curled around our house like sleeping whales and the wind harassed us all night, coming up from the buried fields, the frozen swamp, with its old bugbear chorus of threats and misery. We were afraid of *inside,* the room where we slept. At this time the upstairs of our house was not finished. A brick chimney went up one wall. In the middle of the floor was a square hole, with a wooden railing around it; that was where the stairs came up. On the other side of the stairwell were the things that nobody had any use for any more—a soldiery roll of linoleum, standing on end, a wicker baby carriage, a fern basket, china jugs and basins with cracks in them, a picture of the Battle of Balaclava, very sad to look at. I had told Laird, as soon as he was old enough to understand such things, that bats and skeletons lived over there; whenever a man escaped from the county jail, twenty miles away, I imagined that he had somehow let himself in the window and was hiding behind the linoleum. But we had rules to keep us safe. When the light was on, we were safe as long as we did not step off the square of worn carpet which defined our bedroom-space; when the light was off no place was safe but the beds themselves. I had to turn out the light kneeling on the end of my bed, and stretching as far as I could to reach the cord.

In the dark we lay on our beds, our narrow life rafts, and fixed our eyes on the faint light coming up the stairwell, and sang songs. Laird sang "Jingle Bells," which he would sing any time, whether it was Christmas or not, and I sang "Danny Boy." I loved the sound of my own voice, frail and supplicating, rising in the dark. We could make out the tall frosted shapes of the windows now, gloomy and white. When I came to the part, *When I am dead, as dead I well may be*—a fit of shivering caused not by the cold sheets but by pleasurable emotion almost silenced me. *You'll kneel and say, an Ave there above me*—What was an Ave? Every day I forgot to find out.

Laird went straight from singing to sleep. I could hear his long, satisfied, bubbly breaths. Now for the time that remained to me, the most perfectly private and perhaps the best time of the whole day, I arranged myself tightly under the covers and went on with one of the stories I was telling myself from night to night. These stories were about myself, when I had grown a little older; they took place in a world that was recognizably mine, yet one that presented opportunities for courage, boldness and self-sacrifice, as mine never did. I rescued people from a bombed building (it discouraged me that the real war had gone on so far away from Jubilee). I shot two rabid wolves who were menacing the schoolyard (the teachers cowered terrified at my back). I rode a fine horse spiritedly down the main street of Jubilee, acknowledging the townspeople's gratitude for some yet-to-be-worked-out piece of heroism (nobody ever rode a horse there, except King Billy in the Orangemen's Day parade). There was always riding and shooting in these stories, though I had only been on a horse twice—bareback because we did not own a saddle—and the second time I had slid right around and dropped under the horse's feet; it had stepped placidly over me. I really was learning to shoot, but I could not hit anything yet, not even tin cans on fence posts.

Alive, the foxes inhabited a world my father made for them. It was surrounded by a high guard fence, like a medieval town, with a gate that was padlocked at night. Along the streets of this town were ranged large, sturdy pens. Each of them had a real door that a man could go through, a wooden ramp along the wire, for the foxes to run up and down on, and a kennel—something like a clothes chest with airholes—where they slept and stayed in winter and had their young. There were feeding and watering dishes attached to the wire in such a way that they could be emptied and cleaned from the outside. The dishes were made of old tin cans, and the ramps and kennels of odds and ends of old lumber. Everything was tidy and ingenious; my father was tirelessly inventive and his favourite book in the world was Robinson Crusoe. He had fitted a tin drum on a wheelbarrow, for bringing water down to the pens. This was my job in summer, when the foxes had to have water twice a day. Between nine and ten o'clock in the morning, and again after supper, I filled the drum at the pump and trundled it down through the barnyard to the pens, where I parked it, and filled my watering can and went along the streets. Laird came too, with his little cream and green gardening can, filled too full and knocking against his legs and slopping water on his canvas shoes. I had the real watering can, my father's, though I could only carry it three-quarters full.

The foxes all had names, which were printed on a tin plate and hung beside their doors. They were not named when they were born, but when they survived the first year's pelting and were added to the breeding stock. Those my father had named were called names like Prince, Bob, Wally and Betty. Those I had named were called Star or Turk, or Maureen or Diana. Laird named one Maud after a hired girl we had when he was little, one Harold after a boy at school, and one Mexico, he did not say why.

Naming them did not make pets out of them, or anything like it. Nobody but my father ever went into the pens, and he had twice had blood-poisoning from bites. When I was bringing them their water they prowled up and down on the paths they had made inside their pens, barking seldom—they saved that for nighttime, when they might get up a chorus of community frenzy—but always watching me, their eyes burning, clear gold, in their pointed, malevolent faces. They were beautiful for their delicate legs and heavy, aristocratic tails and the bright fur sprinkled on dark down their backs—which gave them their name—but especially for their faces, drawn exquisitely sharp in pure hostility, and their golden eyes.

Besides carrying water I helped my father when he cut the long grass, and the lamb's quarter and flowering money-musk, that grew between the pens. He cut with the scythe and I raked into piles. Then he took a pitchfork and threw fresh-cut grass all over the top of the pens, to keep the foxes cooler and shade their coats, which were browned by too much sun. My father did not talk to me unless it was about the job we were doing. In this he was quite different from my mother, who, if she was feeling cheerful, would tell me all sorts of things—the name of a dog she had had when she was a little girl, the names of boys she had gone out with later on when she was grown up, and what certain dresses of hers had looked like—she could not imagine now what had become of them. Whatever thoughts and stories my father had were private, and I was shy of him and would never ask him questions. Nevertheless I worked willingly under his eyes, and with a feeling of pride. One time a feed salesman came down into the pens to talk to him and my father said, "Like to have you meet my new hired man." I turned away and raked furiously, red in the face with pleasure.

"Could of fooled me," said the salesman. "I thought it was only a girl."

After the grass was cut, it seemed suddenly much later in the year. I walked on stubble in the earlier evening, aware of the reddening skies, the entering silences, of fall. When I wheeled the tank out of the gate and put the padlock on, it was almost dark. One night at this time I saw my mother and father standing talking on the little rise of ground we called the gangway, in front of the barn. My father had just come from the meathouse; he had his stiff bloody apron on, and a pail of cut-up meat in his hand.

It was an odd thing to see my mother down at the barn. She did not often come out of the house unless it was to do something—hang out the wash or dig potatoes in the garden. She looked out of place, with her bare lumpy legs, not touched by the sun, her apron still on and damp across the stomach from the supper dishes. Her hair was tied up in a kerchief, wisps of it falling out. She would tie her hair up like this in the morning, saying she did not have time to do it properly, and it would stay tied up all day. It was true, too; she really did not have time. These days our back porch was piled with baskets of peaches and grapes and pears, bought in town, and onions and tomatoes and cucumbers grown at home, all waiting to be made into jelly and jam and preserves, pickles and chili sauce. In the kitchen there was a fire in the stove all day, jars clinked in boiling water, sometimes a cheesecloth bag was strung on a pole between two chairs, straining blue-black grape pulp for jelly. I was given jobs to do and I would sit at the table peeling peaches that had been soaked in the hot water, or cutting up onions, my eyes smarting and streaming. As soon as I was done I ran out of the house, trying to get out of earshot before my mother thought of what she wanted me to do next. I hated the hot dark kitchen in summer, the green blinds and the flypapers, the same old oilcloth table and wavy mirror and bumpy linoleum. My mother was too tired and preoccupied to talk to me, she had no heart to tell about the Normal School Graduation Dance; sweat trickled over her face and she was always counting under her breath, pointing at jars, dumping cups of sugar. It seemed to me that work in the house was endless, dreary and peculiarly depressing; work done out of doors, and in my father's service, was ritualistically important.

I wheeled the tank up to the barn, where it was kept, and I heard my mother saying, "Wait till Laird gets a little bigger, then you'll have a real help."

What my father said I did not hear. I was pleased by the way he stood listening, politely as he would to a salesman or a stranger, but with an air of wanting to get on with his real work. I felt my mother had no business down here and I wanted him to feel the same way. What did she mean about Laird? He was no help to anybody. Where was he now? Swinging himself sick on the swing, going around in circles, or trying to catch caterpillars. He never once stayed with me till I was finished.

"And then I can use her more in the house," I heard my mother say. She had a dead-quiet, regretful way of talking about me that always made me uneasy. "I just get my back turned and she runs off. It's not like I had a girl in the family at all."

I went and sat on a feed bag in the corner of the barn, not wanting to appear when this conversation was going on. My mother, I felt, was not to be trusted. She was kinder than my father and more easily fooled, but you could not depend on her, and the real reasons for the things she said and did were not to be known. She loved me, and she sat up late at night making a dress of the difficult style I wanted, for me to wear when school started, but she was also my enemy. She was always plotting. She was plotting now to get me to stay in the house more, although she knew I hated it (*because* she knew I hated it) and keep me from working with my father. It seemed to me she would do this simply out of perversity, and to try her power. It did not occur to me that she could be lonely, or jealous. No grown-up could be; they were too fortunate. I sat and kicked my heels monotonously against a feedbag, raising dust, and did not come out till she was gone.

At any rate, I did not expect my father to pay any attention to what she said. Who could imagine Laird doing my work—Laird remembering the padlock and cleaning out the watering-dishes with a leaf on the end of a stick, or even wheeling the tank without it tumbling over? It showed how little my mother knew about the way things really were.

I have forgotten to say what the foxes were fed. My father's bloody apron reminded me. They were fed horsemeat. At this time most farmers still kept horses, and when a horse got too old to work, or broke a leg or got down and would not get up, as they sometimes did, the owner would call my father, and he and Henry went out to the farm in the truck. Usually they shot and butchered the horse there, paying the farmer from five to twelve dollars. If they had already too much meat on hand, they would bring the horse back alive, and keep it for a few days or weeks in our stable, until the meat was needed. After the war the farmers were buying tractors and gradually getting rid of horses altogether, so it sometimes happened that we got a good healthy horse, that there was just no use for any more. If this happened in the winter we might keep the horse in our stable till spring, for we had plenty of hay and if there was a lot of snow—and the plow did not always get our road cleared—it was convenient to be able to go to town with a horse and cutter.

The winter I was eleven years old we had two horses in the stable. We did not know what names they had had before, so we called them Mack and Flora. Mack was an old black workhorse, sooty and indifferent. Flora was a sorrel mare, a driver. We took them both out in the cutter. Mack was slow and easy to handle. Flora was given to fits of violent alarm, veering at cars and even at other horses, but we loved her speed and high-stepping, her general air of gallantry and abandon. On Saturdays we went down to the stable and as soon as we opened the door on its cosy, animal-smelling darkness Flora threw up her head, rolled her eyes, whinnied despairingly and pulled herself through a crisis of nerves on the spot. It was not safe to go into her stall; she would kick.

This winter also I began to hear a great deal more on the theme my mother had sounded when she had been talking in front of the barn. I no longer felt safe. It seemed that in the minds of the people around me there was a steady undercurrent of thought, not to be deflected, on this one subject. The word *girl* had formerly seemed to me innocent and unburdened, like the word *child;* now it appeared that it was no such thing. A girl was not, as I had supposed, simply what I was; it was what I had to become. It was a definition, always touched with emphasis, with reproach and disappointment. Also it was a joke on me. Once Laird and I were fighting, and for the first time ever I had to use all my strength against him; even so, he caught and pinned my arm for a moment, really hurting me. Henry saw this, and laughed, saying, "Oh, that there Laird's gonna show you, one of these days!" Laird was getting a lot bigger. But I was getting bigger too.

My grandmother came to stay with us for a few weeks and I heard other things. "Girls don't slam doors like that." "Girls keep their knees together when they sit down." And worse still, when I asked some questions, "That's none of girls' business." I continued to slam the doors and sit as awkwardly as possible, thinking that by such measures I kept myself free.

When spring came, the horses were let out in the barnyard. Mack stood against the barn wall trying to scratch his neck and haunches, but Flora trotted up and down and reared at the fences, clattering her hooves against the rails. Snow drifts dwindled quickly, revealing the hard grey and brown earth, the familiar rise and fall of the ground, plain and bare after the fantastic landscape of winter. There was a great feeling of opening-out, of release. We just wore rubbers now, over our shoes; our feet felt ridiculously light. One Saturday we went out to the stable and found all the doors open, letting in the unaccustomed sunlight and fresh air. Henry was there, just idling around looking at his collection of calendars which were tacked up behind the stalls in a part of the stable my mother had probably never seen.

"Come to say goodbye to your old friend Mack?" Henry said. "Here, you give him a taste of oats." He poured some oats into Laird's cupped hands and Laird went to feed Mack. Mack's teeth were in bad shape. He ate very slowly, patiently shifting the oats around in his mouth, trying to find a stump of a molar to grind it on. "Poor old Mack," said Henry mournfully. "When a horse's teeth's gone, he's gone. That's about the way."

"Are you going to shoot him today?" I said. Mack and Flora had been in the stable so long I had almost forgotten they were going to be shot.

Henry didn't answer me. Instead he started to sing in a high, trembly, mocking-sorrowful voice, *Oh, there's no more work, for poor Uncle Ned, he's gone where the good darkies go.* Mack's thick, blackish tongue worked diligently at Laird's hand. I went out before the song was ended and sat down on the gangway.

I had never seen them shoot a horse, but I knew where it was done.

Last summer Laird and I had come upon a horse's entrails before they were buried. We had thought it was a big black snake, coiled up in the sun. That was around in the field that ran up beside the barn. I thought that if we went inside the barn, and found a wide crack or a knothole to look through, we would be able to see them do it. It was not something I wanted to see; just the same, if a thing really happened, it was better to see it, and know.

My father came down from the house, carrying the gun.

"What are you doing here?" he said.

"Nothing."

"Go on up and play around the house."

He sent Laird out of the stable. I said to Laird, "Do you want to see them shoot Mack?" and without waiting for an answer led him around to the front door of the barn, opened it carefully, and went in. "Be quiet or they'll hear us," I said. We could hear Henry and my father talking in the stable, then the heavy, shuffling steps of Mack being backed out of his stall.

In the loft it was cold and dark. Thin, crisscrossed beams of sunlight fell through the cracks. The hay was low. It was a rolling country, hills and hollows, slipping under our feet. About four feet up was a beam going around the walls. We piled hay up in one corner and I boosted Laird up and hoisted myself. The beam was not very wide; we crept along it with our hands flat on the barn walls. There were plenty of knotholes, and I found one that gave me the view I wanted—a corner of the barnyard, the gate, part of the field. Laird did not have a knothole and began to complain.

I showed him a widened crack between two boards. "Be quiet and wait. If they hear you you'll get us in trouble."

My father came in sight carrying the gun. Henry was leading Mack by the halter. He dropped it and took out his cigarette papers and tobacco; he rolled cigarettes for my father and himself. While this was going on Mack nosed around in the old, dead grass along the fence. Then my father opened the gate and they took Mack through. Henry led Mack away from the path to a patch of ground and they talked together, not loud enough for us to hear. Mack again began searching for a mouthful of fresh grass, which was not to be found. My father walked away in a straight line, and stopped short at a distance which seemed to suit him. Henry was walking away from Mack too, but sideways, still negligently holding on to the halter. My father raised the gun and Mack looked up as if he had noticed something and my father shot him.

Mack did not collapse at once but swayed, lurched sideways and fell, first on his side; then he rolled over on his back and, amazingly, kicked his legs for a few seconds in the air. At this Henry laughed, as if Mack had done a trick for him. Laird, who had drawn a long, groaning breath of surprise when the shot was fired, said out loud, "He's not dead." And it seemed to me it might be true. But his legs stopped, he rolled on his side again, his muscles quivered and sank. The two men walked over and looked at him in a businesslike way; they bent down and examined his forehead where the bullet had gone in, and now I saw his blood on the brown grass.

"Now they just skin him and cut him up," I said. "Let's go." My legs were a little shaky and I jumped gratefully down into the hay. "Now you've seen how they shoot a horse," I said in a congratulatory way, as if I had seen it many times before. "Let's see if any barn cat's had kittens in the hay." Laird jumped. He seemed young and obedient again. Suddenly I remembered how, when he was little, I had brought him into the barn and told him to climb the ladder to the top beam. That was in the spring, too, when the hay was low. I had done it out of a need for excitement, a desire for something to happen so that I could tell about it. He was wearing a little bulky brown and white checked coat, made down from one of mine. He went all the way up, just as I told him, and sat down on the top beam with the hay far below him on one side, and the barn floor and some old machinery on the other. Then I ran screaming to my father, "Laird's up on the top beam!" My father came, my mother came, my father went up the ladder talking very quietly and brought Laird down under his arm, at which my mother leaned against the ladder and began to cry. They said to me, "Why weren't you watching him?" but nobody ever knew the truth. Laird did not know enough to tell. But whenever I saw the brown and white checked coat hanging in the closet, or at the bottom of the rag bag, which was where it ended up, I felt a weight in my stomach, the sadness of unexorcized guilt.

I looked at Laird who did not even remember this, and I did not like the look on his thin, winter-pale face. His expression was not frightened or upset, but remote, concentrating. "Listen," I said, in an unusually bright and friendly voice, "you aren't going to tell, are you?"

"No," he said absently.

"Promise."

"Promise," he said. I grabbed the hand behind his back to make sure he was not crossing his fingers. Even so, he might have a nightmare; it might come out that way. I decided I had better work hard to get all thoughts of what he had seen out of his mind—which, it seemed to me, could not hold very many things at a time. I got some money I had saved and that afternoon we went into Jubilee and saw a show, with Judy Canova, at which we both laughed a great deal. After that I thought it would be all right.

Two weeks later I knew they were going to shoot Flora. I knew from the night before, when I heard my mother ask if the hay was holding out all right, and my father said, "Well, after to-morrow there'll just be the cow, and we should be able to put her out to grass in another week." So I knew it was Flora's turn in the morning.

This time I didn't think of watching it. That was something to see just one time. I had not thought about it very often since, but sometimes when I was busy, working at school, or standing in front of the mirror combing my hair and wondering if I would be pretty when I grew up, the whole scene would flash into my mind: I would see the easy, practised way my father raised the gun, and hear Henry laughing when Mack kicked his legs in the air. I did not have any great feeling of horror and opposition, such as a city child might have had; I was too used to seeing the death of animals as a necessity by which we lived. Yet I felt a little ashamed, and there was a new wariness, a sense of holding-off, in my attitude to my father and his work.

It was a fine day, and we were going around the yard picking up tree branches that had been torn off in winter storms. This was something we had been told to do, and also we wanted to use them to make a teepee. We heard Flora whinny, and then my father's voice and Henry's shouting, and we ran down to the barnyard to see what was going on.

The stable door was open. Henry had just brought Flora out, and she had broken away from him. She was running free in the barnyard, from one end to the other. We climbed up on the fence. It was exciting to see her running, whinnying, going up on her hind legs, prancing and threatening like a horse in a Western movie, an unbroken ranch horse, though she was just an old driver, an old sorrel mare. My father and Henry ran after her and tried to grab the dangling halter. They tried to work her into a corner, and they had almost succeeded when she made a run between them, wild-eyed, and disappeared around the corner of the barn. We heard the rails clatter down as she got over the fence, and Henry yelled, "She's into the field now!"

That meant she was in the long L-shaped field that ran up by the house. If she got around the center, heading towards the lane, the gate was open; the truck had been driven into the field this morning. My father shouted to me, because I was on the other side of the fence, nearest the lane, "Go shut the gate!"

I could run very fast. I ran across the garden, past the tree where our swing was hung, and jumped across a ditch into the lane. There was the open gate. She had not got out, I could not see her up on the road; she must have run to the other end of the field. The gate was heavy. I lifted it out of the gravel and carried it across the roadway. I had it half-way across when she came in sight, galloping straight towards me. There was just time to get the chain on. Laird came scrambling through the ditch to help me.

Instead of shutting the gate, I opened it as wide as I could. I did not make any decision to do this, it was just what I did. Flora never slowed down; she galloped straight past me, and Laird jumped up and down yelling, "Shut it, shut it!" even after it was too late. My father and Henry appeared in the field a moment too late to see what I had done. They only saw Flora heading for the township road. They would think I had not got there in time.

They did not waste any time asking about it. They went back to the barn and got the gun and the knives they used, and put these in the truck; then they turned the truck around and came bouncing up the field toward us. Laird called to them, "Let me go too, let me go too!" and Henry stopped the truck and they took him in. I shut the gate after they were all gone.

I supposed Laird would tell. I wondered what would happen to me. I had never disobeyed my father before, and I could not understand why I had done it. Flora would not really get away. They would catch up with her in the truck. Or if they did not catch her this morning somebody would see her and telephone us this afternoon or tomorrow. There was no wild country here for her to run to, only farms. What was more, my father had paid for her, we needed the meat to feed the foxes, we needed the foxes to make our living. All I had done was make more work for my father who worked hard enough already. And when my father found out about it he was not going to trust me any more; he would know that I was not entirely on his side. I was on Flora's side, and that made me no use to anybody, not even to her. Just the same, I did not regret it; when she came running at me and I held the gate open, that was the only thing I could do.

I went back to the house, and my mother said, "What's all the commotion?" I told her that Flora had kicked down the fence and got away. "Your poor father," she said, "now he'll have to go chasing over the countryside. Well, there isn't any use planning dinner before one." She put up the ironing board. I wanted to tell her, but thought better of it and went upstairs and sat on my bed.

Lately I had been trying to make my part of the room fancy, spreading the bed with old lace curtains, and fixing myself a dressing-table with some leftovers of cretonne for a skirt. I planned to put up some kind of barricade between my bed and Laird's, to keep my section separate from his. In the sunlight, the lace curtains were just dusty rags. We did not sing at night any more. One night when I was singing Laird said, "You sound silly," and I went right on but the next night I did not start. There was not so much need to anyway, we were no longer afraid. We knew it was just old furniture over there, old jumble and confusion. We did not keep to the rules. I still stayed awake after Laird was asleep and told myself stories, but even in these stories something different was happening, mysterious alterations took place. A story might start off in the old way, with a spectacular danger, a fire or wild animals, and for a while I might rescue people; then things would change around, and instead, somebody would be rescuing me. It might be a boy from our class at school, or even Mr. Campbell, our teacher, who tickled girls under the arms. And at this point the story concerned itself at great length with what I looked like—how long my hair was, and what kind of dress I had on; by the time I had these details worked out the real excitement of the story was lost.

It was later than one o'clock when the truck came back. The tarpaulin was over the back, which meant there was meat in it. My mother had to heat dinner up all over again. Henry and my father had changed from their bloody overalls into ordinary working overalls in the barn, and they washed their arms and necks and faces at the sink, and splashed water on their hair and combed it. Laird lifted his arm to show off a streak of blood. "We shot old Flora," he said, "and cut her up in fifty pieces."

"Well I don't want to hear about it," my mother said. "And don't come to my table like that."

My father made him go and wash the blood off.

We sat down and my father said grace and Henry pasted his chewing-gum on the end of his fork, the way he always did; when he took it off he would have us admire the pattern. We began to pass the bowls of steaming, overcooked vegetables. Laird looked across the table at me and said proudly, distinctly, "Anyway it was her fault Flora got away."

"What?" my father said.

"She could of shut the gate and she didn't. She just open' it up and Flora run out."

"Is that right?" my father said.

Everybody at the table was looking at me. I nodded, swallowing food with great difficulty. To my shame, tears flooded my eyes.

My father made a curt sound of disgust. "What did you do that for?"

I did not answer. I put down my fork and waited to be sent from the table, still not looking up.

But this did not happen. For some time nobody said anything, then Laird said matter-of-factly, "She's crying."

"Never mind," my father said. He spoke with resignation, even good humour, the words which absolved and dismissed me for good. "She's only a girl," he said.

I didn't protest that, even in my heart. Maybe it was true.

[1964]

· MORDECAI RICHLER ·

1931–

Mordecai Richler was born 27 January 1931 and grew up in the St. Urbain Street area of Montreal that he later immortalized in his fiction. He attended Sir George Williams College for two years, and in 1951 left for Europe where he was to spend most of the next twenty years of his life. He published his first novel when he was twenty-three, and by the age of forty had produced nine books, hundreds of articles and reviews for such magazines as the *Spectator*, the *Nation, Encounter,* the *New Statesman, Punch, Life, Maclean's,* and *Saturday Night,* and numerous scripts for radio, TV, and the movies. Having returned to Montreal in 1972, Richler continues his prolific writing, which has earned him many honours, including the Governor General's Award, the Writers' Guild of America Annual Award, and the Ruth Schwartz Children's Book Award.

Richler is a moralist and a satirist, writing out of a deep-seated frustration with the absurd cruelty of the modern world. In his best work he is also a brilliant creator of character, requiring only the briefest of dialogues to convey subtle nuances of class and cultural background. His sustained portraits, of Duddy Kravitz, for example, or Jake Hersh in *St. Urbain's Horseman* (1971), are complex and incisive. He has the ability to evoke sympathy for the vilest of losers, and at the same time he has nothing but scorn for the modish and the trendy, excoriating the insensitive social climber, of whatever nationality, race, or religion.

His first three novels, while typical of Richler's fiction in their preoccupation with the search for personal values in a world which has rejected communal beliefs, are not representative of the style which readily identifies his mature work. With *The Apprenticeship of Duddy Kravitz* (1959), he found his true style—fast-paced, irreverent, humorous, slangy, marked by abrupt transitions and wildly funny set pieces. In *The Incomparable Atuk* (1963) and *Cocksure* (1968), he moved into the realm of black humour and topical satire, sacrificing complexity of character to comic stereotyping. *St. Urbain's Horseman* triumphantly blends satire and psychological realism in an intricately structured plot that ranges widely in space and time. His most recent novel, *Joshua Then and Now* (1980), offers a similar protagonist in parallel situations, but goes even further than *Horseman* in its narrative complexity. Whatever direction he takes in future works, Richler will continue to be admired (and in some quarters reviled) for his accurate depiction of Jewish Montreal and his devastating satiric wit.

Though best known for his novels, Richler has written some first-class short stories, most of which have been collected in *The Street* (1969). These stories, however autobiographical they may be (and Richler himself is not saying), are obviously rooted in the St. Urbain Street world of the 1940s, but their humour and compassion are universal. "The Summer My Grandmother Was Supposed to Die" is typical of Richler's short fiction in its subtle mingling of elements of comedy and tragedy, of pathos and vulgarity, and his mature style is evident in the brisk narrative pace and deft use of colloquial speech. The hapless father is perhaps the most sympathetic character in the story; completely at sea in every social situation, he is still morally head and shoulders above his glib, hypocritical in-laws.

·———·

Richler's works include *The Acrobats* (1954); *Son of a Smaller Hero* (1955); *A Choice of Enemies* (1957); *The Apprenticeship of Duddy Kravitz* (1959); *The Incomparable Atuk* (1963); *Cocksure* (1968); *Hunting Tigers Under Glass* (1968); *The Street* (1969); *St. Urbain's Horseman* (1971); *Shovelling Trouble* (1972); *Notes on an Endangered Species and Others* (1974); *The Apprenticeship of Duddy Kravitz* (1974, screenplay); *Jacob Two-Two Meets the Hooded Fang* (1975); *The Great Comic Book Heroes and Other Essays* (1978); *Joshua Then and Now* (1980); *Home Sweet Home: My Canadian Album* (1984); *Joshua Then and Now* (1985, screenplay); and *Jacob Two-Two and the Dinosaur* (1987).

Works on Richler include George Woodcock, *Mordecai Richler* (1970); G. David Sheps, ed., *Mordecai Richler* (1971); Michael Darling, "Mordecai Richler: An Annotated Bibliography," *The Annotated Bibliography of Canada's Major Authors,* ed. Robert Lecker and Jack David (1979), 1:155–220; Arnold E. Davidson, *Mordecai Richler* (1983); Victor J. Ramraj, *Mordecai Richler* (1983); Kerry McSweeney, "Mordecai Richler," *Canadian Writers and Their Works,* ed. Robert Lecker, Jack David, and Ellen Quigley (1985), Fiction Series 6: 129–79; and Michael Darling, ed., *Perspectives on Mordecai Richler* (1986).

MICHAEL DARLING

THE SUMMER MY GRANDMOTHER WAS SUPPOSED TO DIE

Dr. Katzman discovered the gangrene on one of his monthly visits. "She won't last a month," he said.

He said the same the second month, the third and the fourth, and now she lay dying in the heat of the back bedroom.

"God in heaven," my mother said, "what's she holding on for?"

The summer my grandmother was supposed to die we did not chip in with the Greenbaums to take a cottage in the Laurentians. My grandmother, already bed-ridden for seven years, could not be moved again. The doctor came twice a week. The only thing was to stay in the city and wait for her to die or, as my mother said, pass away. It was a hot summer, her bedroom was just behind the kitchen, and when we sat down to eat we could smell her. The dressings on my grandmother's left leg had to be changed several times a day and, according to Dr. Katzman, any day might be her last in this world. "It's in the hands of the Almighty," he said.

"It won't be long now," my father said, "and she'll be better off, if you know what I mean?"

A nurse came every day from the Royal Victorian Order. She arrived punctually at noon and at five to twelve I'd join the rest of the boys under the outside staircase to peek up her dress as she climbed to our second-storey flat. Miss Bailey favoured absolutely beguiling pink panties, edged with lace, and that was better than waiting under the stairs for Cousin Bessie, for instance, who wore enormous cotton bloomers, rain or shine.

I was sent out to play as often as possible, because my mother felt it was not good for me to see somebody dying. Usually, I would just roam the scorched streets. There was Duddy, Gas sometimes, Hershey, Stan, Arty and me.

"Before your grandmaw kicks off," Duddy said, "she's going to roll her eyes and gurgle. That's what they call the death-rattle."

"Aw, you know everything. *Putz.*"

"I read it, you jerk," Duddy said, whacking me one, "in Perry Mason."

Home again I would usually find my mother sour and spent. Sometimes she wept.

"She's dying by inches," she said to my father one stifling night, "and none of them ever come to see her. Oh, such children," she added, going on to curse them vehemently in Yiddish.

"They're not behaving right. It's certainly not according to Hoyle," my father said.

Dr. Katzman continued to be astonished. "It must be will-power alone that keeps her going," he said. "That, and your excellent care."

"It's not my mother any more in the back room, Doctor. It's an animal. I want her to die."

"Hush. You don't mean it. You're tired." Dr. Katzman dug into his black bag and produced pills for her to take. "Your wife's a remarkable woman," he told my father.

"You don't so say," my father replied, embarrassed.

"A born nurse."

My sister and I used to lie awake talking about our grandmother. "After she dies," I said, "her hair will go on growing for another twenty-four hours."

"Says who?"

"Duddy Kravitz. Do you think Uncle Lou will come from New York for the funeral?"

"I suppose so."

"Boy, that means another fiver for me. Even more for you."

"You shouldn't say things like that or her ghost will come back to haunt you."

"Well, I'll be able to go to her funeral anyway. I'm not too young any more."

I was only six years old when my grandfather died, and so I wasn't allowed to go to his funeral.

I have one imperishable memory of my grandfather. Once he called me into his study, set me down on his lap, and made a drawing of a horse for me. On the horse he drew a rider. While I watched and giggled he gave the rider a beard and the fur-trimmed round hat of a rabbi, a *straimel*, just like he wore.

My grandfather had been a Zaddik, one of the Righteous, and I've been assured that to study Talmud with him had been an illuminating experience. I wasn't allowed to go to his funeral, but years later I was shown the telegrams of condolence that had come from Eire and Poland and even Japan. My grandfather had written many books: a translation of the Book of Splendour (the Zohar) into modern Hebrew, some twenty years' work, and lots of slender volumes of sermons, hasidic tales, and rabbinical commentaries. His books had been published in Warsaw and later in New York.

"At the funeral," my mother said, "they had to have six motorcycle policemen to control the crowds. It was such a heat that twelve women fainted—and I'm *not* counting Mrs. Waxman from upstairs. With her, you know, *anything* to fall into a man's arms. Even Pinsky's. And did I tell you that there was even a French Canadian priest there?"

"Aw, you're kidding me."

"The priest was some *knacker*. A bishop maybe. He used to study with the *zeyda*. The *zeyda* was a real personality, you know. Spiritual and worldly-wise at the same time. Such personalities they don't make any more. Today rabbis and peanuts come in the same size."

But, according to my father, the *zeyda* (his father-in-law) hadn't been as celebrated as all that. "There are things I could say," he told me. "There was another side to him."

My grandfather had sprung from generations and generations of rabbis, his youngest son was a rabbi, but none of his grandchildren would be one. My Cousin Jerry was already a militant socialist. I once heard him say, "When the men at the kosher bakeries went out on strike the *zeyda* spoke up against them on the streets and in the *shuls*. It was of no consequence to him that the men were grossly underpaid. His superstitious followers had to have bread. Grandpappy," Jerry said, "was a prize reactionary."

A week after my grandfather died my grandmother suffered a stroke. Her right side was completely paralysed. She couldn't speak. At first, it's true, she could manage a coherent word or two and move her right hand enough to write her name in Hebrew. Her name was Malka. But her condition soon began to deteriorate.

My grandmother had six children and seven step-children, for my grandfather had been married before. His first wife had died in the old country. Two years later he had married my grandmother, the only daughter of the most affluent man in the *shtetl*, and their marriage had been a singularly happy one. My grandmother had been a beautiful girl. She had also been a shrewd, resourceful, and patient wife. Qualities, I fear, indispensable to life with a Zaddik. For the synagogue paid my grandfather no stipulated salary and much of the money he picked up here and there he had habitually distributed among rabbinical students, needy immigrants and widows. A vice, for such it was to his impecunious family, which made him as unreliable a provider as a drinker. To carry the analogy further, my grandmother had to make hurried, surreptitious trips to the pawnbroker with her jewellery. Not all of it to be redeemed, either. But her children had been looked after. The youngest, her favourite, was a rabbi in Boston, the oldest was the actor-manager of a Yiddish theatre in New York, and another was a lawyer. One daughter lived in Montreal, two in Toronto. My mother was the youngest daughter and when my grandmother had her stroke there was a family conclave and it was decided that my mother would take care of her. This was my father's fault. All the other husbands spoke up—they protested hotly that their wives had too much work—they could never manage it—but my father detested quarrels and so he was silent. And my grandmother came to stay with us.

Her bedroom, the back bedroom, had actually been promised to me for my seventh birthday, but now I had to go on sharing a room with my sister. So naturally I was resentful when each morning before I left for school my mother insisted that I go in and kiss my grandmother goodbye.

"Bouyo-bouyo," was the only sound my grandmother could make.

During those first hopeful months—"Twenty years ago who would have thought there'd be a cure for diabetes?" my father asked. "Where there's life, you know"—my grandmother would smile and try to speak, her eyes charged with effort; and I wondered if she knew that I was waiting for her room.

Even later there were times when she pressed my hand urgently to her bosom with her surprisingly strong left arm. But as her illness dragged on and on she became a condition in the house, something beyond hope or reproach, like the leaky ice-box, there was less recognition and more ritual in those kisses. I came to dread her room. A clutter of sticky medicine bottles and the cracked toilet chair beside the bed; glazed but imploring eyes and a feeble smile, the wet smack of her crooked lips against my cheeks. I flinched from her touch. And after two years, I protested to my mother, "What's the use of telling her I'm going here or I'm going there? She doesn't even recognize me any more."

"Don't be fresh. She's your grandmother."

My uncle who was in the theatre in New York sent money regularly to help support my grandmother and, for the first few months, so did the other children. But once the initial and sustaining excitement had passed the children seldom came to our house any more. Anxious weekly visits—"And how is she today, poor lamb?"—quickly dwindled to a dutiful monthly looking in, then a semi-annual visit, and these always on the way to somewhere.

When the children did come my mother was severe with them. "I have to lift her on that chair three times a day maybe. And what makes you think I always catch her in time? Sometimes I have to change her linen twice a day. That's a job I'd like to see your wife do," she said to my uncle, the rabbi.

"We could send her to the Old People's Home."

"Now there's an idea," my father said.

"Not so long as I'm alive." My mother shot my father a scalding look, "Say something, Sam."

"Quarrelling will get us nowhere. It only creates bad feelings."

Meanwhile, Dr. Katzman came once a month. "It's astonishing," he would say each time. "She's as strong as a horse."

"Some life for a person," my father said. "She can't speak—she doesn't recognize anybody—what is there for her?"

The doctor was a cultivated man; he spoke often for women's clubs, sometimes on Yiddish literature and other times, his rubicund face hot with menace, the voice taking on a doomsday tone, on the cancer threat. "Who are we to judge?" he asked.

Every evening, during the first few months of my grandmother's illness, my mother would read her a story by Sholem Aleichem. "Tonight she smiled," my mother would report defiantly. "She understood. I can tell."

Bright afternoons my mother would lift the old lady into a wheelchair and put her out in the sun and once a week she gave her a manicure. Somebody always had to stay in the house in case my grandmother called. Often, during the night, she would begin to wail unaccountably and my mother would get up and rock her mother in her arms for hours. But in the fourth year of my grandmother's illness the strain began to tell. Besides looking after my grandmother, my mother had to keep house for a husband and two children. She became scornful of my father and began to find fault with my sister and me. My father started to spend his evenings playing pinochle at Tansky's Cigar & Soda. Weekends he took me to visit his brothers and sisters. Wherever my father went people had little snippets of advice for him.

"Sam, you might as well be a bachelor. One of the other children should take the old lady for a while. You're just going to have to put your foot down for once."

"Yeah, in your face maybe."

My Cousin Libby, who was at McGill, said, "This could have a very damaging effect on the development of your children. These are their formative years, Uncle Samuel, and the omnipresence of death in the house . . ."

"What you need is a boy friend," my father said. "*And how.*"

After supper my mother took to falling asleep in her chair, even in the middle of Lux Radio Theatre. One minute she would be sewing a patch in my breeches or making a list of girls to call for a bingo party, proceeds for the Talmud Torah, and the next she would be snoring. Then, inevitably, there came the morning she just couldn't get out of bed and Dr. Katzman had to come round a week before his regular visit. "Well, well, this won't do, will it?"

Dr. Katzman led my father into the kitchen. "Your wife's got a gallstone condition," he said.

My grandmother's children met again, this time without my mother, and decided to put the old lady in the Jewish Old People's Home on Esplanade Street. While my mother slept an ambulance came to take my grandmother away.

"It's for the best," Dr. Katzman said, but my father was in the back room when my grandmother held on tenaciously to the bedpost, not wanting to be moved by the two men in white.

"Easy does it, granny," the younger man said.

Afterwards my father did not go in to see my mother. He went out for a walk.

When my mother got out of bed two weeks later her cheeks had regained their normal pinkish hue; for the first time in months, she actually joked with me. She became increasingly curious about how I was doing in school and whether or not I shined my shoes regularly. She began to cook special dishes for my father again and resumed old friendships with the girls on the parochial school board. Not only did my father's temper improve, but he stopped going to Tansky's every night and began to come home early from work. But my grandmother's name was seldom mentioned. Until one evening, after I'd had a fight with my sister, I said, "Why can't I move into the back bedroom now?"

My father glared at me. "Big-mouth."

"It's empty, isn't it?"

The next afternoon my mother put on her best dress and coat and new spring hat.

"Don't go looking for trouble," my father said.

"It's been a month. Maybe they're not treating her right."

"They're experts."

"Did you think I was never going to visit her? I'm not inhuman, you know."

"Alright, go." But after she had gone my father stood by the window and said, "I was born lucky, and that's it."

I sat on the outside stoop watching the cars go by. My father waited on the balcony above, cracking peanuts. It was six o'clock, maybe later, when the ambulance slowed down and rocked to a stop right in front of our house. "I knew it," my father said. "I was born with all the luck."

My mother got out first, her eyes red and swollen, and hurried upstairs to make my grandmother's bed.

"You'll get sick again," my father said.

"I'm sorry, Sam, but what could I do? From the moment she saw me she cried and cried. It was terrible."

"They're recognized experts there. They know how to take care of her better than you do."

"Experts? Expert murderers you mean. She's got bedsores, Sam. Those dirty little Irish nurses they don't change her linen often enough they hate her. She must have lost twenty pounds in there."

"Another month and you'll be flat on your back again. I'll write you a guarantee, if you want."

My father became a regular at Tansky's again and, once more, I had to go in and kiss my grandmother in the morning. Amazingly, she had begun to look like a man. Little hairs had sprouted on her chin, she had grown a spiky grey moustache, and she was practically bald.

Yet again my uncles and aunts sent five-dollar bills, though erratically, to help pay for my grandmother's support. Elderly people, former followers of my grandfather, came to inquire about the old lady's health. They sat in the back bedroom with her, leaning on their canes, talking to themselves and rocking to and fro. "The Holy Shakers," my father called them. I avoided the seamed, shrunken old men because they always wanted to pinch my cheeks or trick me with a dash of snuff and laugh when I sneezed. When the visit with my grandmother was over the old people would unfailingly sit in the kitchen with my mother for another hour, watching her make *lokshen*, slurping lemon tea out of a saucer. They would recall the sayings and books and charitable deeds of the late Zaddik.

"At the funeral," my mother never wearied of telling them, "they had to have six motorcycle policemen to control the crowds."

In the next two years there was no significant change in my grandmother's condition, though fatigue, ill-temper, and even morbidity enveloped my mother again. She fought with her brothers and sisters and once, after a particularly bitter quarrel, I found her sitting with her head in her hands. "If, God forbid, I had a stroke," she said, "would you send me to the Old People's Home?"

"Of course not."

"I hope that never in my life do I have to count on my children for anything."

The seventh summer of my grandmother's illness she was supposed to die and we did not know from day to day when it would happen. I was often sent out to eat at an aunt's or at my other grandmother's house. I was hardly ever at home. In those days they let boys into the left-field bleachers of Delormier Downs free during the week and Duddy, Gas sometimes, Hershey, Stan, Arty and me spent many an afternoon at the ball park. The Montreal Royals, kingpin of the Dodger farm system, had a marvellous club at the time. There was Jackie Robinson, Roy Campanella, Lou Ortiz, Red Durrett, Honest John Gabbard, and Kermit

Kitman. Kitman was our hero. It used to give us a charge to watch that crafty little Jew, one of ours, running around out there with all those tall dumb southern crackers. "Hey, Kitman," we would yell, "Hey, shmo-head, if your father knew you played ball on *shabus*—" Kitman, alas, was all field and no hit. He never made the majors. "There goes Kermit Kitman," we would holler, after he had gone down swinging again, "the first Jewish strike-out king of the International League." This we promptly followed up by bellowing choice imprecations in Yiddish.

It was after one of these games, on a Friday afternoon, that I came home to find a crowd gathered in front of our house.

"That's the grandson," somebody said.

A knot of old people stood staring at our front door from across the street. A taxi pulled up and my aunt hurried out, hiding her face in her hands.

"After so many years," a woman said.

"And probably next year they'll discover a cure. Isn't that always the case?"

The flat was clotted. Uncles and aunts from my father's side of the family, strangers, Dr. Katzman, neighbours, were all milling around and talking in hushed voices. My father was in the kitchen, getting out the apricot brandy. "Your grandmother's dead," he said.

"Where's Maw?"

"In the bedroom with . . . You'd better not go in."

"I want to see her."

My mother wore a black shawl and glared down at a knot of hand-kerchief clutched in a fist that had been cracked by washing soda. "Don't come in here," she said.

Several bearded round-shouldered men in shiny black coats sur-rounded the bed. I couldn't see my grandmother.

"Your grandmother's dead."

"Daddy told me."

"Go wash your face and comb your hair."

"Yes."

"You'll have to get your own supper."

"Sure."

"One minute. The *baba* left some jewellery. The necklace is for Rifka and the ring is for your wife."

"Who's getting married?"

"Better go and wash your face. Remember behind the ears, please."

Telegrams were sent, the obligatory long distance calls were made, and all through the evening relatives and neighbours and old followers of the Zaddik poured into the house. Finally, the man from the funeral parlour arrived.

"There goes the only Jewish businessman in town," Segal said, "who wishes all his customers were German."

"This is no time for jokes."

"Listen, life goes on."

My Cousin Jerry had begun to affect a cigarette holder. "Soon the religious mumbo-jumbo starts," he said to me.

"Wha'?"

"Everybody is going to be sickeningly sentimental."

The next day was the sabbath and so, according to law, my grandmother couldn't be buried until Sunday. She would have to lie on the floor all night. Two grizzly women in white came to move and wash the body and a professional mourner arrived to sit up and pray for her. "I don't trust his face," my mother said. "He'll fall asleep."

"He won't fall asleep."

"You watch him, Sam."

"A fat lot of good prayers will do her now. Alright! Okay! I'll watch him."

My father was in a fury with Segal.

"The way he goes after the apricot brandy you'd think he never saw a bottle in his life before."

Rifka and I were sent to bed, but we couldn't sleep. My aunt was sobbing over the body in the living room; there was the old man praying, coughing and spitting into his handkerchief whenever he woke; and the hushed voices and whimpering from the kitchen, where my father and mother sat. Rifka allowed me a few drags off her cigarette.

"Well, *pisherke*, this is our last night together. Tomorow you can take over the back room."

"Are you crazy?"

"You always wanted it for yourself, didn't you?"

"She died in there, but."

"So?"

"I couldn't sleep in there now."

"Good night and happy dreams."

"Hey, let's talk some more."

"Did you know," Rifka said, "that when they hang a man the last thing that happens is that he has an orgasm?"

"A wha'?"

"Skip it. I forgot you were still in kindergarten."

"Kiss my Royal Canadian—"

"At the funeral, they're going to open the coffin and throw dirt in her face. It's supposed to be earth from Eretz. They open it and you're going to have to look."

"Says you."

A little while after the lights had been turned out Rifka approached my bed, her head covered with a sheet and her arms raised high. "Bouyo-bouyo. Who's that sleeping in my bed? Woo-woo."

My uncle who was in the theatre and my aunt from Toronto came to the funeral. My uncle, the rabbi, was there too.

"As long as she was alive," my mother said, "he couldn't even send her five dollars a month. I don't want him in the house, Sam. I can't bear the sight of him."

"You're upset," Dr. Katzman said, "and you don't know what you're saying."

"Maybe you'd better give her a sedative," the rabbi said.

"Sam, will you speak up for once, please."

Flushed, eyes heated, my father stepped up to the rabbi. "I'll tell you this straight to your face, Israel," he said. "You've gone down in my estimation."

The rabbi smiled a little.

"Year by year," my father continued, his face burning a brighter red, "your stock has gone down with me."

My mother began to weep and she was led unwillingly to a bed. While my father tried his utmost to comfort her, as he muttered consoling things, Dr. Katzman plunged a needle into her arm. "There we are," he said.

I went to sit on the stoop outside with Duddy. My uncle, the rabbi, and Dr. Katzman stepped into the sun to light cigarettes.

"I know exactly how you feel," Dr. Katzman said. "There's been a death in the family and the world seems indifferent to your loss. Your heart is broken and yet it's a splendid summer day . . . a day made for love and laughter . . . and that must seem very cruel to you."

The rabbi nodded; he sighed.

"Actually," Dr. Katzman said, "it's remarkable that she held out for so long."

"Remarkable?" the rabbi said. "It's written that if a man has been married twice he will spend as much time with his first wife in heaven as he did on earth. My father, may he rest in peace, was married to his first wife for seven years and my mother, may she rest in peace, has managed to keep alive for seven years. Today in heaven she will be able to join my father, may he rest in peace."

Dr. Katzman shook his head. "It's amazing," he said. He told my uncle that he was writing a book based on his experiences as a healer. "The mysteries of the human heart."

"Yes."

"Astonishing."

My father hurried outside. "Dr. Katzman, please. It's my wife. Maybe the injection wasn't strong enough. She just doesn't stop crying. It's like a tap. Can you come in, please?"

"Excuse me," Dr. Katzman said to my uncle.

"Of course." My uncle turned to Duddy and me. "Well, boys," he said, "what would you like to be when you grow up?"

[1969]

· LEON ROOKE ·

1934–

Leon Rooke was born 11 September 1934 in Roanoke Rapids, North Carolina. His father left home when Rooke was two, and he was raised by his grandparents and his mother, who was a textile-mill worker. He began writing fiction at the age of seventeen, but his earliest success came as a dramatist while attending Mars Hill College (1953–55). After studying drama at the University of North Carolina (B.A. 1957), Rooke travelled throughout the United States and, when drafted into the army, served eighteen months in Alaska. In 1965 he was writer-in-residence at the University of North Carolina. His first book of stories, *Last One Home Sleeps in the Yellow Bed*, was published in 1968. The next year he married and moved with his wife, Constance, to Victoria, British Columbia, where they now live. Rooke's fourth novel, *Shakespeare's Dog* (1983), won the $20,000 Canada-Australia Literary Prize and the 1983 Governor General's Award for fiction.

Like other writers from the American South, Rooke has an acute sense of the richness of language and of the many nuances present in even the most commonplace expressions. Since moving to Canada he has assimilated new voices into his writing, as evidenced by the imitative skills that have characterized his drama (among Rooke's published and produced plays are *Krokodile* [1973] and *Sword/Play* [1974]). But Rooke's verbal inventiveness finds freest expression in his prose fiction. His earliest stories contain realistic settings and scenes, and evocative imagery created by dramatic detail. The novella "Brush Fire" introduces a theme that recurs throughout Rooke's work, that of the purifying renewal following descent or destruction. Generally, the early stories do not exhibit the strong authorial presence that is created in the later fic-

tion by ironic language-play. The two collections of Rooke's stories published in 1977, *The Broad Back of the Angel* and *The Love Parlour: Stories*, show him moving away from mimetic realism and towards an interiorized and more allusive fiction. The publication of *Cry Evil* (1980) marks an intensification of self-conscious narrative, irony, myth, and dark humour in Rooke's short fiction. This writing is firmly postmodernist, but the stories' moral texture keeps Rooke from becoming a game-playing cynic of his own craft. In the rhythmic prose of stories such as "Mama Tuddi Done Over" and "Sixteen-Year-Old Susan March Confesses to the Innocent Murder of All the Devious Strangers Who Would Drag Her Down," both from *Death Suite* (1981), Rooke achieves a narration that is both overwhelming and controlled: such fiction withholds a final resolution, but its flow obscures its deceptive complexity. Because of its Christian symbolism and its motif of transformation, "The Problem Shop," also from this collection, looks forward to the stories in *A Bolt of White Cloth* (1984). The theme of transformation in such stories is not only a moral proposition, it is also relevant to the reading experience itself—because most of Rooke's short fiction requires readers to re-create themselves, to abandon preconceptions about the short-story form, to start anew like experienced explorers in an alien terrain.

Rooke's novels and stories rely less on plot than on language to impel the reader, and they probe the ways in which language defines and creates reality. The protagonist of *Fat Woman* (1980), Ella Mae Hopkins, is bound as much by her language, which limits her perception of life to the realm of clichéd expressions and commonplace thoughts, as by her obesity. In *The Ma-*

384

gician in Love (1981), Rooke challenges the reader's perceptions by offering a narrative sleight-of-hand, in which the author himself becomes the magician who fixes our attention on the story, while secretly manipulating the narrative point of view. Rooke's most acclaimed novel, *Shakespeare's Dog* (1983), is narrated by the poet's dog, who speaks in the delightfully invective idiom of "Elizabethan canine." Rooke has said that literature can redeem the reader, and his fiction is that of an emphatic form-breaker who offers a new world with each story, and who invites the reader to join in his act of narrative creation.

Rooke's works include *Last One Home Sleeps in the Yellow Bed: Stories* (1968); *Krokodile* (1973); *Vault: A Story in Three Parts* (1973); *Sword/Play* (1974); *The Broad Back of the Angel* (1977); *The Love Parlour: Stories* (1977); *Cakewalk* (1980); *Fat Woman* (1980); *Cry Evil* (1980); *Death Suite* (1981); *The Magician in Love* (1981); *The Birth Control King of the Upper Volta* (1982); *Shakespeare's Dog* (1983); *Sing Me No Love Songs I'll Say You No Prayers: Selected Stories* (1984); and *A Bolt of White Cloth* (1984).

Works on Rooke include Stephen Scobie, "The Inner Voice," *Books in Canada* Nov. 1981: 8–10; a special issue of *Canadian Fiction Magazine* 38 (1981); and Russell Brown, "Rooke's Move," *Essays on Canadian Writing* 30 (1984–85): 287–303.

· ——————— ·

MICHAEL HELM

THE PROBLEM SHOP

"AR-SALAR-SALOAM, *of no fixed address and a blight on the soul of this town since you first came to birth, as witnesses against you have put in a No Show and as the Crown's Attorney has thrown up his hands in disgust and had not a shred of evidence in the first place, I have no choice but to declare you a free bird. I want it known, however, by you and by all present that if you ever again appear in my court I shall throw the book at you, guilty or otherwise. You are a reprehensible creature without, so far as I can tell, a single redeeming human trait. You are the bottom of the barrel and in my estimation would frankly be better off hung by the neck. Now get out of here!"*

Ar-Salar-Saloam, the case against him so miraculously concluded, left the judge's chambers where these harsh words had been uttered, and walked out into a muggy Victoria day, to head back to his old stomping grounds in the up-and-coming but still derelict area forming the heart of the old city, the part the bloody English hadn't yet ruined with their tea shoppes and cutesy knick-knack tourist joints.

His child-bride Auriole met him on the steps.

"You old dog!" she exclaimed, smiling, cuffing him hard on the shoulder—"I thought you'd be dead by now!"

To her surprise Ar-Salar-Saloam did not cuff her back. Nor did he speak. He trudged on miserably up the street, looking at his shoes—in what she would call *one of his moods.*

"The reason I didn't visit you," Auriole said brightly, catching up, "is I been busy, real busy, it's been real hard on me out here, not knowing which way to turn."

Ar-Salar-Saloam stumbled on. The way his head hung, the way he slouched, his long arms dangling and his shoes flopping stiffly against the sidewalk, he looked like a man with deep problems—a fact which even occurred to Auriole.

She hung back, biting her nails, wishing he'd git with it.

"Git with it, Dipstick!" she called.

But Ar-Salar-Saloam was already turning the corner.

She found him a few seconds later down on Douglas Street, leaning with his head against a store-front glass, his shoulders scrunched up around his ears and his hands shoved so straight and deep into his pockets that his pants were practically off his hips. She sidled up beside him, silent now, in a mood herself—and for a minute or two both stared at a window poster which had on it the picture of an airplane looking like some kind of bloated python snake, with its front part tied up in a fat knot. THANK GOD IT'S ONLY A MOTION PICTURE, the banner under it read.

Occasional Nudity, the B.C. Censor warned. *Too much swearing. Overall, a negative moral vision curiously copesetic. . . .*

"I seen not one movie," Auriole declared in a lively voice. "I seen not one movie the whole time you were in jail. That's how busy I been!"

Whether responding to this claim or to something revolting in his own nature, Ar-Salar-Saloam's reaction was most curious. With a groan loud enough to startle several passers-by, his body went rigid, he balled up his fists and screwed up his eyes and swayed high up on his toes; Auriole thought he was going to smash his head right through the plate-glass window. She bent her knees, getting set to take off: *"Do it!"* she urged in a fierce whisper. *"Do it! We be to hell and gone before anyone even know what happened!"*

But Ar-Salar-Saloam did nothing of the sort. He straightened up, sighing, shaking off whatever rigours had possessed him, fixing his sad eyes first on Auriole then on the grey street behind her.

They moved on.

To cheer him up Auriole began telling him of all the groovy people she'd met while he'd been locked up. "Great guys!" she said. "Real neat!" A lot of them, she said, would be down at The King's Tattoo this very minute—"probably happy to buy you a suds or two if you've got a real thirst on like I have."

But Ar-Salar-Saloam was off in dreamland or black hole, not even listening to her.

They arrived at Government Street where the Empress Hotel and the Parliament Building hove suddenly into view, like an old and noble but enfeebled couple come together for one last look at the world before going off to gas themselves for what it and they had come to.

They passed on, Auriole chattering, Ar-Salar-Saloam in gloom, looking at her and at the city with a mood of puzzled yet serenely elegiac scorn, moving in a stiff-legged gait, his shoulders bent—much as if he had spent the past six months sitting on his knees in a dark corner.

"Is it that old lady bugging you?" asked Auriole. "Is it you thinking it was your fault that old lady croaked?"

Ar-Salar-Saloam's head slid lower. "I never laid a hand on her," he grumbled, his eyes hooded.

Auriole was rapidly losing her own good edge. She wished he would shape up. She had her own troubles, heaps worse than his, and if this is what marriage was—walking around town to no purpose and with your tongue hanging out—she'd best call it quits right now. Without her hit earlier in the day to boost her along she'd have given him a good dressing-down the minute she saw him. She hadn't shed family and school—hadn't come to the ripe age of sixteen—to put up now with anyone messing round with her good times.

But she was afraid he'd hit her if she said any of this, so she decided to keep her trap shut.

At Johnson Street Ar-Salar-Saloam turned, and they went on down to the water: past the string of junk and pawn shops, past the flop-house rooms, past the littered alleys and dusty doorways where on more agreeable days winos would have been clutching at their sleeves—went on past even The King's Tattoo. Past Man Tung Yi's Foot Parlour, past the City Parkade and the Upper Room and Lum's Foam Factory. Went on past Sally Ann whose great blue three-storey building stood guard over this seedy part of Flower Town like a great blue angel not about to forget which side of the bread her butter came from. Went on down to the water.

"How's it feel to be back in civilization?" chirped Auriole.

Ar-Salar-Saloam gave no answer. Mouth open, his legs wide and bent, he was gawking at something way up in the sky.

The Johnson Street bridge was up, and under its black open tongues, just then passing through towards its anchorage in the Inner Harbour, slid a magnificent long white schooner—banners flying, slicing speedily through the black water, its three huge masts looming higher even than the grey city rim and cold mountain range beyond.

"It's *BEAUTIFUL!*" cried Ar-Salar-Saloam, suddenly beaming, dancing a little jig—"What I wouldn't give to have me one of them!"

"Be a good place to dope up," agreed Auriole, her manner solemn. With a short plump finger the colour of dry seaweed she was busy raking over a number of coins in her palm.

"Dollar forty," she announced—"Plenty enough for two drafts at the Tattoo. Let's go."

But Ar-Salar-Saloam stood with closed eyes, his head thrust back and rhythmically swaying, his expression momentarily blissful—as if from some place far removed from his present location music of divine and tranquil nature was somehow flowing through to him.

"My throat needs wetting," whined Auriole, tugging at an arm—"Are you coming or staying?"

Only after the bridge had cranked down and the line of waiting cars had bolted off to wherever it was their drivers were going—only after the beautiful ship had sailed on—did Auriole get him moving.

They had taken no more than a few dozen paces, however, when Ar-Salar-Saloam halted in his tracks. "What's that?" he demanded. "That up there. What is it?"

Auriole followed the line of his outstretched arm.

"That's the new disco," Auriole told him. She didn't tell him that she had been there the last seventeen nights and that it was the swinginist place inside of a thousand miles. What she told him was: "I hear it's real good."

"I don't care about no disco," replied Ar-Salar-Saloam sullenly. "What I mean is that sign in the window next to it."

"You mean the one with the red hand on a stick pointing around the corner?"

Ar-Salar-Saloam said yeah, that's the one he meant.

Stenciled along the length of the red hand were the words NO PROBLEMS TOO BIG. SEE US FOR SATISFACTION.

"That's Fisheye's new place," Auriole informed him. "He's gone into business. Doing real good, I hear."

"Fisheye!" muttered Ar-Salar-Saloam. "Imagine that!"

Further on up the street, painted on another dusty upper window, was another sign, this one reading IN A RUT? SEE THE PROBLEM SHOP—and in smaller letters, B. Fisheye, prop.

" 'Prop' means he owns it," Auriole explained.

"Oh God in heaven, you think I don't know that?"

"Your face was all screwed up, how could I tell? Stop picking on me."

Auriole pouted. She stared at Ar-Salar-Saloam, hating him, figuring she'd never in her whole life had such a hum-drum, no-account day as this one was turning out to be. He was proving just one big headache and she wished he'd never got out of jail. Then she could be down at The King's Tattoo, having herself a good time.

She wished she had herself a cigarette, or at least some chewing gum.

"I got me a real nicotine fit on," she now told Ar-Salar-Saloam. "You don't want to buy me a pack of Players, do you?"

"I done quit," Ar-Salar-Saloam said.

Auriole backed slowly away from him, filled with rage: her lips puckered, her eyes narrowed. She made up her mind: "I'm cutting out!" she cried. "You can do what you want from here on out! I'm fed up with you! I'm going where I'm appreciated, going to have me some fun!"

Thinking surely he would knock her teeth out, she spat and kicked at him, then sucked in her breath and broke away in a fast run.

A few seconds later she disappeared behind the nearby battered door of The King's Tattoo.

Oh little Auriole, thought Ar-Salar-Saloam, only an inch away from sinking down to weep in his solitude: *All you can think of is having your fun. Life don't mean no more to you than having your glass of beer and your weeds and a place to throw down your head. You are one of the world's lucky ones, and what I wouldn't give to be that way again . . . .*

Poor me, thought Ar-Salar-Saloam. Even so, he wiped his eyes and took a deep breath and locked his shoulders—and trudged on. Onward into gloom. Pedestrians walking two and three abreast parted for him, alert for sudden moves, sensing something menacing and alien in his hooded stare, his scowls, his periodic groans.

Oh, Auriole, he thought, *why me?*

Onward, ever onward into misery, into the odious future. Into remorse and the black pit, into melancholy and hopeless sorrow—hopeless because the further along he ventured the more convinced he became that his was a route allowing no turnarounds. *Problems,* he thought, *so many problems, which way do I turn?* He had no idea what his problem was, only that it was a thing so indeterminate and insuppressible, so vast and impenetrable, that when he was able to glimpse it at all what he was put in mind of was a giant and spidery creature that crawled up out of his ears to drop its black hairy legs over his eyes and spin its sticky black glue over his body head to foot.

Worse yet, all this, he knew, was exactly what he deserved. It was what Ar-Salar-Saloam had been coming to all these years.

Four people were in the waiting room at Fisheye's Problem Shop, five if you counted the dingy-attired man dozing under the iron hat tree in the far corner, six if you counted the proprietor himself. Not nearly as many as Ar-Salar-Saloam had expected. Not for a Fisheye operation. Not with all the troubles loose in this world.

Ar-Salar-Saloam took his place in line.

The real business, he figured, must be going on in a back room. A man with Fisheye's reputation for the fast buck wouldn't be wasting his time on no two-cents operation.

But there was Fisheye at his desk, with a yellow pencil stuck through his mouth and another lodged over his ear, looking as cheerful as you please.

I am the Antichrist, Ar-Salar-Saloam heard someone saying.

The establishment had been fitted out to look something like a church holding-station, with pew-like seats off to the left for the anxious to sit on. Near where the man was sleeping, bolted to the floor, was a stained plywood money-drop box with the words GIVE TO THE NEEDY stamped on its sides. Someone had spray-painted LOVE IS POWER on the side wall. A printed sign off to the right said HOPE I$ BETTER THAN MONEY IN THE BANK. The straw mat by the entrance door said TAKE A LOAD OFF YOUR FEET.

Fly-by-night but not *too* fly-by-night, Ar-Salar-Saloam reasoned.

I am the Antichrist, he heard again. He peered forward and saw that the person speaking was a dumpy, truck-looking woman at the head of the line. Fisheye seemed to be having some trouble with her.

Behind Fisheye, tacked to the wall with masking tape, was a large poster of Mt. St. Helens emitting steam. Next to it was a cardboard print of some yellow flowers in a jug, all sweepy-swirly like the painter had taken his broom to it. It was hanging wrong, and Ar-Salar-Saloam resisted an urge to go and make it right.

A half-dozen carpet remnants of various sizes and colours and weaves had been tossed about the floor.

A fine white mist drifted down from the ceiling.

This gave Ar-Salar-Saloam an eerie feeling, and for the first time he wondered if he had come to the wrong place.

The woman up front continued to rage. "I am the Antichrist!" she shouted.

"You are a pile of you-know-what," Ar-Salar-Saloam heard Fisheye tell her. "Stand aside!"

"That is no way to talk to the Antichrist!" stormed the woman, beating her purse on Fisheye's shaky desk. Papers fluttered to the floor; as Fisheye bent to retrieve them the woman moved over and stood on them. "I am the Antichrist!" she said again. "Do something!" Her face was bloated, the skin purple, as if she had just stepped into a vat of crushed grapes.

Fisheye, too, was losing his temper. "This is a problem shop," he yelled, "what's your problem?" With a rolled newspaper he swatted at the woman's legs until he got his papers back. "Stand aside!" he commanded. "Move on!"

Others in front of Ar-Salar-Saloam were raising their voices as well, saying "Yeah!" and "Git the lead out!" and "We got problems too!" The woman fumed. She banged her purse against the desk and said she was the Antichrist and had her rights the same as anybody else. The dust sifting down from the ceiling seemed to thicken: Ar-Salar-Saloam could see it on the shoulders of the person in front of him, and on the floor in the Antichrist woman's shoeprints as she strode up and down.

Ar-Salar-Saloam trembled; suddenly he felt fearful of his own sanity, wondering whether this strange snowfall was not altogether imagined. It seemed to him that, far from decreasing his troubles, The Problem Shop was only adding to them. A noise behind him made him turn: a small ragged boy, no more than eight or nine, stood poised in the doorway, sobbing wildly. *"Mama Mama Mama,"* wept the boy, *"When will you come home?"*

Ar-Salar-Saloam's own eyes dampened; sobs caught in his throat; the fine white mist went momentarily static, glistening; his knees weakened. He felt himself lifted out of The Problem Shop, transported back to his own stinging childhood: *he* was the boy in the doorway weeping for his lost mother.

Yes, and his mama—worse luck—never *had* come home. She had sent a wire from Reno, saying *Las Vegas next, I'm fed up with working finger to bone, try your Daddy or the church.*

This ragged boy was lucky, he had a mother to look after him. One who could teach him—if not love—then obedience and respect. The Antichrist woman had given up arguing with Fisheye to storm at the miserable boy, to cuff him and shake him, to beat her lessons into his head. *"Get out of here!"* she shrieked. *"I told you never to leave your room! I told you never to bother me while I was doing my work! Am I not the Antichrist?"*

"Yes, Mama," sobbed the throttled boy, "you are the Antichrist."

She ripped at his ear, smacked him hard on the fanny, and slung him back hard against the door. The boy crumpled down, groaning.

"You are, Mama," he whimpered, "I know you are."

"There!" she shouted, turning on Ar-Salar-Saloam and everyone else in the room—"There, you heard my boy! Now you know I am as I say I am!" Her mottled face glistened with perspiration, her glare was furious and would admit no denials. "Tell them again!" she shrieked, spreading her thick legs wide, sweeping both arms high above her head in a victory pose. Cords rippled in her throat; her full bosom heaved.

The boy dragged himself up, to clutch at her: "Oh, Mama," he moaned. *"Oh Mama, come home! Oh Mama, let us take care of you!"* His hands wrapped about her ankles; he slobbered at her feet. *"You are, Mama. You are the Antichrist."*

The woman relented. Her fierce gaze swept over all in the room, she gave the boy another slap or two, but she relented all the same. She was content at last to let the shivering boy hug her knees.

"So long as you understand," she told the silent group. "So long as you know whose problems come first around here!"

The fine white mist leaking from the ceiling appeared to lift and thin; Fisheye's desk chair let out a nasty squeak; over in the far corner the sleeping man was waking up, rubbing knuckles into his swollen eyes and wiping an open hand across the black stubble of his chin.

The Antichrist woman allowed the boy to lead her reluctantly out.

Everyone breathed again.

Half-an-hour later Ar-Salar-Saloam was no nearer to having his problems solved. He did not know what to think, and was ready—as he admitted to the now near-empty room—to throw in the towel.

"I'm on my last lap," he told Fisheye, as it came his turn to stand before the proprietor's desk.

Fisheye was scraping a knife blade under his nails, and did not even consent to look up at him.

A few seconds before, with all clients gone except for Ar-Salar-Saloam, the once-sleeping man had got up and bolted the entrance door.

"My goose is cooked," Ar-Salar-Saloam tried again.

Fisheye gave no indication that he heard. He closed his knife and rolled back in his chair and opened a desk drawer. From inside he pulled out a small sign and when he had placed it on the desk Ar-Salar-Saloam saw that it read GONE FOR COFFEE.

To Ar-Salar-Saloam this seemed too much. He wanted to break down and cry, but instead he squared his shoulders and tried again.

"What's that mean?" he asked.

Finally Fisheye looked at him. His expression registered no opinion one way or another—either of his own actions or of Ar-Salar-Saloam's timid insistence on service. He seemed, with his blue empty eyes, to be looking at something totally to the other side of Ar-Salar-Saloam. He seemed totally disinterested.

"Gone for coffee," he now said—pausing, standing up, reaching for his hat—"It's plain English, can't you read?"

The black pit opened up in Ar-Salar-Saloam's stomach and from there quickly spread. His eyes swirled. One minute he was staring at Fisheye's bland countenance and the next second a full wall of black was where Fisheye had been.

Ar-Salar-Saloam's knees buckled; he sagged down.

The black wall came with him and in another second or two it enlarged to cover everything.

"*You got problems, son,*" someone was saying.

It seemed to Ar-Salar-Saloam, grimacing as pain shot up through his head, that it was his own Daddy's voice speaking to him from the grave.

Oh no, Daddy, not me, not Ar-Salar-Saloam. Your little boy can take care of himself, he has not a care in the world.

This time it was his own voice saying this, yet he knew he had not spoken.

It occurred to him that at last his troubles were over, that he had passed over to the other side.

"Wake up, son," another voice said—"No deadbeats allowed, where you're going."

Ar-Salar-Saloam opened his eyes. The darkness swirled away and in its place there came a rippling tide, a white rippling mist. . . which then cleared and in the clearing, standing with his back to him as he squared-off the scrub-broom print of yellow flowers in a jug, was the once-sleeping man who had earlier bolted the door. Fisheye was gone. His papers had been put away, his desk top clear and shiny now except for one small notepad and two gnawed pencils neatly aligned side by side.

"A hired hand, son," the man explained. "Got to have their coffee breaks, their little privileges—union, you know."

Speechless, Ar-Salar-Saloam studied him. The man was older than he had previously appeared, and had a kindly look, although one faintly cavalier. An unlit fag drooped from his lips, and he stood with his hands in his coat pockets, in half-smile, but shaking his legs as if he had just wet himself.

"My own little problem," he sheepishly admitted. "All of us got to have something."

Ar-Salar-Saloam shook the cobwebs out of his head. The man was clearly a lunatic—maybe worse. Yet he swept aggressively forth, throwing out a hand which Ar-Salar-Saloam accepted in his own limp paw.

"That's right," the man smiled, "you're looking at the brains behind this outfit! You got problems, you come to the right place. Take a load off your feet. I can make no guarantees, but I think I can say that if your heart's in the right place you're as good as cured." He thumped his chest, chuckling, dropping down into the empty chair. "Old Fisheye," he said, "always got his sights on the clock. But I value him, don't get me wrong. He's good at weeding out the snowflakes. Knows his job."

Ar-Salar-Saloam cowered; his inclination was to hit and run.

"Speak up!" continued the man. "I find it pays to get right down to peanuts, no beating around the bush. I can't read minds, you know. What brings a bright-looking fellow like yourself to The Problem Shop?"

Ar-Salar-Saloam could not figure where to begin. It was as if all his problems had flown right out of his head.

"That Antichrist woman," said the man, "is she what's got your tongue? You thinking we can't deliver?" He cast his head down in a state of momentary melancholy, as if sensing that Ar-Salar-Saloam was accusing him of falling down on the job. "With some it takes time," he said, his voice low, caressing fur: "Not everybody can expect relief overnight, ours is not a Magic Shop, you know." He came up smiling, however, casting a mischievous glance over Ar-Salar-Saloam's intent head: "No, for that you have to look elsewhere."

Ar-Salar-Saloam mumbled "Oh yeah, I know what you mean,"—although totally at a loss to understand either what the man was saying or what he himself felt.

A deep pool, he thought, *that's what I've fell into. I've got to get myself out of here.*

"All the same," the man now said, rising, shaking his head at the mystery of it all—"All the same, she's a case, that Antichrist woman. After a hard day like this one I'm half-willing to slit her throat." He fell silent, moping, mulling the issue over.

Too worried about the business, considered Ar-Salar-Saloam, *to give any little thought to me. Rue the day I come in here.*

"Still," the man said, reflecting, striding to a closet door behind the desk—"Still, she's got the boy. We've done that much at least for her."

Ar-Salar-Saloam wisely kept his silence. *Too much going on around here,* he thought. *Too much I don't understand. I'm out of my element in this zoo.*

"What's your name?" he managed. "Who are you?"

"Some folks call me Captain. The Captain, Cap, Old Salt—take your pick."

Ar-Salar-Saloam was watching the ceiling. The white powdery stuff was beginning to sift down again.

"My costume," the Captain said. "Clothes make the man." He had taken from the closet some kind of blue yachtsman's coat, and was pulling it on. It had a gold fringe on the sleeves and a big blue and gold crest on the pocket which said in rounded letters THE PROBLEM SHOP, and a logo that resembled a parking meter.

"How do I look?"

He looked pretty sharp. He looked what Auriole would call a *lulu,* with maybe a touch too many limp shoes thrown in.

But Ar-Salar-Saloam didn't tell him that. "You'll do," he said.

"You're like a lot of people, son," the Captain off-handedly observed: "Too stingy with the praise." He coughed, yanking out a soiled hand-kerchief, blowing his nose. "Let's get out of here. This damned white stuff is killing me. Sinus, you know."

The stairway leading down from The Problem Shop was drab and dingy, unlit except for one naked light bulb flecked with paint. The walls were peeling. The boards creaked. At the bottom a garbage can had been overturned and soup cans and gnawed bones and small balls of cooked rice littered the floor. The moment they hit daylight the Captain came to an abrupt halt.

"Well, my boy," he said, "which way will it be? Right or left?"

Ar-Salar-Saloam was buffaloed. He had hoped that if anyone knew the way this peculiar creature would.

"Or are you the kind that goes whichever way you're pointed? Is that your problem, son?"

Ar-Salar-Saloam dropped his shoulders and shuffled his feet, giving the Captain the full force of his hooded stare. The Captain's mind moved too fast; it took too many devious turns. Ar-Salar-Saloam was beginning to think he was some kind of Show Off, a Dink.

"Spell it out, son. Let me hear in your own words what's troubling you."

Ar-Salar-Saloam had one of his rare brainstorms. He suddenly knew what his problem was, and decided to blurt it out:

"I don't have no future," he said.

The Captain's mouth fell open in surprise, then mild amusement set in, and the next second he was throwing back his head and guffawing. "Why, no one does!" he exclaimed. "Where did you get the idea that anyone did? My my," he said, now strolling along, chuckling to himself, "—this day and age, imagine that!"

Ar-Salar-Saloam scrambled to catch up with him. It seemed to him beyond reason that anyone professing to run a problem shop would fail to understand. He felt angry and betrayed.

"Nothing!" insisted Ar-Salar-Saloam with raised voice: *"I don't have nothing! I might as well be dead!"*

The Captain gave a sympathetic shrug: "In quicksand up to your shoulder blades, is that the way it is, my boy?"

Ar-Salar-Saloam was adamant; he wanted to throttle this grinning man. *"I am without hope! Don't you understand? I don't have nothing and I am plain without hope!"* His fists knotted up as he glared at this man. *"Are you too stupid to understand that? Can't you see I'm in pain?"*

The Captain nodded, unimpressed: "It's a tough life then, you'd say? You find the space a bit tight in your jam jar?" He seemed actually to be enjoying Ar-Salar-Saloam's wretchedness, a gap showing between his teeth as he smiled and once again strolled on.

Ar-Salar-Saloam wanted to put another gap in that man's face. He was outraged by this shoddy treatment, yet at the same time accustomed to it. He groaned. His heart was squeezing up like a small hurt thing, like a tiny bird being slowly crushed, and for a moment black spots floated in front of him as his head swam. He stomped his feet down, summoning up strength for one final appeal: *"I mean it!"* he screeched. *"I'm desperate! I'd rather change places with that Antichrist woman, that's how bad off I am!"*

The Captain did not so much as slow down: "Beyond redemption, would you say?"

Ar-Salar-Saloam felt rooted to the spot. He could feel all his juices deserting him. He was all flagged out; could think of nothing, feel nothing, except for a black recognition of the abiding unfairness of this world. Through dim eyes he watched the Captain stroll jauntily on ahead in his bright blue jacket and his yachtsman's hat, not even glancing back. He thought: *Go on, it's good riddance I say. Prance off all high and mighty, thinking only of yourself. Rue the day I ever met you, go to hell you and your problem shop, I could care less what you do. Yeah, go on, just another big cheese: what do you care, forget Ar-Salar-Saloam, his life is over, when did anyone ever care one whit about me. . . .*

Morbid, dropping down to sit on the curb, slouching over, head down between his legs, groaning to himself *That's it, that's it, I'm down in the gutter now, down here where I belong, where they've always wanted me, where I've been coming to all these years. My trouble was ever thinking I could drag myself up, ever thinking I had a chance. Well it's over now, it's over, I've shot my last wad. I can say it now, I can admit the worst: Ar-Salar-Saloam, you do not have a single redeeming human trait. You'd be better wiped off the face of this earth.*

It penetrated through to him after a time that someone was calling his name. Slowly his head came up, he wiped the wetness from his cheeks; slowly he came back to the life of the street, to the sight of cars whooshing by, of dusty junk windows and tatty curtains behind the glass of upstairs rooms, of smoke spilling up from chimneys and the odd pedestrian coming or going in a slow drift, coming or going as if to or from some far-off dream. Over at Sally Ann's blue building a stringy-haired girl and a fat boy no older than him had their suitcases out and their guitars and were playing some kind of low-down twangy song. Across the street directly in front of him an old man in a droopy coat that wiped the pavement was leaning on two rag-wrapped crutches silently watching him. Further along, outside Man Tung Yi's Foot Parlour, the Antichrist woman was up on a box rattling a tambourine and intoning *I am the Antichrist I am the Antichrist I am the Antichrist* while her boy stood by with pained face, tugging at her dress, saying *Mama come home, Mama come home, Oh Mama come home now.* The sky had turned an unwrinkled blue, shafts of sunlight slanting through drifting clouds like tall perfect skyscrapers belonging to some future day.

The Captain was down near the Johnson Street bridge, waving an arm.

"Come on, boy! Don't lolligag! Hurry up now!"

Ar-Salar-Saloam's black mood vanished; he spun off to catch up with him.

The Captain steered them down to the water. He wore a bemused, lazy expression, now lifting an arm to point out this, now to point out that, approving of one thing, disapproving of another, saying how the breakfast at Smitty's Pancake House was made of chopped-up rubber with a little ratmeat thrown in to sweeten the taste; how the new pedestrian walkway along the Inner Harbour was a step in the right direction, though the city had skimped on it a bit; how the Undersea Gardens was not a bad idea, far as it went, while the Wax Museum was a rip-off and, to his mind, frankly an aberration; how the double-decker busses were a joy to his eyes, while he didn't care a smidgen for the Tally Ho mule-wagon tour; how the black water here surely with a little foresight or old-fashioned ingenuity could have been cleaned up a bit; how, overall, looking at it without bias and with consideration for all the mean problems of this world, the old city hadn't done too badly with its growth; complaining, however, that the government was an abomination naturally—"What else can you expect?"—and how everything cost too much. Reminding Ar-Salar-Saloam how even in a relatively decent city such as this one a body still had to bitch and complain to get a thing done; how you had to watch out for yourself and not let the little stops in life up and knock you flat.

"Your troubles now," he said, "what do they amount to, you still got your youth, you got your health. Now hope, that's another matter, I admit it helps to have that. Certainly it is the A-Number-One problem

I've come up against in my shop, it seems half the people I see have either got too much or not enough." He sighed, shaking his head, guiding Ar-Salar-Saloam on to wherever it was he had in mind going. "Making no bones about it, though, I'd say hopelessness is our speciality, I'd say we've built up a good record on that very issue." He smiled, throwing an arm over Ar-Salar-Saloam's bony shoulder, pushing the visored cap high on his head. "Live and learn," he murmured, "learn and live. So all right, you've got a self-image problem, nothing unique there. But tell me, if you've a mind to, what else has been troubling you. Spit it out, my boy, let the cat fur fly!"

Ar-Salar-Saloam, as if in a trance, gazed out over the Inner Harbour's black water. The big schooner which he had seen earlier in the day passing under the Johnson Street bridge, rocked not more than twenty paces from where he now stood, its three masts shooting up like endless telephone poles above the shining deck.

"There's Auriole," he softly said. "I worry about Auriole, I worried about her the whole time I was in jail. I worried about whether she was being faithful to me, but mostly I worried about her on general accounts."

"Oh, she'll get along," laughed the Captain. "No, a hot ticket like little Auriole, you don't have to be bothered about her. Make a good wife, a good worker, once she gets over loving her dope, over wanting her fun and good times." He paused, then added: "If not for you, then for someone else."

Ar-Salar-Saloam nodded, solemn. "There's that woman who dropped dead," he went on. "That weighs on my mind, what I did to her."

The Captain lightly patted his back. "I should hope so," he said. "A business like that could ruin any poor boy's life. Yet, look at it this way: the lady was old and sick, you couldn't have known. Even her doctor said she was at the edge, could go anytime. Her heart failed, as I recall. No, she was a nice old lady and we can grieve for her, but her illness I think mitigates your guilt." He hesitated, fixing a stern eye on Ar-Salar-Saloam. "Don't get me wrong. Her heart wouldn't have quit if you hadn't come along to snatch her purse. I'm not saying you got any cause to feel scot-free."

Ar-Salar-Saloam turned to the Captain with a sad smile. He wanted to say to this odd man that his life had been hell, that he and little Auriole and a thousand people like them—all that strungout gang down at The King's Tattoo, for instance—had never had a chance, that everything they had ever done and every which way they had ever turned had been wrong and not their choice at the start. But he remained silent, not certain that wasn't fudging the cake. He felt better now, did not have that sunk-down feeling any more. He felt—as maybe Auriole would put it—real strange. Real weird, like his head had zoomed off to some high place. Just walking with the Captain, having this little talk man-to-man, had done it, he guessed. It was like a father and son walk, like the old times he had dreamed about as a kid but never had known. It was wonderful, that's what it was—the Captain's warm hand on his shoulder, the day turned so scrubbed-down and fresh. So beautiful. He didn't even have that cramped feeling in the knees any longer; that iron feeling in the head.

It dawned on Ar-Salar-Saloam that in fact he felt pretty good. That he felt some hope stirring around inside.

There was activity now on the schooner. Someone in a white suit had come out and thrown a gangplank down. Others were scooting over the deck, unlashing the riggings, tying goods down, giving a last buff to gleaming brass rails.

"What's that?" Ar-Salar-Saloam asked, pointing at a small bucket way up high on the centre mast.

"That's the crow's-nest," replied the Captain—and as this did not appear to enlighten Ar-Salar-Saloam, he explained further: "In the old days, say on your arctic or whaling vessel, the lookout man would sit up there and watch for fish. Or pirates. Or land. Whatever needed watching for."

Ar-Salar-Saloam's face brightened. He looked up at the small bucket in amazement. "Now that's a job I could have gone for," he said, "I could have whet my teeth on a job like that."

"Maybe it isn't too late," the Captain answered.

"What you mean?"

The Captain pulled back a sleeve and tapped on a wrist watch: "In about two minutes," he said, "I'm setting sail. You can sign on if you've a mind to."

"*All ready, Captain!*" someone shouted from the ship.

Ar-Salar-Saloam's heart gave a sudden lurch. Striding down the boarding plank, his long black gown whipping up about his ankles, his face frozen into an expression of permanent intolerance and hatred, was none other than the judge who that morning had lectured to Ar-Salar-Saloam so severely.

"Is he a part of this crew!" asked Ar-Salar-Saloam, fearfully.

"Don't bet on it," said the Captain. "No, he's a passenger, I'm afraid. That old toad has got a lot of shaping up to do before I'd trust him with my sails. He has had a thousand chances and ruined every one, while you. . .well you, my boy, you've had nothing, but at least you've wound up no worse than you were at the start. Shall we go aboard?"

Some minutes later the Johnson Street bridge went up for the second time that day, and the ancient schooner with its three tall masts passed through, rocking ever so slightly in the gentle water. From his crow's-nest on the highest mast, Ar-Salar-Saloam looked out over his old haunts, over the full width and length of the city, and already he knew he was going to like this job. Until now it had never crossed his mind that the geography of this or any other place could be remarkable, that this city possessed any noteworthy beauty. Now the water shimmered, all but blinding him, but with his eyes slit so narrowly and his hands up to shade them, he acknowledged that in this respect, as in so many others, he had made a profound mistake. Life was indeed beautiful. Land and water were magic, a dancing pair. It was breathtaking, to tell the truth, and he sensed that from this day he would forever go on thinking so. The sea shimmered, snowcapped mountains all round touched the sky in blissful dignity, clouds hovered within easy reach; the very rooftops of the city seemed to throb and swell and extend to him a personal *bon voyage*. He could see up there on the street beyond The King's Tattoo the Antichrist woman marching at the head of a motley band of fifteen or twenty, and the cars waiting for the bridge to come back down strung back for a block or two and honking their horns—and down there on the corner by the lamppost the rapt face of the Antichrist woman's son waving wildly up at him, now leaving that off to jump up and down and flap out his arms even more wildly and to shout out some excited secret message at him. . . .

The schooner sluiced at good speed through the water, sending out waves to lick at the shore, and even up so high Ar-Salar-Saloam could feel the good spray, the fine slap of untainted air. It was cool and wonderful, better than any possible dream. It was the future, that's what it was—the fearless future splashing him beautifully in the face. It was hope and love and sweet mercy; it was all of these things.

Then at once the schooner turned out of the black ribbon of water that had been its path, and the city fell away and vanished as neatly as if it had never existed, so that only the great sea awaited. Ar-Salar-Saloam at that moment cried out with joy, with an excitement so feverish he would have fallen from his nest had he not been strapped in: "*Fish!*" he screeched in rapture—"*FISH! FISH! FISH!*"

And he went on so screeching, piloted by his own ecstasy as he spotted fish or land or other boats—as he watched for whatever needed watching for—through the entire length of his voyage, which for that matter, has not yet ended.

"*Fish!*. . .

Land!. . .

Heaven, my Captain! It is all here!. . . "

[1979]

· RUDY WIEBE ·

1934–

Rudy Henry Wiebe was born in 1934 at a remote Mennonite community near Fairholme in northern Saskatchewan, the youngest of seven children. In 1947 the family moved to Coaldale, Alberta. Wiebe went on to attend the University of Alberta (B.A. 1956, M.A. 1960), and also studied theology at the Mennonite Brethren Bible College in Winnipeg (Th.B. 1961). He has edited the *Mennonite Brethren Herald* (1962–63), taught at Goshen College, Indiana (1963–67), and in 1967 joined the faculty of the University of Alberta, where he still teaches English (especially Canadian literature) and creative writing.

Wiebe's fiction is remarkable for its ambitious scope and for its continuing sense of moral and religious purpose. His first novel, *Peace Shall Destroy Many* (1962), which he began in a creative writing course, draws for its setting upon his early memories. It portrays a young Mennonite during World War II torn between his community's pacifism and the demands of his country. He moves from the world of youthful innocence to that of painful adult experience as he comes to realize that violence is found within the self and the "peaceful" community as well as in the wicked world outside. Though effective, the novel is too conspicuously didactic. More experimental yet less cohesive, *First and Vital Candle* (1966) centres upon another young man, who has fled a narrow, traditional religious faith, but finds life meaningless in a world that denies God. In both books, a strong plot occasionally bursts rather melodramatically out of earnest but impressive discussions of moral issues.

The Blue Mountains of China (1970) represents a major step forward. This novel encompasses a wide range of characters, both dutiful and lapsed Mennonites, whose combined story is a saga of the Mennonite people. Moving to and fro in time between 1883 and 1967, and in space between Russia, Paraguay, and Canada, the book employs a dazzling array of fictional techniques, which help to make it not only subtler than its predecessors but also artistically far more successful.

At this point, Wiebe turns from an emphasis on his own people to concentrate upon other ethnic minorities in the Canadian West. *The Temptations of Big Bear* (1973) and *The Scorched-Wood People* (1977) are both historical novels concerned with the prairie uprisings of 1885, focusing upon the Cree and Métis peoples respectively. Here Wiebe gets involved in complicated questions of literary and moral perspective, since his re-creations of historical events emphasize the viewpoints of losers rather than victors. Big Bear emerges as a complex and noble figure, while Riel is presented, through a Métis narrator, from an essentially Métis point of view. Both books transcend the category of historical novel to become—in his own phrase—"giant fiction."

In his most recent fiction, Wiebe has returned to more recent subjects. *The Mad Trapper* (1980) interprets the story of Albert Johnson, who defied an immense RCMP manhunt in the Yukon during the winter of 1931–32. (This topic is also treated in his short story "The Naming of Albert Johnson.") *My Lovely Enemy* (1983), in which the protagonist combines Mennonite ancestry with research into nineteenth-century Indian history, is an agonized and controversial novel that examines the vexed interrelations between sexual love and theological *caritas*.

Wiebe's short stories have developed in a similar way. Early stories, like "Tudor King," were written out of his early experiences and portray young people experiencing the complex and often harsh realities of the adult world for the first time. His later work includes experimental stories about the interpretation of history ("Where Is the Voice Coming From?" is now recognized as a classic of this kind) and some recent forays into the world of magic realism (such as "The Angel of the Tar Sands").

.————.

Wiebe's works include *Peace Shall Destroy Many* (1962); *First and Vital Candle* (1966); *The Blue Mountains of China* (1970); *The Temptations of Big Bear* (1973); *Where is the Voice Coming From?* (1974); *The Scorched-Wood People* (1977); *Alberta/A Celebration* (1979); *Far as the Eye Can See* (1979); *The Mad Trapper* (1980); *The Angel of the Tar Sands and Other Stories* (1982); and *My Lovely Enemy* (1983). He has edited a number of anthologies including *The Story Makers* (1970); and *War in the West: Voices of the 1885 Rebellion* (with Bob Beal) (1985).

Works on Wiebe include Allan Dueck, "Rudy Wiebe's Approach to Historical Fiction: A Study of *The Temptations of Big Bear* and *The Scorched-Wood People*," *The Canadian Novel: Here and Now*, ed. John Moss (1978): 187–200; Magdalene Redekop, "Rudy Wiebe," *Profiles in Canadian Literature*, ed. Jeffrey M. Heath (1980), 2; 65–72; W.J. Keith, *Epic Fiction: The Art of Rudy Wiebe* (1981); and W.J. Keith, ed., *A Voice in the Land: Essays by and about Rudy Wiebe* (1981).

W. J. KEITH

WHERE IS THE VOICE COMING FROM?

The problem is to make the story.

One difficulty of this making may have been excellently stated by Teilhard de Chardin: "We are continually inclined to isolate ourselves from the things and events which surround us. . . as though we were spectators, not elements, in what goes on." Arnold Toynbee does venture, "For all that we know, Reality is the undifferentiated unity of the mystical experience," but that need not here be considered. This story ended long ago; it is one of finite acts, of orders, or elemental feelings and reactions, of obvious legal restrictions and requirements.

Presumably all the parts of the story are themselves available. A difficulty is that they are, as always, available only in bits and pieces. Though the acts themselves seem quite clear, some written reports of the acts contradict each other. As if these acts were, at one time, too well-known; as if the original nodule of each particular fact had from somewhere received non-factual accretions; or even more, as if, since the basic facts were so clear perhaps there were a larger number of facts than any one reporter, or several, or even any reporter had ever attempted to record. About facts that are simply told by this mouth to that ear, of course, even less can be expected.

An affair seventy-five years old should acquire some of the shiny transparency of an old man's skin. It should.

Sometimes it would seem that it would be enough—perhaps more than enough—to hear the names only. The grandfather One Arrow; the mother Spotted Calf; the father Sounding Sky; the wife (wives rather, but only one of them seems to have a name, though their fathers are Napaise, Kapahoo, Old Dust, The Rump)—the one wife named, of all things, Pale Face; the cousin Going-Up-To-Sky; the brother-in-law (again, of all things) Dublin. The names of the police sound very much alike; they all begin with Constable or Corporal or Sergeant, but here and there an Inspector, then a Superintendent and eventually all the resonance of an Assistant Commissioner echoes down. More. Herself: Victoria, by the Grace of God etc., etc., QUEEN, defender of the Faith, etc., etc., and witness "Our Right Trusty and Right Well-beloved Cousin and Councillor the Right Honourable Sir John Campbell Hamilton-Gordon, Earl of Aberdeen; Viscount Formartine, Baron Haddo, Methlic, Tarves and Kellie in the Peerage of Scotland; Viscount Gordon of Aberdeen, County of Aberdeen in the Peerage of the United Kingdom; Baronet of Nova Scotia, Knight Grand Cross of Our Most Distinguished Order of Saint Michael and Saint George, etc., Governor General of Canada." And of course himself: in the award proclamation named "Jean-Baptiste" but otherwise known only as Almighty Voice.

But hearing cannot be enough; not even hearing all the thunder of A Proclamation: "Now Hear Ye that a reward of FIVE HUNDRED DOLLARS will be paid to any person or persons who will give such information as will lead . . . (etc., etc.) this Twentieth day of April, in the year of Our Lord one thousand eight hundred and ninety-six, and the Fifty-ninth year of Our Reign . . . " etc. and etc.

Such hearing cannot be enough. The first item to be seen is the piece of white bone. It is almost triangular, slightly convex—concave actually as it is positioned at this moment with its corners slightly raised—graduating from perhaps a strong eighth to a weak quarter of an inch in thickness, its scattered pore structure varying between larger and smaller on its perhaps polished, certainly shiny surface. Precision is difficult since the glass showcase is at least thirteen inches deep and therefore an eye cannot be brought as close as the minute inspection of such a small, though certainly quite adequate, sample of skull would normally require. Also, because of the position it cannot be determined whether the several hairs, well over a foot long, are still in some manner attached to it or not.

The seven-pounder cannon can be seen standing almost shyly between the showcase and the interior wall. Officially it is known as a gun, not a cannon, and clearly its bore is not large enough to admit a large man's fist. Even if it can be believed that this gun was used in the 1885 Rebellion and that on the evening of Saturday, May 29, 1897 (while the nine-pounder, now unidentified, was in the process of arriving with the police on the special train from Regina), seven shells (all that were available in Prince Albert at that time) from it were sent shrieking into the poplar bluffs as night fell, clearly such shelling could not and would not disembowel the whole earth. Its carriage is now nicely lacquered, the perhaps oak spokes of its petite wheels (little higher than a knee) have been recently scraped, puttied and varnished; the brilliant burnish of its brass breeching testifies with what meticulous care charmen and women have used nationally advertised cleaners and restorers.

Though it can also be seen, even a careless glance reveals that the same concern has not been expended on the one (of two) .44 calibre 1866 model Winchesters apparently found at the last in the pit with Almighty Voice. It is also preserved in a glass case; the number 1536735 is still, though barely, distinguishable on the brass cartridge section just below the brass saddle ring. However, perhaps because the case was imperfectly sealed at one time (though sealed enough not to warrant disturbance now), or because of simple neglect, the rifle is obviously spotted here and there with blotches of rust and the brass itself reveals discolorations almost like mildew. The rifle bore, the three long strands of hair themselves, actually bristle with clots of dust. It may be that this museum cannot afford to be as concerned as the other; conversely, the disfiguration may be something inherent in the items themselves.

The small building which was the police guardroom at Duck Lake, Saskatchewan Territory, in 1895 may also be seen. It had subsequently been moved from its original place and used to house small animals, chickens perhaps, or pigs—such as a woman might be expected to have under her responsibility. It is, of course, now perfectly empty, and clean so that the public may enter with no more discomfort than a bend under the doorway and a heavy encounter with disinfectant. The door-jamb has obviously been replaced; the bar network at one window is, however, said to be original; smooth still, very smooth. The logs inside have been smeared again and again with whitewash, perhaps paint, to an insistent point of identity-defying characterlessness. Within the small rectangular box of these logs not a sound can be heard from the streets of the, probably dead, town.

Hey Injun you'll get hung for stealing that steer
Hey Injun for killing that government cow you'll get three weeks on the woodpile
Hey Injun

The place named Kinistino seems to have disappeared from the map but the Minnechinass Hills have not. Whether they have ever been on a map is doubtful but they will, of course, not disappear from the landscape as long as the grass grows and the rivers run. Contrary to general report and belief, the Canadian prairies are rarely, if ever, flat and the

Minnechinass (spelled five different ways and translated sometimes as "The Outside Hill," sometimes as "Beautiful Bare Hills") are dissimilar from any other of the numberless hills that everywhere block out the prairie horizon. They are not bare; poplars lie tattered along their tops, almost black against the straw-pale grass and sharp green against the grey soil of the plowing laid in half-mile rectangular blocks upon their western slopes. Poles holding various wires stick out of the field, back down the bend of the valley; what was once a farmhouse is weathering into the cultivated earth. The poplar bluff where Almighty Voice made his stand has, of course, disappeared.

The policemen he shot and killed (not the ones he wounded, of course) are easily located. Six miles east, thirty-nine miles north in Prince Albert, the English Cemetery, Sergeant Colin Campbell Colebrook, North West Mounted Police Registration Number 605, lies presumably under a gravestone there. His name is seventeenth in a very long "list of non-commissioned officers and men who have died in the service since the inception of the force." The date is October 29, 1895, and the cause of death is anonymous: "Shot by escaping Indian prisoner near Prince Albert." At the foot of this grave are two others: Constable John R. Kerr, No. 3040, and Corporal C.H.S. Hockin, No. 3106. Their cause of death on May 28, 1897 is even more anonymous, but the place is relatively precise: "Shot by Indians at Min-etch-inass Hills, Prince Albert District."

The gravestone, if he has one, of the fourth man Almighty Voice killed is more difficult to locate. Mr. Ernest Grundy, postmaster at Duck Lake in 1897, apparently shut his window the afternoon of Friday, May 28, armed himself, rode east twenty miles, participated in the second charge into the bluff at about 6:30 p.m., and on the third sweep of that charge was shot dead at the edge of the pit. It would seem that he thereby contributed substantially not only to the Indians' bullet supply, but his clothing warmed them as well.

The burial place of Dublin and Going-Up-To-Sky is unknown, as is the grave of Almighty Voice. It is said that a Métis named Henry Smith lifted the latter's body from the pit in the bluff and gave it to Spotted Calf. The place of burial is not, of course, of ultimate significance. A gravestone is always less evidence than a triangular piece of skull, provided it is large enough.

Whatever further evidence there is to be gathered may rest on pictures. There are, presumably, almost numberless pictures of the policemen in the case, but the only one with direct bearing is one of Sergeant Colebrook who apparently insisted on advancing to complete an arrest after being warned three times that if he took another step he would be shot. The picture must have been taken before he joined the force; it reveals him a large-eared young man, hair brush-cut and ascot tie, his eyelids slightly drooping, almost hooded under thick brows. Unfortunately a picture of Constable R.C. Dickson, into whose charge Almighty Voice was apparently committed in that guardroom and who after Colebrook's death was convicted of negligence, sentenced to two months hard labour and discharged, does not seem to be available.

There are no pictures to be found of either Dublin (killed early by rifle fire) or Going-Up-To-Sky (killed in the pit), the two teen-age boys who gave their ultimate fealty to Almighty Voice. There is, however, one said to be of Almighty Voice, Junior. He may have been born to Pale Face during the year, two hundred and twenty-one days that his father was a fugitive. In the picture he is kneeling before what could be a tent, he wears striped denim overalls and displays twin babies whose sex cannot be determined from the double-laced dark bonnets they wear. In the supposed picture of Spotted Calf and Sounding Sky, Sounding Sky stands slightly before his wife; he wears a white shirt and a striped blanket folded over his left shoulder in such a manner that the arm in which he cradles a long rifle cannot be seen. His head is thrown back; the rim of his hat appears as a black half-moon above eyes that are pressed shut in, as it were, profound concentration; above a mouth clenched thin in a downward curve. Spotted Calf wears a long dress, a sweater which could also be a man's dress coat, and a large fringed and embroidered shawl which would appear distinctly Dukhobor in origin if the scroll patterns on it were more irregular. Her head is small and turned slightly towards her husband so as to reveal her right ear. There is what can only be called a quizzical expression on her crumpled face; it may be she does not understand what is happening and that she would have asked a question, perhaps of her husband, perhaps of the photographers, perhaps even of anyone, anywhere in the world if such questioning were possible for an Indian woman.

There is one final picture. That is one of Almighty Voice himself. At least it is purported to be of Almighty Voice himself. In the Royal Canadian Mounted Police Museum on the Barracks Grounds just off Dewdney Avenue in Regina, Saskatchewan, it lies in the same showcase, as a matter of fact immediately beside that triangular piece of skull. Both are unequivocally labelled, and it must be assumed that a police force with a world-wide reputation would not label *such* evidence incorrectly. But here emerges an ultimate problem in making the story.

There are two official descriptions of Almighty Voice. The first reads: "Height about five feet, ten inches, slight build, rather good looking, a sharp hooked nose with a remarkably flat point. Has a bullet scar on the left side of his face about 1-1/2 inches long running from near corner of mouth towards ear. The scar cannot be noticed when his face is painted but otherwise is plain. Skin fair for an Indian." The second description is on the Award Proclamation: "About twenty-two years old, five feet ten inches in height, weight about eleven stone, slightly erect, neat small feet and hands; complexion inclined to be fair, wavy dark hair to shoulders, large dark eyes, broad forehead, sharp features and parrot nose with flat tip, scar on left cheek running from mouth towards ear, feminine appearance."

So run the descriptions that were, presumably, to identify a well-known fugitive in so precise a manner that an informant could collect five hundred dollars—a considerable sum when a police constable earned between one and two dollars a day. The nexus of the problems appears when these supposed official descriptions are compared to the supposed official picture. The man in the picture is standing on a small rug. The fingers of his left hand touch a curved Victorian settee, behind him a photographer's backdrop of scrolled patterns merges to vaguely paradisiacal trees and perhaps a sky. The moccasins he wears make it impossible to deduce whether his feet are "neat small." He may be five feet, ten inches tall, may weigh eleven stone, he certainly is "rather good looking" and, though it is a frontal view, it may be that the point of his long and flaring nose could be "remarkably flat." The photograph is slightly over-illuminated and so the unpainted complexion could be "inclined to be fair"; however, nothing can be seen of a scar, the hair is not wavy and shoulder-length but hangs almost to the waist in two thick straight braids worked through with beads, fur, ribbons and cords. The right hand that holds the corner of the blanket-like coat in position is large and, even in the high illumination, heavily veined. The neck is concealed under coiled beads and the forehead seems more low than "broad."

Perhaps, somehow, these picture details could be reconciled with the official description if the face as a whole were not so devastating.

On a cloth-backed sheet two feet by two and one-half feet in size, under the Great Seal of the Lion and the Unicorn, dignified by the names of the Deputy of the Minister of Justice, the Secretary of State, the Queen herself and all the heaped detail of her "Right Trusty and Right Well-beloved Cousin," this descripton concludes: "feminine appearance." But the picture: any face of history, any believed face that the world acknowledges as *man*—Socrates, Jesus, Attila, Genghis Khan, Mahatma Gandhi, Joseph Stalin—no believed face is more *man* than this face. The mouth, the nose, the clenched brows, the eyes—the eyes are large, yes, and dark, but even in this watered-down reproduction of unending reproductions of that original, a steady look into those eyes cannot be endured. It is a face like an axe.

It is now evident that the de Chardin statement quoted at the beginning has relevance only as it proves itself inadequate to explain what has happened. At the same time, the inadequacy of Aristotle's much more famous statement becomes evident: "The true difference [between the historian and the poet] is that one relates what *has* happened, the other what *may* happen." These statements cannot explain the storymaker's activity since, despite the most rigid application of impersonal investigation, the elements of the story have now run me aground. If ever I could, I can no longer pretend to objective, omnipotent disinterestedness. I am no longer *spectator* of what *has* happened or what *may* happen: I am become *element* in what is happening at this very moment.

For it is, of course, I myself who cannot endure the shadows on that paper which are those eyes. It is I who stand beside this broken veranda post where two corner shingles have been torn away, where barbed wire tangles the dead weeds on the edge of this field. The bluff that sheltered Almighty Voice and his two friends has not disappeared from the slope of the Minnechinass, no more than the sound of Constable Dickson's voice in the guardhouse is silent. The sound of his speaking is there even if it has never been recorded in an official report:

hey injun you'll get
hung
for stealing that steer
hey injun for killing that government
cow you'll get three
weeks on the woodpile hey injun

The unknown contradictory words about an unprovable act that move a boy to defiance, an implacable Cree warrior long after the three-hundred-and-fifty-year war is ended, a war already lost the day the Cree watch Cartier hoist his guns ashore at Hochelaga and they begin the long retreat west; these words of incomprehension, of threatened incomprehensible law are there to be heard just as the unmoving tableau of the three-day siege is there to be seen on the slopes of the Minnechinass. Sounding Sky is somewhere not there, under arrest, but Spotted Calf stands on a shoulder of the Hills a little to the left, her arms upraised to the setting sun. Her mouth is open. A horse rears, riderless, above the scrub willow at the edge of the bluff, smoke puffs, screams tangle in rifle barrage, there are wounds, somewhere. The bluff is so green this spring, it will not burn and the ragged line of seven police and two civilians is staggering through, faces twisted in rage, terror, and rifles sputter. Nothing moves. There is no sound of frogs in the night; twenty-seven policemen and five civilians stand in cordon at thirty-yard intervals and a body also lies in the shelter of a gully. Only a voice rises from the bluff:

We have fought well
You have died like braves
I have worked hard and am hungry
Give me food

but nothing moves. The bluff lies, a bright green island on the grassy slope surrounded by men hunched forward rigid over their long rifles, men clumped out of rifle-range, thirty-five men dressed as for fall hunting on a sharp spring day, a small gun positioned on a ridge above. A crow is falling out of the sky into the bluff, its feathers sprayed as by an explosion. The first gun and the second gun are in position, the beginning and end of the bristling surround of thirty-five Prince Albert Volunteers, thirteen civilians and fifty-six policemen in position relative to the bluff and relative to the unnumbered whites astride their horses, standing up in their carts, staring and pointing across the valley, in position relative to the bluff and the unnumbered Indians squatting silent along the higher ridges of the Hills, motionless mounds, faceless against the Sunday morning sunlight edging between and over them down along the tree tips, down into the shadows of the bluff. Nothing moves. Beside the second gun the red-coated officer has flung a handful of grass into the motionless air, almost to the rim of the red sun.

And there is a voice. It is an incredible voice that rises from among the young poplars ripped of their spring bark, from among the dead somewhere lying there, out of the arm-deep pit shorter than a man; a voice rises over the exploding smoke and thunder of guns that reel back in their positions, worked over, serviced by the grimed motionless men in bright coats and glinting buttons, a voice so high and clear, so unbelievably high and strong in its unending wordless cry.

The voice of "Gitchie-Manitou Wayo"—interpreted as "Voice of the Great Spirit"—that is, The Almighty Voice. His death chant no less incredible in its beauty than in its incomprehensible happiness.

I say "wordless cry" because that is the way it sounds to me. I could be more accurate if I had a reliable interpreter who would make a reliable interpretation. For I do not, of course, understand the Cree myself.

[1971]

· AUDREY THOMAS ·

1935–

It is more than a quarter of a century since Audrey Thomas, American by birth and British by marriage, chose Canada as her country, and twenty years since her first book of stories, *Ten Green Bottles* (1967), was brought out by a relatively unimportant American publisher. Not until 1974 did one of her books, *Blown Figures*, originate with a Canadian house, and then it was a small West Coast enterprise, Talonbooks. But her books almost immediately became underground classics of a kind, read enthusiastically by a small circle of admirers who were convinced that in these painful stories of girls and women a writer of great potential power had appeared on the Canadian literary horizon. They were not disappointed. Since *Ten Green Bottles*, Audrey Thomas has published eleven more volumes of fiction, five of them short stories and six of them novels (though the difference in form between the two genres so far as she is concerned is not always very evident, and perhaps not even very meaningful). The novels, like those of many natural story-writers, tend to be episodic; clusters of connected incidents in which character is more important than plot, and each incident becomes a kind of revelation to character and reader alike, drawing the latter more closely into the shifting predicament. And the collections of stories, for their part, tend to be linked in mood, so that it often seems that the central character—frequently the narrator as well—is really the same person throughout, sometimes changing names, but never changing her way of perceiving.

Her way of perceiving. . . .Of course. For Audrey Thomas writes mostly about women and always through a woman's eye. She is a feminist but, as she says in her introduction to her most recent

collection, *Goodbye Harold, Good Luck*: "I do not, consciously, think of feminism when I am writing a story." She sees politics and art as uneasy bedfellows, and so in her writings one is never aware of the stridency that enters the voices of so many feminists when they approach matters of gender. Men are not vilified in her fiction; rather one senses a compassion for the conventional masculine stances that are imposed on them and which they are often too weak to sustain.

In her fiction Thomas draws freely on her experience, of New York State where she was brought up, of Africa where she lived for almost two years, of the Levant where she travelled, of the Canadian Pacific coast where she has remained—largely in the Gulf Islands—since returning from Ghana in 1966. Much of her writing is strongly autobiographical, a kind of continuing fictionalized memoir, and she has never denied this. As she said to Eleanor Wachtel in an interview:

Yes, I think everybody writes autobiography. I think everybody writes one story, has one thing that really interests them, and I suppose what really interests me is the relationship between men and women and why we lie to one another.

In her quasi-autobiographical fiction Audrey Thomas has demonstrated how small a territory of incident need be in order for the writer to create a continent of psychological complexity. As we have seen, such categories as novel, novella, and short story are not easy to sustain in discussing Thomas's work, for continuities are always present, within and between books. The stories in her first book, *Ten Green Bottles*, for example, are very closely interrelated; all of them are told by an unhappy female who, whether as a girl or as woman, appears to be the same persona, so that in the end the book takes on in one's mind the character of a series of psychologically linked episodes. More loosely, the later collections also appear as real organic unities in their representation of the pain and sadness in sexual relations, and of the reality of generational links.

Similarly, the two novellas (published in a single volume) "Munchmeyer" and "Prospero on the Island," are not in reality separate works. They are linked by the fact that "Munchmeyer" (itself a kind of mirror work in which it is hard to tell what is meant as plot and what is the novelist-hero's fantasizing) is presented as the novel that has been written by Miranda, the narrator in "Prospero on the Island," and is being discussed by her with "Prospero," an elderly painter friend who lives in retreat on the same British Columbian island. And the novels *Mrs. Blood, Songs My Mother Taught Me, Latakia* and *Intertidal Life*, are in turn constructed within loose frameworks, so that structurally there are considerable resemblances between the groups of interrelated stories and the highly episodic novels.

It soon becomes evident that the structural principle of Thomas's fictions is one in which the psychological patterns take precedence over the aesthetic or self-consciously formal. The experience of their characters, in merely physical terms, is limited and largely repetitive, since it runs fairly closely parallel to Thomas's own life. Yet though the central persona of the *oeuvre* appears to be the same, it seems at times to be treated unchronologically, since a middle-period book, *Songs My Mother Taught Me*, deals, in a rather shapelessly flowing narrative, with childhood recollections that already occur as memories in earlier stories. *Mrs. Blood,*

a harrowing novel which depicts a perilous pregnancy in West Africa, also incorporates the persona's sentimental journeys in England, while in the novella "Prospero on the Island," creation and memory meld together with the persona-now-turned-novelist reflecting on the creative present to which all these pasts contribute.

Throughout Thomas's fictions is the constant fact of suffering, and an acute awareness of the psychological results of suffering—its power to distort our perceptions and our memories. A recurrent situation takes us to the appalling borderland between sanity and madness; on that knife edge of mental anguish appears the terror that haunts all Thomas's fiction. Yet the essential quality of her work does not lie in the nightmare that shadows her psychologically complex characters and loosens their grasp of experience; but rather in the precarious equilibrium—which they achieve so intermittently—between the fear and the joy of existence.

· ———— ·

Works by Audrey Thomas include *Ten Green Bottles* (1967); *Mrs. Blood: A Novel* (1970); *Munchmeyer and Prospero on the Island* (1971); *Songs My Mother Taught Me* (1973); *Blown Figures* (1974); *Ladies and Escorts* (1977); *Latakia: A Novel* (1979); *Real Mothers: Short Stories* (1981); *Intertidal Life* (1984) and *Goodbye Harold, Good Luck* (1986).

Works on Audrey Thomas include Elizabeth Komisar, "Audrey Thomas: A Review/Interview," *Open Letter* 3rd ser. 3.3 (1975): 59–64; "Audrey Thomas Section" *Capilano Review* 7 (1975): 24–113; Robert Diotte, "The Romance of Penelope: Audrey Thomas's Isobel Carpenter Trilogy," *Canadian Literature* 86 (1980): 60–68; and Joan Coldwell, "Memory Organized: The Novels of Audrey Thomas," *Canadian Literature* 92 (1982): 46–56.

GEORGE WOODCOCK

DÉJEUNER SUR L'HERBE

They travelled together as brother and sister and even made a game of it, volunteering this "fact," if it did not somehow come up naturally in conversation; but the truth of the matter was that they were old (and Platonic) friends. Once, years ago, at a time when both of them were still married, they had gone to bed together and ended up laughing. They knew too much about each other, even then, to start a romance. He knew all about her stretch marks and deep depressions; she knew all about the zinc ointment that he used for his haemorrhoids and his not being allowed, at age thirteen, to attend his mother's funeral. There was no mystery. And her husband was his close friend; the bed that they had "gone to bed" in was the large comfortable bed that her husband, who was clever with his hands, had built. Eventually, both marriages broke up, for reasons that had nothing to do with the "going to bed": he left his wife; five years later, her husband left her. There were periods when they saw very little of one another; he moved to a different part of the city, miles away, and he had a series of live-in girlfriends, all much younger than he was (his wife had taken the children and gone back to Halifax, where she was born). Sometimes, when he was a little bit drunk, he would say things like, "When my wife left," and it would make her furious, for he had forced her to leave. She thought that he was a show-off and a hypocrite; and his passion for girls who were at least fifteen years younger than he was, amused and affronted her. He thought that she was a neurotic, judgmental bitch, who treated her husband, his friend, as though he were a cross between her father and the hired hand.

Yet somehow, they always came back together, wrote letters, talked on the telephone, met each other for a meal or a drink. One night, when they were both quite drunk, he told her that he would never desert her and she looked at him and knew that it was true.

Last autumn, after her latest lover left, she called Robert on the telephone long distance (she was teaching in another city at the time) and told him, bravely, that she had started saving money to go to France. He heard what she was really saying, for often she had a child's way of dealing with the world, indirectly, through insinuation. "I don't suppose that you'd be interested in going with me?"

He'd been a bit drunk when she called, having just lived through another unholy row with his girlfriend.

"Bon voyage," he said. "This fish ain't biting."

But a few days later, sitting at the kitchen table, utterly exhausted by yet another scene, he picked up the telephone.

"All right," he said. "You're on. I haven't got a dime, but we'll figure it out."

She went downtown the next day and made airplane reservations for two, bought a Michelin guide and a Berlitz *French for Travellers,* and mailed them off to him.

"Thank you," she wrote. She did not tell him how desperate she had been feeling when the phone rang, how she had been standing in the bathroom, naked, staring at the medicine cabinet and wondering whether or not she should get dressed and go for help. When she was in the bookstore, she looked in the Berlitz book under "doctor".

"I've got a pain here."

"How long have you had this pain?"

She felt like one of those queens in the fairytales, who have to get a certain thing to eat or drink or they will die. Only, what she wanted was love; to be loved. Her latest lover told her that she was "too independent." Her husband told her that she "leaned on him" too much.

"I have had this pain," she told the imaginary doctor, "all my life."

"Ôtez votre pantalon et votre slip, s'il vous plaît."

"Please remove your trousers and your underpants."

Friends sometimes asked her if, really—tell the truth now—weren't she and Robert lovers?

"No," she said, "that would be incest." And she added, "Besides, *I'm* over twenty-five!" But she knew that there was more to it than that.

In spite of the many small economies, standing at the bar rather than sitting at a table if they stopped somewhere to have a drink, treating the ubiquitous *pâtisserie* windows as gorgeous still lifes (all on the general theme of sweetness), rather than as invitations to enter and buy; in spite of the *Résidence Lutèce,* where the morning coffee tasted of chicory, and the *douche* cost extra and was two floors up, Paris was proving to be more expensive than their worst imaginings. So, they always carried their lunch with them when they went out for the day—a *baguette* or two, sausage, a piece of cheese, a tomato, and of course, a bottle of cheap wine (although, even there, the price was no longer *ordinaire*).

They eyed longingly the fruits and vegetables at the *primeur*'s next door: the thick white asparagus with its pale purple tip, the fennel, the aubergines! It would be lovely to have a little flat where they could cook. Next time—if either or both of them ever came back. And they wanted to come back, both of them. They loved Paris; they loved it all! Except for the litter in the streets (but London was like that—and New York and Montréal) and the incredible prices (but there again—London, New York), they found little with which to quarrel. One evening, sitting side by side, in one of the *vedettes* which took sightseers up and down the Seine, watching the slow spread of the sunset, learning the names and histories of the bridges (her favourite was the Pont Neuf; his, the Pont Royal), they confessed to each other that Paris had turned out to be as beautiful and as charming as they had hoped.

"Sometimes," she said, "I build up such high expectations of a place that I am bound to be disappointed when I see it. But Paris *feels* the way I wanted it to. It feels like my dream Paris."

"Did you walk so much or so far in your dream Paris?"

"Maybe not. I suppose that I rode in taxicabs and carriages; but I don't mind the walking, I really don't. Maybe I'll even lose some weight."

"You ought to do that," he said. "Seriously. I can't understand how you could let yourself get so fat. You're really a very attractive woman— or were."

"I don't think that I want to be attractive anymore," she said. "I think that I've had it up to here with being 'attractive'."

"Then do it for your own sake," he said. "You're too young to be so overweight and middle-aged. I worry about you."

"Thanks," she said, and she turned away from him, staring out over the water. She thought, "How cruel he is to me! Why can't he leave me alone?"

He had fallen in love again, between the buying of the tickets and their actual departure, and had admitted on the plane to London that he nearly hadn't come. His new girl had just moved in with him and he was uneasy and distressed at leaving her. This time, it seemed like the real thing. He said that he was surprised at himself, at how much in love he was. "God, I love that woman!" he would say as they walked the streets or chatted over lunch. And she would look at him with her cynical smile and say, "So you keep telling me." Robert's girls never got any older, or rather, the ratio of years between him and them stayed pretty much the same. When she teased him, he told her, quite seriously, that she did not understand "the aesthetics of the flesh."

"I suppose not. I do understand, however, that line in *Beautiful Losers:* 'When I was sixteen, I stopped fucking faces'."

But he confessed, also, while they moved slowly under the bridges, that he really was enjoying the trip, that he was loving it.

They spent a few days in London first, where the time change made them wide awake at 4:30 a.m., and so, they got up and dressed and walked and talked, each morning, the streets almost totally deserted. They took pictures of each other on Westminster Bridge, listening to Big Ben strike 6 a.m. (Yet, when he told the story of their early walks to a distant cousin who had taken them out to dinner, he said, "I knew Marguerite was also awake, because she wasn't snoring." Cruel! He was always cutting her down! When she defended herself in front of the cousin, by pointing out that he snored too, he said, "Oh yes, but it doesn't bother you.")

Everywhere, there were warning signs about unattended parcels:

DON'T TOUCH
DON'T GET INVOLVED

and whom to notify.

There was a picture of Margaret Thatcher in the papers, attending the memorial service for the M.P. who was blown up. In Victoria Station, while she waited in a huge crowd and Robert went off to check that they were in the correct line for the boat train, she suddenly noticed a small case, like a child's suitcase, off to one side. She did not know the right thing to do. Robert was coming towards her; he was so tall that she could see his head above the crowd. Did she call out, "Robert, there's a bomb!" Did she go and stand in front of it? Could she get to a guard before it went off? Then, a mother, dragging a crying child, came along and scooped up the parcel. It was not a bomb at all—of course not. She was so afraid that she thought that she was going to be sick. How could people live with such possibilities? It seemed to her that, all her life, she had been lacking some sort of insulating material that kept other people from feeling things so deeply. Her mouth had already opened for the calling of Robert's name when the woman with the child came hurrying up. The M.P. had survived World War II, only to be blown up when he started his car. She remembered being hit in the back of the head with a snowball when she was young. The snowball had a lump of coal in it and it hurt terribly, even through her toque. And the shock of it, the outrage. Did the M.P. have time to feel that stunned anger before he died?

In spite of the morning walks, and the pubs and plays, she was glad to get out of London. One night, walking in Soho, there had been two young men in thick boots, bashing each other with bits of pipe. And all the sex shops. *Rubber* magazine, the models advertising leather and bondage. At the National Gallery, her handbag was examined; his briefcase. Cruelty and suspicion were everywhere. "Don't Touch. Don't Get Involved."

In conversation with another friend, male, he had once said, several years ago, that no woman could really give you the orgasm that you got from jacking off. She objected.

"If that's all you really want!" she said. "Surely, there's more to it than that? Being held, cuddled; the other body which is always, even when people have been together for years, a mystery." To her surprise, his friend had agreed with her. He had always seemed, to her, even more callous than Robert. She had been very sad that night, missing her husband, and her children who were spending a year with him. Robert phoned and she asked him to come over. He brought his friend, whose name she could not remember, and two bottles of wine. After the first bottle of wine, she asked if they would wash her hair for her—it was very long and thick—and she knelt on a chair at the kitchen sink, while they took turns pouring warm water over her head. Then, they took turns drying her hair with towels and kissed her and went away. Later, the friend—Peter? Paul?—sent her a poem about that night and washing her hair; and she was very touched. But she also remembered how they laughed about some woman that they had both fucked. They liked to go downtown and watch strippers, inviting them back to the table for a drink.

At the *Résidence Lutèce,* the patronne was surprised that they wanted two beds. It was so much more expensive. You could see from her face that she was interested in them and wondered what their history was, if there had been a quarrel. They explained that they were brother and sister on a long-awaited holiday. Ah, how charming—and, of course, they must have two beds! They were on the fifth floor, facing the street, where they could hear the constant sound of the traffic down the rue Monge, and the hee-haw of the ambulances. They had tall windows that opened in, and a small, beautifully-wrought ironwork safety railing. They came in at night, after a leisurely meal and a long walk, and drank and talked, she, in her nightgown; he, in his dressing gown, at the small table by the window. They liked walking the city so much that they hardly ever took the Métro. Robert wore the star-shaped key to their room like a sheriff's badge, sticking out of his jacket pocket, on the way up and down to the desk. But he wore a *béret* and a soft woollen scarf, a present from the new girl, and he looked so continental that it was hard to believe that he was from Canada. He kept the map and the "kitty" and she was content, for the most part, merely to go wherever he suggested. The fights with her last lover had worn her out and she felt as though she were still convalescing from some awful illness. Robert said to her one day that something seemed to have gone out of her, some kind of necessary, absolutely fundamental energy. When she mentioned her lover, he told her to leave it alone, let it go. "I'm an impressionist myself," he said. "I deal with the moment and don't always look for the eternal aspect of things." Later, she saw a sundial in the Jardin des Plantes. It said: "I only count the happy hours." She resolved to do better.

But always, he was there with his little hammer, tapping away at her. "Why don't you lose weight?" "Why are you so bitter?" "Why do you always fall in love with losers?" When she came back from the Ladies Room in the swank restaurant in London, he was telling his cousin the history of his marriages and girlfriends. "Marilyn!" she said. "If he's only got to Marilyn, we might as well forget about the play!" For she had her little hammer too and she wasn't afraid to use it. But he just laughed and said, "You're just jealous because you haven't had as many husbands and boyfriends as I have had wives and girls." "*Jealous,*" she said scornfully. "Jealous!" The cousin looked from one to the other of them with a puzzled smile.

But most of the time, they got on very well. He could always make her laugh, as well as make her cry. One Sunday, they walked to the Place des Vosges. The weather was stormy and the grey sky threatened behind a row of brick houses, pricked out the grey stone. The square was something of a disappointment; the statue of one of the Louis on his horse was poor, and the fountains, non-descript. But they had walked a long way and they decided to have lunch on a bench. It was May 27th, *La*

Fête des Mères, and when a young woman, her blouse unbuttoned, strolled by carrying a bunch of roses in clear cellophane, Robert whispered, "See that? That's a whore taking flowers to her mother." A very sad-looking woman sat two benches over, smoking cigarettes. She smiled at their laughter and called out to them, "Bon appétit!" She probably thought that they were two lovers having a picnic. Because the woman looked so sad, Marguerite almost thought that she should go over and explain the situation. "Voyez, you see, we are only friends travelling as brother and sister. He never touches me."

Robert bought two large macaroons as a special Sunday treat, but as soon as he unwrapped them, a huge flock of pigeons descended on them, pushing for crumbs. One of the pigeons had a horrible growth on its neck, a kind of caul, and Robert, who was squeamish about such things, tried to shoo it away. It kept coming back, however, and they became hysterical with laughter, screaming at the pigeons in French and English, and flapping their arms. When the rain came, they ran for shelter, still laughing, across the square.

"Now," Marguerite thought, "now she will see that we are not real lovers or he would be kissing me in this doorway, licking the sweet crumbs from my lips."

They walked and walked—they bought postcards along the Seine and walked to the bird market, which bothered both of them, because of the cages—to the Tuileries, where the slender metal chairs, made to look like the delicate gilt chairs of far-off salons, had been left in groups which seemed, to them, to tell stories. It was raining that day, too, but very gently. They were the only people in the gardens and they took two of the chairs under a large tree, so that they could eat their lunch.

"That group," she said, "that is a father and mother, very respectable— see how their chairs face the path unflinchingly and directly—and their teenage daughter, who would rather be anywhere else, but who is too well brought-up to say so. See how the one chair is just slightly apart from the others?"

"That group," he said, "is a bunch of tourists, very noisy. They are taking pictures of everything, especially of one another in front of every-thing. I think they are German."

"Why do you think that?"

"I won't tell. Yes, they are German."

"That chair all by itself, under a tree. That is the lady's chair."

"And those two, facing each other. . ."

"The lovers, of course."

In the end, he took a series of photos of the chairs; they really were strangely eloquent. The whole day turned out to be lovely and they felt very close to one another.

"You're beginning to look better," he said and she squeezed his arm. "I wish that you were really my brother," she said, but that wasn't quite what she wished.

"Sartre est vivant!" was scrawled with red paint on a wall.

"Well," he said, "it would be nice to live 'across the park' or whatever it was they did, Sartre and Simone."

"Don't you ever want that?" she said. "Don't you ever want, as your companion, someone who is your intellectual equal?"

"Oh, I get enough of that anyway. And the women that I love aren't stupid, although you may think them so."

"I never said that."

"You don't have to." And she didn't pursue it, because it was such a lovely afternoon and they had been so close. It was as though she had put her hand in her pocket and felt her little hammer, and then, taken her hand away. For he had called them stupid himself, some of them anyway, the early ones, the ones just after his first wife, whom he had also called stupid. "You stupid cow!" Shouting at her, out on the front lawn, with his children standing together and watching it all, not really understanding, or maybe not even hearing the actual words, just the tone of contempt. Later, when her husband said such terrible things to her that she thought that she could never get over them, never walk down a street on a May afternoon and feel even a quiet sort of happiness, Robert said to her, as comfort, that she had to understand that there was something called "the exaggeration of desperation," and the things said were all part of that. And she and Robert did it to one another, sometimes said terrible things. Was that the same though? If so, what were *they* desperate about? Each could leave; was free to leave at any time. It wasn't the same thing; it couldn't be.

As they came out of the Jeu de Paume, he said, "My God, we've seen a lot of painted flesh in the past few days!" So, as an antidote, they went and laughed at Napoleon's stuffed dog and looked at case after case of dress-up clothes that Frenchmen had worn for killing, the "officers and gentlemen." At what point did man begin to kill his fellow man? Was it over a bone, a cave, a woman? It began back in the water, perhaps, and was carried forward onto land. "Mine, it's mine, it's mine." And the women accepting it, or at least pretending to, even urging the men on. Napoleon's dog did not know that Napoleon was emperor, but he would have known who was master. In the end, they were sickened by all the uniforms and firearms, and hurried out into the sunshine. Her ex-lover had written to her that it had been a "battle" between them, and then added, "No, a war! *La lutte continue.*" Because he had been younger than she was, she thought that things would be easier, that there could be an equality between them, a "mutuality," but it had not worked out.

When a pretty French girl went by, Robert said, "Oh God, I'd like to fuck that one!"

"You'd like to go home and say you'd fucked a French girl?"

"Well, why not? What's wrong with that? It would be like drinking at their well."

(And everywhere there were the statues—"Mort pour la France"—as though it were the feminine that was, *au fond,* responsible for all the conquests, the cannonballs, the screams, the fountains of blood.)

At the restaurant, last night, there had been a stupid Englishman, in a party of six, who had asked to see their *sentier* map. She had it spread out on the table, as they were planning a walking tour in the valley of the Loire. In minuscule letters, above the French word for "beacon" on the map, she had written the word "markers." The Englishman was drunk. "What is this in your country?" he said. "What are snackers? Something sexy?"

"Such a stupid man," she said afterwards. "Such a stupid, stupid man."

Robert disagreed. "We can't be judgmental. That poor man had been cast as the life of the party."

"Do we have to play out roles that other people impose on us?"

"It's easier."

"Do you think women impose rules on men?"

"That's more complicated. Certain agreements are reached, especially in marriage; certain contracts are made."

(He had come in one night, years ago, after his marriage broke up, but hers was still intact. He had been to see a movie of *The Picture of Dorian Gray.* It had affected him in a curious way, as though he had only, just then, in the darkened movie theatre, become aware of his own mortality. "I want to fly!" he cried to them. And then, laughing at himself, "Before my feathers fall off!" A year later, he married a girl who was nineteen. His role, from then on, was always one of provider or protector, at least insofar as his wives, or the various women with whom he lived, were concerned. Yet, in the end, there would be fights and rebellions and pettiness and he would find somebody new.)

"Even the excitement of a new body in the bed," he told her once, "the aesthetics of the flesh." The women who did not love him hated him. It was about fifty-fifty each way. He brought his new girls to her for her approval—or disapproval, which amused him more—and often, months later, the girls would sit on her couch and sob. She never knew what to say.

In the phrase book:

I'm ill.
I'm lost.
I've lost my _____.
Keep your hands to yourself.
Leave me alone.
Lie down.
Listen to me.
Stop or I'll scream.

He had a way of making friends with anyone, anywhere. It came from a certain arrogance, a belief that he was always right. On their way back from the Place des Vosges, he stopped at a stall and bought flowers for Madame la Patronne of their pension. She had discovered their washing hanging over the bidet and the wash basin.

"Je vous en prie!" her note began. "Je vous en prie! Il est interdit. . ."

He gave her the flowers and told her, in his terrible accent, that she was the loveliest flower of all. She laughed and told him that he was foolish, but there were no more notes about the washing.

He came into her room at the hospital, the day after her third child was born. She was sharing with a young Italian girl and the whole family had been visiting. He stood in the doorway, laughing, carrying an enormous bunch of white and yellow daisies. "Well," he said, "have they found out who the father is yet?" He had the nurses scurrying for vases, and soon knew where the Italian family lived, shared the joy of their first grandson, etc. He seemed to know always just the right thing to do, as well as just how much he could get away with. But he had a dark side, too. ("You stupid cow." The young women sobbing on her couch.)

"Does it bother you," she said to him one night, as they sat in front of the high windows in their night clothes, drinking wine and looking down at the street, "Does it bother you that I've just been trailing along after you, letting you study the map, make all the decisions, just like the sort of woman that I've always despised? Following you around like a faithful dog?"

"No," he said, "that doesn't bother me. You're a good companion. What bothers me is that something seems to have died in you."

"What?" she said desperately. "What has died?"

"Oh, I don't know. Some self-love. Some necessary self-respect. You seem so old to me. You seem to have collapsed all of a sudden, to have stopped trying. You've let yourself go."

"And you?" she said. "What about *you*? What have you done with your life?"

"I'm happy," he said. "I enjoy my life."

"How can you? How *can* you?"

Later, she watched him as he walked to the corner to try and phone home. She pretended to be asleep when he came back, but he ignored her pretence.

"I did it! Only for a minute, but I could hear her as though she were next door."

She kept her eyes shut.

"Would it bother you," he said, "if I sat at the table and smoked my pipe for a while? I want to jot down a few things."

"No," she said, "it wouldn't bother me at all." And she turned on her side, away from him, where he was sitting at the window. She heard him open another bottle of wine and light his pipe.

"Oh God!" he said. "Oh God, I love that woman!"

And then, softly, "Marguerite, do you think I'm too hard on you?"

but she didn't answer. She felt like an unattended parcel, ticking away in the corner of the room. If he touched her in any way, she would explode.

On their last day in Paris, they decided to visit Montmartre and Sacré Coeur. The *Blue Guide* warned them not to; it put down the basilica as "only too visible from almost every part of Paris" and lamented the fact that hardly anything remained of old Montmartre. They wanted to go anyway, climb the steps and look out over the city. But they were late getting started and it was nearly noon by the time they got off the bus. They had planned to spend an hour just mooching around the streets before going up to Sacré Coeur itself.

"I think that we should eat first," Robert said. "We're still a long ways away." It was getting hot as well and they both thought that they could do with a drink.

"Are there any parks around?" she asked. "Let's make it someplace nice for our last *déjeuner* in Paris."

He looked at the map. "What about the cemetery?"

They were standing in the middle of a bridge and they could see the cemetery, or part of it, below them. There were trees and paths; it might be pleasant.

"It's probably illegal, as well as a mortal sin," she said, "to picnic in a cemetery. We might get arrested and get our pictures in the paper: 'FOREIGN PIGS SHOW NO RESPECT FOR WAR DEAD'."

"I think that most of the war dead are somewhere else." He was looking in the *Guide*. "There seem to be a lot of famous people buried here."

She hesitated.

"Oh, come on," he said. "We're hungry and thirsty and we have a chance to picnic with Degas and Nijinsky. I'll take your photograph."

But once they got over the bridge, they could not find a way in. A wall seemed to run around the cemetery for miles, and they began to wonder if there was any public access at all. The sun was hot on their necks when they turned a corner onto a narrow street which reeked of dog shit. They had to be careful where they stepped.

"Christ," he said, "do you think all the dogs come here for the bones?"

And still the high brick wall was on their left side—and no entrance. A woman came walking along behind them, and then, in front, pulling a small boy by the arm.

"Rue Merde," she sniffed. "Rue Merde" and she warned the boy to watch where he was stepping. Robert and Marguerite began to laugh.

"Shall we give it up?" he asked. "I'm starving."

"Oh, we can't give up now, it's all too funny."

So, they went back to the bridge and started again, and this time, they found the entrance.

The cemetery was like a small town of narrow houses, with steep roofs. Most of the paths had names, like streets, and it was all very peaceful.

They sat side by side on a stone bench and began their lunch, although, for propriety's sake, they kept the wine bottle in the carry-all.

"I feel as though we ought to pour a libation." he said. He looked at the *Guide* again and raised his glass. "Salut, vous fantômes vénérables!"

"It is impossible for me to believe," she said, "that it's all just snuffed out, at the end, like a candle."

"Yes, and that Yorick's skull probably looked just like Stendhal's, that Nijinsky's thigh bone could just be something for a dog to chew on."

He drank some more wine and then he took her hand. The gesture was so strange and intimate, coming from him, that she was terrified.

"Well," he said, "what on earth are we going to do about you?"

A woman in a flowered dress came up the path. She was carrying a kitten and talking to it, or to herself, it was hard to tell. She did not so much as glance at them as she passed by, and yet Marguerite withdrew her hand.

"I'll be all right." She leaned over to pour some more wine from the carry-all. "I'm just feeling unloved right now. It will pass. I'm enjoying this trip though. Thank you for coming with me."

He looked at her and shook his head. She laughed. "Oh, we'll probably ride off into the sunset together some day." And she laughed again. "On separate horses, of course. Like our *chambre avec deux lits*. Do you think that we could be buried that way, in the same grave, but in twin coffins, or in one of these mausoleums, side by side, in drawers?"

They began to take pictures, tipsy on the wine and the heat and the sense that they were doing something rather shocking. He posed on a large black gravestone, smoking his pipe; she leant against the iron grille of a mausoleum. He even went so far as to kiss a pretty angel. She took his picture while he kissed the angel and put his hand on her marble thigh.

"Watch out!" she said. "What if she wakes up?"

"What if I turn to stone instead?"

It was a strange game that they were playing, there in the cemetery, while the pigeons fluttered around the stone bench where they had eaten their lunch. "I love you," she wanted to say to him. "How can I love you so much and hate you so much all at the same time?"

They did not notice the woman coming back along the path, still muttering, until she stopped in front of Robert, who had been absorbed in arranging Marguerite beside a wreath of artificial poppies. She said something unintelligible, then held out her hands to him, then went on.

Robert and Marguerite looked at one another.

"Where's the kitten?" she said. "Robert, where's the little kitten?"

"There's nothing that we can do," he said.

"But her hands were covered with dirt! We've got to do something. Suppose that it's still alive?"

"I think that's what she was trying to tell me," he said.

"What?"

"That the kitten was sick. That she killed it."

"Are you *sure*?"

"No, I'm not sure. But there really is nothing that we can do."

"Don't Touch!" Marguerite shouted at him. "Don't Get Involved!" He looked bewildered.

"What the hell are you talking about?"

But she was already running down the path. "I'm going to find that kitten. You made it up, about what the woman said!"

He grabbed the carry-all and camera and started after her. It would be easy to get lost in here. He was really angry with her now.

"And what if you do?" he called after her. "What then?"

[1981]

· JOHN METCALF ·

1938–

Born in Carlisle, England, in 1938, the son of a Methodist minister, John Metcalf grew up surrounded by a large library of theological works and English literature. He graduated from the University of Bristol in 1961 and came to Canada in 1962. Before devoting himself full time to writing, he taught high school and college, and has been writer-in-residence at the University of New Brunswick, the University of Ottawa, Loyola and Concordia University in Montreal, and also the University of Bologna. In addition to writing seven books of fiction and essays, Metcalf has edited over twenty anthologies of short stories and maintains a lively interest in the genre's enrichment by editing (with Leon Rooke) the annual *New Press Anthology: Best Canadian Short Fiction.* For his own fiction he has received the President's Medal of the University of Western Ontario, *Canadian Fiction Magazine*'s Contributor's Prize, and the Periodical Distributors' Association Prize. He lives in Ottawa.

Increasingly, Metcalf's fiction and essays have tended toward a wry and self-deprecating sense of the individual—especially the artist—uncomfortably resident in an ersatz culture. It is a debased culture he portrays; both in his first novel, *Going Down Slow* (1972), a deeply ironic view of a young English immigrant teaching at a high school in Montreal; as well as in his second novel, *General Ludd* (1980), concerning an iconoclastic poet-in-residence at a Canadian university.

Never forgetting the important role of little magazines and discerning editors, Metcalf has fashioned his career around the belief that most writers are engaged in a protracted struggle against isolation, neglect, and small sales—and must therefore be encouraged by older writers who share more or less the same

ordeal. A tireless anthologizer, he has sought at the same time (and with increasing effect) to create a critical climate for his own writing. Among Metcalf's first principles is a strong insistence upon the word as an embodiment of the concrete world. He has said, commenting upon inattentive reading of his stories: "it's out of giving yourself totally to the evoked *thing* that meanings and significances arise. Some of my stories, though concrete, are very mysterious. 'Keys and Watercress' is a good example. That seems to me a persuasively *real* story and real because of its wealth of detail. . . . Symbols *have* no life. Words and the way they're marshalled have life."

John Metcalf's reputation as a stylist derives especially from the weight and texture of his shorter fiction, since the short story and novella are forms he has found particularly conducive to his painstaking methods of composition. "The Lady Who Sold Furniture," "Private Parts: A Memoir," and "Girl in Gingham," are all wonderful examples of the subtle interweaving of process and theme, risk-taking and equilibrium—worked out at novella length. Self-conscious, particular, comic, and elegiac; the tone of Metcalf's fiction is unmistakable. His inflections, he is perhaps more willing than other writers to admit, are the product of his tinkerings.

It was at Metcalf's suggestion that Montreal Story Tellers came into existence in the early seventies, a group of public readers who included Clark Blaise, Hugh Hood, Ray Smith, Ray Fraser, and Metcalf himself. As a boy, he was used to hearing two of his father's sermons every Sunday, and became attuned to links between conversational and literary styles. Metcalf claims that as a result his sense of rhetorical structures developed early. So must a sense of evangelism. His latest novella, "Travelling Northward," again develops the theme of literary culture, and, among other trials along the way, examines the dubious benefit to a steadfast author of reading from his work in a northern Ontario town. The compass direction of the title is as much metaphorical as it is geographical.

. ———— .

Metcalf's works include *The Lady Who Sold Furniture* (1970); *Going Down Slow* (1972); *The Teeth of My Father* (1975); *Girl in Gingham* (1978); *General Ludd* (1980); *Selected Stories* (1982); *Kicking Against the Pricks* (1982); and *Adult Entertainment* (1986).

Works on Metcalf include Barry Cameron, "Invention in *Girl in Gingham*," *Fiddlehead* 114 (1977): 120–29; and "An Approximation of Poetry: The Short Stories of John Metcalf," *Studies in Canadian Literature* 2 (1977): 17–35; Robert Lecker, "John Metcalf: Unburdening the Mystery," *On the Line* (1982): 59–97; Geoff Hancock, "Communiqué: Interview with John Metcalf—February 16, 1981," *Kicking Against the Pricks* (1982): 1–28; a special issue of *Malahat Review* 70 (1985); Doug Rollins, "John Metcalf," *Canadian Writers and Their Works*, ed. Robert Lecker, Jack David, and Ellen Quigley (1985), Fiction Series 7: 155–211; and Barry Cameron, *John Metcalf* (1986).

LOUISE VANIER -GAGNON

KEYS AND WATERCRESS

David, with great concentration, worked the tip of his thumbnail under the fat scab on his knee. He carefully lifted the edges of the scab enjoying the tingling sensation as it tore free. His rod was propped against his other leg and he could just see the red blur of his float from the corner of his eye. He started to probe the centre of the crust.

"Had any luck?" a voice behind him said suddenly.

Startled, his thumbnail jumped, ripping the scab away. A bright bead of blood welled into the pit. The sun, breaking from behind the clouds, swept the meadow into a brighter green and made the bead of blood glisten like the bezel of a ring.

"Had any luck?" the old man said again. David twisted round to look at him. He wasn't in uniform and he wasn't wearing a badge and anyway he was far too old to be a bailiff. Unless he was a Club Member—and they could report you, too. And break your fishing rod.

David glanced down the river towards the bridge and the forbidding white sign. "I'm only fishing for eels," he said. "With a seahook."

"Slippery fellows, eels," said the old man. "Difficult to catch."

"I haven't caught any yet," said David, hoping the old man wouldn't notice the grey eel-slime on the bank and the smeared fishing-bag.

The old man started to sit down. Wheezing harshly with the effort, he lowered himself until he was kneeling, and then, supporting himself on his hands, laboriously stretched out each leg like a dying insect in a jam jar. His anguished breathing eased slowly away into a throaty mutter. David felt more confident because he knew he could run nearly to the bridge by the time the old man had struggled to his feet.

Taking a blue silk handkerchief from the top pocket of his linen jacket, the old man dabbed at his forehead. "My word, yes!" he said. "Extremely slippery fellows." He took off his straw hat and rubbed his bald head with the blue handkerchief.

"They're a nuisance," said David. "The Club Members don't like catching them."

"And why is that?"

"Because they swallow the hook right down and you can't get it out," said David.

"You've hurt your knee," said the old man. The bead of blood had grown too large and toppled over, trickling down his knee to run into the top of his stocking.

"Oh, that's nothing," said David. "Only a scab."

"Yes," said the old man reflectively, "it's a pleasant day. A beautiful sky—beautiful afternoon clouds."

They sat silently staring across the flow of the river. Near the far bank in the shallows under the elderberry bushes the huge roach and chub basked in the sunshine, rising every now and then to nose soft circles in the water.

"Do you know the name of clouds like those?" asked the old man suddenly. "The *proper* name, I mean."

"No," said David.

"Well, the correct name is cumulus. Cumulus. You say it yourself."

"Cumulus," said David.

"Good! You won't forget, will you? Promise me you won't forget." There was a silence while the old man put on his spectacles from a tin case. Then, taking a fountain pen and a small black book from his inside pocket, he said, "But boys forget things. It's no use denying it—boys forget. So I'm going to write it down." He tore a page from the notebook and printed on it: Cumulus (clouds).

As David tucked the paper into his shirt-pocket, he looked across at the old man who was staring into the water, a vague and absent look in his eyes. David watched him for a moment and then turned back to his float, watching the current break and flow past it in a constant flurry. He tried to follow the invisible nylon line down into the depths where it ended in a ledger-weight and a turning, twisting worm.

"Every evening," said the old man, speaking slowly and more to himself than David, "when the light begins to fail, the cattle come down here to drink. Just as the night closes in."

"They've trampled the bank down further up-stream," said David.

"And I watch them coming across the fields," said the old man as though he hadn't heard. "I see them from my window."

The old man's voice died away into silence but suddenly, without warning, he belched loudly—long, rumbling, unforced belches of which he seemed quite unaware. David looked away. To cover his embarrassment, he started reeling in his line to check the bait and the clack of the ratchet seemed to arouse the old man. He groped inside his jacket and pulled out a large flat watch. With a click the lid sprang open. "Have you ever seen such a watch before?" he asked. "Such a beautiful watch?" He held it out on the palm of his hand.

"Do you know what watches like these are called?"

"No," said David. "I've never seen one before."

"They're called Hunters. And numbers like these are called roman numerals."

As the old man counted off the numbers on the watch-face, David stared at the old man's hand. The mottled flesh was puffy and gorged with fat blue veins which stood beneath the skin. He tried to take the watch without touching the hand which held it.

"What time does the watch say?" asked the old man.

"Half-past four," said David.

"Well, then, it's time we had our tea," said the old man. "And you shall come and have tea with me."

"Thank you," said David, "but I've got to go home."

"But tea's prepared," said the old man, and as he spoke he started to struggle to his feet. "Tea's prepared. In the house across the bridge— in the house with the big garden."

"But I really have to go," said David. "My mother'll be angry if I'm late."

"Nonsense!" said the old man loudly. "Quite untrue."

"Really. I do have to. . . ."

"We won't be long," said the old man. "You like my watch, don't you? You *do* like my watch."

"Oh, yes."

"Well, there you are then. What more proof do you need? *And*," said the old man, "I have many treasures in my house." He stared at David angrily. "You would be a rude boy to refuse."

"Well. . ." said David. "I really mustn't be long."

"Do you go to school?" the old man asked suddenly.

"Parkview Junior," said David.

"Yes," said the old man. "I went to school when I was a boy."

As David was sliding the rod-sections into the cloth case, the old man gripped his arm and said, "You may keep the watch in your pocket until we reach the bridge. Or you could hold it in your hand. Whichever you like." Then stopping David again he said, "And such a watch is called a. . .?"

"A Hunter," said David.

The old man relaxed his hold on David's arm and said, "Excellent! Quite excellent! Always be attentive. Always accumulate *facts*." He seemed very pleased and as they walked slowly along the river-path towards the bridge made little chuckling sounds inside his throat.

His breath labouring again after the incline from the bridge, the old man rested for a few moments with his hand on the garden gate. Then, pushing the gate open, he said, "Come along, boy. Come along. Raspberry canes everywhere, just as I told you."

David followed the old man along the path and into the cool hall. His eyes were bewildered at first after the strong sunlight, and he stumbled against the dark shape of the hall-stand.

"Just leave your things here," said the old man, "and we'll go straight in to tea."

David dropped his fishing-bag behind the door and stood his rod in the umbrella-stand. The old man went ahead down the passage and ushered him into the sitting room.

The room was long and, in spite of the French windows at the far end, rather dark. It was stuffy and smelled like his grandma.

In the centre of the room stood a table covered with green baize, but tea was laid out on a small cardtable at the far end of the room in front of the French windows.

Bookshelves lined the walls and books ran from ceiling to floor. The floor, too, was covered with piles of books and papers; old books with leather covers, musty and smelling of damp and dust, and perilous stacks of yellow *National Geographic* magazines.

A vast mirror, the biggest he'd ever seen, bigger even than the one in the barber's, stood above the fireplace, carved and golden with golden statues on each side.

David stared and stared about him, but his eyes kept returning to the lion which stood in front of the fireplace.

"Do you like it?" asked the old man. "It's stuffed."

"Oh, yes!" exclaimed David. "Can I touch it?"

"I've often wondered," said the old man, "if it's in good taste."

"Where did it come from?"

"Oh, Africa. Undoubtedly Africa. They all do, you know."

"I think it's terrific," said David.

"You may stay here, then, and I will go and put the kettle on," said the old man. As soon as the door had closed, David went and stuck his hand into the lion's snarling mouth and stroked the dusty orbs of its eyes with his fingertips. When he heard the old man's footsteps shuffling back down the passage, he moved away from the lion and pretended to be looking at a book.

"Do you take sugar?" asked the old man as they sat down at the cardtable in front of the French windows.

"No thank you," said David. "Just milk."

"No? Most interesting! *Most* interesting. In my experience, boys like sweet things. A deplorable taste, of course. Youth and inexperience."

He passed the teacup across the table and said sternly, "The palate must be educated." David didn't know what to say and because the old man was staring at him looked away and moved the teaspoon in his saucer. Putting down the silver teapot, the old man wrote in his notebook: The love of sweetness is an uneducated love. Handing the note across the table he said, "Facts, eh? *Facts.*" He chuckled again inside his throat.

"And now," he continued—but then broke off again as he saw David staring out of the window into the orchard. "If you're quite ready? We have brown bread. Wholemeal. Thin-cut. And with Cornish butter." He ticked off each point on his fingers. "To be eaten with fresh watercress. Do you think that will please you?"

"Very nice, thank you," said David politely.

"But it's not simply a matter of *taste*, you see," said the old man fixing David with his eye. He shook his head slowly.

"Not simple at all."

"What isn't?" asked David.

"Not at all simple. Taste, yes, I grant you," said the old man, "but what about texture? Umm? Umm? What about vision?"

"What isn't simple?" David asked again.

The old man clicked his tongue in annoyance and said, "Come along, boy!" He glared across the table. "Your attention is lax. Always be attentive." He leaned across the cardtable and held up his finger. "Observe!" he said. "Observe the tablecloth. Cotton? Dear me, no! Irish linen. And *this*." His fingertips rubbed slowly over the facets of the bowl. "Waterford glass—brilliant. Can you see the colours? The green of the cress and the drops of water like diamonds? Brilliant. A question of the lead-content, you see. You *do* see, don't you. You do understand what I'm telling you."

"Well. . .please," said David, "what's a texture?"

And once again the old man took out his notebook and his fountain pen.

When tea was finished, the old man wiped his lips with a linen napkin and said eagerly, "Well? Do you think you're ready? Shall you see them?"

"Please," said David, "I'd like to very much."

The old man pulled on the thick, tasselled rope which hung by the side of the window and slowly closed the red velvet curtains. "We don't want to be overlooked," he whispered.

"But there's no one there," said David. The old man was excitedly brushing the green baize and didn't seem to hear. With the red curtains closed, the room smelled even more stuffy, hot and stifling, as if the air itself were thick and red. And in the warm gloom the lion lost its colour and turned into a dark shape, a pinpoint of light glinting off its dusty eye. As David crossed over to the table he saw himself moving in the mysterious depths of the mirror.

"Come along, boy!" said the old man impatiently. "We'll start with the yellow box. There. Under the table."

The old man lifted the lid of the box and took out three small leather sacks. They were like the pictures in pirate books and as he laid them on the baize they chinked and jangled. Slowly, while David watched, very slowly, the old fingers trembled at the knots, and then suddenly the old man tipped the first sack spreading keys across the tabletop.

There were hundreds of keys; long rusted keys, flat keys, keys with little round numbers tied to them, keys bunched together on rings, here and there sparkling new Yale keys, keys to fit clocks, and keys for clock-work toys. The old man's fingers played greedily among them, spreading them, separating large and small.

"Well?" he said, looking up suddenly.

"I've never seen so many," said David.

"Few people have," said the old man. "Few people have." His eyes turned back to the table, and he moved one or two of the keys as though they were not in their proper place. And then, as if remembering his manners, he said, "You may touch them. I don't mind if you do."

David picked up a few keys and looked at them. His hands became red with rust, and he dropped the keys back on the table, stirring them about idly with his fingertip.

"Not like that!" snapped the old man suddenly. "Do it properly! You have to heap them up and scatter them. If you're going to do it do it properly."

He pulled at the strings on the other bag and cascaded a stream of keys onto the table. The air swam with red rust. David sneezed loudly and the old man said, "Pay attention!"

He raked the keys together into a large heap and burrowed his hands deep into them. When they were quite buried, he stopped, his eyes gleaming with a tense excitement. His breathing was loud and shallow. He looked up at David, and his eyes widened. "Now!" he shouted, and heaved his hands into the air.

Keys rained and rattled about the room, clicking against the mirror, breaking a cup on the cardtable, slapping against the leather-covered books, and falling loudly on the floor-boards. A small key hit David on the forehead. The old man remained bent across the table as if the excitement had exhausted him. The silence deepened.

Suddenly, a key which had landed on the edge of the mantelpiece overbalanced and fell, rattling loudly on the tiles of the hearth. Still the old man did not move. David shifted his weight restlessly and said into the silence, "I think I'll have to be getting home now. My mother's expecting me."

The old man gave no sign that he had heard. David said again, "I'll have to be going now." His voice sounded flat and awkward in the silent room.

The old man pushed himself up from the table. Deep lines of irritation scored the side of his mouth. David began to blush under the fierceness of the old man's eyes. "I can't quite make up my mind about you," the old man said slowly. He did not take his eyes from David's face.

"Sometimes I think you're a polite boy and sometimes I think you're a rude boy," He paused. "It's unsettling." David looked down and fiddled with one of the buttons on his shirt.

"Lift up another box of keys," said the old man suddenly.

"But I have to go home," said David.

"Quite untrue," said the old man.

"Really I do."

"A lie!" shouted the old man. "You are lying. You are telling lies!" He pounded on the table with his fist so that the keys jumped. "I will not tolerate the telling of lies!"

"Please," said David, "can I open the curtains?"

"I'm beginning to suspect," said the old man slowly, "that you don't really like my keys. I'm beginning to think that I was mistaken in you."

"Please. Honest. I have to," said David, his voice high and tight with fear of the old man's anger.

"Very well," said the old man curtly. "But you are a rude boy with very little appreciation. I want you to know that." Reaching inside his jacket, leaving brown rust marks on the lapel, he took out his notebook and wrote in it. He passed the piece of paper across the table. David read: You have very little appreciation.

The old man turned away, presenting his silent and offended back. David didn't know what to do. Hesitantly he said, "I do like the keys. Really I do. And the lion. And thank you for the tea."

"So you're going now, are you?" asked the old man without turning around.

"Well, I have to," said David.

"It's a great pity because I don't show it to many people," said the old man.

"Show what?"

"It would only take a moment," said the old man turning round, "but you're in too much of a hurry."

"What is it?"

"Can you really spare me two minutes? Could you bear to stay with me that long?" Suddenly he chuckled. "Of *course* you want to," he said, "Go and sit on the settee over there and I'll bring it to you."

"Can I open the curtains now?" asked David. "I don't. . .I mean, it's hot with them closed."

"Don't touch them! No. You mustn't!" said the old man. He was struggling to take something from one of the bookshelves. He came and stood over David and then stooped so that David could see the black leather case in his hands. It was so stuffy in the room that it was difficult to breathe properly, and when the old man was so close to him David became aware of a strong smell of urine. He tried to move away.

Almost reverently, the old man opened the leather case. Lying on the red silk lining was a small grey ball. They looked at it in silence.

"There!" breathed the old man. "Do you know what it is?"

"No," said David.

"Go on! Go on!" urged the old man.

"I don't know," said David.

"Try."

"A marble?"

"A marble!" shouted the old man. "Why would I keep a marble in a leather case! Of course it isn't a marble! That's one of the most stupid remarks I've ever heard."

"I'm sorry," said David, frightened again by the anger in the old man's glaring face.

"You're an extremely silly boy. A brainless boy. A stupid boy." He slammed shut the leather case. "Stupid! Silly!" shouted the old man.

"I want to go home now," said David, beginning to get up from the settee. The old man pushed him back. "A marble!" he muttered.

"Please. . ." said David.

"It's a bullet!" shouted the old man. "A rifle bullet."

"I didn't know," said David. He tried to get up again, but he was hemmed in by an occasional table and the crowding presence of the old man. The dim light in the room seemed to be failing into darkness. David's throat was dry and aching.

"This bullet," said the old man, "was cut out of my leg in 1899. December 1899. Next I suppose you'll tell me that you've never heard of the Boer War!"

David said nothing, and the old man's black shape loomed over him.

"*Have* you heard of the Boer War?"

David began to cry.

"*Have* you?"

"I want to go home," said David in a small and uncertain voice.

"Quite untrue," said the old man. "I will not tolerate liars. You told me you went to school, and yet you claim not to have heard of the Boer War." He gripped David by the shoulder. "Why? Why are you lying to me?"

"Please," said David, "I'm not telling lies. Please let me go."

"Oh, very well," said the old man. "Maybe you aren't. But stop crying. It irritates me. Here. You may touch the bullet." He opened and held out the leather case.

"There's no need to cry."

"I want to go home," snuffled David.

"I know!" said the old man. "I know what you'd like. I'll show you my leg. The bullet smashed the bone, you know. You *would* like that, wouldn't you?"

"No," said David.

"Of course you would."

The old man moved even nearer to the settee, and leaning forward over David, lifting with his hands, slowly raised his leg until his foot was resting on the cushion. The harsh wheezing of his breath seemed to fill the silent room. The smell of stale urine was strong on the still air. Slowly he began to tug at his trouser-leg, inching it upwards. The calf of his leg was white and hairless. The flesh sank deep, seamed and puckered, shiny, livid white and purple, towards a central pit.

"If you press hard," said the old man, "it sinks right in."

David shrank further away from the white leg. The old man reached down and grasped David's hand. "Give me your finger," he said.

David tore his hand free and, kicking over the coffee table, rolled off the settee. At first, in his panic, he wrenched the doorknob the wrong way. As he ran out of the darkened room, he heard the old man saying, "I've tried to teach you. I've tried to teach you. But you have *no appreciation.*"

[1970]

· MARGARET ATWOOD ·

1939–

Note: A biography of Margaret Atwood appears in the poetry section.

THE SIN EATER

This is Joseph, in maroon leather bedroom slippers, flattened at the heels, scuffed at the toes, wearing also a seedy cardigan of muddy off-yellow that reeks of bargain basements, sucking at his pipe, his hair greying and stringy, his articulation as beautiful and precise and English as ever:

"In Wales," he says, "mostly in the rural areas, there was a personage known as the Sin Eater. When someone was dying the Sin Eater would be sent for. The people of the house would prepare a meal and place it on the coffin. They would have the coffin all ready, of course: once they'd decided you were going off, you had scarcely any choice in the matter. According to other versions, the meal would be placed on the dead person's body, which must have made for some sloppy eating, one would have thought. In any case the Sin Eater would devour this meal and would also be given a sum of money. It was believed that all the sins the dying person had accumulated during his lifetime would be removed from him and transmitted to the Sin Eater. The Sin Eater thus became absolutely bloated with other people's sins. She'd accumulate such a heavy load of them that nobody wanted to have anything to do with her; a kind of syphilitic of the soul, you might say. They'd even avoid speaking to her, except of course when it was time to summon her to another meal."

"Her?" I say.

Joseph smiles, that lopsided grin that shows the teeth in one side of his mouth, the side not engaged with the stem of his pipe. An ironic grin, wolfish, picking up on what? What have I given away this time?

"I think of them as old women," he says, "though there's no reason why they shouldn't have been men, I suppose. They could be anything as long as they were willing to eat the sins. Destitute old creatures who had no other way of keeping body and soul together, wouldn't you think? A sort of geriatric spiritual whoring."

He gazes at me, grinning away, and I remember certain stories I've heard about him, him and women. He's had three wives, to begin with. Nothing with me though, ever, though he does try to help me on with my coat a bit too lingeringly. Why should I worry? It's not as though I'm susceptible. Besides which he's at least sixty, and the cardigan is truly gross, as my sons would say.

"It was bad luck to kill one of them, though," he says, "and there must have been other perks. In point of fact I think Sin Eating has a lot to be said for it."

Joseph's not one of the kind who'll wait in sensitive, indulgent silence when you've frozen on him or run out of things to say. If you won't talk to him, he'll bloody well talk to you, about the most boring things he can think of, usually. I've heard all about his flower beds and his three wives and how to raise calla lilies in your cellar; I've heard all about the cellar, too, I could give guided tours. He says he thinks it's healthy for his patients—he won't call them "clients," no pussyfooting around, with Joseph—to know he's a human being too, and God do we know it. He'll drone on and on until you figure out that you aren't paying him so you can listen to him talk about his house plants, you're paying him so he can listen to you talk about yours.

Sometimes, though, he's really telling you something. I pick up my coffee cup, wondering whether this is one of those occasions.

"Okay," I say, "I'll bite. Why?"

"It's obvious," he says, lighting his pipe again, spewing out fumes, "First, the patients have to wait until they're dying. A true life crisis, no fakery and invention. They aren't permitted to bother you until then, until they can demonstrate that they're serious, you might say. Second, somebody gets a good square meal out of it." He laughs ruefully. We both know that half his patients don't bother to pay him, not even the money the government pays them. Joseph has a habit of taking on people nobody else will touch with a barge pole, not because they're too sick but because they're too poor. Mothers on welfare and so on; bad credit risks, like Joseph himself. He once got fired from a loony bin for trying to institute worker control.

"And think of the time saving," he goes on. "A couple of hours per patient, sum total, as opposed to twice a week for years and years, with the same result in the end."

"That's pretty cynical," I say disapprovingly. I'm supposed to be the cynical one, but maybe he's outflanking me, to force me to give up this corner. Cynicism is a defence, according to Joseph.

"You wouldn't even have to listen to them," he says. "Not a blessed word. The sins are transmitted in the food."

Suddenly he looks sad and tired.

"You're telling me I'm wasting your time?" I say.

"Not mine, my dear," he says, "I've got all the time in the world."

I interpret this as condenscension, the one thing above all that I can't stand. I don't throw my coffee cup at him, however. I'm not as angry as I would have been once.

We've spent a lot of time on it, this anger of mine. It was only because I found reality so unsatisfactory; that was my story. So unfinished, so sloppy, so pointless, so endless. I wanted things to make sense.

I thought Joseph would try to convince me that reality was actually fine and dandy and then try to adjust me to it, but he didn't do that. Instead he agreed with me, cheerfully and at once. Life in most ways was a big pile of shit, he said. That was axiomatic. "Think of it as a desert island," he said. "You're stuck on it, now you have to decide how best to cope."

"Until rescued?" I said.

"Forget about the rescue," he said.

"I can't," I said.

This conversation is taking place in Joseph's office, which is just as tatty as he is and smells of unemptied ash-trays, feet, misery and twice-breathed air. But it's also taking place in my bedroom, on the day of the funeral. Joseph's, who didn't have all the time in the world.

"He fell out of a tree," said Karen, notifying me. She'd come to do this in person, rather than using the phone. Joseph didn't trust phones. Most of the message in any act of communication, he said, was non-verbal.

Karen stood in my doorway, oozing tears. She was one of his too, one of us; it was through her I'd got him. By now there's a network of us, it's like recommending a hairdresser, we've passed him from hand to hand like the proverbial eye or tooth. Smart women with detachable husbands or genius afflicted children with nervous tics, smart women with deranged lives, overjoyed to find someone who wouldn't tell us we were too smart for our own good and should all have frontal lobotomies. Smartness was an asset, Joseph maintained. We should only see what happened to the dumb ones.

"Out of a *tree*?" I said, almost screaming.

"Sixty feet, onto his head," said Karen. She began weeping again. I wanted to shake her.

"What the bloody hell was he doing up at the top of a sixty-foot *tree*?" I said.

"Pruning it," said Karen. "It was in his garden. It was cutting off the light to his flower beds."

"The old fart," I said. I was furious with him. It was an act of desertion. What made him think he had the right to go climbing up to the top of a sixty-foot tree, risking all our lives? Did his flower beds mean more to him than we did?

"What are we going to do?" said Karen.

What am I going to do? is one question. It can always be replaced by *What am I going to wear?* For some people it's the same thing. I go through the cupboard, looking for the blackest things I can find. What I wear will be the non-verbal part of the communication. Joseph will notice. I have a horrible feeling I'll turn up at the funeral home and find they've laid him out in his awful yellow cardigan and those tacky maroon leather bedroom slippers.

I needn't have bothered with the black. It's no longer demanded. The three wives are in pastels, the first in blue, the second in mauve, the third, the current one, in beige. I know a lot about the three wives, from those off-days of mine when I didn't feel like talking.

Karen is here too, in an Indian-print dress, snivelling softly to herself. I envy her. I want to feel grief, but I can't quite believe Joseph is dead. It seems like some joke he's playing, some anecdote that's supposed to make us learn something. Fakery and invention. *All right, Joseph,* I want to call, *we have the answer, you can come out now.* But nothing happens, the closed coffin remains closed, no wisps of smoke issue from it to show there's life.

The closed coffin is the third wife's idea. She thinks it's more dignified, says the grapevine, and it probably is. The coffin is of dark wood, in good taste, no showy trim. No one has made a meal and placed it on this coffin, no one has eaten from it. No destitute old creature, gobbling down the turnips and mash and the heavy secrecies of Joseph's life along with them. I have no idea what Joseph might have had on his conscience. Nevertheless I feel this as an omission: what then has become of Joseph's sins? They hover around us, in the air, over the bowed heads, while a male relative of Joseph's, unknown to me, tells us all what a fine man he was.

After the funeral we go back to Joseph's house, to the third wife's house, for what used to be called the wake. Not anymore: now it's coffee and refreshments.

The flower beds are tidy, gladioli at this time of year, already fading and a little ragged. The tree branch, the one that broke, is still on the lawn.

"I kept having the feeling he wasn't really there," says Karen as we go up the walk.

"Really where?" I say.

"There," says Karen. "In the coffin."

"For Christ's sake," I say, "don't start that." I can tolerate that kind of sentimental fiction in myself, just barely, as long as I don't do it out loud. "Dead is dead, that's what he'd say. Deal with here and now, remember?"

Karen, who'd once tried suicide, nodded and started to cry again. Joseph is an expert on people who try suicide. He's never lost one yet.

"How does he do it?" I asked Karen once. Suicide wasn't one of my addictions, so I didn't know.

"He makes it sound so *boring*," she said.

"That can't be all," I said.

"He makes you imagine," she said, "what it's like to be dead."

There are people moving around quietly, in the living room and in the dining room, where the table stands, arranged by the third wife with a silver tea urn and a vase of chrysanthemums, pink and yellow. Nothing too funereal, you can hear her thinking. On the white tablecloth there are cups, plates, cookies, coffee, cakes. I don't know why funerals are supposed to make people hungry, but they do. If you can still chew you know you're alive.

Karen is beside me, stuffing down a piece of chocolate cake. On the other side is the first wife.

"I hope you aren't one of the loonies," she says to me abruptly. I've never really met her before, she's just been pointed out to me, by Karen, at the funeral. She's wiping her fingers on a paper napkin. On her powder-blue lapel is a gold brooch in the shape of a bird's nest, complete with the eggs. It reminds me of high school: felt skirts with appliqués of cats and telephones, a world of replicas.

I ponder my reply. Does she mean *client,* or is she asking whether I am by chance genuinely out of my mind?

"No," I say.

"Didn't think so," says the first wife. "You don't look like it. A lot of them were, the place was crawling with them. I was afraid there might be an *incident.* When I lived with Joseph there were always these *incidents*, phone calls at two in the morning, always killing themselves, throwing themselves all over him, you couldn't believe what went on. Some of them were *devoted* to him. If he'd told them to shoot the Pope or something, they'd have done it just like that."

"He was very highly thought of," I say carefully.

"You're telling *me*," says the first wife. "Had the idea he was God himself, some of them. Not that he minded all that much."

The paper napkin isn't adequate, she's licking her fingers. "Too rich," she says. "*Hers.*" She jerks her head in the direction of the second wife, who is wispier than the first wife and is walking past us, somewhat aimlessly, in the direction of the living room. "You can have it, I told him finally. I just want some peace and quiet before I have to start pushing up the daisies." Despite the richness, she helps herself to another piece of chocolate cake. "*She* had this nutty idea that we should have some of them stand up and give little testimonies about him, right at the ceremony. Are you totally out of your tree? I told her. It's your funeral, but if I was you I'd try to keep it in mind that some of the people there are going to be a whole lot saner than others. Luckily she listened to me."

"Yes," I say. There's chocolate icing on her cheek: I wonder if I should tell her.

"I did what I could," she says, "which wasn't that much, but still. I was fond of him in a way. You can't just wipe out ten years of your life. I brought the cookies," she adds, rather smugly. "Least I could do."

I look down at the cookies. They're white, cut into the shapes of stars and moons and decorated with coloured sugar and little silver balls. They remind me of Christmas, of festivals and celebrations. They're the kind of cookies you make to please someone; to please a child.

I've been here long enough. I look around for the third wife, the one in charge, to say good-bye. I finally locate her, standing in an open doorway. She's crying, something she didn't do at the funeral. The first wife is beside her, holding her hand.

"I'm keeping it just like this," says the third wife, to no one in particular. Past her shoulder I can see into the room, Joseph's study evidently. It would take a lot of strength to leave that rummage sale untouched, untidied. Not to mention the begonias withering on the sill. But for her it will take no strength at all, because Joseph is in this room, unfinished, a huge boxful of loose ends. He refuses to be packed up and put away.

"Who do you hate the most?" says Joseph. This, in the middle of a lecture he's been giving me about the proper kind of birdbath for one's garden. He knows of course that I don't have a garden.

"I have absolutely no idea," I say.

"Then you should find out," says Joseph. "I myself cherish an abiding hatred for the boy who lived next door to me when I was eight."

"Why is that?" I ask, pleased to be let off the hook.

"He picked my sunflower," he says. "I grew up in a slum, you know. We had an area of sorts at the front, but it was solid cinders. However I did manage to grow this one stunted little sunflower, God knows how. I used to get up early every morning just to look at it. And the little bugger picked it. Pure bloody malice. I've forgiven a lot of later transgressions but if I ran into the little sod tomorrow I'd stick a knife into him."

I'm shocked, as Joseph intends me to be. "He was only a child," I say.

"So was I," he says. "The early ones are the hardest to forgive. Children have no charity; it has to be learned."

Is this Joseph proving yet once more that he's a human being, or am I intended to understand something about myself? Maybe, maybe not. Sometimes Joseph's stories are parables, but sometimes, they're just running off at the mouth.

In the front hall the second wife, she of the mauve wisps, ambushes me. "He didn't fall," she whispers.

"Pardon?" I say.

The three wives have a family resemblance—they're all blondish and vague around the edges—but there's something else about this one, a glittering of the eyes. Maybe it's grief; or maybe Joseph didn't always draw a totally firm line between his personal and his professional lives. The second wife has a faint aroma of client.

"He wasn't happy," she says. "I could tell. We were still very close, you know."

What she wants me to infer is that he jumped. "He seemed all right to me," I say.

"He was good at keeping up a front," she says. She takes a breath, she's about to confide in me, but whatever these revelations are I don't want to hear them. I want Joseph to remain as he appeared; solid, capable, wise, and sane. I do not need his darkness.

I go back to the apartment. My sons are away for the weekend. I wonder whether I should bother making dinner just for myself. It's hardly worth it. I wander around the too-small living room, picking things up. No longer my husband's: as befits the half-divorced, he lives elsewhere.

One of my sons has just reached the shower-and-shave phase, the other hasn't, but both of them leave a deposit every time they pass through a room. A sort of bathtub ring of objects—socks, paperback books left facedown and open in the middle, sandwiches with bites taken out of them, and, lately, cigarette butts.

Under a dirty T-shirt I discover the Hare Krishna magazine my younger son brought home a week ago. I was worried that it was a spate of adolescent religious mania, but no, he'd given them a quarter because he felt sorry for them. He was a dead-robin-burier as a child. I take the magazine into the kitchen to put it in the trash. On the front there's a picture of Krishna playing the flute, surrounded by adoring maidens. His face is bright blue, which makes me think of corpses: some things are not cross-cultural. If I read on I could find out why meat and sex are bad for you. Not such a poor idea when you think about it: no more terrified cows, no more divorces. A life of abstinence and prayer. I think of myself, standing on a street corner, ringing a bell, swathed in flowing garments. Selfless and removed, free from sin. Sin is this world, says Krishna. This world is all we have, says Joseph. It's all you have to work with. It is not too much for you. You will not be rescued.

I could walk to the corner for a hamburger or I could phone out for a pizza. I decide on the pizza.

"Do you like me?" Joseph says from his armchair.

"What do you mean, do I *like* you?" I say. It's early on; I haven't given any thought to whether or not I like Joseph.

"Well, do you?" he says.

"Look," I say. I'm speaking calmly but in fact I'm outraged. This is a demand, and Joseph is not supposed to make demands of me. There are too many demands being made of me already. That's why I'm here, isn't it? Because the demands exceed the supply. "You're like my dentist," I say. "I don't think about whether or not I like my dentist. I don't *have* to like him. I'm paying him to fix my teeth. You and my dentist are the only people in the whole world that I don't *have* to like."

"But if you met me under other circumstances," Joseph persists, "would you like me?"

"I have no idea," I say. "I can't imagine any other circumstances."

This is a room at night, a night empty except for me. I'm looking at the ceiling, across which the light from a car passing outside is slowly moving. My apartment is on the first floor: I don't like heights. Before this I always lived in a house.

I've been having a dream about Joseph. Joseph was never much interested in dreams. At the beginning I used to save them up for him and tell them to him, the ones I thought were of interest, but he would always refuse to say what they meant. He'd make me tell him, instead. Being awake, according to Joseph, was more important than being asleep. He wanted me to prefer it.

Nevertheless, there was Joseph in my dream. It's the first time he's made an appearance. I think that it will please him to have made it, finally, after all those other dreams about preparations for dinner parties, always one plate short. But then I remember that he's no longer around to be told. Here it is, finally, the shape of my bereavement: Joseph is no longer around to be told. There is no one left in my life who is there only to be told.

I'm in an airport terminal. The plane's been delayed, all the planes have been delayed, perhaps there's a strike, and people are crammed in and milling around. Some of them are upset, there are children crying, some of the women are crying too, they've lost people, they push through the crowd calling out names, but elsewhere there are clumps of men and women laughing and singing, they've had the foresight to bring cases of beer with them to the airport and they're passing the bottles around. I try to get some information but there's no one at any of the ticket counters. Then I realize I've forgotten my passport. I decide to take a taxi home to get it, and by the time I make it back maybe they'll have everything straightened out.

I push towards the exit doors, but someone is waving to me across the heads of the crowd. It's Joseph. I'm not at all surprised to see him, though I do wonder about the winter overcoat he's wearing, since it's still summer. He also has a yellow muffler wound around his neck, and a hat. I've never seen him in any of these clothes before. Of course, I think, he's cold, but now he's pushed through the people, he's beside me. He's wearing a pair of heavy leather gloves and he takes the right one off to shake my hand. His own hand is bright blue, a flat tempera-paint blue, a picture-book blue. I hesitate, then I shake the hand, but he doesn't let go, he holds my hand, confidingly, like a child, smiling at me as if we haven't met for a long time.

"I'm glad you got the invitation," he says.

Now he's leading me towards a doorway. There are fewer people now. To one side there's a stand selling orange juice. Joseph's three wives are behind the counter, all in identical costumes, white hats and frilly aprons, like waitresses of the forties. We go through the doorway; inside, people are sitting at small round tables, though there's nothing on the tables in front of them, they appear to be waiting.

I sit down at one of the tables and Joseph sits opposite me. He doesn't take off his hat or his coat, but his hands are on the table, no gloves, they're the normal colour again. There's a man standing beside us, trying to attract our attention. He's holding out a small white card covered with symbols, hands and fingers. A deaf-mute, I decide, and sure enough when I look his mouth is sewn shut. Now he's tugging at Joseph's arm, he's holding out something else, it's a large yellow flower. Joseph doesn't see him.

"Look," I say to Joseph, but the man is already gone and one of the waitresses has come instead. I resent the interruption, I have so much to tell Joseph and there's so little time, the plane will go in a minute, in the other room I can already hear the crackle of announcements, but the woman pushes in between us, smiling officiously. It's the first wife; behind her, the other two wives stand in attendance. She sets a large plate in front of us on the table.

"Will that be all?" she says, before she retreats.

The plate is filled with cookies, children's-party cookies, white ones, cut into the shapes of moons and stars, decorated with silver balls and coloured sugar. They look too rich.

"My sins," Joseph says. His voice sounds wistful but when I glance up he's smiling at me. Is he making a joke?

I look down at the plate again. I have a moment of panic: this is not what I ordered, it's too much for me, I might get sick. Maybe I could send it back; but I know this isn't possible.

I remember now that Joseph is dead. The plate floats up towards me, there is no table, around us is dark space. There are thousands of stars, thousands of moons, and as I reach out for one they begin to shine.

[1982]

· CLARK BLAISE ·

1940–

"Sociologically, I am an American. Psychologically, a Canadian. Sentimentally, a Québécois. By marriage, part of the Third World. My passport says Canadian, but I was born in America; my legal status says immigrant." This is Clark Blaise's description, in *Resident Alien* (1986), of the dualities that have shaped his life. He was born in Fargo, North Dakota, to an English-Canadian mother and a French-Canadian father. He records that "I lived my childhood in the deep, segregated South, my adolescence in Pittsburgh, my manhood in Montreal, and have started my middle age somewhere in middle America," in Iowa.

As his words suggest, Blaise's short stories and novels are marked by their preoccupation with the tensions between a host of extremes. He is attracted to raw experience, spontaneous impulse, grotesque realism, and uncultured thought; simultaneously, he is a polymath who needs reason, order, intellect, and learning in order to survive. For Blaise, these two worlds can never coincide; yet his fiction is driven by the strategies he employs in his attempt to *make* them coincide. The most obvious strategy involves doubling and superimposition. Blaise's characters are often two-sided, and their stories detail—through extended use of archetype and symbol—a profound desire to discover an integrated and authentic self. A list of the authors who influenced Blaise—including Pascal, Flaubert, Proust, Faulkner, and Céline—indicates that his work is philosophical, realistic, epic, eschatological, and existential. It is important to note this range, if only because Blaise has been viewed as a purely realistic writer involved with the tragic implications of the events of his era. This perspective seems curious when one considers the extent to which Blaise's stories become self-conscious explorations of their own mode of articulation. Their ultimate reality is internal, psychological, personal, and self-reflective. To trace Blaise's growing preoccupation with this self-reflective mode is to describe the evolution of his fiction.

Blaise's first collection of linked short stories is marked by its multi-levelled revelation of the fears, obsessions, and aesthetic values that shape the book's three central narrators. The distanced third-person perspective of the opening eventually gives way to a revealing, fragmented, first-person mode that details the various narrators' personal and narrative collapse. Blaise makes it clear that his protagonists will never be satisfied with their creations, or with themselves. Yet they continue to deceive themselves, in the belief that "anything dreamt had to become real, eventually." The dreams shared by Blaise's narrators are always highly symbolic and archetypal in form, a conclusion that is supported by even the most cursory reading of Blaise's second short-story collection, *Tribal Justice* (1974). Here, in some of his richest and most evocative fiction, Blaise returns again and again to his narrators' meditations on their art.

Blaise's first two books established him as one of the finest short-story writers in Canada at the very time he decided to explore a different genre. While *Lunar Attractions* (1979) proved that Blaise could master the novel form, it also demonstrated that his fundamental attraction to self-reflective writing remained central to his art. After all, *Lunar Attractions* is a semi-autobiographical account of a writer's development: David Greenwood insists on seeing himself in every aspect of his creation, so much so that his fiction becomes an intricate confession of his failure to get beyond himself. Yet *Lunar Attractions* is by no means purely solipsistic; it is a book about our times, about growing up in our times, and about the symbols and systems we use to explain our lives. Blaise has written that he wanted "to create the portrait of the authentically Jungian or even Freudian whole mind," which "sees every aspect of the natural and historical world being played out in its own imagination, and it literally creates the world that it sees."

These words suggest that for Blaise the writer can never be merely a recorder or even the interpreter of events. He must give form to experience and must be responsible to that form. The nature of this responsibility is the focus of Blaise's second and most recent novel—*Lusts* (1983). Here the nature of writing is explored through Richard Durgin's struggle to understand the suicide of his wife, who was a successful poet, and who challenged Durgin's assumptions about the social and political implications of art.

If Rachel is Richard's "other self" then her death is doubly significant: it suggests that Blaise may have overcome the personal divisions that kept his successive narrators from becoming whole. Does this mean that he has found the integrated self he has sought through-out his work? No. *Resident Alien* (1986), his most recent collection of autobiographical fiction, shows that Blaise's ongoing attempt "to find the centre of my imagination" is essential to his art, for the quality of his writing—its permutations, obsessions, and complex use of voice—is tragically dependent on Blaise's constant inability to find himself, or his final story.

. ——————— .

Works by Blaise include *A North American Education: A Book of Short Fiction* (1973); *Tribal Justice* (1974); *Days and Nights in Calcutta* [with Bharati Mukherjee] (1977); *Lunar Attractions* (1979); *Lusts* (1983); and *Resident Alien* (1986).

Works on Blaise include Frank Davey, "Impressionable Realism: The Stories of Clark Blaise," *Open Letter* 3rd ser. 5 (1976): 65–74; Geoff Hancock, "An Interview with Clark Blaise," *Canadian Fiction Magazine* 34–35 (1980): 46–64; Robert Lecker, "Murals Deep in Nature," *On the Line: Readings in the Short Fiction of Clark Blaise, John Metcalf, and Hugh Hood* (1982) 17–58; Barry Cameron, "Clark Blaise," *Canadian Writers and Their Works*, ed. Robert Lecker, Jack David, and Ellen Quigley (1985), Fiction Series 7: 21–92; and Robert Lecker, *An Other I* (1988).

ROBERT LECKER

THE BRIDGE

Studio One reached Fort Lauderdale from the Dumont station in Miami, and in the summer I was allowed up late enough to watch it. We had no set at home, having recently come down from Montreal. I watched it at Rifkin Brothers Furniture and Appliance Center, where my father was the furniture buyer. The sets were round with magnifying lenses bracketed in front. The hostess of *Studio One* was Betty Furness, the Westinghouse lady.

An enormous sense of power, watching television behind locked doors while people press their faces to the windows—a seven-year-old responds to that. Behind me in the dark, mannequins in evening dresses stood by their washing machines, and upstairs my father worked on the books.

Around seven o'clock his secretary would come down from the office and sit with me in front of the television, and talk. She had a northern voice, and a harsh one, but no demands were in it. I knew (in the way of a boss's son) that she liked me. I knew, in fact, she thought I was amazing. She took me out to get the coffee and sandwiches, a high-point of the evening. A child hungers for that. There's something illicit in going out with a pretty secretary for coffee and sandwiches.

Joan was her name. She'd been introduced to me as Joan and a boss's son has that privilege, even when he is fast becoming a *yes ma'am—no ma'am* southern boy and is otherwise overly polite. I called her Joan because I never learned her last name. Born a Larivière up in New Hampshire (where they pronounced it "Larry Veer"), she had been divorced from a Georgian named Holman after being widowed in the war by a man named Paulson. Widowed at eighteen and divorced on the rebound, and still only twenty-five. She was tiny but ample, and depending on the day and what she wore, became a trifle plump or unbearably voluptuous. The word, I know now, was *ripe*. Her arms were full and downy, her waistline faultless but a little too sudden, no room for a curving back and leisurely midriff, the gentle reach and suppression of breasts and hips, and I, at seven, responded to that. She was old enough to be my sister, but *just* to be my sister, and that accounted for the whistles she got on the way to the carryout counter at the big Walgreen's a block away.

With the television on and my father in the back behind the door, I would prowl the darkened store, trying chairs and sofas, and far from the windows where people could watch me, I dug my well-scrubbed hands into the mannequins' dresses, over their cold unnippled breasts and up their fused and icy thighs. All of the mannequins immobile, unprotesting, Betty Furnesses. By the middle of the evening, I'd have all the girls unbuttoned, then by ten o'clock, have them proper once again.

2

We Thibidaults went to the beach one weekday, a day of perfect calm. My parents lay on a blanket sleeping and I ventured out. I couldn't swim. The Atlantic was glassy, even calmer than the Gulf but without the slime of jellyfish. Just the weeds with spotted crabs. I walked out in the perfect neutral warmth, in piss-warm water, not flinching with the darts of minnows against my legs, not worried about sand sharks and manta rays, barracuda beyond the jetties. I'd read of the fishes, knew the dangers, but still I walked. No waves in sight, the convoy of giant tankers steamed across the horizon, and the illusion was firm that I could walk that day to Dakar or Lisbon. I bounced to shoulder-depth, knowing that if I stumbled or if something large should strike my legs, if a wave or undertow should suddenly arise, I would drown. At chin-depth I tried to turn and couldn't without taking another half-step forward to gain my balance. I opened my mouth to call, but only whimpered, and water entered. I thought I saw the dark funneling shapes of my worst nightmares, and my throat closed with fear. I tried to walk backward and stumbled. My head went under, water invaded my ears, and then I was lifted, carried back a step or two, and set down in shoulder-depth water. My chest was still locked and my father struck me, hard, as he turned. I coughed as I ran behind him, afraid to look back. *"Dites rien à Maman,"* he said, and joined my mother who had not wakened. He never spoke of it to me, or to her.

3

Fort Lauderdale had a city pool, a Spanish-style fortress across from the beach. Swimming lessons were free in fresh, icy water under a murderous summer sun. We lived four miles from the ocean on a brackish, unswimmable estuary called the Tarpon River. The river swarmed with eels, crabs, mullet, and catfish, and I had caught and studied them all, and lost yards of line and dozens of hooks to the garbage fish that gasped and bubbled under our dock. But such is access to the ocean; before you charter a boat you haul up eels; before skin-diving you learn to paddle. And you learn the ocean in the Municipal Pool.

I never learned. The water stunned me with its iciness. It was a July day in the upper nineties. The noon-time sun was a lamp that bleached the skies and burned through the droplets of water on my back. I tried to float and felt torn by the scalding sun on my back and the numbing cold that gripped my legs and belly. I wanted to sink into the dancing blueness, the cold Canadianness of the water. No one watched, and bronzed Florida kids played dangerous games in the deep end. I left.

I had biked out barefoot, towel around my shoulders, feeling very Floridian and almost at home. It was four miles from our house to the pool, down Las Olas Boulevard. A scorching day. Las Olas was intersected by an old swing bridge over the Inland Waterway which I, returning from the pool, towel on the handle bars drying, now approached. The bridge was out to let a string of yachts pass under. It wasn't returning in time to allow the backed-up cars to start and finally my bicycle began to wobble. I put my bare foot down to steady it and suddenly I screamed. The black-top was gummy from the sun, my foot already tar-stained and burning. The bicycle toppled, spilling the towel on the crushed limestone shoulder. The wooden bridge was now back in place and the guardrail was lifting, but I was crouched in the burning limestone. My bike and towel had rolled several feet behind me. The stones gave way to a sheer drop to the waterway about fifty feet below; my only hope was in dashing to the bridge, a splintery weathered thing, itself hot, but equipped with a rail that I could lean over until my feet quit burning. And then my bike was farther away than ever and walking to it barefoot over the burning limestone or over the soggy black-top seemed almost Fijian, something natives did in the *National Geographic.* My eyes watered in the blank sunlight. I looked at my arms and shoulders and they were as white as a slice of baker's bread.

Cars whizzed past, glittering in the sun, their windshields, hoods, and chromework so bright that I couldn't face them. Everywhere I looked there was a haze of pink. It was like coming out of a Saturday matinee after three hours in the dark and letting the white buildings blind you. No one was out walking, not at noontime over the unshaded bridge with just a bait and tackle shop at the far end. No one ever walked in the States, my mother had said.

The door of the bait shop opened. Way in the distance an old man started my way, drinking a bottle of orange and carrying a white carton of live bait-shrimp. He was still talking to the owner as he walked away, and finally he laughed loudly and waved. I could taste the orangeade prickling my mouth as the man shambled toward me. An old man, dressed warmly on a blistering day, took a final swig leaving an inch or so on the bottom, and flung the bottle over the railing and into the Waterway.

"Sir!" I called, long before the man could hear. My voice was weak against the traffic and seemed to be whining, like the voices of tourist kids in restaurants.

"Sir!"

The man drew near, holding the shrimp by a frail wire loop. The shrimp smelled, the water sloshed. I knew I could drink it.

"Sir—would you get my bike for me, please?"

The man walked past, smiling at his shrimp, squinting against the oncoming cars. "Sir—please, please. My feet are burnt and I can't walk—" but my voice was coming out a whimper and he didn't turn around. He just crunched on over the limestone in his thick oily boots and was past my bike without looking down. Then he faded and I had to blink to keep him in sight. He climbed down the bank and settled by the water to fish.

I lowered myself to the wooden planks. My shadow had made the wood bearable for my knees, then my legs, and finally I curled myself on the wood against the railings. There was a tiny knothole by my toes and I bent over, until my back seemed ready to split, like a roasted pig's I'd once seen in the *National Geographic.* The limestone looked like white-hot coals.

Through the knothole the water seemed even closer, like Coke at the bottom of a bottle. If I'd had a straw, I could suck it through, and I remembered the day I almost drowned, when ocean water hadn't tasted all that bad. Now, blue, running and deep, it seemed a cool blanket to wrap my shoulders in.

And when the water became olive-dark, strange shapes began to flutter; the channel seemed opaque, then shallow. I clung to the railing now, so large did the knothole seem; so close did the lapping of water against the pilings sound. The channel bottom was heaving and rolling; bubbles rose, currents dimpled, needlefish glided on the surface, mullet teemed around the pilings, snook leaped, a cabin cruiser that didn't need the bridge to turn, gurgled under me, shattering the water for several minutes, the old people on board drinking beer from ice chests, maybe trawling, and playing cards. I thought of taking down my swimsuit and pissing through the knothole on the next boat that passed. Maybe if I took off my pants and stood naked on the bridge someone would stop and give me water; but I was afraid of getting in trouble. I lifted my head a minute and stared at the highway, now vague and white. I had the impression that I was going to die and that dying on the bridge with hundreds of cars passing would be more pathetic than anything. People would know how I had felt. The old man fishing on the bank would be caught and thrown in jail. The bait man at the end of the bridge and the bridge man who must have been watching for the past two or three hours from his little perch at the far end, and the people on the boats who had passed underneath and all the cars that had hissed past on a film of melted asphalt; all guilty of letting me die. If I'd wanted to talk now I couldn't, my mouth was as dry as my back, and my tongue had grown to my palate. The water under the bridge was olive now and my gaze penetrated far below the surface. The wooden railing jiggled slightly. I held on, afraid that I might tip head-first through the peephole. I couldn't feel my body against the wood; it was as though I were asleep in bed with my head sinking into the cool pillow and my feet rising slowly. In the water, which now seemed shallow, something enormous, flat and brown, tipped a wing and then settled back. The surface shuddered in response.

"I think—" A voice that seemed to be coming from the wood of the bridge, and I had to force myself to remember that I was just a foot or two from the highway, and in the middle of a sidewalk. I tried to look up to see who it was, for the voice was familiar, but, as in a dream, I couldn't. I felt now as though my feet were waving high and I was somehow balancing on the sharpened pupil of my eye. But when a hand came down on my back, I twitched, banging my nose.

"My God, the skin—look at his back! I told you that was his bike, didn't I? Go down to that bait shop and bring me some water. He's unconscious."

My father.

I couldn't waken to speak. His hands were under me now, trying to lift me in my bent position, but any movement was like palming hot sand over broken blisters, and the moment I was lifted from the knothole, the instant water was removed and everything again turned white and wooden, I began to shiver, then to retch. I wanted only to be dropped in cool water and allowed to sleep. I opened one eye, just enough for light to enter, and saw the waterway, and on the surface, as though I had conjured them at last, a school of manta rays, skimming the surface and slapping their way out of sight. Then I slept hearing voices and my father's response, "I'm taking him home, yes, I'm his father, yes, I've been searching all over . . ."

When I wakened it was shady, in a car, in the arms—I could tell even with my eyes closed—of a young woman who had recently showered. The doors of the car were open, I could feel a warm breeze, though I shivered, and the ashtrays had not been cleaned.

"It's frightening," she said. "How close—"

My back was cooler but the pain was deep, more like cuts than a burn. I would have vomited but felt too weak. "I mean if we hadn't of . . . You'd better take him now," she said, "he feels a little cooler." The doors slammed and my father said, "I'll let you off first," I fluttered my eyes but couldn't keep them open. "All right," she said, and I could feel her looking down at me, stroking my hair, "Such a little boy, really," and then, "It would be bad if he saw me here," she said in that harsh Yankee voice. And before I slept she added in that soft Canadian French of her childhood, and mine, "Mal s'il me voit."

[1973]

· KEATH FRASER ·

1944–

Keath Fraser was born in Vancouver on 25 December 1944. He received a B.A. and an M.A. from the University of British Columbia, and then went to London University, where he received his Ph.D. in 1973. After teaching at the University of Calgary for five years, he resigned with tenure in 1978 to devote himself full-time to writing. He wrote two full-length plays before turning to fiction in 1980, and since then has published short stories and novellas in a variety of journals and anthologies, including *Descant, 82: Best Canadian Fiction,* and *The New Press Anthology: Best Canadian Short Fiction.* In 1982 he received the Contributor's Prize from *Canadian Fiction Magazine.* His collection of stories, *Foreign Affairs* (1985), was short-listed for the Governor General's Award, and won the Ethel Wilson Fiction Prize for 1986. Fraser has travelled extensively, including Europe, Southeast Asia, Australia, New Zealand, and Central America. He currently lives in Vancouver.

Fraser's fiction is concerned with the multifarious dislocations of which life in contemporary society consists. Throughout his stories the characters attempt to communicate about the things that matter most to them: the unfamiliarity of their own words and emotions, death and its curious immanence, the fascination of merely being alive. At times, the characters achieve some greater understanding by struggling to articulate their daily predicaments; at other times, this attempt at explication only causes greater confusion.

Yet despite these disconnections, Fraser's fiction is not always pessimistic. Moving along various declining pathways, there are many adventures, philosophical musings, and stories that help to pass the time. For Fraser, words

themselves, and the way words enter our senses and imaginations, provide welcome relief. In such stories as "Roget's Thesaurus" and "Foreign Affairs" the strange world of words—with their attendant puns, clichés, and games—is central. In almost all the stories there is a wealth of allusions and references to other writers: Plato, Shakespeare, Conrad, and Yeats among them. Throughout Fraser's fiction there is also a concern with the intricacies of various cultures, such as those of Cambodia, India, Vancouver. Each locale seems simultaneously foreign and familiar, as though the characters, and Fraser himself, are discovering anew traditions that seem to have been in existence for millennia.

In an essay entitled "Notes Toward a Supreme Fiction" Fraser says: "I am talking about fiction that overturns expectation by juxtaposition, nexus, dislocation. I am talking about fiction that aspires to an understanding of cultural anorexy; fiction that creates the complexity capable of engaging our imaginations; fiction capable of perceiving the many ways that our received culture, for all its splendours of cohesion, for all our diplomacy, is suffering from edema of the soul." It is Fraser's examination of these questions and dilemmas that makes his writing at times richly textured, at times frustratingly desperate, and always full of wonder.

· ——————— ·

Works by Keath Fraser include "Notes From a Bus Ride to Tehran," *Queen's Quarterly* 78.3 (1971): 421–30; *Taking Cover* (1982); "Notes Toward a Supreme Fiction" *Canadian Literature* 100 (1984): 109–17; and *Foreign Affairs* (1985).

Works on Fraser include David Watmough, "New Talents," *Canadian Literature* 97 (1983): 97–98; Geoff Hancock, introduction, *Canadian Fiction Magazine* 49 (1984): 4–5; and Bronwyn Drainie, "Evoking the Exotic," *The Canadian Forum*, Feb. 1986: 37–38.

PETER O'BRIEN

TAKING COVER

Ladies and gentlemen, to kick off we'd like to welcome you officially. Children and singles too.

WHOOP WHOOP WHOOP WHOOP WHOOP. . . .

This is the emergency distress call for anybody locked out of their rooms during a red alert. Knowing how to whoop may save your lives.

In a few minutes you will all be shown to rooms that are sealed hermetically. The different corridors have coloured handrails and you should remember the colour of yours. For your own protection it's imperative to stay inside your rooms as much as possible, because corridors are less well protected from the radiation outside—and incidentally more likely to harbour other people's germs. Visiting hours you'll find posted on the back of every door. But as the corridors are narrow you should make plans to visit other rooms well ahead of time to avoid congestion. If the contamination level in the corridors is high they may be closed for extended periods. Suddenly and without warning. It should be remembered this auditorium will be closed till further notice and no public meetings scheduled after you are admitted to your rooms. This space is contaminated.

The world is contaminated. It's a fate worse than death.

To pet-owners apologies are due. Noah was kinder to pets but Noah had fewer people to accommodate. Since there's a limited supply of uncontaminated air everybody here is in competition. Children shouldn't lose heart. Their pets may prove defiantly resilient outside and even survive this internecine war. Suffice to say the penalty for smuggling in an animal is the pet itself. So no dogs, cats, hamsters, crocs or cockatiels.

On the subject of breath you ought to be aware of the Tibetan Monk Chant. This consumes less oxygen than normal breathing, and has the additional advantage of exercising the lungs. It's also helpful in meditation and relaxation, and serves as a warning to others that introspection is in progress.

m m m m m m m m m m m m m m m m m m m m m m m m m m m m m m m m m m m m m m m m m m m m m m m m m A A A A A A A A H H H H H H H H H H H H H H. . . .

This teaches you how to hold your breath for long periods at a stretch by exhaling slowly from the bottom of the spine.

As you will all be here for quite a while, learning how to pass the time is an important means of understanding how to survive. How to manage, how to cope, how to keep your heads above water. You're all in the same boat. So to weather the storm and tide you over, to keep you high and dry as well as steering clear of disaster, here are some rules:

No dumping on your neighbour, okay? No hogging hot water during the shower hour. No showers more than once a week. No loud tape decks. No flushing of toilets in the middle of the night unless absolutely necessary. No metal in the garburetor, olive pits, sanitary napkins, pencil stubs. No pissing in the shower. Otherwise we have a lot of happy-go-lucky refugees doing what they feel like with no regard for the community and the business to hand, ie, survival through mutual co-operation.

Privacy is privilege. Social shame remains an ethical system. The ways of doing time are oriental.

No people whose word for "yesterday" is different from their word for "tomorrow" can be said to have a loose grip on time.

You are requested to make your beds wash your dishes flush your excrement mop off your tiles dust the furniture polish your mirrors vacuum the carpet recycle your water but remember:

This is no place for the morose. This is a clean well-lighted place. A place in need of your decorating ideas. The vigorous here are in one another's minds the sick in one another's arms the young in one another's dreams. Our theory of space is transformational. This is no place for the languid. No place for the worn-out and despairing, for the self-important the mean the small-talkers. This is no place for the unregenerative. This place is no place you thought would save you.

Nothing transfigures all that dread but you.

Breathe normally so as not to use up more than your share of oxygen. No jogging in the corridors, around rooms, on the spot. Light torso movements all right, likewise isometrics, toe-touching, but no pushups or arm-wrestling. And definitely no aerobics. Dancing's allowed in your own rooms during our hour of recorded dance music every evening, but don't expect heavy rock, Strauss or hoedown. Nor any mournful melodies. Count on foxtrots and the Bossa Nova. Discourage your thirst: the supply of uncontaminated water is strictly rationed.

Where you are going space is constricted and time capacious. Time makes everything happen but space is what you perceive. Being under siege will entice you to temporize. Taking cover will incite feelings of living in a glass house. Resist these temptations. Time's in the imperative. Throw stones against empty walls. You might even survive.

Expect to receive broadcast messages from the theatre of war when and if available. Expect these in nutshells. Don't expect them to harp upon the long and short of expiration. Forget about obituaries. Listen for new ways of understanding old expressions. Of grief, of eating your heart out, of passing away. Of being smashed to smithereens. Give voice from the bottoms of your hearts. Be wise after the event.

Anybody who wants to broadcast on our community station we will list in our weekly program: topics like ceramics, self-improvement, memoirs. Nothing discouraging please. Nothing negative. No goddamn whining to see the stars again. And for heaven's sake, no gardening tips.

Those of you with children will find games and correspondence courses provided. It will be up to parents to educate their children to the new constriction. Unlike some shelters this one encourages children, but it would be delinquent not to remind you that having any more at this time would require a sacrifice you might not like. Childless couples should realize their own space is limited and no new rooms are available should they suddenly give birth. We inform you of this with a heavy heart.

Singles among you should remember that no doubling-up is permitted. The single rooms are just not adequate. Those found co-habiting will be asked to give up one of their rooms to families in need of additional space. A single room needn't be lonely for anybody involved in community activities. We have a small bank of information available about other singles listing their interests and aspirations. Dial the number in the manual by your telephone. Be brief. This shelter is on a party-line and many of you may not be familiar with party-line etiquette.

This is the case with children in the habit of using phones whenever they feel like it. Children should be discouraged from using the phone unless they ask permission. Please, no goddamn pranks. In the last war no-one, let alone children, had access to a phone in the underground bogs they used to call shelters. The telephone has been installed to prevent you feeling down in the mouth. Use it wisely.

What else? Golfers are reminded to give up their clubs and putters. They are going to have to replay a lot of life's links in their heads. They're going to have to mow them and hoe them and irrigate them alone. By the way, ladies, there is one hibiscus in every apartment, which likes to be watered once a week with a pinch of fertilizer once a month. If you spot thrips, murder them or they'll eat your root.

WHOOP WHOOP WHOOP—

Always whoop from the abdomen, never the thorax. The worst whoopers will not survive in the event of another bomb. Fallout in the corridors may cause a slow and painful—

Give up what you knew about the good old ways of taking cover. Lay the groundwork for a new way of feeling at home. Lick your rooms into shape. Gird up your loins for a long lean time.

During which it would be better to toy with new ideas and mince no words. Your perception is idiomatic and begs other space. War is hell. War lasts. It is the original sin. Heaven blazing in the head.

When you feel like throwing in the towel when you feel like burning your bridges when you feel like kicking the bucket

just remember: to get a new lease on your room refurbish it. You are apt to believe that grass is greener on the other side of the fence. This is a fatal mistake. Nothing here is the same old story. Not looking for greener pastures, not keeping up with the Joneses, not making a beeline for security. Nothing flies the way of the crow. Out there is definitely no man's land.

You're all in for a long haul. Feeling down in the dumps will become a residential virus. By the look of you, it already has. Expect to find yourselves up the creek without a paddle, fishing in troubled waters, going down for the last time. . . But don't give up. The war in the world may disappear. Don't presume, so may the world. Acquire detachment.

In a moment you will be asked to take off your clothes. This act will be your final preparation. Your first precaution to ensure that as little fallout as possible reaches your rooms. There's no need to be embarrassed. In the end we'll turn out the lights and you may shed your clothes by the light of the Exit sign.

Remember—what you are used to is now old hat. Like pulling up your socks or flying by the seat of your pants. You are accustomed to buttoning up, belting up, pulling yourselves up by the bootstraps. You used to be clotheshorses.

No more. Here your baggage will be stored in lockers until it's safe to return it to you. Everything you require, showers and robes, will be found inside your rooms. Inside your covenants. Inside yourselves. You're among the lucky. You're taking cover.

All your troubles are packed in old kit bags. You've decided that discretion is the better part of valour. Displaced and anxious you are willing to turn the other cheek because the alternative is a slow and painful death.

But cross that river when you come to it. Right now you're tired and anxious to retreat to your rooms where you can cherish old possibilities. Like wading out with the tide on a clear August day dreaming of your best friend's wife's buttocks. Like barbecuing fritters for the gang on your backyard Hibachi. Or playing tag with your spaniel in the park, where he did his business, scratched up the lawn and came bouncing back. Down here we encourage the exchange of snapshot albums. We delight to imagine you seated here. Spitting images.

Yet these are erstwhile pleasures because in the end you may suffer nausea, run out of oxygen, deplete your food, fall apart inside from radiation. Waste away, suffer, go up like smoke under a direct hit, perish.

For the succor of all you will discover in residence an interior decorator. He's another reason to keep your phone free. We encourage the arts and feel the cost of a decorator will meet with your approval. He comes with the shelter and although you will never meet him he'll help to brighten up the dark days and months ahead. His services are subsidized by the questions you admit.

Does anybody exist at the end of the line if he doesn't speak? How else do you know if the forest exists? Why do we need a voice at the end of the line anyway?

Anybody interested in receiving one of his calls can count themselves eligible. He wants you to know he is not a crackpot. He merely wants to change the way you listen. So when your phone rings and he refuses to speak—give him the time of day. Sit back and take a load off your feet. Let him breathe in your ear.

He speaks in no pictures you'll recognize. He may not even be a he. Listen to him breathe. He is used to reticence, indifference, hangups. He hates darkness and isolation. The darkness he finds obscene. He breathes and even pants.

Your world may light up. It may not. You may call him an impostor. He may be one. Greatness lies not in being strong, but in the right use of strength. Our decorator's strength is in his fingers. He dials, he calls you up with new sets of old numbers, old combinations with new prefixes. He'll try to turn you into voyeurs. The effect could be narcotic. You may feel like rearranging your rooms. You may begin to see the forest for the trees, that you're still in the swim, that unlike Heraclitus you are able to dip your foot in the same river twice.

Pay attention when our decorator in residence rings and fails to reveal himself fails to tip his hand fails to live up to his promise fails to meet you half-way fails to darken your door...

For in here your received notions of human nature will undergo change. Nature will not survive man's assault on himself. The luxury of ideologies leads only to the grave.

Your blood cannot survive invading anaemia. Your senses cannot survive radiation that blisters your skin cooks your eyes gnaws your eardrums ulcerates your tongue oxidizes your nose.

The sensible thing is to check for leakage every day. Check your gauges. Report changes in levels of radioactivity.

You are all contaminated. All victims of what is everywhere in the air. Take stock of changes in yourselves, any desiccation, any deterioration, any convulsions of your tongues. The way you speak measures your degree of resistance to residential virus. To severe dislocation. The penalty down here for talking shop is fallout. It hangs in the air like dust.

m m m m m m m m m m m m m m m m m m m m m m m m m m m m m m m m m m m m m m m m m m m m m m m A A A A A A A A A H H H H H H H H H H H H H....

Make up your minds to empty them. The dialect here is new. Old-fashioned war permitted a return to normal life every morning. This is no longer possible. Your nightmares last all day every day. There is no way of distinguishing day from night. What you forget no longer exists, what you don't remember no longer infects you:

no more clover in July no more asters in September no more plane trees or lotus or dragonflies in autumn no more milliners no more pianos no more concert halls no more stadiums no more theatres no more chicken coops no more Toyotas not to mention legislatures congresses courts no more brass bands no more lexicography no more Chinese food no more trust company officers no more archery no more bicycles no more comstockery no more Visa and Mastercard no more libraries no more junk mail no more Constantinople no more capuccino ice cream no more gerrymandering no more Sunday newspapers no more hindsight no more friends in cafés no more parachuting no more Hovis bread no more popery no more waterbeds no more stockbrokers no more siroccos no more adjudications no more blueberry-picking no more lapis lazuli no more ferry schedules no more hugger-muggers no more topping lifts no more donut diners no more cosmography no more eggs no more area codes no more Malvern Hills no more simony no more butter lettuce no more butter no more mystagogues no more jujubes no more store detectives no more Latinists no more cryptography no more kid gloves no more tabernacle choirs no more mergansers no more oysters no more pointillism no more natural light.

No more fresh air. Those who insist on poking your heads outside will return with radiation sickness. You will keep throwing up. You'll lose control of your bowels. You'll bleed from your noses and your ears. Your hair will fall out. You will probably die.

Here while it lasts is a less noxious world. Breathe in, breathe out. You will discover you have noses. You will smell what is denied your common sense. You will smell apple skin in the air, cologne on dogs, chocolate in daffodils. Grass bleeding, a lake stirring, the sea rotting. You will smell the engine-rooms of freighters on the night wind. Train stations, golf balls. Hair in the sun, motel swimming-pools, metronomes. Chicken feed, $10 bills, printer's glue in the spines of books. Shingles in heat, cat gut in racquets, missals in church. Baseballs, teabags, tarpaper. Bark on trees, violins at concerts, cement in mixers, turkey in the straw. Salt marshes and roller-skates. Fingernail filings, African violets, decaying teeth, watchstraps. You will smell turpentine in sagebrush, ammonia in brie, popcorn in lobsters. Sprinklers, pitch, tires on asphalt, suitcase handles, blow holes, Bombay, holy water in fonts, goose shit. You will smell furniture polish at parties. Sewing-machine oil in rifle barrels, lights at a play. Spider monkeys, newsprint, lobelia.

Do not believe the source of life is extinguished. Do not believe it isn't. Do not be generous without being kind. Don't believe the quiet person has less to say. Don't be sanguine about the place you're going to. Don't, on the other hand, repine. This is no place for the senseless. Not even if the place makes no sense at all. Your sentence now is life. The idiom can be translated but never commuted. Love starts here in the vernacular.

You may not be Chinese. But you're becoming oriental. You have glittering eyes. Your eyes amid many wrinkles are wise.

The world is on fire. This place is covered. Take off your coats. The light is going out. Stand up and shed all your clothes. Do not be ashamed. Use the light of the Exit sign. Stand up.

Tell yourselves not to be afraid. Tell yourselves the fear is in your minds. Address yourselves to the cave inside. Take off all your clothes. The light is going out. Tell yourselves you are taking cover. Tell yourselves to shed the jejune remains of style, your flirtations with persistence, your resolutions to lead less solemn lives. Tell yourselves this place is ideal. Tell yourselves the world is on fire. Tell yourselves the light is going out. Tell yourselves to stand up and take off your clothes. Don't be ashamed. Use the light of the Exit sign. Leave your clothes where they are. Leave yourselves by the Exit light. Stand up. Do not be afraid.

[1982]

ACKNOWLEDGEMENTS

ACORN, MILTON

"Charlottetown Harbour," "I've Tasted My Blood," "The Idea," and "The Natural History of Elephants" from *Dig Up My Heart: Selected Poems 1952-83* (Toronto: McClelland and Stewart, 1983). Used by permission of The Canadian Publishers, McClelland and Stewart Limited, Toronto.

ATWOOD, MARGARET

"This Is a Photograph of Me," from *The Circle Game*. Copyright © 1966 by Margaret Atwood (Toronto: House of Anansi Press, 1966). Reprinted by permission. "The Animals in That Country" and "Progressive Insanities of a Pioneer" from *The Animals in That Country* by Margaret Atwood (Toronto: Oxford University Press Canada, 1968). Copyright © Oxford University Press 1968. Reprinted by permission of Oxford University Press Canada. "Departure from the Bush" from *The Journals of Susanna Moodie* by Margaret Atwood (Toronto: Oxford University Press, 1970). Copyright © Oxford University Press Canada 1970. Reprinted by permission of Oxford University Press Canada. "There Is Only One of Everything" from *You Are Happy* (Toronto: Oxford University Press, 1974). Copyright © Margaret Atwood 1974. Reprinted by permission of the author and Oxford University Press Canada. "Trainride, Vienna-Bonn" from *True Stories* (Toronto: Oxford University Press, 1981). Copyright © Margaret Atwood 1981. Reprinted by permission of the author, Oxford University Press Canada, and Jonathan Cape Ltd., London. "The Sin Eater" from *Bluebeard's Egg* (Toronto: McClelland and Stewart, 1983). Reprinted by permission of Margaret Atwood from *Bluebeard's Egg* published by McClelland and Stewart © 1983. Also by permission of The Canadian Publishers, McClelland and Stewart Limited, Toronto and Jonathan Cape Ltd., London.

AVISON, MARGARET

"Voluptuaries and Others," "Butterfly Bones or Sonnet Against Sonnets," "The Swimmer's Moment," and "Black-White Under Green: May 18, 1965" from *Winter Sun/The Dumbfoundling Poems 1940-66* (Toronto: McClelland and Stewart, 1982). Used by permission of The Canadian Publishers, McClelland and Stewart Limited, Toronto. "Stone's Secret" from *Sunblue*, 1978. Reprinted by permission of Lancelot Press Limited, Hantsport, Nova Scotia.

BIRNEY, EARLE

"Bushed," "The Bear on the Delhi Road," "El Greco: *Espolio*," "Billboards Build Freedom of Choice," and "Canada Council" from *The Collected Poems of Earle Birney* (Toronto: McClelland and Stewart, 1975). "Father Grouse" and "My Love Is Young" from *Fall By Fury* (Toronto: McClelland and Stewart, 1978). Used by permission of The Canadian Publishers, McClelland and Stewart Limited, Toronto.

BLAISE, CLARK

"The Bridge" from *A North American Education* (New York: Doubleday & Company, 1973). Copyright © 1973 by Clark Blaise. Reprinted by permission of Doubleday & Company, Inc.

BORSON, ROO

"At Night You Can Almost See the Corona of Bodies," "Now and Again,"

"Jacaranda," and "Gray Glove" from *A Sad Device* (Dunvegan, Ontario: Quadrant Editions, 1981). Reprinted by permission of the author.

BOWERING, GEORGE
"Grandfather" from *Particular Accidents: Selected Poems* (Vancouver: Talon Books, 1980). Reprinted by permission of the author. "Against Description" from *West Window: The Selected Poetry of George Bowering* (Toronto: Stoddart Publishing Co., 1982). Reprinted by permission of the author and Stoddart Publishing Co. Limited, Toronto, Canada. "The House" from *Touch: Selected Poems 1960-1970* (Toronto: McClelland and Stewart, 1971). Used by permission of the author and The Canadian Publishers, McClelland and Stewart Limited, Toronto. "Thru" from *The Gangs of Kosmos* (Toronto: House of Anansi Press, 1969). Reprinted by permission of the author. "Summer Solstice" from *The Catch* (Toronto: McClelland and Stewart, 1976). Used by permission of the author and The Canadian Publishers, McClelland and Stewart Limited, Toronto.

CALLAGHAN, MORLEY
"Now That April's Here" from *Morley Callaghan's Stories* (Toronto: Macmillan of Canada, 1959). Reprinted by permission of Macmillan of Canada, A Division of Canada Publishing Corporation. Also used by permission of Don Congdon Associates.

CARMAN, BLISS
"Low Tide on Grand Pré," "A Vagabond Son," "I Loved Thee, Atthis, in the Long Ago," and "Vestigia" from *The Poems of Bliss Carman*, New Canadian Library No. 9 (Toronto: McClelland and Stewart, 1976). Used by permission of The Canadian Publishers, McClelland and Stewart Limited, Toronto. "Low Tide on Grand Pré" and "A Vagabond Song" also used by permission of Dodd, Mead & Company, New York.

COHEN, LEONARD
"I Have Not Lingered in European Monasteries," "For E.J.P.," "What I'm Doing Here," and "Two Went to Sleep" from *Leonard Cohen: Selected Poems 1956-1968* (Toronto: McClelland and Stewart, 1968). Copyright © Leonard Cohen. All rights reserved. "Welcome to These Lines" from *The Energy of Slaves* (Toronto: McClelland and Stewart, 1972). Reprinted by permission of the author and The Canadian Publishers, McClelland and Stewart Limited, Toronto.

CRAWFORD, ISABELLA VALANCY
"The Roman Rose-Seller from *'Old Spookses' Pass', 'Malcom's Katie' and Other Poems* (Toronto: Bain, 1884). "The Dark Stag," "Said the Canoe," and "The Lily Bed" from *Collected Poems* (1905; rpt. Toronto: University of Toronto Press, 1972).

di MICHELE, MARY
"The Disgrace" from *Bread and Chocolate/Marrying into the Family* (Ottawa: Oberon Press, 1980). "Poem for My Daughter" from *Necessary Sugar* (Ottawa: Oberon Press, 1983). Both poems reprinted by permission of the author and Oberon Press. "As in the Beginning" from *The New Canadian Poets 1970-1985* (Toronto: McClelland and Stewart, 1985). Used by permission of The Canadian Publishers, McClelland and Stewart Limited, Toronto.

DUDEK, LOUIS
"The Pomegranate," "Europe," and "Coming Suddenly to the Sea" from *Collected Poetry* (Montreal: Delta Canada, 1971). "Tao" from *Cross-Section:*

Poems 1940-1980 (Toronto: Coach House Press, 1980). Copyright © Louis Dudek.

FRASER, KEATH

"Taking Cover" from *Taking Cover* (Ottawa: Oberon Press, 1982). Copyright © 1982 by Keath Fraser. Reprinted by permission of the author.

GALLANT, MAVIS

"The Accident" originally published in *The New Yorker*, October 28, 1967. Reprinted by permission of Georges Borchardt, Inc. and the author. Copyright © 1967 by Mavis Gallant.

HOOD, HUGH

"Ghosts At Jarry" from *None Genuine Without This Signature* (Downsview, Ontario: ECW Press, 1980). Used by permission of ECW Press, Toronto.

KLEIN, A. M.

"Heirloom," "Portrait of the Poet as Landscape," "The Rocking Chair," and "Political Meeting" from *The Collected Poems of A. M. Klein* (Toronto: McGraw Hill Ryerson, 1974). Reprinted by permission of McGraw-Hill Ryerson Limited. "Sestina on the Dialectic" reprinted by permission of Colman Klein and Sandor J. Klein.

KROETSCH, ROBERT

"The Sad Phoenician 'A' 'N' 'W'" from *Field Notes: The Collected Poetry of Robert Kroetsch* (Toronto: Stoddart Publishing Co., 1981). Reprinted by permission of the author and Stoddart Publishing Co. Limited, Toronto, Canada. "Mile Zero" from *Advice to My Friends* (Toronto: Stoddart Publishing Co., 1985). Reprinted by permission of the author and Stoddart Publishing Co. Limited, Toronto, Canada.

LAMPMAN, ARCHIBALD

"Among the Timothy," "Heat," "In November," "On the Companionship with Nature," "The City of the End of Things," and "Winter Uplands" from *The Poems of Archibald Lampman* (Toronto: University of Toronto Press, 1974) and *Lyrics of Earth* (1895; rpt. Ottawa: The Tecumseh Press, 1978).

LAURENCE, MARGARET

"A Bird in the House" from *A Bird in the House* (Toronto: McClelland and Stewart, 1970). Used by permission of The Canadian Publishers, McClelland and Stewart Limited, Toronto. Reprinted by permission of JCA Literary Agency as agents for the Estate of Margaret Laurence. Copyright © 1970 by Margaret Laurence. Also used by permission of A. P. Watt Ltd. on behalf of the estate of Margaret Laurence.

LAYTON, IRVING

"The Swimmer," "The Cold Green Element," "The Bull Calf," "The Fertile Muck," "Whatever Else Poetry Is Freedom," and "Keine Lazarovitch: 1870-1959" from *A Wild Peculiar Joy: Selected Poems 1945-1982* (Toronto: McClelland and Stewart, 1982). Copyright © 1982 by Irving Layton. Used by permission of The Canadian Publishers, McClelland and Stewart Limited, Toronto, and Lucinda Vardey Agency.

LIVESAY, DOROTHY

"Fire and Reason," "Green Rain," "Bartok and the Geranium," "Lament" and "On Looking into Henry Moore" from *Collected Poems: The Two Seasons* (Toronto: McGraw-Hill Ryerson, 1972). Reprinted by permission of Dorothy Livesay. "Ice Age" from *Ice Age* (Erin, Ontario: Press Porcepic, 1975). Reprinted by permission of Press Porcepic Ltd., Victoria and Toronto.

MACPHERSON, JAY
"The Anagogic Man," "The Boatman," "What Falada Said," and "Umbrella Poem" from *Poems Twice Told* (Toronto: Oxford University Press, 1981). Reprinted by permission of Oxford University Press Canada.

MANDEL, ELI
"Notes from the Underground" from *Dreaming Backwards* (Toronto: General Publishing Co., 1981). Reprinted by permission of the author and General Publishing Co., Ltd. "The Double World:" from *Out of Place* (Erin, Ontario: Press Porcepic, 1977). Copyright © 1977 by Eli Mandel. "In My 57th Year" and " 'Grandfather's Painting': David Thauberger" from *Life Sentence* (Toronto and Victoria: Press Porcepic, 1981). Copyright © 1981 by Eli Mandel. Reprinted by permission of Press Porcepic Ltd., Victoria and Toronto.

MARLATT, DAPHNE
"So Cocksure" and "Seeing Your World from the Outside" from *Net Work* (Vancouver: Talon Books, 1980). "Imagine: A Town" from Steveston (Edmonton: Longspoon Press, 1974). "From Somewhere" from *Here & There* (Lantzville, B.C.: Island Writing Series, 1981). "Delphiniums Blue & Geraniums Red" from *How Hug a Stone* (Winnipeg: Turnstone Press, 1983). Reprinted by permission of the author.

METCALF, JOHN
"Keys and Watercress" from *The Lady Who Sold Furniture* (Toronto: Clarke, Irwin, 1970). Used by permission of ECW Press, Toronto.

MUNRO, ALICE
"Boys and Girls" from *Dance of the Happy Shades* (Toronto: Ryerson, 1968). Copyright © 1968 by Alice Munro. Reprinted by permission of McGraw-Hill Ryerson Limited and Virgina Barber Literary Agency, Inc.

NEWLOVE, JOHN
"The Flowers," "Samuel Hearne in Wintertime," and "Crazy Riel" from *The Fat Man: Selected Poems 1962-1972* (Toronto: McClelland and Stewart, 1977). Used by permission of The Canadian Publishers, McClelland and Stewart Limited, Toronto. "Driving," "The Green Plain," and "The Permanent Tourist Comes Home" from *The Night the Dog Smiled* (Toronto: ECW Press, 1986). Reprinted by permission of ECW Press, Toronto.

NICHOL, bp
"1335 Comox Avenue," "Dada Lama," "Blues," and "Two Words: A Wedding" from *As Elected* (Vancouver: Talon Books, Ltd., 1980). The typography on "Blues" is by Vivien Halas. "A Small Song That Is His" from *Love: A Book of Remembrances* (Vancouver: Talon Books, 1974). Reprinted by permission of the author.

NOWLAN, ALDEN
"The Bull Moose" and "The Execution" from *The Things Which Are* (Toronto: Irwin Publishing Inc., 1962). Reprinted by permission of the Estate of Alden Nowlan. "The Mysterious Naked Man" from *The Mysterious Naked Man* (Toronto: Clarke Irwin & Company Limited, 1969). Copyright © 1969 Clarke Irwin & Company Limited and used by permission of Irwin Publishing Inc. "The Broadcaster's Poem" from *I'm a Stranger Here Myself* (Toronto: Clarke Irwin & Company, 1974). Copyright © 1974 by Clarke Irwin & Company Limited and used by permission of Irwin Publishing Inc.

ONDAATJE, MICHAEL
"King Kong Meets Wallace Stevens," "White Dwarfs," and " 'The Gate in His Head' " from *There's a Trick with a Knife I'm Learning To Do* (Toronto:

McClelland and Stewart, 1979). "The Cinnamon Peeler" from *Running in the Family* (Toronto: McClelland and Stewart, 1982). Reprinted by permission of the author.

PAGE, P. K.
"Stories of Snow," "T-Bar," and "After Rain" from *Cry Ararat! Poems New and Selected* (Toronto: McClelland and Stewart, 1967). "After Reading *Albino Pheasants*" from *Evening Dance of the Grey Flies* (Toronto: Oxford University Press, 1981). "Deaf-Mute in the Pear Tree" from *The Glass Air* (Toronto: Oxford University Press, 1985.) Reprinted by permission of P. K. Page.

PRATT, E. J.
"Newfoundland," "The Shark," "[From] *Brébeuf and His Brethren*," "The Truant," and "Missing: Believed Dead: Returned" from *The Collected Poems of E. J. Pratt* (Toronto: Macmillan, 1958). Reprinted by permission of the University of Toronto Press.

'URDY, AL
"The Country North of Belleville," "The Cariboo Horses," "Eskimo Graveyard," "Wilderness Gothic," and "Lament for the Dorsets" from *Collected Poems of Al Purdy* (Toronto: McClelland and Stewart, 1986). Used by permission of the author and The Canadian Publishers, McClelland and Stewart Limited, Toronto.

REANEY, JAMES
"Antichrist as a Child," "The Red Heart," "The Sundogs," and "The Alphabet" from *Selected Shorter Poems* (Erin, Ontario: Press Porcepic, 1975). Copyright © 1975 by James Reaney. Reprinted by permission of the author and Press Porcepic Ltd., Victoria and Toronto.

RICHLER, MORDECAI
"The Summer My Grandmother Was Supposed to Die" from *The Street* (Toronto: McClelland and Stewart, 1969). Reprinted by permission of the author.

ROBERTS, CHARLES G. D.
"Tantramar Revisited," "The Sower," "The Potato Harvest," and "In an Old Barn" from *The Collected Poems of Sir Charles G. D. Roberts* (Wolfville, Nova Scotia: Wombat, 1985). Reprinted by permission of Lady Joan Roberts. "Do Seek Their Meat from God" from *The Last Barrier and Other Stories* (Toronto: McClelland and Stewart, 1958). Used by permission of The Canadian Publishers, McClelland and Stewart Limited, Toronto.

ROOKE, LEON
"The Problem Shop" from *Death Suite* (Downsview, Ontario: ECW Press, 1981). Used by permission of ECW Press, Toronto.

ROSS, SINCLAIR
"The Painted Door" from *The Lamp at Noon and Other Stories* New Canadian Library No. 62 (Toronto: McClelland and Stewart, 1968). Used by permission of The Canadian Publishers, McClelland and Stewart Limited, Toronto.

ROSS, W. W. E.
"The Creek," "The Diver," "This Form," and "Rocky Bay" from *Shapes and Sounds* (Toronto: Longman Canada, 1968). Reprinted by permission of Mary L. Hutton.

SCOTT, D. C.
"The Onondaga Madonna," "The Forsaken," "On the Way to the Mission," and "At Gull Lake: August, 1810" from *Duncan Campbell Scott: Selected Poetry*

(Ottawa: The Tecumseh Press, 1974). The work of Duncan Campbell Scott is published with the permission of John G. Aylen, Ottawa, Canada.

SCOTT, F. R.

"The Canadian Authors Meet," "March Field," "Trans Canada," "Overture," and "Lakeshore" from *The Collected Poems of F. R. Scott* (Toronto: McClelland and Stewart Limited, 1981). Used by permission of The Canadian Publishers, McClelland and Stewart Limited, Toronto.

SMITH, A. J. M.

"The Lonely Land," "Swift Current," "Like an Old Proud King in a Parable," "News of the Phoenix," "The Archer," and "Metamorphosis" from *The Classic Shade: Selected Poems* (Toronto: McClelland and Stewart, 1978). Used by permission of The Canadian Publisher, McClelland and Stewart Limited, Toronto).

SOUSTER, RAYMOND

"Yonge Street Saturday Night," "Downtown Corner Newsstand," "Study: The Bath," and "Two Dead Robins" from *Collected Poems of Raymond Souster, Volume One 1940-55* (Ottawa: Oberon Press, 1980). "Pigeons on George Street" from *Hanging In* (Ottawa: Oberon Press, 1979). Reprinted by permission of Oberon Press.

THOMAS, AUDREY

Déjeuner Sur l'Herbe from *Real Mothers* (Vancouver: Talon Books, 1981). Copyright © Audrey Thomas. Reprinted by permission of Talon Books Ltd.

WEBB, PHYLLIS

"Marvell's Garden" from *Selected Poems, 1954-1965* (Vancouver: Talon Books, 1971). "From The Kropotkin Poems" from *Wilson's Bowl* (Toronto: Coach House Press, 1980). "Messages" from *Talking* (Montreal: Quadrant, 1982). "Leaning" from *Water and Light: Ghazals and Anti Ghazals* (Toronto: Coach House Press, 1984). Reprinted by permission of the author.

WIEBE, RUDY

"Where Is the Voice Coming From?" from *Where Is the Voice Coming From?* (Toronto: McClelland and Stewart, 1974). Reprinted by permission of the author.

WILSON, ETHEL

"From Flores" from *Mrs. Golightly and Other Stories* (Toronto: Macmillan of Canada, 1961). Reprinted by permission of Macmillan of Canada, A Division of Canada Publishing Corporation.

· INDEX ·